THE EAGLE'S TALONS

Dedicated to
my wife
Virginia Posvar Smith

THE EAGLE'S TALONS

A MILITARY VIEW OF
CIVIL CONTROL OF THE MILITARY

MAJ. GEN. DALE O. SMITH, USAF (RET.)

SPARTAN BOOKS
Washington, D. C.

FOREWORD

Americans respect the concept of civil control of the military, and we are repeatedly reminded of the virtue of this control, but rarely do we hear an analysis of this virtue. Almost never do we hear of civil control of the military being associated with evil. Yet the capture of the German military establishment by Adolf Hitler was without question the ultimate expression of civil control of the military. So, too, is the Commissar system employed by the Soviet Union. Firm civil control of the Soviet divisions is thus assured.

General Smith breaks new ground by daring to question the unalloyed goodness of all civil control of the military. He makes a convincing case for the proposition that too much civil control of the military is at least as dangerous to individual freedom and constitutional government as too little control. Through a fascinating historical analysis unique to this kind of literature he has shown that when civil control of the military becomes too domineering, the military virtues of honesty, of moral courage, and of devotion to the State, are broken down. Substituted in their place is a blind obedience to the political leadership. Thus the military becomes a tool for dictatorship rather than a bulwark of free government.

I share with General Smith the belief that at this time in our history the United States has gone too far with its measures for increased civil control of the military. As it is exercised today in the Pentagon civil control is counter productive and leading the United States into dangerous waters. Military men have lost much of the necessary authority to do their jobs well, or even to govern their own affairs.

Their last refuge, military ethics, is now dictated by the civilian echelon of the Office of the Secretary of Defense. The quibble–the shrewd manipulation of statistics and other data—is brazenly accepted if it makes a political point or protects an administrator. This has been extended to the reporting of intelligence. The reevaluation downward of the strength of Soviet ground forces in Europe is an example. The Secretary of Defense presumably wanted NATO to rely less on our nuclear weapons (there was much talk about the need for options short of a nuclear holocaust), so he had to show allied conventional strength *vis-a-vis* the Soviets in a more favorable light. Intelligence estimates were conveniently juggled to make us look good on the ground. Thus the new case for conventional warfare versus nuclear warfare in Europe upset years of the highest objective military planning by the fifteen NATO countries.

Another example of this quibble by the use of statistics is in the adjustment of accuracy and reliability figures. For example, if it can be shown that our ICBMs are more accurate and reliable than had been previously estimated, we will need fewer of them. It has been reported to me that the Secretary of Defense has revised the CEPs (Circular Error Probable) of our ICBMs in order to make them appear more accurate, and that this was done over the protest of the JCS. Thus is a case made to reduce the number of ICBMs which we require to defend ourselves.

Revelation of intelligence methods, as was done during the Cuban missile crisis of 1962, has become an acceptable technique for making the Administration look good. The military man's deep concern of what this might do to future intelligence gathering and to the security of our country is arrogantly ignored. We all remember Secretary of Defense McNamara's TV show with aerial photographs and his explanation of how our photo interpreters analyzed the signs which disclosed the nuclear missile sites in Cuba. A show which, by the way, was in progress at the same time when members of the Senate Armed Services Committee were being briefed, in strict secrecy, by the head of the CIA on the same points.

After this rather thorough disclosure of our intelligence methods, does anyone doubt that the Soviets henceforth paid more attention to camouflage wherever they built missile sites? And so today, how can we be sure just how many Soviet ICBMs are deployed and aimed at our own missile sites, SAC bases and cities?

Civil leadership has established conflict of interest ethics for military men, prohibiting them from being entertained in any way by those doing business with the government. Even a lunch is forbidden. Yet the TFX scandal, which gave a $6.5 billion contract to the higher bidder on a second best airplane under most peculiar circumstances involving a brash manifestation of conflict of interest by a former Deputy Secretary of Defense, goes unpunished.

Our military men have been gagged. They can't protect themselves from those who would use them as political footballs and put words in their mouths. They testified in favor of the nuclear test ban under great pressure from their civilian superiors. The public relations activities of all military services have been centralized at the Defense and Service Secretarial levels. Writings and speeches by uniformed men are heavily censored for policy considerations. Testimony before Congressional committees is canned, cleared by the Office of the Secretary of Defense. The public gets a loud, clear, common voice from the Pentagon, right from the Secretary of Defense. Everything is simply peachy, just peachy.

And our military strategy, our weapons, our military commands, and our military doctrines are all determined by the Secretary of Defense. Military decisions by military men are almost a thing of the past. Even unanimous Joint Chiefs of Staff agreements are overruled without compunction. Who will ever know? All JCS papers are classified Top Secret and the JCS has no public relations whatsoever.

The country has been informed by the Secretary that we were not too thinly spread at anytime during the war in South Vietnam and that we were not short of ammunition of certain types—both of these statements were false and the Secretary either knew they were false or spoke in ignorance.

My own view is that General Smith pulls too many punches. The cases he presents are soundly and factually drawn, with ample documentation, but the danger is greater than he suggests. If we continue to debase our military establishment by making it the puppet of the party in power, we are not long for honest representative government.

Perhaps more important, if we let our military survival be dictated by amateur strategists—"Whiz Kids" working for the Secretary of Defense—we will not be long for this world.

Barry Goldwater
Maj. Gen., USAFR

PREFACE

Almost every book has a message, and this one is no exception. Having served thirty-four years in both the Army and the Air Force of the United States, with three tours of duty in the Pentagon, it is not unreasonable to assume that I have acquired some strong convictions about civil-military relations. Call them biases or prejudices if you will. They have been acquired honestly and are not without foundation. I make no pretensions of objectivity in this regard.

I have come to believe that there is a profound misunderstanding in America of the role of military leadership and its proper place in the administration of the United States Government. Through a system of myths and legends the American military has been maligned, stigmatized and made out to be intrinsically dangerous to democratic government and American traditions. I am convinced that these beliefs are not only largely false but that they stimulate the civil-military practices which handicap the proper development of the military profession and threaten the very democratic processes that "civil-control" is designed to preserve.

Having become thoroughly convinced in 1956 that the military side of the story was not being told, I applied for and was awarded a research grant-in-aid from the Social Science Research Council. I hoped to discover the roots of the civil-military doctrines which so rigidly shape the structures and guide the practices of our national defense. The many gross distortions in writings about the military profession had puzzled and worried me. I wanted to do what I could to shed some light on the truth. Being still on active military service, however, I found it impossible to get manuscripts on this subject cleared for publication. This demonstrates one of the ills I intend to expose—the arbitrary, unjust and unnecessary denial to military men of certain fundamental rights and freedoms of

American citizenship. I wish to acknowledge my debt of gratitude to the now-extinct Committee for National Security Policy Research of the Social Science Research Council for its patient assistance.

It was not until I retired from the Air Force in 1964, and was provided another grant, this time from the Institute for Social Science Research, that I was able to complete my inquiry and report it in this book. I am deeply grateful for the generous assistance of this Institute.

Many important and busy people have taken the time to read this manuscript and let me profit from their wise remarks. In particular I wish to mention Earl H. Voss, Elaine Fowler, Major William M. Crabbe, Jr., Vice Admiral T. G. W. Settle, and my father, Alfred Merritt Smith. I am in their debt.

I make no claim to polished research. I have not attempted to run down primary source materials. This has been done by historians and scholars far more able than I and I have been content to rely on a number of highly informative and accurate secondary works. Like Erasmus, I have made it my purpose not to dig out detailed beginnings, but to reinterpret what has already been discovered and written by reliable authorities. To the authors of those works I acknowledge my debt.

Since I am convinced that most traditional interpretations of civil-military relations have been incorrect, I have attempted to examine these events in the light of my military experience and study. Admittedly an *a priori* approach, it is hoped that this will at least provoke more study from the military point of view and at most that the novel interpretations I suggest here may find some adherents among our civil leaders.

It is, of course, too much to hope that this effort will dissipate the many spurious and cynical beliefs which have harassed and hog-tied the military with distrust and which have prevented it from doing what it is best trained and dedicated to do—to protect the United States against its enemies. But it may help. And something must be done if we are to survive as a nation. Should shortsighted civil-control practices lead to military catastrophe, we will have no one to blame but ourselves.

I have tried to pursue five lines of inquiry and analysis. These are:

1. To trace the pertinent history of the military profession and assess its assets and liabilities to good government.

2. To show how the doctrine of civil control of the military evolved.

3. To examine the relationships between national defense and the military profession.

4. To counter the antimilitary myths and the derogatory and inaccurate propaganda found in current literature dealing with civil-military relations.

5. To suggest changes which would improve national defense through a more effective military profession and through more meaningful and appropriate civil-military relations at no danger to Constitutional government or American traditions.

Finally, I wish to express my appreciation to those many fine secretaries who have typed manuscripts and kept files and notes for this study throughout the years, at the Operations Coordinating Board of the White House, the Pentagon, Dhahran, Okinawa, Stewart Air Force Base, and the Joint Staff; and to Frances McGavin who so carefully typed the final pages. My wife Virginia Posvar Smith has cheerfully and patiently typed draft after draft and corrected my abominable spelling and syntax. But for her I would not have started. Thanks, also, to lively sons Drew and Dale for giving up a lot of time we might have had together.

Dale O. Smith
Major General, USAF (Ret.)

CONTENTS

xi

PART I

PROFESSIONAL PROBLEMS

CHAPTER 1

INTRODUCTION

Many learned men believe that war has become so terrible that it will never again be waged except possibly in a very limited sense with, by tacit agreement, the most powerful weapons kept in check by each side. The "unthinkableness" of war is not entirely a new idea. History is replete with prophets who have assured the world that war had become too horrible for contemplation.

The invention of gunpowder provided the first quantum jump in the violence of war and some soothsayers were quick to predict the futility of fortifications. They believed that the increase in destructive power would render "the triumph of barbarism impossible." [1] Upon witnessing the first Montgolfier balloon ascension in Paris, Benjamin Franklin wrote that this discovery should convince sovereigns "of the folly of wars . . . since it will be impossible for the most potent of them to guard his domains. . . ." [2] Orville Wright came to the same conclusion. He once said, "When my brother and I built the first man-made flying machine we thought that we . . . would make further war practically impossible." [3]

Horrible, impossible or foolish wars have continued and their scope and intensity have steadily grown. Excepting the short period of limited wars since 1945, history shows a trend "toward totalitarian military organization of the belligerents and totalitarian military operations during war." [4]

The arguments today that nuclear war is impossible echo the frequent yearnings for peace which have been heard throughout history. Dubois, Erasmus, More, Penn, Saint-Pierre, Sully, Grotius, Rousseau and Kant, to name a few, have all voiced these fervent hopes of mankind.

American history has been marked with a persistent idealism which visualizes a world of peace. In 1784, after winning the Revolution, Congress reduced the army to seventy men for guarding the stores at West Point. No officer above the rank of captain remained.[5] Yet Indians on our western frontiers were massacring American settlers. In 1807 President Thomas Jefferson attempted to avoid war with the Embargo Act which tied up all our shipping in home ports. The measure failed to prevent war with England five years later but it very nearly destroyed the American economy. In 1842 a Congressman announced that "We have no prospect of war." Four years later the United States was at war with Mexico.[6] Just before the Civil War an effort was made to abolish the Navy.[7] In 1896 Congressman Livingstone of Georgia said, "I do not take much stock in the danger of an early war with Spain," and Speaker "Uncle Joe" Cannon voiced the same belief, yet we fought with Spain within two years.[8] At the turn of the century reputable studies were published and broadly discussed which "proved" war to be "impossible from military, economic and political points of view." One such study argued that the "mechanisms of war have rendered war impractical, an economic impossibility . . . [and] a catastrophe which would destroy all existing political organizations." [9]

Just a few months before the First World War blazed in all its fury, David Starr Jordan, president of Stanford University, predicted that "It is apparently not possible for another real war among the nations of Europe to take place." His book *War and Waste* [10] which espoused the doctrine of war's impossibility fulfilled the perennial wish of man.

The Kellogg-Briand Pact signed by fifteen countries in 1928 was another expression of the conviction that war was no longer feasible. All signatories agreed to outlaw war as an instrument of national policy.[11] In Congress an idealistic member proposed a Constitutional amendment to make it illegal to "prepare for, declare, engage in or carry on war." [12]

Human nature itself seems to impel man toward war. As Quincy Wright has written, "Peace is today menaced by idealists who consider their causes so valuable that they justify the sacrifices even of war, no less than by the realist who thinks, because war has a long history, it is inevitable and must be prepared for." [13] Yet he continues by suggesting that the cost of war may be too great to justify any purpose in waging it. Few will dispute the truth of this statement in terms of economic values. But some idealists still persist in believing that death is preferable to certain intolerable conditions of life. Then too, we now know that there lurks in everyone a subliminal *Gotterdammerung* mood or Freudian "death wish" which can cause less idealistic people to actively seek self-destruction as an escape from grinding hardship or emotional depression.

In the final analysis the mortality rate of all human beings is exactly 100 percent. With this in mind, as long as people are subject to intense wants, fears, and hates, and as long as people are capable of organizing themselves, war of whatever intensity appears to be a distinct possibility. The people of the United States would hardly accept a 50 billion dollar annual defense budget if this were not generally believed.

The concept of deterrence beguiles us with an ultimate answer to war, but there is little in history to promise unlimited confidence in the concept. Deterrence is not a new idea. It is a human response created by fear and prudence. Still, the cruel suffering in past wars, the masses of men, women and children slaughtered, the utter destruction of cities from Nineveh, Troy, and Carthage to Magdeburg and Hiroshima, have not seemed to check the awful march of the Fourth Horseman. Nor has international organization, co-operation or negotiation promised any lasting relief from the scourge of war. The prudent man, then, be he realist or idealist, must look to keeping his powder dry. He does not wish to become a victim of Santayana's prophecy that "Those who cannot remember the past are condemned to repeat it."

THE DISEASE OF WAR

Before the invention of nuclear power, Pendleton Herring wrote that "War is a violent reaction to failure at adjustment through peaceful methods. . . . Too often those most strategically placed in political office have contented themselves with sitting on the lid." [14] He continued:

> If war is faced not as a moral but simply as a human phenomenon, we observe that it is so persistently recurrent that it must be accepted as one of the uniformities of social behavior. It is inevitable in the sense that any persistent uniformity of human behavior is so regarded. From this point of view an understanding of our problem is not enhanced merely through the denunciation of violence. [15]

Going to the heart of the matter, Pendleton Herring compared war to disease and suggested that therapy does not come by condemnation or incantations but through the application of knowledge gained from prolonged study. This proposition has become more than ever valid with the coming of nuclear power which, as General Eisenhower wrote, ". . . left no doubt . . . that a new era of warfare had begun." [16]

If we regard war as some sort of human disease it seems reasonable to believe that we can better control it and lessen its devastating consequences through study. This is the job of the professional military man—the study of war. He bends every effort toward preventing war, but if his political leaders determine it must be waged, the soldier attempts to wage it in such a way as to restore an acceptable peace as soon as possible at the least possible cost in human lives.

DETERRENCE OF WAR

If we cannot afford to hope for an assured end to war in our lifetime it behooves us at least to do all we can to forestall it. Deterrence, even though a weak reed, is still our best support and the only support which has yet revealed a modicum of success. While continuing to grope for other means of bottling the nuclear (and the chemical and biological) genie we must nevertheless continue to whet our nuclear sword. Only with an exceedingly sharp weapon can we impress upon our major competitor that we insist on peace—and our kind of peace. "Power, however limited and qualified, is the value which international politics recognizes as supreme." [17]

Deterrence is not simply a matter of piling up armaments. It requires an amalgam of military skills, professional understanding and confident direction in order to be credible. Narrow and simplistic views of war, more often than not held by civilian leaders, may lead to a failure in deterrence.[18] For example, there was much self-congratulation over the establishment of a "hot line" communication system between Washington and Moscow in 1963. The civilian view asserted that this would provide an instant avenue for chiefs of state to explain nuclear blunders or accidents. The concept was vividly revealed in a wildly imaginative best-seller novel, *Fail-Safe*,[19] which depicted an unauthorized nuclear attack on Moscow by American bombers. After a highly improbable conversation on the "hot line," the city of New York was destroyed by the American President as a concession for the accidental attack on Moscow. Nuclear holocaust apparently was averted.

From the military view, so much depends on surprise in future war that an aggressor can be expected to use the "hot line" not to alert his victim, but rather to deceive him—to delay his retaliation until it is too late. Such a stratagem is as old as man.[20] One should not forget that Japanese diplomats were busily negotiating a *rapprochement* in Washington while the Japanese fleet steamed for Pearl Harbor with war orders.[21]

Professional military men have been repeatedly trained to suspect surprise. Clausewitz said that the "strongest weapon of offensive warfare is surprise attack"[22] and this maxim has proved true too often to be ignored. A most enlightening study on this subject was made after the First World War by a German general, Waldemar Erfurth,[23] who confirmed the Clausewitz maxim with overwhelming experience in war.

APPEASEMENT

Appeasement, too, a more likely attitude of civil than of military leadership, may just as well contribute to war as to peace, as Munich revealed. Vannevar Bush observed that the fiascoes of Abyssinia, the Rhineland and Munich in the 1930's resulted from Guilio Douhet's doctrine of city bombardment and the "terror of the air fleet that weakened the will to resist."[24] Those not familiar with war through experience and study are more apt to become paralyzed and unable to think clearly by its imminence. Some believe that nuclear war will bring on the extinction of mankind so frequently depicted in science fiction novels such as Nevil Schute's *On the Beach* [25]—a fascinating story based upon ludicrous technical inaccuracies seldom understood by civilian leaders. Those who expect the end of the world are more apt to blink in a crucial nuclear confrontation. But as Vannevar Bush noted,

> A new great war would not end the progress of civilization, even in the days of the riven atom, even with the threat of disease marshaled for conquest. . . . It need not destroy democracy, for the organization of free men tends to become refined under stress, whether the stress be hot or cold, and meets its greatest hazards when the times are soft.[26]

This thought is less dramatic than human extinction, the theme so prevalent in popular science fiction and arms control literature. But it may have more validity. Military men, however, who so much as suggest that civilization might survive a war are frequently branded as warmongers and "dangerous." But faith in our arms and in our future seldom leads to appeasement.

With his piercing insight, Winston Churchill disposed of the appeasement question in a few brief sentences. "What we really mean," he said, ". . . is no appeasement through fear. Appeasement in itself may be good or bad according to the circumstances. Appeasement from weakness and fear is alike futile and fatal. Appeasement from strength is magnanimous and noble and might be the surest and only path to world peace." [27] Churchill often quoted the Roman dictum, "Spare the conquered and confront the proud," but he deplored the fact that in modern times we oftener "punished the defeated and groveled to the strong." [28] Churchill, with a military beginning, was a master at blending the military and the political in his decision making.

ANTIMILITARY BIAS

On the whole, however, the modern concept of civil control of the military has tended to stifle and ridicule military thought and expression. "History is almost bare of soldiers who have anything to say," wrote H. L. Mencken,[29] and this bias persists more today than ever before.

> . . . I have said [he pontificated] that the military career tends to slow down the mind but it may be that the thing works the other way—that it does not usually attract men who are excessively intellectual . . . of all the arts practiced by man the art of the soldier seems to call for the least intelligence and to develop the least professional competence. Every battle record in history appears as a series of almost incredible blunders and imbecilities. . . . Whenever at the practice of their art in the field they confront a problem of any complexity they have to get help from civilians. . . .[30]

Mencken vividly expresses the attitudes of some present-day civilian leaders. Caught off guard, they often disclose similar feelings about the military. Such prejudices are fundamental to our civilization.[31] They might better be termed myths because they bear such little relation to the truth. Myths are the "value-impregnated beliefs and notions that men hold, that they live by or live for," wrote R. M. MacIver in *The Web of Government*.[32] "Every society is held together by a myth-system, a complex of dominating thought-forms that determine and sustain all its activities."

The false myth-system which regards American military men as not quite bright, believers in dictatorship, prone to war, and striving for control of civil government, is a truly dangerous feature of our national ethos. Military men are first of all Americans with American values, ideals and dreams. They are neither more nor less stupid or intellectual than their civilian counterparts. But they *are* trained in a unique and vital profession which, as Omar

Bradley succinctly put it, is "to prevent war if possible, or to win it if it occurs." [33]

ATTITUDES TOWARD THE MILITARY AFTER 1945

World War II saw a revival of the military spirit in America and an increase in the prestige and authority of military leaders. Following V-J Day, however, concerted efforts were made to cut the military again down to size. Public charges were made in the press of the "caste system," of unfair treatment of enlisted men, of arbitrary punishment under the Articles of War, and of the domination of civil leadership by "the brass." Some writers argued that this was a Communist-inspired campaign to weaken the country which had demonstrated conclusively that its muscles were significantly larger than those of any other country—or combination of countries. Whether or not a Communist effort was afoot to tarnish the American military image, there already existed in the American culture a natural tendency to think ill of the military. Had not the Cold War and Korea intervened it is conceivable that the military posture of the United States would have sunk to that level of near extinction which obtained between the two World Wars.

The detractors of the armed forces finally shifted their sights to a more subtle target: civil control of the military. Review of an annotated bibliography published in 1954 by the Committee on Civil-Military Relations Research of the Social Science Research Council [34] reveals an amazingly large number of literary attacks on the military establishment. The success of this antimilitary literary campaign was described by Hanson W. Baldwin in 1953 in a widely discussed article, "What's Wrong with the Regulars?" [35] He noted that the regular military services were not attracting new men and that veterans were leaving because the country seemed to be slighting them. Baldwin warned that "Men, not machines, make war, and it is men, not machines that are our sure shield against military disaster." And the men obviously were not inspired.

NEED FOR MILITARY VIRTUES

As long ago as 1910 it was noted by the philosopher William James, himself a pacifist, that every virile and progressive country needs "The Moral Equivalent of War." [36] To preserve peace, he said, a state must preserve army discipline and cultivate the martial virtues of "intrepidity, contempt of softness, surrender of private interests [and] obedience to command." His idea was not to have a true army but to attempt to achieve these virtues by declaring war on disease and unsanitary conditions. William James failed to appreciate that the high ideals of a dedicated military man are inspired by a cause associated with great and real danger, danger not only to himself but to his country. Perhaps a similar élan could be achieved in a peaceful campaign against less threatening and immediate dangers to life, but this has yet to be demonstrated.

There need be no artificial equivalent of war created today in order to achieve the military virtues. Over two and a half million Americans are in uniform and the military virtues can be adequately engendered by fair treatment and due regard from their employers—the American people. The military system of itself cannot assure these virtues in an unwholesome environment of distrust and, in some cases, of outright animosity.

On the same date that the Declaration of Independence set the United States free from King George III of England, the great economist and philospher, Adam Smith, published his *Wealth of Nations*. In order to carry the military art to an adequate degree of perfection, Adam Smith noted, ". . . it is necessary that it should become the sole and principal occupation of a particular class of citizens. . . ."[37] The United States has reluctantly come to agree with Adam Smith that a professional military establishment is necessary in order to train its members appropriately in the complicated and varied arts necessary to win battles. This includes the development of the fundamental military virtues which assure an army's loyalty, discipline and courage. Yet neither the skills nor the virtues will be fully realized as long as the public is skeptical and suspicious of its armed forces. Loyalty and confidence go in two directions. As General George S. Patton wrote, "To be a good soldier a man must have discipline, self-respect, pride in his unit *and in his country*. . . ."[38] General Patton deplored as a "tragic fact" that in our attempts to prevent war "we have taught our people to belittle the heroic qualities of a soldier." Are we losing the military virtues in which William James believed?

OBJECTIVE OF THIS STUDY

Many people who have proudly worn the uniform in peace and war believe, more than ever before, that the civilian overcontrol of the military now being exercised in the Pentagon is eroding military pride and self-respect. Our national sword is becoming blunted and corroded through the usurpation of professional command and staff duties by the civilian echelon of the Department of Defense. It is because of this pressing problem, and because the underlying reason given for more and more civil control is the imaginary military threat to democratic government, that a thorough analysis should be made of the presumed dangers presented by the military profession.

The objective of this study, therefore, is to examine the antimilitary bias so prevalent in America, to identify and analyze its historical beginnings, its effects on national defense and its relationship to the civil control of the military. An effort is made in this light to determine the degree, scope and kind of civil control of the military which will best contribute to American ideals and to practical national defense.

CHAPTER 2

TRADITIONAL FEARS OF THE MILITARY

It has long been axiomatic in the American society to consider the military as intrinsically dangerous to democracy. Much of this attitude is a residue from the Roundhead domination of the Long Parliament of England in the mid-17th Century, reinforced by historical examples of the usurpation of government by Julius Caesar, Napoleon, and other military autocrats. Little has been written of the *creation* and *preservation* of democracies by military force: of how General George Monk's Roundheads reestablished the free Parliament in England or of the many revolutionary armies which have fought for representative government, not the least of which was Washington's Continentals. It might be well for us to examine more closely some of the traditional antimilitary attitudes in an effort to understand them better.

THE CIVILIAN CONTROL PREMISE

In *Civil-Military Relationships in American Life,* Paul H. Appleby, a well-known critic of the military, lumped two related antimilitary premises into one sentence: "Recognizing that danger to civilian control of national defense is danger to democracy, we must recognize that danger to civilian control has been made enormously more critical by the new military potential." [1] There seemed to be no need in Appleby's mind to question these two premises that (1) reduced civilian control of national defense endangers democracy or that (2) the danger is more critical today because of our new military potential. These biases were "givens."

Leaving the second proposition for another chapter, let us examine Appleby's major premise. Unquestionably it is the traditional American view. But is it true? Is it borne out by evidence, or by emotion? How did Appleby come by it? Simply because it is traditional, it cannot be justified as a rock-bottom premise for constructive reasoning.

In defense of his premises Appleby noted "a certain tendency, even in this country, to accept authority as an escape from individual and democratically organized responsibility." This is a truism which almost anyone will accept as a fundamental characteristic of human personality, in this country or elsewhere, applicable under both civilian and military leadership. But does it support his basic premise?

AUTHORITY VERSUS FREEDOM

It must be clear to anyone, whether analyzing himself or his environment, that people seek *both* authority and freedom. The fact that authority and freedom in the absolute are incompatible does not prevent human beings from desiring both. It has been well established by psychologists that all people are to some extent ambivalent. They love and hate at the same time and harbor any number of conflicting emotions and desires. This explains so many apparent human inconsistencies.

The problem is not one of choice between authority and freedom, therefore, but between relative *degrees* of each, and of mixing them together in a harmonious society so as to permit the greatest individual happiness, initiative and opportunity compatible with national security and the general welfare. In other more ringing words, ". . . life, liberty and the pursuit of happiness." As to what constitues human welfare, this should, of course, be determined by the people themselves. As to what constitutes national security, this has usually been a decision of government because of its highly technical nature. We do not go so far as to suggest, however, that governments should have sole authority to wage war. This, too, is an intimate concern of the people because they are the ones who must do the fighting. Hence national defense must always be a public matter.

HOW AUTHORITARIAN IS THE MILITARY?

Most writers on this subject, like Appleby, tend to equate authority with antidemocracy, and both with the military. There can be slight question that the military is generally authoritarian, but it is not *absolutely* so. In time of peace particularly, people in the United States military services have almost as much freedom as civilians. They have certain rights and privileges established by law which cannot be arbitrarily suspended or superseded by order of military authority. And these "freedoms" do not necessarily cause inefficiency in the military machine. In fact, they as often tend to enhance military effectiveness. Considerable individuality is encouraged along productive lines, tending toward re-evaluation and improvement of organizations and weapon systems.

It might surprise the layman to know how many military decisions are arrived at through the so-called democratic processes of conferences, staff meetings, objective studies, seminars, forums and whatnot. Authoritative decisions are not infrequently reversed through the same democratic processes. In general, military decisions are made in no more an authoritative manner than are decisions reached in nonmilitary governmental agencies* or in organized business. In fact, the opposite is more often true because military people have more job security and thus tend to speak with less fear than men who might lose their livelihood by speaking out.

One might assume that the military is authoritarian because it has so many rules and regulations but this does not necessarily follow. The military seeks orderly practices established by regulation. In itself this tendency toward order is no more undemocratic than is the Constitution or the public law. And since military regulations are in almost every instance established through the so-called democratic processes, they are no more arbitrary than any other governmental regulations.

Where orderly rules and policies are not established to regulate behavior in an institution, one is more likely to experience arbitrary one-time decisions and unfair practices. This is most likely to happen in a nonmilitary institution simply because there is less emphasis on systematic behavior. It is a fallacy to concede that regulations in themselves tend to restrict. They may just as often define liberties, privileges and opportunities.

If justice is a feature of democracy and freedom, then the military should rank high among human institutions in this regard. At least military men know where they stand and what to expect. They are not quite as subject to whimsical or authoritarian treatment as are members of many other institutions. For example, military men would be quick to agree that the General Service Administration regulations which govern the Pentagon are far less permissive than are the regulations governing military bases.

---

*The story is told that when Lincoln asked for a Cabinet vote which went against his views he remarked, "Eight nays, one aye. The ayes have it."

MAN-ON-HORSEBACK MYTH

Like so many other exponents of the antimilitary bias, Appleby identified the military with the man-on-horseback myth. "There is significance in the fact," he wrote, "that when we speak of the possible arrival of a man on horseback we are thinking of the military." [2] This is another popular misconception. True, there have been many military dictators, but there have probably been as many civilian dictators—at least in modern times. True, also, a non-military man-on-horseback sometimes gets control of the military system and uses its backing to enforce his *coup d'etat*. But more often, the civilian dictator first wrests control from civilian authority, which in turn controls the military. One remembers the *Reichstag* fire and the vote for Hitler the following day. A few years earlier Mussolini was given extraordinary authority by civilian leadership. "The dangers of usurpation . . . arise not so much from the military," wrote Harvard professor Carl Friedrich, "but from political and other civilan elements who employ the military to achieve their ends." [3]

In a *U.S. Naval Institute Proceedings* article intitled "The Ivy-Clad Man on Horseback," Captain Paul R. Schratz commented that ". . . the military man now finds himself outflanked by a civilian on horseback, as, each day, the flag of the Secretary of Defense casts an ever-lengthening shadow." [4] He added that:

> No military man remotely dreams of a real possibility for a military takeover in America. But the McNamara era broke into our soliloquy to pose an entirely unanticipated problem. The situation is now reversed. Deeply entrenched and supported by the Commander-in-Chief, the Congress, and the people, the military itself is in danger of being outflanked. . . . We who placidly mused on a military takeover which could not happen suddenly face a civilian authority which may reduce the military influence to the impotency of a latter-day General Board.

Stalin and Hitler and Mussolini did not achieve their power positions through subverting state military establishments. Once in control of the civil authority and the police, Stalin controlled the military legitimately. Although Hitler's irregular Brown Shirts provided him with some strong-armed force, such irregulars can hardly be considered military in the modern sense. They were, in effect, organized political gangs devoted to their leader's will. Earlier, Mussolini had utilized the same technique with his Black Shirts.

During the Second World War the "garrison state" concept was put forward by Harold Laswell.[5] Laswell's theory raised ·another

fear that total war would result in a government and society indefinitely geared to war. Imminence of conflict would be used by
government as the excuse to keep the economy on a total war footing
with all resources of the country devoted to national defense, and
with all able-bodied citizens undergoing military training. This
draws up the picture of George Orwell's world of *Nineteen Eighty-
Four*.[6]

Postwar events, even with the constant Cold War threat to security, have proved Laswell's fears of a garrison state to be groundless, but one still sees the phantom in literature from time to time.
It was a false prediction which became so embedded in the literature as to assume a pseudo reality. It has contributed to the equally
false notion of a controlling military-industrial complex.

THE MILITARY CAN BE GOOD OR BAD

It can be argued that the military have just as often restored
popular government as they have destroyed it. Not only can this
be said for the American Revolution, but, to a lesser extent, for the
American Civil War and the Spanish-American War. The First
World War saw the general downfall of autocracy in Europe and
the creation of several new democracies. The military forces of ancient Athens, the Roman Republic and Switzerland repeatedly protected governments by the people. As J. W. Masland has put it,
". . . military power can be employed for good as well as for evil
purposes and . . . the [U.S.] armed forces serve as a shield for the
protection of the democratic institutions and values that we preserve." [7]

In our time railing against the evils of the military is reminis-
cent of earlier attacks made on technology and the machine. In
England during the Industrial Revolution mobs destroyed the "evil"
textile mills on several occasions. To the machines were imparted
human characteristics of guilt for depriving craftsmen of their
jobs. Today the nuclear weapon suffers even more virulent attacks,
if not physically, at least indirectly through popular literature
which would, in fact, physically obliterate the bomb. This anthro-
pomorphism encompasses all too often the military institution itself.

Being the servant of the state, the military institution is morally
neutral with respect to the employment of nuclear weapons. They
can be used for good or evil depending upon the orders given by
the *civilian* authority. Except in the most extreme circumstances of
presumed immortality the military leaders are not expected to ques-

tion their orders from constituted civilian authority. No American airman can or should be held responsible for the bombing of German cities or Vietnam villages. *He* does not make such decisions. He is only the instrument of execution.

The military is capable of course of destroying whole cities and populations. Also, by its mere existence, the military *prevents* this from happening through deterrence. Thus the military is the instrument which permits millions of people to live happy, peaceful and productive lives.

It is a feature of the technical age that people are sometimes prone to deplore technology *per se* as something that has degraded and endangered civilization. Raymond Aron took the opposite view when he wrote:

> The profit and loss account is not yet closed. Even in the matter of war, it has not been proved that the debts outweigh the credits. Medicine saves more lives than explosives destroy. Sparta and Athens did not need radio-guided missiles and atomic bombs to exhaust themselves in fighting. Pestilence and famine have ruined communities which the demon of knowledge had spared. The population of Germany after the Thirty Years' War had fallen by more than half. That of Western Europe had risen by ten per cent in 1939.[8]

Military force is an essential characteristic of sovereignty and thus of any state, and may be good or bad, virtuous or evil, loyal or disloyal, autocratic or democratic depending much upon the character of the state itself. In itself, simply because it is military, it is none of these. The American military institution, therefore, should not be treated or regarded as alien to the American way of life and untrustworthy without cause simply because it is military.

DANGERS FROM "MILITARY PRESTIGE"

Paul Appleby warned that "the glamor and prestige conferred by history and crisis on wearers of military uniforms" is another danger to civilian control. Arthur A. Ekrich wrote that civil authority may become "a willing dupe of military men, overwhelmed by their prestige. . . ."[9] If this were ever true in the United States, the fear is indeed unwarranted today since all the evidence seems to point in the other direction. Objective polls have repeatedly revealed that most people in uniform have a minor interest in following a military career—an attitude that hardly indicates "glamor and prestige." Pay scales, living conditions, and general social status find the military far down the ladder of professions. In fact few Americans today accord the military the prestige of the term "profession," tending to regard it instead more as a uniformed civil service or government-run business. In his analysis of the American mind, Henry Steele Commager has noted that America has never acknowledged a military caste and rarely rewarded military service with social prestige.[10]

It is not unreasonable to surmise that anyone of the military who has served in Washington, D. C., would testify to the fact that his status is exceedingly low in comparison to that of civilians in official or unofficial positions. Prior to the Second World War the military status was so low that officers from the field who visited the nation's Capital were under orders to shed their uniforms and don mufti. Civilian wear was the official uniform of our highest military headquarters.

As noted by Michael Howard, looking upon the American phenomenon from England, "the regular officer, far from being an object of social deference, was often an object of scorn." [11] He recalled that when Lieutenant Grant rode into Cincinnati in his new uniform he was jeered with "Soldier, will you work? No siree, I'll sell my shirt first!" [12] Although World War II raised some public regard for the military, few military men today prefer uniform to civilian dress when off duty. Neither the rank of a military man, his length of loyal service, the risks of life he has made for his country, nor the degree of his education or ability can overcome the antimilitary bias which pervades the American culture and which so sweepingly justifies the civilian control premise.

As for the "better remuneration . . . better retirement benefits . . . and other perquisites" [13] which Appleby considers to be superior for the military as opposed to civil servants, enough studies have been made (such as the Compton Report,[14] Strauss Report,[15] and Cordiner Report) [16] to prove rather conclusively that the opposite is more close to the truth. But irrefutable evidence is found in the fact that military manpower must be drafted. When civil service positions go unwanted to the extent that civilians must be coerced with conscription into accepting them, then there may be reason to assert that civil service holds less status than military service.

MILITARY THINKING AND INVENTION

Another argument for civil control deals with the popular assumption that the military are rigidly doctrinaire and this "involves danger that national defense will not be sufficiently imaginative, flexible and dynamic. . . ." [17] There is indeed some historical evidence of this. The military was slow to accept the airplane, for example, and the tank. But if one carefully examines the cases of military shortsightedness one will observe that they seem to extend more often than not from oppressive civilian control. Penurious military budgets for the purpose of keeping the military weak (and thus less threatening to the democracy—a reason sometimes voiced in the 19th Century) [18] do not lead to experiments in new weaponry or to discarding old weapons for costly new ones. The inventor of the fast Christie tank in the 1930's had to peddle his product in Europe. There seems to be no lack of military imagination and inventiveness, however, if funds are available to make this possible. Nuclear bombs, jet engines, guided missiles and space boosters, to name a few, are largely products of military ingenuity. Blunder and shortsightedness are endemic in mankind. The military has had and will continue to possess its share of these universal shortcomings. But to single out the military as suffering with the lion's share of mankind's stupidity is simply another manifestation of groundless and unreasoned antimilitary bias. If the American military has not been generally successful in its forecasts of weapons and strategy there would be few democratic institutions left in the United States today, if indeed there were a United States.

When the U.S. Army fought with single-shot Civil War rifles against American Indians armed with Winchester repeaters it was not because the military chose to fight at such a disadvantage. Civil leadership was considerably more responsible for this military lack, as the record demonstrates.[19] Unfortunately the military usually reap the discredit for the tragic consequences of inept civilian control. Soldiers have long been the docile whipping boys of their civilian leaders.

EXAMPLES OF POISON GAS AND TANKS

The military historian H. A. DeWeerd contributed to this stereotype of the backward military mind when he wrote that in World War I the military "distrusted the introduction of new elements in the struggle." He continued:

> The history of the misuse of gas by the German High Command and of the tanks by the British High Command offer illustrations in point. Both of these weapons were forced on the military by civilian pressure. But when they were employed it was done so timidly and so experimentally, with such a limited view of the potentialities of both weapons, that

> the surprise factor was wasted for trivial local gains. . . . Professional
> soldiers could not invent; invention had been properly drilled out of
> them. Pride and traditional reserve restrained them in some cases from
> using the devices of "outsiders." [20]

It is, of course, easy to visualize the worth of a new weapon
after it has been developed and employed. Twenty-twenty hind-
sight is a happy faculty of historians, but it is a different matter
when a commander is pressured to use a volatile poison gas such
as Chlorine, or a lumbering mechanical monster.

Bernard Brodie provides a more balanced judgment of the
military mind:

> . . . Men who have been condemned out of hand as unimaginative or
> unprogressive may simply have been much more acutely aware of
> technical difficulties to be overcome before a certain invention could
> be useful than were their more optimistic contemporaries. The mere
> circumstances that one man was proved wrong in his predictions and
> another right does not prove that the latter was the more discerning
> observer. [21]

Seldom does a new weapon or machine spring full-blown from
the inventor's drawing board. Usually, like Fulton's steamboat and
Marconi's wireless, it clearly demonstrates a potential only after
innumerable subsequent failures, refinements and adjustments.
The same held true for gas and the tank as used in World War I.
Both innovations had potential. But to assume that these early
weapons were initially capable of any unusual strategic consequences runs contrary to the history of invention. One exception
to this rule, of course, is the atomic bomb.

Chlorine gas, as first attempted by the Germans at Ypres and
Neuve Chapelle was dispensed in generators and delivered by the
wind. This seemed a logical tactic to the proponents of this weapon.
Unfortunately, the wind shifted and blew the lethal fumes back
over the Germans. In its first application, gas was far from reliable.
Later, mustard gas fired in artillery shells was more effective, but
in general gas did not prove to be a very good weapon.

As for the first tanks, which were clumsily armored caterpillar
tractors driven by far from reliable internal combustion engines,
an initial surprise at Cambrai was quickly overcome when the
Germans discovered their vulnerability. Standing bulky on the sky-
line, as cumbersome and slow as tortoises, and frequently immobilized by their own crudity, the tanks were of minor consequence
in World War I. [22] These examples of the early use of gas and tanks,
when carefully examined, serve more to demonstrate the wisdom

of careful, professional military decisions as against the optimistic impetuosity of civilian amateurs. In World War II, when tanks were stalled by hedgerows in Normandy, an earth-cutting tank attachment was invented within a few weeks. Three soldiers were the inventors: Captain James Depew, Lt. Steve Litton and Sgt. Curtis Culin. The tank dozers sliced forward in the historic St. Lô breakthrough.[23]

EXAMPLE OF THE ATOMIC BOMB AND OTHER WEAPONS

"But what of the atomic bomb?" one may ask. "Was not it a civilian development?" The idea was born in civilian laboratories and seminars. As soon as Einstein's formula $E=MC^2$ was established, the awful potential of atomic power began to be appreciated. It was even postulated in science fiction as early as 1939. But the catch was how to release this energy. Until a method was developed, the atomic bomb was just a dream.[24]

The military can hardly be disparaged for not producing an Einstein to discover $E=MC^2$ earlier or even to exploit this discovery. Before World War II there were meager funds provided for research and development, and none in the field of basic research, the area in which Einstein studied. Only a handful of practicing physicists wore uniforms.

But scientists continued to study and experiment. Finally, the power of the atom was unleashed by the first chain reaction at the University of Chicago on December 2, 1942.[25] This dramatic breakthrough pointed the way for developing an atomic bomb with a high probability of success. Einstein presented the possibility to the President and the two billion dollar Manhattan Project was formed with enthusiastic military support. The project soon became one of the greatest and most costly single programs ever undertaken by the country up to that time. Although largely a civilian undertaking, it was successfully managed and directed by the United States Army. The military was neither backward nor shortsighted in this stupendous venture. But in passing one might note that this development left civilians as culpable as the military in war making.

Nor did the armed forces hinder the employment of the resultant atomic bomb. Although President Harry S. Truman made the final decision, he was provided with positive recommendations from the Joint Chiefs of Staff and his civilian advisors. Then the military simply followed civilian orders. The actual dropping of the two atomic bombs was the culmination of an exceedingly well-planned and well-timed military operation.

Radar presents another, though less dramatic, instance of enthusiastic acceptance by the military of a scientific breakthrough. Imaginative military use of radar was instrumental in achieving the Royal Air Force victory in the Battle of Britain. After observing the remarkable success of radar in England in 1939, General H. H. Arnold of the U.S. Army Air Corps recommended to General George C. Marshall that the Army establish a Scientific Advisory Board to assist in weapons development. This was done with signal success, and the Navy followed suit with the Office of Naval Research.

The charge can be made and supported with abundant evidence that *civilian* direction often puts a dead hand upon military efforts to introduce new weapons. The story of General Billy Mitchell's efforts to advance military aviation following the First World War are too well known to repeat. What is not well known is President Calvin Coolidge's support of the reactionary military elements which attempted to downgrade the results of the battleship bombing experiments. Admiral William E. Moffett was having similar troubles getting aviation accepted by the Navy.[26]

In France young Captain Charles de Gaulle was attempting to interest his government in tanks and aircraft, but a conservative government instead spent vast sums on super defense works—the Maginot Line.

Even in Germany the myopic military vision of Hitler contributed to his ultimate defeat. General Ernst Udet tried to interest the *Fuehrer* in a newly developed jet fighter, the ME262, which might have cleared the skies of allied bombers. But Hitler arrogantly ordered the ME262 to be redesigned as a dive bomber. This delayed manufacture of the aircraft for over a year and prevented it from becoming a significant weapon.[27]

When weapons are developed that can pass the test of military knowledge, there is ample evidence that they are eagerly accepted by the military—although this is not to presume that the soldiers are incapable of error. In partnership with civilian science, and given adequate funds and authority from the civilian control echelons of government, the military is as progressive and farsighted as any other segment of the American society.

MILITARY ARE MORE CIRCUMSPECT

In defense of Appleby, it must be admitted that he attempted a dubious compliment by commending the military as a responsible element of national life. "In general," he wrote, "the professional military men in America are much more aware of the proper limitations of their roles than are reservists, temporary officers, and many civilians."[28] Professional military men are, by and large, less anxious to assert themselves politically and more content with an orderly life than the highly competitive civilians. And one must keep in mind that inactive reservist and temporary officers are essentially civilians with civilian attitudes. Might it not be logical to assume, therefore, that more responsible and sober leadership— leadership less subject to personal desires and ambitions—would be found in the professional military?

This thought is seldom expressed in literature dealing with civil-military relations. Yet it is not uncommon for Presidents to be chosen from the American military profession[29] and on rare occasions for high government officials (such as General George C. Marshall) to be appointed, although not without a hue and cry being raised by those who see grave danger in this practice. Almost without exception, however, such high posts held by military men have been discharged honorably and in the best democratic tradition. How can this be generally true if leaders are nurtured in an environment which presumably engenders so many dangerous attitudes?

There is absolutely no truth in the frequent charge, for example, that a military man is of a more violent nature than a civilian. Genocides practiced by civilians Stalin and Hitler exceeded any mass slaughters in history. History also provides examples of military leaders advising the milder course in opposition to political leadership. This was evident in 1871 when von Moltke refused to shell Paris, a tactic urged by civilian Chancellor Bismarck. History was to repeat itself in 1944 when General von Choltitz refused to obey Hitler's orders to blow up Paris after German evacuation.[30]

The new German army has been unjustly accused of somehow contributing to Hitler's depredations. Under a jaundiced allied eye of guidance, the German army was organized in 1953 along "democratic" lines. There are no real commanders in uniform. Instead, commanders are called "inspectors" who cannot give orders to subordinates and enforce them. Only the minister of defense, who must be a civilian, can give an order without reference to higher authority.[31]

This unmilitary system of command has defeat built into it with its similarity to the Soviet commissar system practiced during the disastrous war with little Finland in 1940. Yet the sheer illogic of the German army command system can be recognized in the American trends for increasing civilian control as a safeguard against a potentially dangerous military.

Military leaders have been barbarous, as with Tamerlane and Genghis Khan, but donning a uniform in modern societies does not give military men a corner on cruelty or violence. It seems more likely that individual and cultural attitudes combined with the passion of the moment will determine the degrees of compassion or violence, rather than a man's profession.

EDUCATION OF THE MILITARY

Appleby suggested that military men are narrowly educated. There is an element of truth in this, although if years in school and hours of study are criteria, the evidence will point to the fact that the military is one of the most intensively educated of all professions. Military education may well be narrow in its specialization, although this same charge can be leveled with equal justification against almost any other profession. One hears it said of medicine, business, education, and even politics. Parochialism is a product of our age, in which highly specialized professions demand so much study of the individual that he loses touch with other areas of learning.

The education of public administrators is similarly wanting. Since the large majority of senior public administrators are nurtured in law or business, it is difficult to perceive how this training prepares them to advance to eminence in politico-military areas. Yet they do so, as opposed to those who are trained in the military. No doubt this preference for nonmilitary men in government stems from both a fear of military control and the supporting fallacy that the military are poorly educated for responsible government work.

A broader education with more cross-training for both military and civil servants might improve the conduct of government. This recommendation has often been put forward by discerning students of civil-military problems. In the Preface to the bibliography on *Civil-Military Relations* published under the auspices of the Social Science Research Council, William T. R. Fox wrote:

> ... Today public concern is not so much directed toward preventing the armed services from becoming either pawns or prime movers in domestic politics as it is toward energizing our cumbersome defense machinery, enabling our soldiers, sailors, and airmen to formulate a military policy precisely calculated to support the specific foreign policies of the country, and developing the civilian capacities necessary if political

aims and military means are to be rationally reconciled. Civil-military relationships today, then, must meet the requirements of national security, as well as the need for maintaining civilian controls.[32]

If education is to be broadened in both civil and military areas in preparation for administrative posts dealing with politico-military matters, military men must be offered much more political material in their service schools, and the civilians, much more military material. There will be a blending of the two, with each approaching the other in terms of specialized knowledge. The question then arises, will not the distinction between civil and military control become blurred? It will at least become increasingly difficult to identify a public administrator as a civilian or a military man. Perhaps some of the antimilitary bias could thus be dispelled.

EXERCISE OF CIVILIAN AND MILITARY AUTHORITY

Although Quincy Wright said that "throughout most of its history the military mind has probably had too little rather than too much influence in the United States; and the military has probably generally been too small rather than too large,"[33] he nonetheless reasoned that the military presents a threat to the democratic way of life because "Military organization relies on discipline and compulsion, and the line of authority flows from the top down. Democratic organization relies on individual initiative and consent, and the line of authority flows from public opinion at the grass roots up to the top."[34]

There is much good reasoning in this statement but it bears analysis. In the first place the military and democracy are not mutually exclusive in their characteristics. In both, lines of authority go both up *and* down. No military commander has ever been successful unless he were accorded the loyal support which leads to true authority over his troops. Nor has any democratic leader been worth his salt without exerting some authority upon those who placed him in power.

Armies can be both democratic and autocratic, but never are they all of one or the other. Democracy, on the other hand, must have organized leadership with laws enforced from the top. Without this top-down aspect of democracy it no longer fits the definition. It becomes anarchy.

What is seldom considered is that military men can be inspired by the same concepts of liberty and freedom as are civilians. They can be so loyal to these democratic precepts as to deny themselves certain personal liberties derived from the democratic system itself in order to assure the perpetuation of these very same self-denied liberties for their children and loved ones. For example, a professional military man may not engage in active political work. He may vote, but he may not campaign or run for office or publicly debate or make political speeches. This does not gainsay that he does not fully approve of such democratic ways. There is no reason to believe, therefore, that military men would crave a soldier-state any more than would a businessman or a lawyer.

CONCLUSION

In view of the foregoing it appears that the often-cited dangers to civilian control presented by the military are illusory. They are habitual and unreasoned fears bearing little relationship to the realities of our modern American society. The American military is not entirely authoritarian, while democracy is not entirely the exercise of freedom. The military has no monopoly over the man-on-horseback, and soldiers fight to support free government just as often as to support autocracy. The "prestige and glamor" of military life and its special perquisites have not yet made the military a desired profession by any means, and although military thinking and education have their shortcomings, these are shared with the civilians. If such traditional fears could only be laid to rest where they belong the subject of civilian control of the military might be examined with less heat and more light.

CHAPTER 3

THE MILITARY STEREOTYPE

Social scientists have made several comprehensive and objective studies of the personal characteristics of American military leaders and of the military profession.[1] It seems to come as a surprise to some of these researchers when their findings reveal that professional military men in America are much like average civilians. The antimilitary bias is so strongly held, however, that the stereotype of the military leader which fits the bias is an almost indestructible image.

Morris Janowitz has pointed out that military officers, especially those who occupy posts at the highest echelons, are only dimly perceived as persons and human beings.[2] What is more unfortunate for the profession, as well as for national security which so greatly depends on this profession, these military leaders often appear as hard-eyed, insensitive Prussian martinets, a little on the stupid side and somewhat loud-mouthed.

One has only to watch television Westerns to see this distorted image in action. Modern tolerance usually makes out the early American Indian to be a misunderstood but basically benign tribesman[3] fighting against the forces of aggression as typified by the military. The civilian scout, on the other hand, understands and is sympathetic with the Redskins. Opposed to the scout is the bungling army colonel whose concept of strategy is as crude as Custer's but not as heroic. By illegally assuming the military authority and disobeying his orders, the civilian scout invariably saves from disaster the civilian settlers in their wagon train. It seems that the only reason the settlers got into trouble in the first place was because the army colonel had stupidly antagonized the Indians and then galloped off on some wild goose chase to leave the settlers defenseless. Civilian settlers are heroes, of course. It seldom enters the mind of the uncritical viewer that the soldiers were there to protect the settlers—or that the settlers themselves were the true aggressors. It is a much more plausible thesis to make the troopers out as the aggressors. But here again there is another invidious distinction made among the soldiers themselves.

The ordinary private soldier is a pretty good guy, caught in the web of circumstances and the blind, coercive military system represented by the military leader. If there has to be a villain in the small detachment, he is invariably the smart-aleck second lieutenant just out of West Point. But the poor soldier is only in the service because of hard times. Either his side was defeated in the Civil War, or he is a broke cowboy, or a lovable drunk, or a misunderstood criminal. But not the army officer. Too often the officer is characterized as an insensitive and stupid villain. Of course in the grand finale the U.S. Cavalry gallops to the aid of the besieged settlers in their wagon train. More often than not this cavalry charge is led by the heroic civilian scout, the colonel having fallen into justifiable disgrace of some sort.

So the stereotype of the military leader is drawn and reenforced upon the formative young minds which view television daily. Some exceptions such as "Battle Report" and "Twelve O'Clock High" have been unable to alter the unfavorable image if the low enlistment and reenlistment rates are any measure of appeal. Popular literature adds its stamp. Antimilitary novels have been highly successful from *Mr. Roberts* and *The Quick and the Dead* to *Seven Days in May* and *Fail-Safe*. It is no wonder that objective-minded researchers are amazed to find this stereotype to be a weird distortion. It is a pity that the sober and enlightening studies they publish have had such little influence in changing the picture held in the public mind. In this age it is almost impossible for serious and informative literature to compete with popular media in the intense daily contest for the minds of America.

PRESTIGE OF THE MILITARY

In a classical understatement Janowitz repeated the truism that "In the United States the military profession does not carry great prestige." He noted accurately that there is a "tradition of hostility against the military establishment." A 1955 opinion sampling found the prestige of the officer in the armed services to be below that of physician, scientist, college professor, minister and public school teacher.[4]

In 1964 Dr. Glenn Seaborg, Chairman of the Atomic Energy Commission (AEC), noted in a speech that The National Opinion Research Center of the University of Chicago published a study of occupational prestige in the United States between the years 1925 and 1962. The first nine occupations ranked according to prestige did not include a military man, even a general. In rank order those on the list were: Supreme Court Justice, physician, nuclear physicist, scientist, government scientist, state governor, cabinet member, college professor, and representative to Congress.[5]

In speculating why the prestige of the nuclear scientist (together with the garden-variety "scientist" and even "government scientist") had risen so high, Dr. Seaborg suggested that it was because people knew he was a man responsible for nuclear weapons and that "the nuclear scientist has become the most articulate representative of the scientific community." He went on to say that the

> . . . soul-searching among scientists of the Manhattan Project . . . is too well evident in subsequent events to need retelling. There is hardly a one of the major contributors to the project who has not felt the need to participate in developing public policy with regard to the control of nuclear energy in its military and peaceful uses.

This illustrates the power of propaganda. Because nuclear scientists are "articulate" there is no opprobrium attached to their creation of the nuclear bomb. In fact, because of all the bleeding-heart remorse reported in the press, the public is actually sympathetic. But how about the military? Unable even to defend itself because of the restrictions on clearing writings for publication, let alone create a sympathetic image, the military is dismayed to find that its relationship with nuclear explosives forbodes nothing but evil in the public mind.

A poll of 450 college freshmen at Antioch College revealed similar findings regarding military prestige. Students were asked to name the ten most prominent human beings who have lived during the 20th Century. Not one military leader was mentioned, not even Generals Eisenhower, MacArthur, Marshall or Pershing.[6] It is incredible that we can forget so quickly. In the words of a character in "South Pacific" who deplored prejudice, "You have to be carefully taught." A similar national poll of college students rated the military low among those institutions "which evoke their respect and admiration."[7]

Another view of the military sees it as the major element in our society devoted to force as the means for solving all national and international problems. Thus devoted to force, goes the oversim-

plified argument, the military is opposed to peace and inimical to
our highest cultural motives and aspirations. Identifying the military with violence (some social scientists have referred to the military as "managers of violence"[8]) unrealistically tends to separate
the military from the American environment. The military becomes
an institution and a profession apart, beyond the pale, hostile to
the peaceful American way.

As an institution the military is not a self-generated, self-perpetuating entity. Armies, navies and air forces are established by
the will of the general populace to perform functions not only
approved but assigned by the elected representatives of those people.
The military is merely one of several instruments of national power.
It exercises no more violence in time of peace than does the Atomic
Energy Commission or the Central Intelligence Agency. In time of
war all public institutions become violent. It was the President of
the United States who decided to drop the atomic bomb. The military is, totally, the child of the state, and hence, in democratic
America, of the people. It is as American as apple pie. But for some
strange reasons it has become a rather bitter dish.

Unfortunately the distorted stereotype of the professional military leader drives people away from and out of the Services. Were
the prestige of military service higher, military budgets, already
prohibitive, could be considerably less. The huge turnover of personnel which necessitates fabulously expensive training establishments would be materially reduced if the Services presented more
attractive careers. Even the matter of pay would be less acute if
young men were clamoring to volunteer. In 1957 a survey of army
lieutenants revealed that the most promising officers tended to resign after completing their obligatory term of service. Resignations
of academy graduates had increased from 1951 to the level where
one out of every four or five left the service within five years after
being commissioned.[9]

In the five years since 1960 this problem has grown increasingly
acute. An average of 54 percent of Air Force officers left the Service
at the earliest permitted date, while between 60 and 70 percent of
the enlisted men left at the end of their first enlistment. Army
resignations increased 50 percent and Air Force resignations by
137 percent.[10]

CONTRACTING FOR MILITARY SERVICE

Because of the inability of the Services to retain skilled men, resort to contracting with civilian concerns has been more commonly

practiced. The operation and maintenance of some Air Force bases, such as Dhahran Air Force Base in Saudi Arabia, is handled under a civilian contract. Many equipment maintenance and service contracts are in effect, as are training and educational contracts. The Air Force conducts primary flying training, for example, at a number of civilian contract schools.

One of the largest service contracts and one which performs what would appear to be a purely military task is the operation of the Distant Early Warning (DEW) Line in the Arctic. This air defense radar warning net extends from Iceland to Alaska with approximately forty stations. The single contract in 1961 for manning this vital air defense barrier ran just under forty million dollars.*

Of course, there are many other radar stations in the Arctic manned by military personnel. The military tour of one year in this frigid and inhospitable environment includes no increase in pay for the airman, and of course he must leave his wife and family behind. There are no volunteers for this work, and none ever asks to extend his tour beyond one year. Usually those subjected to this duty understandably elect not to reenlist when their tours of service are completed. So new men must be trained in the operation and maintenance of the complicated electronics gear and ordered north. It is an expensive treadmill.

Should the discharged airman decide to pursue this work at considerably more profit to himself he might be hired by the DEW line contractor. His pay would then be from two to four times as much as it had been in the Service doing precisely the same kind of work—except that he would be free to quit at will in the civilian setup. Leaves, bonuses and pay raises might encourage him to remain in the Arctic with the civilian firm for two, three or even four years. When he returned he might have a stake of several thousand dollars. These are strong inducements for a young man which far exceed any dubious attraction of the military life in the Arctic.

Where should the line be drawn between civilian and uniform for military tasks? Some say that only the special legal status of the military which prohibits absence-without-leave and desertion on pain of stiff penalties can assure that people will be available for orders when danger strikes. But what validity is there in this? Some civilian enterprises are exceedingly dangerous, such as min-

---

* The author commanded this along with other Arctic warning establishments in 1961.

ing, test flying, or construction of high voltage power lines. Yet civilians can be hired who stand up to these risks with all the courage of soldiers in combat.

Before the days of standing armies professional military companies were available for hire. The word of the military unit, "company," has the same beginning as the word for the commercial organization, "company." Swiss companies, hired by any sovereign who could pay their price, fought valiantly and well. From the 12th to the 17th century in Europe these bands of mercenaries appeared in almost every highly organized society. In the 18th century 22,000 Hessian troops were hired by Britain for about three million pounds to fight the American colonies. In the 20th century Chennault's Flying Tigers in China fought valiantly as did the Eagle Squadron in Great Britain. Mercenaries all, by any definition. They garnered all the honor and tradition of military companies raised among the citizens of the government at war. Is this the direction in which we are headed today? We seem to be incapable of attracting men to the colors.

CAN THE DRAFT BE AVOIDED?

Our military system today is rigidly indoctrinated with the *levee en masse* and the conscription principles which have governed the military institutions of all great powers for the past century and a half. Large numbers of men are called up for short periods—a few years at the very most—and then returned to civilian life when the crises of war have subsided. It would be impossible for a country to pay such vast numbers of men what they are truly worth; to attempt to do so would surely bankrupt the government concerned. So a substandard wage for men in the Service has become acceptable. Economic necessity combined with the compelling needs of national defense have led to rationalizations of the natural injustice of coerced military service. Some have become so confused as to call conscription "democratic." Others with more logic insist that loss of freedom and liberty by coercion is slavery, whether for military necessity or not. Unless we intend to perpetuate a fundamental contradiction in our social and political philosophy, a way must be found to correct the anomaly of the draft in an otherwise free society. Of course this must not be done at the risk of survival of that society. The last thing I would advocate would be abolition of the draft without substituting a more effective system for recruiting the necessary military manpower.

Today, in the age of nuclear missilry, we must maintain a constantly ready military force. The military jobs are now highly technical. Years of training are required to develop the skilled specialist. We want such men to remain in service. But we can't keep them there on the low salaries which are so out of step with the salaries of civilian life. Since our greatest concern is national defense, what, then, are we to do? If we wish truly to have the free society we profess, there are only a few alternatives.

1) We can improve our national attitude toward the military and thus increase its prestige and attractiveness; that is, correct the stereotype.

2) We can pay its members more.

3) We can hire civilians to do the military job, paying them whatever might be required to perform the military tasks.

4) Any combination of these. Whichever course we take we should move rapidly, for time is running out and our international competition becomes stiffer each year.

MARTIAL SPIRIT FADES

The martial spirit and the "heroic" image of the soldier are fading in today's efforts to avoid hostilities. The United States Air Force Strategic Air Command (SAC) advertises the motto "Peace is our Profession." The Air Force itself has assured the country that it is devoted to "Aerospace Power for Peace." Manning hundreds of radar stations, watching cathode ray scopes and picking up electronic emissions, day after day, are routine jobs, monotonous and decidedly nonheroic. So, too, is the manning of Nike batteries and Minuteman ICBM's whose crews in subterranean concrete shelters seldom see the light of day. Some of the old spirit is revived among those engaged in the Vietnamese war. But generally speaking, military service grows less exciting. Refueling at sea keeps sailors away from port. It's a waiting game. Fighter and bomber aircraft are wearing out and decreasing in number. The requirement for rated flying officers steadily declined until 1965 when many World War II pilots retired with twenty years of service. But for the long term, the curve points down. Under these circumstances the romance of Service life is lessening and other attractions must be found to induce enlistments.

Does the preoccupation of the military with "defense" and "peace" weaken our deterrent force? Deterrence is not a matter solely of defense, but of the offense. A credible deterrent must include attack and counterattack in its bag of tricks. A potential enemy, to be deterred from incorporating weak nations whom we have pledged to protect, must believe that we have the capability and the will power, if need be, to attack, to punish.

Our national problem is not just to deter a nuclear attack upon our own country. It is, as well, to deter the gradual encroachment of Communism on the free countries of the world. We can't expect to deter this advance with mere words. We must have the military strength to stop it and the courage to use this military strength if necessary. How can we do this if we destroy the martial spirit?

As Morris Janowitz says:

> With the increase in the importance of deterrence of hostilities, the military elite become more and more involved in diplomatic and political warfare, regardless of their preparation for such tasks. Yet, the specific and unique contribution of the military to deterrence is the plausible threat of violence, a threat which can be taken seriously because of the real possibility of violence. Old or new types of weapons do not alter this basic formula. Effective deterrence is, in part, a political strategy.[11]

During World War II there was a lot of behind-the-lines talk about the unpleasant "dirty job" we had to do; how we had to get it over with as soon as possible and get back home to Mom, the girls and the gang. But the men who really fought and bled considered the war to be more than a necessary dirty job. It had to be more. No one is likely to lay down his life simply to accomplish an unpleasant *job*—if that is all it is.

Those who fought hard, who stuck their necks out again and again, were pursuing a high and noble purpose. In the words of General Dwight D. Eisenhower they were on a crusade.[12] The shoulder patch he adopted for SHAFE[13] depicted a crusader's sword. It had real meaning to fighting men. Troops with this crusading ardor were those who won the war.

The war may have been a great engineering accomplishment for the large majority who provided the weapons and supplies to the fighting men, but this logistical support would have been worthless had not the weapons been put into the hands of the people who had the dedication of a high calling. In World War II less than one percent of the military pilots became aces with five or more victories, but these crusaders accounted for roughly thirty to forty percent of the destruction of enemy aircraft in the air. Also, less than one-quarter of the ground troops fired their weapons in battle. Victory depended on a relative handful of those who were *not* behaving in a strictly business-like manner.

Napoleon's maxim has never been proved invalid that "Morale is to the physical as three is to one." An army doesn't get this kind of morale by considering itself a workaday enterprise. The so-called scientific approach to human relations has had some success in the military service but it is not all a positive gain. Beginning with the theories of Frederick Winslow Taylor[14] in the first decade of this century, the concepts of scientific management have been eagerly grasped by the military. Long before industry had adopted these practices the government arsenal at Watertown, Massachusetts, was testing Taylor's principles. Congressional action brought on by union pressure abolished this testing in the military about the time industry was growing interested. In more recent years the Services have adopted industrial personnel practices in whole cloth, with machine records, intelligence tests, comptroller procedures, cost accounting, etc. There can be no question but what these business practices have improved the orderly functioning of military service and have led to many kinds of efficient practices. The one thing they have not done, however, and what they have tended to endanger, is the inspirational character of military service. One cannot get inspired about a code number behind one's name which designates his special skills, particularly when he realizes his job will be determined by an unfeeling machine which matches this number code with a corresponding requirement.[15] To preserve what is left of the martial spirit we must humanize our personnel practices.

SPACE EXPLORATION

Step by step, the public antimilitary tradition is eroding the pride of country and service which cause men to fight. In the past, for example, great explorations and national accomplishments have been a province of the military. Lewis and Clark, Lt. Zebulon Pike, General John Frémont, Admiral Robert Peary, General Adolphus Greely, General George Goethals, and Admiral Richard E. Byrd carried the Stars and Stripes to new lands. Now, when the time has come to explore space, it is felt best to give this task to a nonmilitary organization. Even the military men flying the missions must be cast in a civilian image. Why? Because our political leaders believe this will better demonstrate our peaceful purposes to the world.

Does this make sense? If we find military uses for technical discoveries in our peaceful space explorations will we not exploit this military knowledge? Will we not build military space craft just as soon as a true requirement is revealed? Just as soon as it seems necessary in order to protect ourselves? Does any Soviet citizen doubt this? Any Congo native? Any Cuban "socialist?" Why must we insist on this oversimplified and naïve moralism of "peaceful uses?" Do we truly believe anyone is deceived?

Simply stated, it was our antimilitary hair shirt which caused us to lose the race to put a man in space. Both the Army and the Air Force had ballistic missile boosters capable of this but we insisted on a "peaceful" Vanguard program. Orbiting an object and a man were significant milestones in mankind's progress, yet we accepted second place in each great undertaking—by default.

There was some excuse, but not much, for losing the race to put the first object in orbit about the earth. We were trying to balance the budget in 1955 and were niggardly in supporting the Vanguard project with funds. Our leaders were not impressed by the psychological advantage of putting up a satellite and they could envision no military advantage.[16]

At the Department of Defense level it had been decided to give the Vanguard project to the Navy because the Navy had been left out of appropriations for missiles. In other words, the project was given to the least experienced service as a sop since both the Air Force and the Army were well along in developing Thor, Atlas, Redstone and Jupiter ballistic missiles. The Navy had nothing comparable at the time. No criticism to the Navy is intended. It was in no way responsible for its inexperience. But is there any wonder that Sputnik flew first? Or that the Vanguard program was such a disheartening flop?

After Sputnik there was much frantic activity in government. Money was no longer a problem for space explorations. We magnanimously admitted that the Soviets were ahead and we pretended we were little concerned. But we were. Vitally. No public official likes to see the United States come in second best even if it's in a race we profess not to be running.

To solve this problem, to catch up, we made the same mistake we made in assigning Vanguard to the Navy. Only this time we organized an entirely new administration and put it in charge of space exploration. This new agency was even less experienced than the Navy on matters of space.

Either the Air Force or the Army was prepared to take this ball and run it to the goal. Both the Air Force and the Army were well

on the way. They had developed rocket boosters for long range ballistic missiles of great power and high reliability. The new civilian
space administration was, in the final analysis, obliged to borrow Air
Force and Army facilities, equipment and people to get started.

The National Advisory Committee for Aeronautics (NACA) was
the agency selected to carry on the race for space. For decades this
had been a most effective research agency for aviation technology
but it was totally unprepared for the new task assigned. Nor did
a change in its name to the National Aeronautics and Space Administration (NASA) correct this shortcoming. Again it was the
hair shirt of antimilitarism that influenced this decision.

Six military officers were borrowed from the Air Force, Navy and
Marine Corps to become the first United States astronauts. Immediately their military affiliation was deemphasized. The astronauts
were encouraged not to wear uniforms or use their military rank.
They later appeared before the President in civilian clothes for a
civilian award. It seemed that every step possible was taken to deny
the honor and pride which our military service might have gained
by putting men into space.

The next act could have been predicted. The new NASA established the slow, methodical Mercury Program to put a man in space
without giving more than passing concern to the far-reaching
political and military implications. We *were* in a race, whether admitted or not, and the winning country would be found most attractive to our allies and to the many uncommitted peoples of the earth.
Moreover, the pride, confidence and self-respect of Americans themselves were involved. A great nation cannot be contented with
second place. To be so would be to renounce greatness itself.

NASA plodded along, making test after test, taking no risks. A
new agency could not afford a failure. The public was lulled by
propaganda that it was not possible to catch up with the Soviets for
years to come. According to one report over a million tests were
made of one configuration, and in another case a half million tests
were made on a single piece of electronics gear.[17] This super caution
was not the mark of a winner. Commander Alan B. Shepard, Jr., the
first United States astronaut,[18] remarked at a press conference [19]
that he believed the manned shot could have been made somewhat
earlier; that they were ready enough when the successful flight was
made with the chimpanzee, Ham, which occurred before the Russian
success in orbiting Cosmonaut Yuri Gagarin, on April 12, 1961.[20]
From this it appears that the military astronauts were far ahead

of the NASA scientists who were more concerned with cautious methodology and safety than with the international implications of winning the space race.

In 1964 there were 2,944 United States servicemen killed by accidents, almost all "in line of duty." One hundred and forty of these were in "peacetime" combat in South Vietnam. This clearly demonstrates that the American serviceman is, willing to risk his life in order to advance his country's national interest.[21]

History will not credit the United States with humanitarian motives for making the first manned flight safe for the astronauts. Nor will it condemn the Soviet Union for attempting flights which might have killed its pilots. Many people will be killed in space flight just as air flight has claimed countless lives. This is one price for progress. Innumerable loyal Americans are willing to pay that price. More than military pride was lost in this space race. Few Americans have not experienced a personal loss, a sense of failure, a sad admission that the luster of American greatness has, been tarnished.

Let us hope we shall lose no more races of this sort. To win we must renounce the dog-in-the-manger attitude that we weren't racing in the first place. Not even a great nation can win unless it tries. A measured scientific pace (some have referred to a scientific WPA) with too high a value put on human safety will cause us to fail the great challenges of our age. Our military leaders are eager and able to accept these challenges. But without public trust and confidence in them they are helpless.

COUNTER ARGUMENTS

When the proposition is presented before a civilian audience that there exists a fundamental antimilitary tradition in America, one is sometimes met with a defensive response. Defenders of the American attitude toward the military will point to the huge defense budgets, to the almost universal military training as represented by the draft, to the prestige which is paid by many to those in uniform, to the fact that a good proportion of our national heroes are ex-military men, and to much other evidence which seems to point to the high regard of the nation for its military establishment and military people. As we have seen, however, a student of civil-military relations perceives an undercurrent of aversion to the military.

In his book *The Citizen Army*, Frederick Martin Stern makes the point quite clearly:

This country has long failed to create a military establishment fully acceptable to the people. Almost nobody seems satisfied with it— neither the young men who are drafted nor the military leaders and officers; neither the spokesmen of the Administration nor the members of Congress; neither the educators nor the families. As a result, the military establishment is in a state of continuing experimentation, while grave dissensions divide its leaders.[22]

Those who defend the military reputation are prone to point out that in the Air Force, the Navy and the Marine Corps, billets are filled entirely with volunteers, that only a portion of the Army personnel are drafted. It has been well established that these wholly volunteer services, however, could not meet their manpower requirements without the draft for men to fill the Army. It happens that young men, realizing that the draft is almost inevitable and that by law they must serve a few years in one of the armed services, elect to volunteer in the service of their choice. It is for this reason that the Air Force, Navy and Marine Corps are able to acquire the number of men they need to fill out their manpower authorizations. Young men are forced to volunteer because of the draft.

IDLENESS IN THE MILITARY

Stern differs from most of the other scholarly analysts and authors who have studied the military profession in that he tends to believe another popular stereotype. He has the odd impression that much idleness abounds in the services. My own impression after thirty-four years of service is one of sixty, eighty and hundred hour weeks, Sunday work, night work, and a constant scramble to get jobs done, not tomorrow, not today, but "yesterday."

No one questions that in some former days life as a soldier or sailor was not particularly exacting and there were many idle periods during an enlistment. The writings of Frederick Winslow Taylor [23] refer frequently to "soldiering on the job." This reflected the military image found during the first decade of this century. "Soldiering on the job" meant shirking one's work, or simply loafing. This impression persists as a feature of the antimilitary stereotype. The thesis of Stern's book rests upon the concept that time hangs heavy on the hands of soldiers, sailors and airmen. Hence he feels that what they must learn can be learned better by civilians in short periods of intensive training.

... they are idle for a great part of the time, with the unhappy results to morale—and morals—that idleness always breeds. Of course, armies have always striven to overcome, or at least to hide, such idleness with drills, parades, cleaning, and polishing.[24]

It is quite clear from this passage that Stern looks upon military service as it was performed prior to World War II when funds were so low as to prohibit the procurement of basic weapons. He goes on to say that modern armies achieve the same wasteful results in a more subtle way by training men for jobs to which they are never assigned. He is half right in noting that many skills, and perhaps valuable skills, are not always utilized in the military service. But this can be said of any other large institution. An employee is utilized where he is needed. If he isn't able to perform a particular needed skill, then he is trained to do it, although he may be possessed of many other personal skills which are not then required. The military, like anything purposeful, is not a make-work endeavor. Certain tasks must be done. The incidental available skills of its manpower do not create the tasks.

As long as progress and change persist, there always will be some people who are trained for jobs which they will never undertake. Training takes time and sometimes by the time a course of study has been completed, the piece of gear, an engine or a radar, has been superseded with a new model. In other cases, a technical reorganization may result from a change in national or military policy, as with the cancellation of Bomarc or Dyna-Soar weapon systems. Nothing remains fixed for long.

The all-too-prevalent concept of a professional army, or of any professional military service, is the one gained from history. In the past, the term "standing army" was commonly used. This meant, in effect, that the army was standing ready to defend a nation against an aggressor who crossed its borders. Such an army was normally situated in barracks or in camps near the borders and much of its time was spent in simply waiting. There can be no question that barracks life under these circumstances was often boring and dull, leading to misconduct and public criticism. A French author, Hippolite de Guibert, wrote in 1770 that "all armies consist of the vilest and most miserable part of the citizenry." This was indeed a not uncommon attitude toward the military of that age. Idle soldiers were often unruly and a public problem. The army was employed to stand in defense of the regime and, once trained, required little more activity than to polish equipment and appear on parade. According to de Guibert, discipline was merely a means of keeping the troops out of trouble. No doubt discipline contributed to well-mannered troops, but the purpose of discipline in those days, as today, was to achieve a reliable and effective military force.

THE RIGHT TO BEAR ARMS AND REVOLT

Some of the fundamental doctrines of our society, such as the right to bear arms, are related to the antimilitary tradition and contribute to the stereotype. In England the citizens' right to bear arms had been well established in the 17th century. This right, it was believed, protected the common citizen from despotic lords and kings as the legend of Robin Hood illustrates. It was only natural for the English settlers in America to bring along this fundamental principle. The musket over the fireplace mantel helped the Minuteman feel more secure from oppression. The target of this homespun defense force was, of course, the established government's regiments.

No less an authority on democracy in action than Thomas Jefferson believed strongly in this "right of resistance." Or, to state it more simply, the right to revolt against the government. In a letter to William S. Smith written in 1784, Jefferson wrote:

> What country can preserve its liberties if their rulers are not warned from time to time that their people preserve their spirit of resistance? Let them take arms. The remedy is to set them right as to facts, pardon and pacify them. What signify a few lives lost in a century or two? The tree of liberty must be refreshed from time to time with the blood of patriots and tyrants. It is its natural manure.[25]

In another letter Jefferson wrote to Madison: "I hold it that a little rebellion now and then is a good thing, and as necessary in the political world as storms in the physical. . . . It is a medicine necessary for the sound health of government." [26]

The great English philosopher John Locke stated that whenever force is applied by government which is in the wrong, then the citizen has every right to defend himself against this force, that "all former ties are cancelled, all other rights cease, and everyone has the right to defend himself and resist the aggressor." [27]

In a government such as ours where the professional military forces are governed entirely by the rule of the people expressed through their elected representatives, such a philosophy of revolt appears entirely out of place and unnecessary. The citizens of America can, by their vote, abolish all the military forces now serving if they so choose. The secret ballot, as long as it is honored, is more powerful than the sword. The concept of armed revolt applies only when the government of a nation becomes lost to the people and when the people have no further recourse. Only then as a last resort would there be any purpose in revolt. Sound as were the concepts of Thomas Jefferson and John Locke, they applied strictly to their age and not to ours. This concept of armed revolt against the established authority of government is now more typical of the Communist doctrine. It definitely has merit in a society where the people have no control, or little control, over the government which dictates to them. In present-day United States the concept has little validity.

Of course it can be argued that some day our government may become dictatorial and therefore we should still honor the right to revolt. Should this day come, we shall certainly not save ourselves with hunting rifles stored in our closets. Nor will any semi-trained militia provide us with the protection we might need. The freedom fighters of Hungary in 1956 were helpless against the well-organized professional divisions of the Soviet Union supplied with tanks and all the implements of modern warfare. Any freedom fighters of the future will have to organize and equip themselves similarly to have any hope of success. The Viet Cong guerrillas in South Vietnam, for example, are provided weapons from North Vietnam. With these and the large stocks of American ordnance which they are able to capture the Viet Cong manage to put up a formidable resistance. In the United States the old "right to bear arms" was incorporated into the Bill of Rights of the Constitution in 1798. Although few now consider their hunting rifles as anything more than weapons for sport, the ancient fear persists that professional military forces may back a tyrannical government. Some believe that this can be prevented by keeping the military impotent, hence anything which contributes to this, such as the degradation of military prestige, is a step in the right direction.

IMAGE OF THE PRUSSIAN ARMY

Some Americans persist in comparing their regular military establishment with the stereotype of the Prussian counterpart. The grounds for this thesis will be discussed at length in a later section of this study but a quick reference is necessary here.

The Prussian armies of the 19th and early 20th centuries exerted some political influence,[28] even though their doctrine was to remain aloof from politics. Arguments have been made that this influence led to war, although equally strong arguments can be made that

German generals as frequently recommended peaceful moves. Nevertheless, the vision of a diabolical Prussian military machine leading the world to war remains in the public mind. It is a pity that so many writers such as Gordon A. Craig, Frederick Martin Stern, and Isaac Don Levine, have associated the American regulars with the familiar Prussian military establishments of their mother country. Although Stern specifically warns the reader not to confuse his references to professional army officers with those of the American or British establishments he failed to follow his own warning since his argument rests on the proposition that regular armies are essentially dangerous instruments of government and the citizen can only be protected by the creation of a part-time militia.[29]

A passage from Stern's book clearly reveals his conception and disapproval of the Prussian regular army:

> The grotesque parade step, the "goose step," invented in the eighteenth century for the express purpose of numbing the soldier's senses to anything except the execution of orders, was only a small part of the endless stupefying exercises on the barrack grounds. And besides drill, the soldiers were subjected to all kinds of humiliations and cruel nightly visitations that had nothing to do with training. An official and frequently used method of promoting habits of violence among the soldiers was collective punishment by excessive extra drill. The soldiers were invited to take it out later on some of their comrades. A great many Germans emigrated to America to escape the ordeal of military service.[30]

Stern notes that this system produced professional corporals and sergeants who were imbued with the spirit of brutality.[31] Yet the irregular forces of Brown Shirts and Storm Troopers which Hitler raised were not without brutality. Was the brutality a military or a cultural phenomenon? One wonders whether the cause for this effect might be misplaced.

BRITISH IMAGE OF THE MILITARY

The British also contribute to certain antimilitary stereotypes, among them that of the army of dunces or of the dull-witted. In his *War Memoires* Lloyd George discusses the British army of 1914: "The Army was never considered to be a career for the talents. Rather the reverse. Those who were endowed with brains above their fellows sought other professions where talents were more welcome and better requited. . . ."[32] Winston Churchill's father, Lord Randolph Churchill, held the same belief. Young Winston Churchill was found somewhat wanting in academic attainments at Harrow, so his father sent him to Sandhurst, the British military academy.

Understandably, Churchill never harbored the low opinion of the military held by Lloyd George who believed that independent thinking was impossible in the professional army and that the army encouraged conformity in order to guard against mutiny. Lloyd George felt that training towards mental subservience and absolute obedience caused by army discipline cramped a "suppleness of intellect" and that it was unlikely that this kind of training would ever develop resourceful leaders of men. Winston Churchill's career adequately refutes this prejudice.

The same sort of criticism is often leveled against any well-organized institution. An integrated institution has its doctrines, its rules and its customs which it attempts to enforce. Obviously it cannot be too flexible and remain an institution. Whether the institution be that of medicine, law, religion, or education, the same criticisms can be heard as those of Lloyd George against the professional military.

The unpopularity that the professional military endures in Britain is demonstrated rather clearly by the fact that in 1937, in spite of Britain's then chronic mass unemployment, the Army was 20,000 men short of the planned size.[33] Conscription was introduced as an absolute necessity but not until just three months before the outbreak of World War II. This was considerably too late to prevent the collapse of France.

COMPARING MILITARY AND CIVILIAN EMOLUMENTS

A further illustration of the unpopularity of military service caused by the unhappy stereotype in this country can be found right after the Second World War when the draft was ended temporarily. In order to gain a higher quality of enlistees, the passing marks of intelligence tests were raised modestly from fifty-nine to seventy. This resulted in half of the number of applicants for enlistment being turned down. By the end of 1947 the regular Army and the Air Force were almost 170,000 men below authorized strength. Many inducements for additional education and higher pay proved of little avail in attracting young men to the Services at this time, possibly because the inducements were relatively minor compared to the rewards the "G.I. Bill" provided the veterans for remaining *out* of the service. Stern uses this as an argument for his so-called citizen army. It certainly illustrates the unpopularity of

military service at that time and possibly the inadequacy of inducements which would make military service a truly attractive career,
comparable with careers in civilian life. The pay adjustments which
resulted from the excellent Cordiner Committee studies in 1957 were
of some minor help in increasing the attractiveness of military
service but the full recommendations were never adopted. The Uniformed Services Pay Act of 1963 was another half-hearted effort
to reduce the wide disparity between military compensation and
compensation in other sectors of the economy. Subsequent pay
raises have been so small as to be no more than tokens save for that
achieved by L. Mendel Rivers against Administration opposition
in 1965. Military careers today still compare most unfavorably with
similar careers in civilian life, in terms of pay, benefits, prestige,
retirement and survivor compensations. Ultimate opportunities and
the promise of stability for raising families are missing from
military service.

With all the emphasis placed on improving military conditions
after the Korean experience and throughout the Cold War, for
example, adequate housing for military personnel has yet to materialize. The Capehart program which built houses for military
people at a *net profit* to the government has been allowed to lapse.
True, some small percentage of the professional military are fairly
well housed, but there are still so many thousands of families either
without homes or living in substandard dwellings or trailers that
it is not hard to understand why this sort of life presents such little
attraction.

PROVISIONS IN THE CONSTITUTION

Stern recognized that the supreme command of our regular
forces is vested in the President, with Congress exerting considerable control by holding the purse strings. He also recognized that
our armed forces are aware of their subordination to the civil government and behave accordingly. But he asserts that since the
Constitution makes an issue of this subordination of the regular
military forces, and also that no issue was made with respect to
police forces or other government services, that the need to maintain this civilian subordination must be constantly stressed. He
assumes that the fact that the subordination of the armed services
to the civilian government had to be firmly established and that it
is being discussed from time to time indicates that there is a problem.[34] This reasoning is rather complicated, if not spurious. If noth-

ing else it again reveals the stereotype. The issue at the Constitutional Convention of 1787 was not one of civil-military relations but one of centralized versus decentralized government. No issue was made of the subordination of regular military forces as is often contended. The armed forces were subordinate to the President, of course, while Congress, as a check on the President was authorized to "raise and support armies."

CONCLUSION

The military stereotype which Stern and others have so vividly depicted is a universal monster: often idle, bent on destroying personal liberty, devoted to violence as a solution to all problems both private and public, arbitrary and dogmatic, ignorant and somewhat vacuous, striving for power and waiting in the wings to usurp legitimate civil government at the first opportunity. Because of the presumed gulf between the civilian and the professional soldier it is often impossible for them to communicate. They are sealed from one another.

But this separation is one more of form than of substance. The stereotype is a cruelly twisted and exaggerated caricature. The typical civilian sees this twisted image, or something like it, when he regards a military man because his vision has been conditioned. Thus the illusion tends to become the mother to the fact.

Pay and emolument of the military services are so poor as often to border on poverty. The martial spirit has become discredited and the elan and dedication of service are waning. Only the draft keeps military spaces filled, but with green, inexperienced men the best of whom separate at their first opportunity. Unless the military stereotype can be corrected it might be necessary to contract for more military services in order to maintain an adequate posture for defense.

CHAPTER 4

COLD WAR ESSENTIALS

A humorous and secretly approving chord in the American personality is struck when one hears that "the British lose every battle but the last one," or that "the British always seem to muddle through." This subtle admiration for disorder and confusion may stem from a deep-seated Anglo-Saxon temper for revolt against established authority in any form. Order and purpose, of course, are manifestations of authority. Whatever the antecedent may be to this implicit faith in success, no matter how poorly prepared we may be, it is one British inheritance which has had a great influence on our lives and fortunes. Herodotus said, "Given time enough, anything will happen," and we seem to feel that we have plenty of time and whatever happens will always be to our ultimate favor. Will the nuclear missile age permit us the time to muddle through again? That is the pressing question of our day which demands an answer.

An Old Testament proverb says, "Where there is no vision, the people perish." In the past, time permitted us to cut and try, to hang on grimly, until the solution was revealed to us. And we survived.

In the future as in the past it will be the loss of hope rather than the loss of life which will decide our wars.[1] When men reach the point where they see and feel that further effort and sacrifice are futile they bow to the inevitable. In the past, too, this moment of truth sometimes has come before fighting broke out. Even more likely in the future, considering the awesome character of nuclear war, the end may well come with a whimper because the consequences of resistance would seem to be so devastating. Thus the great nuclear holocaust that has been so widely predicted in the last twenty years may never occur, yet the possibility of defeat and slavery remains with Western man as never before.

George Kennan once likened the contest between the free world and the Communist world to "two scorpions in a bottle." Perhaps this oversimplifies the problem because scorpions are not as likely to change their habits as are the social systems of mankind, but until a very great deal of change occurs to bring the free world and Communism closer together there can be no question about each side's capability to sting the other. Should the sting of the Western scorpion become less lethal than the sting of the Eastern scorpion, and this fact becomes known, the chances of war will be slight but the consequences of peace will be devastating.

Another oversimplified parable frequently heard is that the world resembles two men in a gas-filled room, each with a match in his hand. Now the conclusion desired by purveyors of these neat analogies is that neither man should strike his match because all the world would be blown up. Therefore the *only* solution is de-matching both men. No one is supposed to suggest that a window be opened because that would leave the two men capable of fighting again—and fighting must be ended, once and for all. Some people prefer to keep the room full of gas in order to assure the ultimate de-matching even though the mutual trust necessary would introduce vast and unknown risks to survival, keeping in mind that matches are easily hidden. The military man, on the other hand, would like to find a way to purge the room of gas or introduce a new chemical which would prevent the inflammatory gas from igniting.

A most unattractive course of action would be to stand there in the room with matches poised to strike. The time has passed when America can rock along hoping that something good will turn up and resting her survival on a kind of blind faith in the inevitability of the "good" American way. If at no other time in our history, this is the time for purpose. In the words of Demosthenes, ". . . nothing, if you take precaution, is to be feared; nothing, if you are negligent, goes as you desire." [2]

THE MILITARY PLATEAU

The dilemma created by the awful facts of nuclear war has caused a rebellion against what certain civilian specialists claim to be outdated military doctrine.[3] The conception that military superiority over potential enemies is the best defense which has guided successful statecraft and military operation throughout the ages has given way to esoteric concepts such as "mutual deterrence," "minimum or finite deterrence" and "parity." Since the United States enjoys a military superiority it is an easy matter to achieve parity by a slow-down of military development. We are sometimes told that a plateau has been reached where no further technological break-throughs can be anticipated and that all we need do now is to hold our own, making minor improvements in existing weapons. In other words, we are led to believe that the pattern for nuclear war has been established for a long time to come and that we can now settle back and relax.

It might be appropriate at this point to quote a passage from Vannevar Bush's *Modern Arms and Free Men*. Perhaps he saw coming the hopeless and despairing attitude which has character-ized the recent decisions of our highest Defense leaders.

> The course of history [wrote our wartime chief scientist] is determined by the faith that men are guided by. If they misread the lesson of expanding knowledge and in their brazen egotism believe that all things are knowable, then they will see nothing but an endless repeating pattern of sordid strife, the ascendancy of ruthlessness and cunning, man damned to exist a little time on earth where there is nothing higher than to seize and kill and dominate. If they see beyond this they will see by faith, and not by reading instruments or combining numbers.[4]

History has provided few plateaus in human experience where progress ceased. But in modern history, in this era of exploding tech-nology in which we find ourselves, it is foolhardy indeed to suggest that scientific discovery and military technical progress have begun to level off. Weapons which appear to be invincible today may be duds tomorrow. A laser beam, a trail of fine sand orbiting the earth, a certain kind of radiation, or an entirely new development of science may pull the fuse from all nuclear weapons. The plateau is a harpy, a siren song to complacency. As Dr. Edward Teller said, "We live in an 'Alice in Wonderland' world: we must run very fast just to stay in the same place." Unless we continue to strive, might-ily, our Communist competition may achieve the weapon defenses which we have denied could be found. Then, defeat with a whimper will mark our epitaph.

Seneca said, "Worse than war is the fear of war." It is the fear of nuclear war that is causing a rebellion against the traditional military doctrine of superiority.[5] This fear will not be dispelled by attempting to change the immutable characteristics of mankind, but it might well be allayed by surrender.

APPEALS TO REASON

Even pacifist Bernard Shaw once said that "Peace shall not prevail save with a sword in her hand," and the Goddess of Justice is so typified. Yet we are perpetually bombarded with advice from starry-eyed idealists who urge the lamb to lie down with the lion. The novelist Thomas Mann speaking in Zurich on his seventy-fifth birthday said "the United States should take the initiative for a universal peace conference whose task would be an over-all financing of millions of people. This would be humanistic communism." The United States did something like this with its Marshall Plan but the lion is still stalking us. The architect Frank Lloyd Wright assured us in 1950 that "We have nothing to fear in abandoning the atom arms race. Russia wants peace just as much as we do." [6] These remarks were just the beginning of those which have been raised to a crescendo today. And the current experts are often as little qualified as the novelist and the architect to speak on national policy. But the nuclear weapon, possibly because of its universal threat, has created a strange variety of international and military experts. There are those who sincerely believe that our danger is caused not by the Communists but by a "military industrial partnership" in this country which is keyed to perpetual fear and patriotic fervor bent on nothing more than the extension and preservation of capitalism and privilege.[7]

There has been much talk along this line in relation to the arms control and disarmament philosophies now at large. It is argued that the arms race was started by the United States and can only be halted by a unilateral United States initiative. In spite of the fact that the Western world scrapped its arms and demobilized its armies after 1945 while the Soviet Union moved boldly into the power vacuums of Eastern Europe, the proposition is repeated that our strength now leaves the Soviets in fear of our possible aggression.

IRRATIONAL NATURE OF WAR

During World War II a rash of literature was published in an effort to understand better the nature of the war we were then fighting. A Study of War, by Quincy Wright,[8] was one massive, two-volume effort. Another by Mark A. May [9] attempted to analyze the socio-psychology of war. Neither effort ascribed to war the simplistic causes so popular today among the arms control and disarmament followers. May listed at least seven motives for fighting and another seven counter-motives for not fighting.[10] The general conclusion one draws from thoughtful works of this nature is that there is no simple cause of war but that a multiplicity of conflicting motivations are at work, many of them irrational and frequently associated with fear and hate. The human mind, May points out, is "tempted to select some one principle and exaggerate its importance at the expense of alternate possibilities." [11] We search for simple logical explanations to complex and often illogical situations.

The proposition has many times been expressed by philosophers and analysts of the past two World Wars that "The modern world, highly skeptical of war as a useful institution, encounters it as a disaster, and whomever the particular combatant blames for the disaster he will seek to exterminate. Such an approach makes for unrestricted warfare and destroys the basis for any kind of international law of war." [12] In other words, because wars are no longer acceptable in terms of international law as expressed by Hugo Grotius [12] and susequent jurists, wars must be accounted for in moral rather than legal terms. This unleashes the passions and leaves little room for reconciliation or negotiation. The consequence is a bloody fight to the death with total war since our side is always "right" and the opponent always "wrong." With war so regarded, the chances of nuclear war and the extermination of populations are more likely. We cannot be saved by mere protestations that such a war would be too horrible.

After the first World War Europeans were obsessed with the horrors of war and the theory grew that no individual in his right mind could be cruel enough to take the initiative in starting a war. Thus, it was reasoned, wars burst out through "an enigmatical chain of circumstances," something like a social disease. This idea was expressed vividly in Tolstoy's *War and Peace* in which he portrayed the defeat of Napoleon, not to mention Napoleon's invasion itself, as a consequence of interacting chance events. This theory of war led to the inevitability notion which is just one step away from the fatalistic nothing-can-be-done-to-prevent-it attitude.[13]

Although much can be said for the disease theory of war, it would be a mistake to accept it as an enigmatic phenomenon not subject to rational analysis or control. The fatalistic approach in any area of human endeavor can lead only to stagnation, ignorance, and eventual extinction.

But it may be just as dangerous to let the pendulum swing to the other extreme and assume that all war can be prevented if we will it so with enough determination. One approach to this is the effort to wipe war from our minds by calling it "unthinkable." Obviously, a phenomenon which becomes "unthinkable" cannot be examined, studied or controlled and the end result is not far removed from the "inevitable" attitude. Both approaches are fatalistic.

Generally speaking, however (disregarding the ambitious nation for the moment), a country goes to war when its national interests are threatened to the degree that it feels peace would present even more dangers than war. This fear of the peace may be irrational and closely associated with the passions of hate but it is nonetheless real.

SOME CONCEPTS OF WAR CAUSE

There was much talk at the time of the Taiwan Straits Crisis of 1958 that we should not consider going to war over Quemoy and Matsu Islands. They were militarily indefensible, said the hand-wringers, and besides, the offshore islands meant nothing to us.[14]

Should we have had to fight, it would most certainly not have been to save Quemoy. It would have been to defend a great principle without which we could well become Communist subjects. This principle is the backbone of United States foreign policy today and the credo of the United Nations as well: naked, unprovoked armed aggression must be everywhere resisted by the Free World. One of our most peace-loving Presidents, Thomas Jefferson, found it necessary to subdue the Barbary Pirates even though we were well able to pay their "tribute."

United States tradition is steeped in this principle. Nor did we fight the Civil War over Fort Sumter because this small Federal fortification in Charleston Harbor was overcome by a Confederate artillery blockade. The Civil War was not fought to return Fort Sumter to the Union but rather to uphold the principle that armed insurrection was no way to solve a domestic political problem.

The United States did not fight the Spanish American War to gain an indemnity for the battleship *Maine* sunk in Havana Harbor. We fought to free our friends and neighbors from what we believed to be a cruel subjugation. Our ideals were not quite as lofty and courageous during Cuba's trials in 1961.

Certainly we did not enter the first World War simply because Germany had torpedoed the *Lusitania*. Here again we were convinced that armed aggression was on the loose and if we rested supinely in the face of this unleashed force, we would be the next victim.

Nor did we fight World War II over Pearl Harbor. This angered us, to be sure, and it certainly proved that armed aggression was running wild. But it wasn't the ships and men we lost, as such, for which we fought. It was to convince aggressors that we and our peaceful friends were not to be kicked around.

We didn't fight in 1950 to save South Korea, although some policy-makers must have believed so considering the unsatisfactory outcome. We fought in Korea because we believed it wrong for the Communists to march into any undefended country, particularly a country which looked to us for help. Our actions were punitive but they fizzled out through fear of greater involvement.

Some of our leaders were unduly concerned about extending this war with atomic weapons, so when the Chinese Reds attacked us under the blatantly transparent disguise of "volunteers," we failed to retaliate. The end result was something of a stalemate, the bitter fruits of which we picked at Dien Bien Phu, with the loss to the Free World of North Vietnam, and with the later bitter struggle in South Vietnam.

Our announced purpose in the Vietnam struggle is to assist our friends, the South Vietnamese, to build a free and stable country. But the great resources in blood and treasure which we have devoted to this conflict would indicate that our motives are somewhat more comprehensive. It seems obvious that we wish to check the expansion of Communism in Asia but that we fear to use the force necessary because of the risk of becoming embroiled in another war with China, or even the U.S.S.R. How far should we go? That is the daily question.

A bully remains a bully unless he is "clobbered good." And we failed to teach the Red Chinese bully a lesson in Korea. Instead we gave him encouragement. He learned he could confront us with impunity. He still believes armed aggression will pay off at the opportune time. Communist China does not subscribe to peaceful co-existence, not even the Soviet brand. Because we feared to enlarge the Korean War, Red China thinks we will eventually knuckle under. Mao Tse-tung should consult a textbook of United States history. He might be surprised to learn that the Korean War was atypical of the American political philosophy.

Speaking in San Marios, Texas on April 10, 1965, President Lyndon B. Johnson clearly expressed the traditional United States policy. The President warned that the Communist world should not misjudge the United States purpose. In measured phrases he said, ". . . when we have given our commitments to others we shall keep them." The course of history was set on a "tragic direction in the 1930's by men who "misread our American purpose, misjudged our American will and—not least of all—miscalculated the spirit and stamina of American youth."

Talk of Quemoy being militarily indefensible in 1958 was pure defeatism. Quemoy or any area can be adequately defended if the United States is determined to use whatever force is necessary to do the job. Careless and ignorant talk of the hopelessness of defending any position whether South Vietnam or Berlin, can contribute to the fact. This invites the despair which leads to surrender. Unless we stop the many small leaks in the dikes of the Free World bastion we may suffer a Red inundation which itself could lead to general war.

THE HYPERBOLIC INTERPRETATION

It is frequently overlooked, however, that wars themselves change the motives which led to them in the first place. Wars are ideal breeding grounds for hates, superstitions, misconceptions, strong beliefs, violent passions, new national attitudes and altered national interests. The Thirty Years' War began as a religious conflict and ended a dynastic struggle with Catholics fighting Catholics. The disgraceful defeat of France at Sedan in 1871 led to the *revanchism* which welcomed the war of 1914. The slaughter of the Somme offensive in 1916, and the senseless blood bath of Verdun, led to the Anglo-French pacifism which encouraged Hitler to launch the second World War believing that he could get away with a quick and easy victory. Perhaps no other influence has such a marked effect on national interests than war itself, and when it is waged the initial causes of the war are sometimes subordinated into oblivion by the white-hot issues generated in combat. It is for this reason that a true statesman is slow to anger and slower to commit his country to a dangerous course of action.

National interests are, of course, dynamic. Some, such as those principles written into the Constitution have great lasting power but these, too, are subject to constant reinterpretation and amendment. Considerably more volatile are our foreign policies which may change from day to day on the decision of the Chief Executive, as witness the aboutface of the United States toward France and Great Britain at the time of the Suez crisis of 1956. It would be foolhardy indeed to go to war to protect a national interest which might change before the war ended. National interests, too, when poorly defined, can encourage aggression. The clear indication given by the United States that South Korea was not a part of its strategic defense perimeter was a direct contribution to the North Korean aggression of 1950.

Raymond Aron notes that:

> One can conceive of a society living in one way in time of peace and another way in wartime, but this depends on the war and peace being two distinctly separate states. The cold war and the risk of surprise attack are condemning the democracies to permanent mobilization.[14]

Thus the hyperbolic nature of war is felt even in peacetime, which actually is not peace at all in the traditional sense.

With the heating up of cold war and the intensification of hot war, human attitudes and passions rise accordingly. Once on the slippery slope of war the management of government and of men becomes less and less predictable. The ultimate end of this trend is a complete breakdown of human society with anarchy and chaos in the saddle like that after the fall of Rome. The counter to this is, of course, discipline, but disclipine threatens individual freedom and initiative. It is upon this dilemma that modern democracy rests.

But democracy *can* be sufficiently sophisticated to steer a middle course between too much discipline and too much freedom, as the history of our country attests. One of the most vital questions of our times is: are we straying from the middle course? And the middle course in today's nuclear environment may not be the same middle course of the past.

DENIGRATION THE MILITARY

Associated with the belief that America is threatening the Soviet Union and causing the arms race is the belief that men in uniform are primarily responsible. If not that, at least it is the uniformed men who fight to retain the arms they believe to be necessary for national defense. Therefore it stands to reason that if any progress in arms reduction is to be made the professional military advice must be discredited.

It is not likely that there is a conscious conspiracy to cut the uniformed leaders down to size, but the dynamic arms control movement has certainly encouraged such action. Much more pervasive and effective than a conspiracy is a sincere revolution in thought and doctrine. This movement continues to recruit adherents from all walks of life.

A spate of books, articles and motion pictures has gained much popularity, some reaching best-seller proportions, by ridiculing the man in uniform. A theme of particular popularity is that a military leader may suddenly become insane and plunge the world into nuclear war.[17] Some of these wild stories are passed off as being based upon truth, a prevarication as vicious as yelling "Fire!" in a crowded theater. As John F. Loosbrock has written, ". . . there *is* a growing case of antimilitary zealotry in the land. . . . Much of it, we suspect, finds its roots in the internal frustration of the intellectual utopian. He sees an imperfect world tense and divided when he desperately wants to see a world that is unified and perfect." [18]

Of all the people to come to the defense of the military in this crisis of confidence, Roswell L. Gilpatric, former Deputy Secretary of Defense, was the least likely to do so. Yet he did.[19] After describing how smooth and congenial were the civil-military relations in the Pentagon, he went on to explain that "a wide array of physical restraints on nuclear firing," and coded locks on nuclear weapons called "permissive action links," make it almost impossible for anyone but the President to fire a nuclear weapon. This hardly demonstrates the confidence in the military he implied. Mr. Gilpatric makes it quite clear that the military role "is one of professional advice and judgment, not decision making." In other words the man in uniform is relegated to the position of a mere technician who may not even make decisions on technical matters. If a military leader were actually denied the right to make decisions he would be worthless indeed. In fact most analysts of the essential characteristics for military leadership put "decisiveness" well toward the top.[20] But such is the role of military subordination visualized by a former top civilian Defense administrator.

A more real but less dramatic danger to the country was expressed by Jack Raymond, a *New York Times* Pentagon correspondent and author of the excellent book, *Power at the Pentagon*.[21] The militarism so feared, he told an audience at the Pentagon, "may be brought about by civilian leaders." [22] He decried the trend toward concentration of power in the defense establishment which is exerted "not by military officers but by appointed civilians."

TIME FOR COURAGE

Raymond Aron wrote that democracies are in danger of being contaminated by the enemy. "But," he said, "those who use this argument in order to refuse measures of resistance should imagine what contamination there would be if the democracies should, un-luckily, succumb." [23] The contamination, however, is real, and the enemy is as much fear itself as it is the antithetical doctrine of Communism. Military men have been thoroughly discredited and muzzled. The defense strategy of the nation, from policy to common tactics, is being dictated by "thermonuclear strategists" whose theories began to reshape American policy with the advent of the Kennedy Administration in 1961.

Civil-military relations have been rapidly changing in the new environment and the indispensible values of the past are being cavalierly thrust aside in the name of the new "logic." Some claim that military men have so alienated themselves in the ideological battle as to become ineffectual. Others assert that ". . . their claims and remonstrances in a world preoccupied with survival must not be thrust aside with a yawn or branded as puerile and self-seeking by intellectuals and politicans who cannot see beyond the transient political harmonies that have assured their own place in the sys-tem." [24] Yet George Kelly has warned against a dangerous imbal-ance of "unrepresented elements" (the military) seeking ways of solving the nuclear dilemma which do not command the consensus of the community. As long as the military is gagged, its traditional ethics and motives questioned, and its professional doctrines ridi-culed, it is little wonder that it fails to generate a consensus. Inter-estingly, Kelly believes military men protest too much about their "representativesness" as Americans. (Just how representative the military is of the American public will be discussed later although this feature of the civil-military contest seems to be a relatively minor one.) But should the military ever break its professional code and, as many other federal employees do, organize politically and vote as a body, the representativeness of the military would no longer be at issue. No one wants this, particularly the military. How-ever, I submit that the "unrepresented" military *can* command a consensus of the community. Should it ever happen that the military became truly representative, i.e., exercised the political prerogatives of other American citizens, the character of American government would, to say the least, be radically changed. But even this might be preferable to the options of Communism or nuclear war.

To avoid such radical possibilities, we must do just one thing. We must stiffen our spines and determine to protect ourselves. We must adopt a policy like that voiced by Winston Churchill in 1952. "Our policy is, by hard sacrifice and constant toil, to increase the deterrents upon an aggressor. We shall do our utmost short of going bankrupt to increase these deterrents. . . ." [25]

The American military profession rests upon measures to deter an aggressor from war. The philosophy is as old as mankind, as old as fear itself: If you have superior power and your adversary knows it, he will not attack. This works. Without exception wars have begun because the initiator believed he could win. The doctrine of superiority is old and hoary. It needs no logic. Its proof is in the cocoon of history. Those countries who have ignored the lesson no longer exist.

PART II

ORIGINS OF THE MILITARY PROFESSION

CHAPTER 5

THE PRAETORIAN LEGEND

In early classical times military command and statecraft were integral. "War is the trade of kings," wrote John Dryden although this applied more truly to the ancients than to his era. Ancient rulers were the principal generals: Darius, Alexander, Caesar, Hadrian. War was a primary function of the rulers. There was no such thing as civilian supremacy over the military because of the absence of nonmilitary leaders.[1] In Greece, military service was a prerequisite to citizenship and a high place in government. Separation of the military from citizenship and statecraft in order to prevent the military from controlling the state was never an issue in itself. To be sure there were continued power plays between rival factions, but there were no civil-military distinctions made.[2]

BEGINNINGS OF SEPARATION

Separation of the military from politics began first to manifest itself during the days of the Roman Empire. This came about when the Roman government began to incorporate barbarians into its defense establishment.[3] The decadence of the declining Empire inevitably led to finding unsophisticated provincials to undertake the hard work of defense.[4] Before long many military chieftains in the provinces of questionable loyalty to Rome held the reins of power. Through the Praetorian Guard in Rome they sometimes influenced the selection of the Emperor.[5] This Praetorian Guard example is repeatedly called up to illustrate the dreadful consequences of allowing the military to exercise the prerogatives of civilian citizens. But the example is often grotesquely distorted, particularly when applied to our American military system.

THE PRAETORIAN GUARD

The Praetorian Guard was usually the only body of troops in

Rome and thus similar to the *Guardia Civil* of many modern Latin American states. Composed of nine thousand picked men,[6] it was obvious that any aspirant to the throne would have to gain support of this military-police force in order to survive.[7] Even so, the Praetorian Guard rarely exercised its influence except in a crisis, and it must be admitted that its selections were not all bad.[8]

Claudius was the first to become emperor through the Guard support in A.D. 41. He replaced Caligula, a manifestly insane ruler. Although not popular, Claudius carried forward the progressive program established by Augustus with considerable statesmanship. Client-states were absorbed, southern Britain was incorporated, and public works advanced. Claudius was succeeded by the odious Nero, who was *not* a Praetorian selection.

Nero's excesses caused the household Praetorians again to step in with Oltho as their candidate. But troops in the provinces likewise had candidates. Vespasian, leading a coalition of armies of the Danube and the Euphrates, prevailed and assumed the throne. It must be noted that Vespasian was not a Praetorian Guard champion, although he might be termed a man on horseback—one who achieves his place with military force. However, this was not an uncommon method of accession throughout ancient times, even during the Greco-Roman republics.

Vespasian was followed by two sons, Titus and Domitian. The cruel excesses of the latter resulted in his not unjustified assassination by his wife and secretaries, with Guard assistance. Nerva, a Guard selection, proved an upright and honorable emperor. His adopted son and successor, Trajan, himself a tough soldier, dominated the Praetorian Guard and sent it off to war in the Provinces.[9]

There followed three capable adoptive emperors: Hadrian, Antonius and Marcus Aurelius. The last reigned with signal success and devotion to duty until his death in 180 A.D. During this period the boundaries of the Roman Empire crept forward and reached their maximum extent. Historians usually do not attribute selection of these emperors to excessive Praetorian influence, although the age was marked by increasing centralization and bureaucratic control and the Guard was definitely an instrument of power.[10] Marcus Aurelius was followed by a worthless son, Commodius, who ushered in a century of war and disorder "during which nothing but the stern rule of soldier-emperors saved the empire from dissolution." [11]

From this evidence it would seem that it was by no means the

Praetorian Guard which caused the degeneration of Imperial Rome. Had it not been for the stiffening influence of the Guard, Rome probably would have collapsed much sooner. The Guard's influence on the Empire was but one symptom of a cultural disease, not the disease itself. "When decline and defeat finally overtook the legion, Rome's military institutions had outlasted the Empire they were preserving. The kernel had rotted before the shell showed signs of cracking." [12]

RULE OF PROVINCIAL CHIEFTAINS

Disintegration was rapid as the various provincial armies put forward their claimants to the purple. The barbaric Goths, Persians and Franks broke through the weakened frontiers in the third century. Provincial chieftains ceased to pay allegiance to Rome and the Empire split up. Thus began the completely autocratic rule in Rome which was to prevail through the Middle Ages.

Whether autocracy is better government when conducted by civilians or by soldiers is open to some question. Certainly autocracy is not necessarily government *by* the military as witness modern civilians Stalin, Hitler and Mussolini. On the other hand, the autocracies of Alexander, Caesar, Augustus, Vespasian, Trajan, Hadrian, Frederick II, and Napoleon (all military men) have been regarded as fairly progressive and enlightened—as autocracies go.

PAX ROMANA

Detractors of the Praetorian Guard usually fail to point out that the first two centuries of the Roman Empire when the Guard was most influential was also the period of the *Pax Romana*. At least, if the Praetorian Guard controlled the Roman emperors, it was able to do so in such a manner as to provide the longest period of peace in recorded history.[13] Moreover, this period from the accession of Augustus in 14 B.C. to the murder of Commodius in 192 A.D., a period of peace marred only by the brief civil wars of 68-69 A.D., was marked by great progress in law, colonial government, art, literature, philosophy and science. It was the age of Plutarch the historian, of Marcus Aurelius the scholar-emperor, of Ptolemy the Greek astronomer and mathematician, and of the authors Quintillian, Seneca and Pliny. This "Golden Age of Rome" which coincided with the period of the Praetorian Guard's eminence has never been matched before or since as a protracted period of human peace, prosperity and progress. It marked the climax of classical civilization.[14]

When the *pax* came to an end with the murder of Commodius by his servants in 192, the Praetorian Guard tried to auction the throne but failed. The Guard had lost its influence over forces in the field.[15] The armies on the frontiers then put forward their candidates and the empire burst into civil war which was to extend, off and on, for almost a century. Septimius Severus, originally a citizen of Punic Africa who commanded the army on the Danube, won the prize after Commodius. He did nothing for Rome and after his death there were thirty emperors in fifty-three years, many of whom like Severus were generals of barbarian stock. Roman legions were filled with Germans, Britons, Numidians and other foreigners. Wealthy Romans were habitually executed and their lands confiscated to pay the troops. Plunder became a regular practice. Terrible inroads were made on the Empire's economy and Rome's leadership crumbled.[16] Was this degradation of Rome caused by the Praetorian Guard? Or was it because the Roman Guard had lost its power and influence to hold Rome up?

COMPARISON OF GUARD AND SENATE

When the Guard had been a leading influence in Rome, Rome prospered and peace reigned. Indeed, the Praetorian Guard did a much better job of securing peace and prosperity than the Roman Senate ever did even in the days of its true power during the Republic.

Nor was the Guard responsible for the imperial system. It was the Senate that gradually allowed its powers to be whittled away by strong men such as the Gracchi, Sulla, Pompey, and Crassus until Julius Caesar finally assumed supreme authority.[17] One might say, too, that the Roman citizen grew indifferent to popular government and its responsibilities. He was degraded with bread and circuses and exempted from military service.[18]

It might be noted here that in the last days of the Republic the Roman Senate had become a corrupt oligarchy which resorted to murder to rid itself of reformers like Tiberius Gracchus and his followers. For this despicable practice one seldom hears a condemnation of the Roman Senate *as an institution* as one so frequently hears condemnation of the Praetorian Guard. The Senate was at least as power-mad as the Guard became and as nonrepresentative of the body politic. One might ask which institution was more legitimate? Which was better for Rome and its citizens? Which made the greater contribution to history?

Probably no institution of history has been so unjustly maligned as the Praetorian Guard. The literature of the modern Western world seems to have distorted this history as a consequence of the growing separation of the military from civilian society, and because of the aversion of civilian authors to things military.

SOCIAL DISINTEGRATION OF ROME

To blame the degeneration of Rome on the Praetorian Guard is grossly to oversimplify a vast and complicated social disintegration in all areas, from agriculture to economics, from government to patriotism, from law to morality. Who can say which one factor was most responsible? It took a whole matrix of disparate and debilitating influences operating over centuries of time to bring mighty Rome to her demise, and she died hard. Because Rome had been the ultimate world power for so many centuries, her end was never fully conceded. The spiritual symbol of Rome inspired Charlemagne no less than Napoleon and justified the Holy Roman Empire which survived until 1806. In this century even Mussolini tried to revive the Roman spirit and today the Roman Catholic Church is to some degree supported on the pillars of ancient Roman prestige.[19]

It can be argued just as strongly that Rome's separation of military matters from statecraft was as responsible for her destruction as was the influence of the Praetorian Guard in affairs of state during the first three centuries A.D. When the rulers and governing officials turned matters of defense over to military experts of doubtful loyalty, the rulers lost touch with the major realities of politics.[20]

As Rome's disintegration progressed, the military repeatedly stepped in and provided, if not peace, at least some semblance of order. And once again military leadership and state leadership became one and the same, prevailing through the feudalistic period of the Middle Ages. Not until nationalism and commercialism gained such dominance and power as to control governments and hire armies was the military again separated from direct dealings in affairs of state.

CHAPTER 6

THE CROMWELLIAN LEGACY

Literature dealing with civil control of the military contains two principal villians: the Prussian General Staff and Oliver Cromwell. It might be well to examine some of the Cromwellian legends in the light of their history. From a military point of view this approach suggests some novel interpretations.

THE REVOLUTIONARY ARMY

Much of the English tradition for separation of civil and military affairs originates as a consequence of the Great Rebellion during the first part of the 17th century. During this period in which Cromwell rose to dictatorship, the army of Parliament was a highly political organization and on several occasions controlled the government itself. It can hardly be claimed, however, that this New Model Army (as it was called after Cromwell made several reforms of discipline and gave it regular pay and a uniform) was a professional force comparable to today's professional establishments. The New Model Army was a revolutionary army, and like all revolutionary armies, it was steeped in the political hatreds, convictions and philosophies which had caused the revolution.[1]

This is not to say that the New Model Army did not become a most effective military instrument. Before Cromwell died his army was respected and feared throughout Europe. Nevertheless, it was largely Cromwell's private army and had little professional tradition except to serve him, the Protector and Captain-General. In this capacity it was a true political force and provided Cromwell with the ultimate authority of government in defiance of Parliament. It was not praetorian. It did not lead. It was the dictator's instrument. Its modern counterpart would be more akin to the Nazi Storm Troops or the *Waffen* SS than to any of today's regular establishments.[2]

BEGINNING OF THE GREAT REBELLION

The Great Rebellion came about initially as a result of Parliament's extreme dissatisfaction with King Charles I. His disregard of the Commons, double-dealing, illegal taxation, unpopular religious policies (his wife was a Catholic), and what were considered to be treasonous acts in deals with Spain, the Irish and the Scots, led Parliament to assume all of the functions of government. This required the raising of an army which by all military standards (except for Cromwell's horse) was an undisciplined rabble. At one point Manchester [3] was reluctant to accept the order to march against the King because he claimed that the army "cannot be commanded by Parliament without consent of the association of provinces which raised it for its own defense." [4]

In 1642 King Charles fled from his capital in fear of the mobs of London. The King had had the temerity a few days earlier to invade the House of Commons with three or four hundred swordsmen to arrest its leaders. The violent reaction to this illegal act touched off the conflict that had been brewing for some years. [5] Actual fighting began between the King's Cavaliers and the forces of Parliament (called the "Roundheads" for their close-cropped hair, or later "Ironsides" for Cromwell's original regiment) at Edgehill in October where the battle "was marked by abundant ignorance on both sides" [6] and ended in a draw. [7] The war dragged on for four bloody years. Roundhead fortunes went badly at first under the leadership of Essex [8] as commander-in-chief and Manchester who commanded the forces of East Anglia. The army was eroded by desertion and disease. Even a resounding Roundhead victory at Marston Moor in July 1644 failed to turn the tables because King Charles later managed to outmaneuver and defeat Essex who had available twice the manpower of the King. [9]

CROMWELL REFORMS THE ARMY

That winter Cromwell returned to London in order to assume his duties as a Member of Parliament. A devout Independent Puritan with no sympathy for the Presbyterianism of the Scots who had allied themselves with Parliament, Cromwell violently disagreed with the way the war was being conducted. He also attacked Essex and Manchester for incompetence and urged a complete reconstruction of the army along the lines of his own successful cavalry regiments. [10]

To purge the army of officer-politicians who also held memberships in Parliament, a "Self-denying Ordinance" was passed. This excluded members of either House from the army. The few lords, Essex and Manchester in particular, who remained in Parliament and those who had had charge of the war up to then were thus eliminated from the forces. Cromwell also resigned his commission. But the new Commander-in-Chief, Sir Thomas Fairfax, needed Cromwell, the man-of-the-hour. So Parliament authorized a single exception to the Self-denying Ordinance and permitted Cromwell to serve as "General of the Horse." [11]

Under Cromwell's guidance the army was reorganized from top to bottom. The essence of this reorganization achieved unity of command without regard to local interests or aristocratic birth. "The Puritan faith equaled the Spartan ethic in making invincible soldiers." [12] Cromwell instituted a tightened discipline and raised morale with regular supply and pay. He fired his troops with an *esprit* backed by a religious fervor which had not been seen in armies since the conquests of Islam almost a millenium earlier.

END OF THE FIRST CIVIL WAR

The reorganized army of Parliament met King Charles at Naseby on June 14, 1645 and inflicted a crushing defeat on the Royalists. This battle was the decisive clash which caused the war eventually to end in favor of the Roundheads, although mopping up continued for almost a year. After the last of the royal forces surrendered at Oxford in 1646, Parliament had successfully seized every vestige of sovereignty.[13] But even after the Self-denying Ordinance the Ironsides never ceased being a political influence. This was an inevitable consequence of revolution and the questionable legitimacy of the instruments of government, but it was accentuated by an unappreciative House of Commons.

The fighting over, Parliament promulgated military policies so heartless and shortsighted as to invite outright military revolt. It made a deal with King Charles, the object of the Rebellion, and attempted to disband most of the army without satisfying arrears in pay. In March 1647 the infantry had not been paid for over four months and the cavalry for over ten.[14] What was left of the army was to be shipped off to Ireland.

THE ARMY VERSUS PARLIAMENT

The army refused to disband and presented a well-justified petition to Parliament with its grievances. The Presbyterian leaders in

Commons then proposed and carried a resolution that the petition-
ers were "enemies of the State." [15] To call the winners of the war
treasonous had gone too far even for Cromwell and he went over to
the army.

Still suffering rancor against the government and encouraged by
its political success, the army next began angrily to question the
entire social structure. Being deeply religious, most of the soldiers
were seeking guarantees for free conscience and parliamentary
representation for all Christian groups. These enlightened precepts,
over a century ahead of their time, were later to be adopted by the
American and French Revolutions. Why is it that the agitation by
the New Model Army for freedom of religion and truly representative government is seldom referred to in literature? Is it because
armies are not supposed to have enlightened thoughts or to encourage social advance?

The majority of the members of Parliament sought a close relationship between the Presbyterian Church and the State. This presented little change from the Episcopacy which the deposed King
had supported as a state religion. The army would have none of it.
Both the Roundheads and Parliament bargained with the King in
order to gain some legitimacy for their causes. On the army side
this bargaining was done by the generals and was disapproved of
by the rank and file.

After his defeat in 1646 the King had placed himself in the hands
of the Scots who held him virtually a prisoner for almost a year at
Newcastle. The Scots attempted without success to convert him to
the Presbyterian faith which was violently opposed to the Episcopacy of the Anglican Church. Finally the Scots, having been paid
half of what was owed them for their assistance in the war, turned
the King over to the Parliament.

Weary of war, many factions in England would have been glad
to see the King return to the throne provided his power could be
curbed and that he would recognize Parliament's supremacy. But
the King attempted to take advantage of the differences between
the army and Parliament over the issue of religious freedom. The
army was bitterly opposed to being subjected to either Presbyterianism or Episcopacy because both sects attempted to force conformity to their doctrines.

In hope that they might gain some support for their cause from
the king, the generals seized Charles from Parliamentary control.
There followed months of negotiations between the generals, the

King, and Parliament. A written constitution known at the "Heads of the Proposals" was drafted by the army to which Charles agreed, but Parliament rejected it.[16] More radical elements in the army urged social reforms and a democratic republic. It soon became apparent that the Ironsides would not accept the King under any circumstances.

Fearing for his life, Charles fled to the Isle of Wight. Here he signed a secret "engagement" with the Scots allying Royalism with Presbyterianism.[17] This brought on the Second Civil War when Royalist forces in the north joined with the Scots and marched south.

In the meantime a revolt of the New Model Army had been put down by the generals. The rank and file were seeking soldiers' rights but discipline prevailed under the genius of Cromwell. He then marched north and quelled the Royalist uprising in less than six months.

EXECUTION OF CHARLES I

Now the Roundheads, having lost all patience, demanded Charles' head. The New Model Army simply could not afford to have Charles regain his power. There would have been scant mercy for the many soldiers who had ridden down the King's gentlemen.[18] But the House of Commons failed to draw charges against the King and so the officers of the army drove out the Presbyterians in Parliament who still favored a royal restoration. Since the King had unsuccessfully attempted only a few years earlier to drive out his own opponents by force of arms, the pattern had been set.

This act is known as Pride's Purge because a Colonel Thomas Pride forced the expulsion. By so doing the army gained nearly absolute control of Parliament. Pride's Purge has the invidious distinction of being regarded as a dark crime perpetrated by the military against civil leadership. But was it truly a crime? Or was it justified?

First of all, how legitimate was the revolutionary Parliament itself? The last election had taken place eight years earlier in 1640 under a rigged system of small "rotten" boroughs who packed the Commons with landed gentry. Only seventy-odd merchants of some 500 members managed to get elected.[19] There was no pretense of democracy.[20] The House of Commons was rather evenly split in the early struggle with Charles (159 to 148 on the Grand Remonstrance) while the House of Lords was strongly for the King.[21]

When the London mobs who supported the majority in the Commons caused the King to flee, most of the Royalists followed. Thus the "Long Parliament" remaining was forced to assert its legitimacy with the sword against the King. When it comes down to the sword, one sword seems no more legitimate than another.

Nor was the Long Parliament representative of the people. Since most of the Royalists had fled, the House was now dominated by Presbyterians who enjoyed a questionably popular majority in England where the Independent sects of Puritanism were the rage.[22] In all probability the Ironsides of the army themselves were far more representative of the English people. All faiths were found in the ranks, but Independent sects espousing religious freedom predominated.[23] The soldiers had made their petitions to Parliament, moreover, through the democratic processes of debate and vote and had been peremptorily rebuffed and insulted. Then when Parliament proved so inept as to permit the victorious first civil war to drift into a second war, forcing the Roundheads to face death and hardship again, their patience had understandably worn thin. They felt that Parliament had betrayed them at every turn.

It is little wonder that the army seized the King on the Isle of Wight and then purged Parliament of Roundhead enemies. Forty-five members were arrested of a total of about 500. Three hundred members remained absent after the purge. Thus the "Rump Parliament" [24] was formed by force of arms, as legitimate or as illegitimate as its predecessor, the self-perpetrated Long Parliament, which had also been supported by force of arms.[25]

Charles I was accordingly tried by sixty members of the Commons, convicted, and beheaded on January 30, 1649. Few regicides have been more justified. He had been loyal to no faction in the country save his own Cavaliers and had sacrificed every principle of patriotism and good government, to the point of treason, for his throne. He felt himself above the people and beyond the law.[26] This execution was to leave no doubt in the minds of succeeding monarchs that they were subordinate to the Parliament and the people.[27]

THE ENGLISH REPUBLIC

The functions of the English government were then shared by the officer-dominated Parliament and the elected Council of the Army, Cromwell being a member of both. Laws were passed abolishing the House of Lords and the monarchy, and a republic was proclaimed. This republic might have flourished had Cromwell and his supporters been patient enough to allow the inefficiencies and the growing pains of a new order to work themselves out. Or if the Puritan Ironsides had been more tolerant of "Merry England."

The country was beset by constant strife, internally and externally. Religious issues hounded the age with vicious and intolerant persecutions, fanatical reprisals and counter-reprisals. A century earlier Mary Tudor had burned alive 300 Protestants.[28] Cromwell subdued Ireland by killing 2,000 Catholics. The sanctimonious nature of the Puritan New Model Army galled the English populace who suffered under innumerable arbitrary blue-laws. Revolts flared from every quarter and the Royalists, now championing Charles II, the son of the executed King, continued to stir up trouble abroad. Yet the New Model Army under Cromwell's great leadership remained the one source of stability and success. It was almost inevitable that as "Protector of the Commonwealth," Cromwell would finally assume full dictatorial powers.

Success crowned Cromwell's leadership at every hand. He had never consciously sought authority but found it increasingly thrust upon him. At one point the army offered him the title of king but he refused it. Perhaps George Washington at Newburgh over a century later, when he was proffered the same title by the Continentals, had Cromwell's noble example in mind. Nonetheless, unlike Washington, Cromwell believed he had a divine calling to rule as Protector. Under these circumstances the army continued to exert political pressure.

TAMING THE ARMY

Gradually Cromwell separated the army from politics by retiring the more actively political officers. A few, such as William Thompson, whose views on equal rights of property were too liberal even for Cromwell, were shot for mutiny. Others who failed to volunteer for the Irish war were discharged without pay.[29] Despite his use of the army for many civil functions, as when he placed civil government in the provinces under major generals (a practice which the United States copied during the reconstruction following the Civil War), the beginnings of a truly professional, nonpolitical military force emerged. This tradition grew steadily after Cromwell's time. Effort was lent henceforth to keep the army divorced from influence over either the legislative or the executive powers of government. The Anglo-Saxon apolitical military tradition thus had its quiet birth in England following the civil wars, although it took a strong military dictator to start it on the right track.

DISBANDING THE ARMY

Civil control of the military was to enjoy its major growth, however, in the reaction following the restoration of Charles II. After Cromwell's death his lieutenants, Parliament, and the Royalists jockeyed for control of the government. As the chaos mounted General George Monk came to the forefront. He was a professional soldier who commanded the Roundheads in Scotland and who had brought that land into complete subjection, "but without incurring any lasting animosity." [30] Supported by the Scots, Monk marched south in 1660 to restore order. Covered with success he took London and recalled the Presbyterian members of Parliament who had been expelled by Pride's Purge. Having been trained in Holland, Monk did not approve of "soldiers councils" and other manifestations of democracy in the army.[31] Convinced that the people wanted the King back, Monk was instrumental in restoring Charles II to the throne. The Great Rebellion had come full circle although now there remained no doubt whatsoever about the supremacy of Parliament over the Crown.

The relationship of Parliament to the army was another matter. This problem was solved by cutting the Gordian knot and disbanding the army altogether. Having grown to a strength of some 40,000 men, having pacified Ireland and Scotland, having subdued England's enemies throughout Europe and gained a respect for the country not known since the days of Queen Elizabeth, and finally, having, through Monk, restored a free and superior Parliament, the Ironsides were destroyed. It was decided to have no standing army whatsoever! The goose that laid the golden egg was killed.

Popular opinion was virtually unanimous about doing away with the Ironsides. They were universally detested for their hot-eyed evangelism, their priggish sanctimony and their harsh religious laws which had placed a pall of gloom over England for almost fourteen years. But for its unpopular Puritanical attitudes, the army might have prevailed as a respected "estate" of the government. Instead this "omnipotent, invincible machine . . . vanished in the civil population," [32] a practice which became habitual in England and the United States following successful wars until the modern Cold War made standing armies a necessity.

Fortunately for Britain, her insular geography and her strong-navy policy permitted her to survive without a peacetime army. But toward the end of the 17th century France began to push England off the continent and an army had to be formed. To guard against an army dictatorship, Parliament passed the Mutiny Act in 1689 which stipulated that the very existence of the army would be approved annually.[33] This idea of an annual review turned up in the United States Constitution as a biennial appropriation of funds, although practice has copied the British tradition of an annual budgetary review.

The Napoleonic Wars found Britain raising another army. After Waterloo, the victorious Duke of Wellington became a political leader, eventually rising to Prime Minister. There were repeated accusations that he aspired to military dictatorship although he gave no cause for such alarm. The ghost of Cromwell still roamed the land.[34]

It is interesting to note that at the beginning of the civil war there seemed to be too much civil control of the Parliamentary army and as a consequence it was of little value as a military instrument. This typifies the kind of "subjective" control deplored by Huntington.[35] The military establishment is weakened by civilian intrusion, thus forcing civilian standards on the military. Not only did members of Parliament, acting also as officers, bring political pressures to bear on the conduct of the campaigns, but local civilian authorities who had helped raise the troops felt that they had authority to direct them. It later became necessary to remove from the army those members of Parliament who were providing the most civil control.

The Self-denying Ordinance was necessary *not* for the purpose of achieving civil control, which had all but destroyed the army as a fighting machine, but to lessen civil control over forces in the field and make the army as a whole more responsive to Parliament as a corporate governing body, a higher civil authority. For example, when Charles was threatening Oxford in October 1644, command of Parliament's army was handled by a civilian committee and Oxford fell to the King. The Self-denying Ordinance was also a step toward putting the army in the hands of those who were more concerned with taking orders and winning battles than with debating orders and questioning the need for battles.

Direct Parliamentary influence over subordinate segments of the army was eliminated to achieve unity-of-command and discipline. Purpose and zeal were injected with Cromwell's leadership and religious inspiration. Orderly and fair administrative procedures rounded out the reforms to produce the New Model.

But in the beginning Parliament had set the precedent of condoning political action by the army itself and so the army continued with the election of agitators, soldier councils, and committees of generals to deal with Parliament. The Ironsides overreacted to civilian control by becoming a powerful political instrument in their own right, and the army remained a political institution until it was finally abolished altogether by General Monk.

When one considers the temper of the times, the political nature of the army becomes more understandable. Traditional political and religious institutions had collapsed while new and radical substitutions were being advanced. It was a period of social upheaval and religious ferment unlike anything the world had ever seen. This was so not only in England, but likewise on the Continent where the terrible Thirty Years' War had raged in chaotic fury. In such a confusing world environment the army was undoubtedly a haven of order and purpose. Had the Roundheads not stepped in to stabilize the arguing Parliament and provided consistency to the aims of the revolution, the political gains, paid in blood, would have gone for naught.

SOCIAL INNOVATION IN THE ARMY

Following the end of the first civil war, when the Army was defying Parliament's order to disband and when the Roundhead generals were negotiating for arrears in pay, the rank and file of the army itself became a hotbed of social revolution not unlike what was experienced in Russia almost three centuries later. Not only did the army petition for its back pay but for indemnity for damages done to property in war, guarantees against arbitrary conscription, and pensions for disabled soldiers and their widows and children. For weeks at Putney in the autumn of 1647 the army considered all kinds of farsighted social and political matters in open debate.[36] One of the radical groups led by John Lilburne called themselves the Levellers, a term descriptive of their equalitarian concepts. The Levellers worked on various drafts of the Agreement of the People which affirmed that no person was to be drafted for military service in a foreign war nor for service at home except to repel invasion. And no man was to be compelled to serve against his conscience.[37] These ideas all reappeared in various American doctrines over a century later.

Other proposals presented by the Ironsides espoused the natural rights of man. Milton wrote at the time that "no man who knows right can be so stupid to deny that all men were naturally born free." [38] Political equality was preached in such sayings as "A man is not bound to a system of government which he hath not had any hand in setting over him."[39] But the generals countered with the modern reactionary principle that only property owners with "a stake in the country" could vote.[40] Still the Roundheads talked of manhood suffrage at twenty-one, equal electoral districts and biennial Parliaments.[41] Inspired and guided by religious scriptures, the soldiers were taking giant strides into the future. Fired by this revolutionary mood they often came near to mutiny, particularly when the generals dealt with the King whom the Roundheads called the "Man of Blood"—the one primarily responsible for the war.[42] One can marvel not only at the enlightened thought of the Ironsides, centuries ahead of their age, but at the heights of leadership which Cromwell must have achieved in order to control such a volatile revolutionary force.

Had it not been for the extreme popularity of Cromwell with the rank and file of the army, and for Cromwell's wisdom and skill in wresting authority away from army agitators and political leaders (thus starting the nonpolitical military tradition), it is not unreasonable to assume that at this point in British history a system could have been created in which both the Parliament and the ruler might have been selected or at least strongly influenced by a voting army. Even though Cromwell's authority rested fundamentally with the New Model Army, and even though he sometimes employed the army as a constabulary to enforce his edicts, the army eventually became responsive to him and was not a dominating power in itself.[43] His work had been done so well that when General Monk ordered the army's demise, it obeyed without question.

THE MAN ON HORSEBACK

The legend of the man on horseback stems from the Cromwellian dictatorship. It is a major antecedent of the American fear of excessive military power. The antimilitary tradition in Britain (and subsequently in America) continued to grow from the period of the Great Rebellion, reinforced by the frequently biased accounts of the parts played by Parliament, the Crown, the people, the dictator, the Church and the New Model Army. Edmund Burke said in 1790, "An armed, disciplined body is, in essence, dangerous to liberty;

undisciplined it is ruinous to society." [44] Invariably the military, being nonpolitical, generally inarticulate and usually gagged, and hence less able to defend itself against popular indictment, became the evil character in the historical drama which actually had enough villains in the cast to go around to all actors.

WHAT MAKES A POLITICAL ARMY

Misconceptions of the New Model Army can be seen in statements such as one made not long ago by John J. Lindsay in *The Nation:* ". . . a Cromwell-like military establishment . . . fully capable, if history means anything, of turning, in time of crisis, as easily and catastrophically upon its civilian authority as upon the enemy." [45] As we have seen there was some question of the legitimacy of the civilian authority in Cromwell's time while the army itself had a much clearer idea than Parliament of the purposes of the revolution. It was Parliament that had created the crisis by failing to try the King and by refusing to provide religious liberty, both aims of the revolt. Historians agree that the Great Rebellion was *not* a civil-military struggle. It was a contest between Parliament and the Crown. The army got caught in the middle and for a time became the dominant governing power, but, when ordered to do so by a competent and representative authority in 1660, peacefully disbanded.

If guilt is to be charged, Parliament was equally culpable for turning on the army. Parliament even accused the Roundhead heroes of being traitors. A government which asks its citizens to defend it and then turns against those very citizens and sells out to the enemy after victory has been won, is a government which can expect military revolt. A government which shows such duplicity and disloyalty to its defenders, who have sacrificed their lives and suffered most from the cruelties of war, may well be worse than the army which overthrows it.

SIMILAR PROBLEMS OF WASHINGTON'S CONTINENTALS

As we have noted, an interesting parallel can be found in United States history. After Yorktown the Continental army was held at Newburgh under General Washington until the terms of peace were negotiated and Congress finally made provisions for the army's payment and demobilization. But this action was unduly delayed and the army became restless. Protests were sent to Congress. Had the Continentals been nearer Philadelphia, perhaps General

Washington could not have restrained them as easily as he did at Newburgh. It is conceivable that Washington might have been forced by his Continentals, as was Cromwell, to assume the reins of government.

Yet the final outcome, as in England, would probably still have been democratic government. Let us not forget that the first popular expression of the natural rights of man and political equality came from the rank and file of the Roundhead army, almost a century before Rousseau and Kant popularized them. This fact seems to have gone unnoticed in a society that would rather think of the military as an autocratic force bent on dictatorship.

CONCLUSION

The early New Model Army was a political instrument raised and officered by politicians who were in revolt against the King. Such an organization cannot honestly be compared with the non-political regular forces of the modern Anglo-American military establishments who traditionally bestow their loyalty on the constituted civil authority. In fact, the defeated King's men would be more comparable to our modern forces.

The complete demobilization of the New Model Army after the restoration of Charles II was accompanied by a curious Anglo-Saxon phenomenon of military forgetfulness. With the physical and peaceful destruction of the army went a blackout of military thought which has persisted to modern times. The whole military subject was swept into a closet and locked there. As Alfred Vagts has said, the defense policies of liberal and democratic nations reveal "Spurts of activity alternated with long periods of relapse, sudden scares with surprising forgetfulness. . . ." [46] Rational thought on military matters has been looked upon with disfavor, if not with distaste, and any necessary military mobilization in a national crisis has been achieved through a resort to emotionalism. Outside the small regular military establishments there have been no institutions to nourish a continuity of interest in military subjects. "In the absence of an informed civilian public democracy had to be frightened into its own proper defense. . . ." [47]

Excepting for the recent pullulation of arms control and disarmament writing and teaching, the absence of military thought can be noted in the colleges and in English language literature. At least two strictly American wars, the Revolution and the Civil War, produced striking changes in the technology and strategy of armed conflict. This knowledge was distilled in German literature but not in the liberal democratic press which tended to believe that knowledge of war would lead either to more war or to military dictatorship, both of which were in opposition to the American dream.

"Neither in Europe nor anywhere else," wrote Vagts, "has Liberalism produced a military literature."

> Hostile to war, which was glibly said 'never to decide anything,' and confusing the proper study of defense with its excuses of militarism, Liberals shunned discussion of any aspect of the subject. They would not study the control and direction of the forces that most menaced their chosen way of life.[48]

Along with this public attitude goes the degradation of the soldier. To prevent him from seizing civil powers his prestige and stature must be held down, mocked and even defiled. This undoubtedly enhances his subservience to civilian control but at the expense of eroding his usefulness and risking the very dangers which civil control seeks to avoid. It seems unreasonable that the modern military should be caused to suffer suspicions and curbs of its legitimate and lawful activities for the legendary offenses perpetrated by the New Model Army of an ancient day. Might it not be more sensible to re-examine the Anglo-American military traditions of civil control in the light of objective history? Civil control may not be an unalloyed blessing in every instance, as the civil over-controlled army of Parliament would suggest.

CHAPTER 7

EUROPEAN INFLUENCES
ON THE MILITARY

Although the Cromwellian period in Britain during the early
17th century had much to do with influencing subsequent Anglo-
American civil-military relations, events on the Continent had been
taking place which were also to shape these relations. Germany had
been undergoing the Thirty Years' War. The Catholic Holy Roman
Empire under the Hapsburgs in Vienna, allied with Spain, had been
threatened by the Protestant Evangelical Union of German princes
combined with Denmark, Sweden, and finally Catholic France, who
hated the Hapsburgs more than Protestantism. The Hapsburgs managed to prevail over the Protestant combinations in the first decade
of the war by hiring two able professional soldiers: Johan Tilly
and Albrecht von Wallenstein. The latter veteran raised his own
army of 20,000 (including, strangely, many Protestants) and insisted that he have a free hand in the war. Thus armed with
hard-fighting mercenaries he defeated the Protestant forces at
Dessau in 1626 and, allied with Tilly's army, subdued Christian of
Denmark at Lutter.[1]

The ambitious General Wallenstein became governor of territories he had conquered and favored religious tolerance.[2] It was
not surprising that the vested interests of the Catholic League attempted to force his dismissal. This was badly timed because in
the summer of 1630 Gustavus Adolphus of Sweden took up the
Protestant cause and swept through Germany in triumph, defeating
Tilly near Leipzig. Emperor Ferdinand II had to eat humble pie
and appeal to Wallenstein to save the day. For this Wallenstein
exacted concessions of supreme command over imperial forces as
well as authority to make treaties.

79

If Wallenstein had won, it is not inconceivable that a kind of military dictatorship could have been established over the Holy Roman Empire. But he did not win. At Lutzen in 1632 Wallenstein was defeated by Gustavus. Then, after two more years of desultory and unsuccessful campaigning, Wallenstein was relieved from command and soon thereafter assassinated. So ended a threat by an independent military leader to the constituted royal authority. It was a lesson not to be regarded lightly and the mercenary forces that had been so prevalent during this vicious war began to lose favor.

France, dominated by Cardinal Richelieu, actively entered the war in 1635 and pushed the battered Hapsburgs to the wall with a decisive victory at Rocroi in 1643. The long and bloody Thirty Years' War petered to a close although France and Spain continued to fight for eleven years more. The Peace of Westphalia in 1648 made Prussia a new European power.[3]

EFFECT ON MILITARY ART

Military art had lain dormant as long as it had been left to hired hands of the sort Wallenstein led.[4] "Free Companies" such as the *Condottieri* in Italy provided most of the military strength. They were military societies like the trading guilds who were paid by levy money, loot and land. Kings could not afford to pay these bands for not fighting so they were laid off between wars and often reverted to banditry. Still they were the best soldiers available.[5] As Charles Oman observed, "Such a system was, of course, unfavorable to the rise of great generals or the framing of broad strategic plans." [6] The mercenary leaders were simply old soldiers who had won distinction by hard fighting but whose wider experience was little different from the men under them. There was little distinction of rank and a council of war was like a veterans' meeting.[7] Tactics, of course, assumed far more importance than strategy, for strategy is always a function of government and the mercenary leaders were rarely admitted to these inner circles. But Gustavus Adolphus had proven successful by again integrating the military art with statecraft as had so many of the classical rulers.[8]

Some professionalism emerged in France under Louis XIV when Vauban developed new kinds of fortifications. Military engineering had been born and was becoming a respectable study. So were studies of geography, diplomacy and government.[9] This military enlightenment and the practice of integrating the military and statecraft were carried to new heights of achievement under Frederick the Great of Prussia a little over a century later.[10]

FREDERICK THE GREAT

In the War of the Austrian Succession (1740-48) Frederick II (the Great) defeated the armies of Maria Theresa of Austria and acquired Silesia through a series of brilliantly led battles. A few years later, however, he found himself virtually surrounded by enemies whose purpose was to dismember all of Prussia. Frederick fought gallantly against an overwhelming alliance of Russia, Austria, France, Saxony, and Sweden. His sole ally was England-Hanover whose support was essentially financial. Oddly enough, this Seven Years' War had begun in America between French and English colonists. England's alliance with Prussia, and France's with Austria, caused the two German states again to take up arms against each other. This war exemplifies the escalation concept which is discussed so much today.

Frederick's grand strategy was to keep his enemies from uniting and to defeat them in detail by use of his interior lines. By striking each enemy separately, then wheeling to contain another, he was able to keep them off balance and apart. This strategy worked well against his vastly superior foes until the Austrian and Russian armies managed to join each other in 1759 at Kunersdorf. Here Frederick suffered his worst defeat. The end looked near for Prussia but the wildest kind of luck came to Frederick's assistance. A change of regime with the death of Empress Elizabeth in Russia caused a change in sympathies and Russia switched sides. England and France patched up their quarrel causing France to lose interest in fighting Prussia. At this juncture Maria Theresa of Austria thought it prudent to negotiate a peace and Prussia was saved.

But there was more than clever strategy and luck in Frederick's success. He had gained the complete allegiance of his nobles and "the officer corps became the embodiment of the spirit of devotion to the Crown and the state, while the common foot-soldier[s] . . . [became] the finest soldiers in Europe. . . ." [11] Frederick believed, however, that conscription should be held to a minimum because his subjects served the state better as taxpayers and producers of goods than as soldiers. Thus foreigners outnumbered natives in his army by two to one. He sometimes forcibly enrolled prisoners of war and subjects of occupied states rather than draft his own population.[12]

Some fourteen years after the Seven Years' War, Frederick again challenged Austria, but this War of the Bavarian Succession came to an end without fighting and with Austria renouncing its claims to Bavaria. Frederick, like all good generals before and since, had no desire to fight if his country's aims could be achieved by diplomacy. Here he again demonstrated the smooth merger of the military function with statecraft. Seldom in history has a ruler executed both functions with such consummate skill as did the Prussian king.

Had Frederick lived longer he might have been successful in achieving the unification of Germany, a task eventually accomplished by the Bismarck-Moltke team a century later. Frederick's unification effort was begun in 1785, when a league of German princes was formed which gave the dream some promise, but the league was dissolved after Frederick's death the following year.[13]

MILITARY ART AND STATECRAFT

The French Revolution saw the military art again become an integral part of government under Napoleon. Strategy assumed a dominant role in statecraft, and vice versa. Archduke Karl, who led the Austrians against the French, and probably felt the lack of this integration in his own forces, put it this way:

> ... The strategic design, as a rule, depends on the decisions of cabinets and upon the resources placed at the disposal of the commander. Therefore, the leading statesmen should either have correct views of the science of war or should make up for their ignorance by giving their entire confidence to the man to whom the supreme command of the army is entrusted.[14]

But integration of the military with statecraft was as shortlived as Napoleon, who succumbed to a coalition led by mercantile England which was dedicated to keeping the military in its place. Perhaps the need for civil control of the military began to be felt on the Continent as a consequence of the fear which Napoleon had spread throughout Europe for half a generation. Fear and evil are unquestionably related in human conclusions. Therefore lack of civil control of the military could have been regarded as dangerous; particularly by those merchant princes who were beginning to wrest control of statecraft from the hereditary nobility. To them wars were only acceptable if they improved business and military men seldom recognized such objectives. Certainly the Napoleonic wars had been unprofitable. Moreover the military were fundamentally loyal to the sovereign rather than to the emerging democratic elements of government and the sovereign was the target for the new commercially inspired reforms.

Analyzing Napoleon's successes, Karl von Clausewitz theorized on the integration of politics and war. "None of the principal plans which are required for a war," he wrote, "can be made without an insight into political relations." [15] Yet Clausewitz noted certain cleavages of the military from statecraft that even then were beginning to be practiced in Prussia. To correct this tendency he urged crosstraining between statesman and soldiers.

The emerging military-political dichotomy during Clausewitz's time was revealed by his cautions for greater unity and for civil-military mutual understanding. "War is only a part of social intercourse," he wrote, "therefore by no means an independent thing in itself . . . accordingly war can never be separated from political intercourse." To do so, he maintained, would cause war to be "a useless thing, without an objective . . . the unbridled element of hostility.[16]

Splitting off the military from the state itself at this stage of history and thereafter did not come about entirely as a measure to keep the military from threatening the state. It was as much if not more a consequence of a general cultural trend. Hereditary control of property and power, as established by the feudal system and later by the divine right kingdoms, concentrated the wealth in the hands of a few who became disinclined to practice the rough game of self-defense. As long as the military could be hired and loyalty of a sort bought, as long as the hereditary succession of property and power was accepted as the natural course of events, there was no need for statesmen to practice the military arts. There is little evidence that this division of labor came about through any conscious effort to keep the military within bounds as is popularly imagined today.

As commercialism grew, the concept of divine right lost credence—in Germany as elsewhere. Although the Congress of Vienna following Napoleon's downfall at first appeared to restore the old order, popular government had captured the imagination of all Western countries and the military, aligned with the old order, was generally regarded as an enemy to this reform.

Separation of the military took many forms. One such form was an intellectual division. Military matters began to be discussed in a political vacuum as "pure" military strategy. The renowned French and Russian military philosopher of Swiss birth, Antoine Henry

Jomini, scoffed at there being anything like a purely military decision. The principal plans which are necessary for war, he said, cannot be made without an understanding of the political conditions, ". . . war is not an aberration of human life with a history of its own and alien to other kinds of history, but . . . an integral part of the history of civilization." [17] Policy and strategy should be one and the same.

Clausewitz held the same view and ridiculed the idea that there could be a "purely political opinion" as was frequently asked for by cabinets who wanted to keep the military divorced from affairs of state.[18] Clausewitz wrote that:

> . . . If war is to correspond entirely with the intentions of policy, and policy is to accommodate itself to the means available for war, in case statesmen and soldiers are not combined in one person, there is only one satisfactory alternative left, which is to make the commander-in-chief a member of the cabinet.

Generally speaking, however, the Prussian military leaders were not accepted in the ruling circles. They had few ambitions beyond mastering the sword and improving Germany's military posture. In Britain, too, the hereditary leaders securely held the power of the state and, after the trials with the Roundheads of the New Model Army, the civilian leaders were determined to leave the army out in the cold. Being an island nation with a great navy, England was able to pursue this policy without being overcome by another power. British political leaders were thus largely civilian in background and amateurs in military affairs.

Too often civilian rulers in their military ignorance would turn uncritically to military advice in time of crisis. "War is the province for soldiers," was too readily recited, while on the other hand the political ignorance on the part of soldiers led to equally grave consequences. Bismarck was one of the few statesmen who recognized the dangers in letting the military run a war in a political vacuum.[19] He appreciated the genius of von Moltke who defeated Austria in seven weeks and subdued France in four, but, by dictating magnanimous terms, Bismarck was permitted by his former enemies to consolidate the German Empire.

As warfare grew more encompassing with modern organization and technology, its relationship to politics became increasingly evident. Yet this evidence has not caused an amalgamation of the citizen and the soldier. If anything the opposite has taken place, with the general and the statesman growing further apart. And, since the time of Cromwell, the military has been regarded with increasing suspicion as a threat to representative government. This ancient civil/military dichotomy is fervently justified in America as a means to retain civil control over the military which, it is felt, is necessary to assure democratic principles.[20]

Because of mutual ignorance of the others' aims and methods, politicians and generals have argued bitterly in every Western country which has practiced this civil-military separation. Each class fears the other as a threat to peace and security. The military are alarmed at policies promulgated by governments which fail to consider military strategy or capacity, while civil leaders look upon the military as a necessary evil, dangerous to freedom and only to be called on when all other means of statecraft fail. This is typified by Woodrow Wilson's remarks that soldiers should have nothing to do with boundary drawing. "It is the military who have led us from one disaster to another," [21] he said at Versailles. He even blamed the military for the Treaty of Vienna (1815) which was wholly drawn by civilian diplomats and sovereigns.

It might be of some concern to note here that the free city of Danzig was established by the Treaty of Versailles at which Wilson was in conspicuous attendance, and at which his military advisor, Tasker H. Bliss, was virtually disregarded. Isolated in Poland, this German city was separated from its Prussian neighbors on either side. One of the issues which sparked World War II was Germany's desire to correct this geographical and political anomaly. Having fought the Second World War the victorious allies similarly isolated Berlin and left it an island in a sea of Soviet-controlled territory. Again, as Vagts admits, the "military and naval men . . . [were] only rarely consulted." [22] This was where we came in with respect to Danzig, and the Berlin issue has several times put us on the brink of World War III. One can readily understand why military men would like to sit at the peace table and in the cabinets where such decisions seem to be made in a military vacuum, for it is the military who are usually called upon to correct these mistakes by force of arms.

On the other side of the coin is the narrow military attitude which eschews political considerations in military decision making, either as being of minor consequence or as somehow having an immoral connotation. This attitude was expressed by Payton C. March in 1919 when he pointed out that our military program "frames entirely on its merits, without any relation whatsoever to national or international politics." [23]

It can be seen from history that a separation of the military profession from statecraft and politics is not a United States invention by any means. It was common to most Western countries long before the American Revolution and it has been religiously practiced ever since for various reasons, valid or not. Much of the American antipathy to the soldier, for example, was related to the frontiersman's rejection of rank and discipline. As Henry Steele Commager noted in his study, *The American Mind*, ". . . the principle that the civilian was superior to the soldier was as much an expression of the suspicion of military standards as of the fear of military usurpation." [24] In recent times efforts have been made to achieve more coordination between political and military elements of government in order to arrive at reasonable national policies. The establishment of the National Security Council was directed to this end, but the overall effort to coordinate has achieved considerably more form than substance, especially since 1961 when the NSC system was all but abandoned.

SOLDIER VERSUS DIPLOMAT

A most comprehensive study of the role of the soldier in the conduct of foreign relations, *Defense and Diplomacy*, was made in 1956 by Alfred Vagts under the auspices of the Institute of War and Peace Studies of Columbia University. In the foreword to this work, William T. R. Fox of the Institute notes that,

> Dr. Vagts has deliberately let his materials speak for themselves, and his conclusions remain largely implicit. Much of this illustrative material is drawn from the experience of Continental armed forces before World War I. This is natural since archival data for this earlier period are more accessible and the important memoirs have all been written. As a consequence, the normal civil-military relationship and the normal behavior of soldiers when working with politicians, diplomats and other bureaucrats, may appear to be the pre-1914 Continental pattern. Whether it is also the post-1914 Anglo-American, constitutional-democratic pattern will surely be a matter for debate. . . .

These remarks by Fox are most revealing and provide the clearest possible analysis of the entire study. Generalizations are sometimes made by Vagts of the Continental pre-World War I military events without qualifying them by their time and place. Consequently this exceptional and voluminous piece of research must be utilized in light of the environment from which the many examples are taken. However, in his preface Vagts makes a sound observation with respect to the general roles of the soldier and the diplomat in any culture where these two roles are separated into specialties and given specific missions as they are in western governments, including our own:

> . . . Since they started upon their separate establishments, diplomats and military men have frequently clashed. Their basic outlooks have only too often been antagonistic, even when both were members of the same 'ruling class.' Their views on whether, when and how to undertake a war have differed many times, and most acutely over the question of undertaking a preventive war, an enterprise more often proposed from a military rather than from a diplomatic point of view.

Whether military men are more prone to advocate preventive war than are diplomats is open to some question. It must be remembered that the examples found by Vagts in the archives follow the pre-1914 Continental pattern and were generated against a background of limited war. The wars of the later 17th, 18th and 19th Centuries on the Continent of Europe, except for the Napoleonic wars, were generally dynastic in nature and did not result in such great destruction and loss of life as did earlier and certainly modern wars. Thus, not only the soldiers but diplomats in this benign era could toy with the idea of preventive war as a solution to a pressing national threat. As war became more dangerous and destructive in the 20th Century, one can find the military arguing against war, with diplomats and chiefs of state as often advocating it. Hitler, it will be remembered, was advised by his top military advisers not to undertake the attack on Poland which started World War II.

It must be noted that Alfred Vagts is another of those brilliant refugees from Hitler's Germany who has revealed an understandable antimilitary prejudice in his writings. His works thus bear a certain unreality and tend to pander to and enhance the existing bias found in the American culture. His most famous book, published in 1937, was *A History of Militarism*.[25] This highly entertaining and vitriolic treatise condemned the military from every direction. It left no doubt that the writer, having come from an environment in Germany which was again thriving on a growing militarism, was getting something off his chest. It is not surprising, therefore, that in *Defense and Diplomacy* Vagts draws largely on materials from the German situation and reaches conclusions from these data. For example, he states that, "More often than not, a soldier was considered the 'first man in the whole state.' "[26] No doubt this statement is correct when applied to pre-1914 Germany, but it is anything but true for other modern countries and certainly not for the

United States at any period. The reference which he used to support this statement came from a German ditty.

The major thesis of *Defense and Diplomacy* is that soldiers make poor diplomats and should be kept in their place. But unless military and political decisions become grossly unrealistic by "hardening of the categories," soldiers must be made privy to and become participants in diplomacy. As former President Dwight D. Eisenhower put it, "There is hardly a political decision in the international field that does not have some security aspects. And, similarly, there are very few high-level military decisions which do not necessarily have profound moral, political and economic implications." [27]

"HONOR" AS A CAUSE OF WAR

A comparison of soldiers and diplomats brings up the question of honor as a *casus belli*. There was much talk in 19th Century Europe about the honor of nations but it was seldom heard in the United States. The American Civil War was not fought on the question of honor but on a much more pragmatic question of human justice and the political necessity of having a federal government from which no state could secede.

There can be little question that military men are jealous of their personal honor; that it is one of the military codes for officers to speak up without equivocation and as honestly as conscience and common sense can dictate. This is an ancient precept. Herodotus wrote of the Persian leaders: "Their sons are carefully instructed from their fifth to their twentieth year in three things alone—to ride, to draw the bow, and to speak the truth." [28] Only in time of war against an announced enemy is deception "honorable." Diplomacy on the other hand has been known to use double-talk, innuendoes and outright deceit even with friends in efforts to gain necessary political ends. In *The Diplomat*, by Charles Wheeler Thayer,[29] this point is clearly revealed. However, Thayer believes that modern diplomacy can best be achieved by outright honesty, the kind of honesty that the military man extols. It is noteworthy that Thayer, himself, may be tainted with the military ethic. He is a graduate of the United States Military Academy, although he never served in the army but went immediately into the Foreign Service.

Honor in war makes sense only when one knows his enemies and friends and when these relationships have been clearly announced in formal declarations by constituted authority. Throughout the ages rules of war were slowly developed which made armed conflict less cruel and more predictable. The term "civilized warfare" was used until extreme reformists insisted there was no such thing. Yet Hugo Grotius and others had codified these rules of war as a basis for international law, and the several Geneva Conventions made even more progress along these lines. But the wanton excesses of the two "total" world wars which were waged with almost religious fury left little room for rules. In particular the practice of "declaring" war has become passé. Germany in 1940 and Japan in 1941 did not wish to forego the advantage of surprise against Russia in the first instance and against the United States in the second. The United States in 1950 and again in 1965 preferred the legal pretense that war was not being waged at all in Korea and Vietnam. It was feared that a declaration of war might cause enemy alliances to solidify.

Undeclared war debases military honor because of the difficulty of distinguishing friend from enemy. It places the military professional in a compromising position. When captured his status is unclear. He cannot claim to be a "prisoner of war." He is little better off than an uncivilized tribesman. Instead of high ideals and worthy political aims clearly expressed, war tends to degenerate into expressions of hate, revenge, and blood lust.

Undeclared war also sets up cruel paradoxes. Any country can trade legitimately with the enemy. We cannot blockade an enemy without violating international law. Thus we may be providing economic and military aid to a friendly country which is trading with our undeclared enemy who in turn is killing our soldiers.

There are indeed some aspects of the code of honor which may be dangerous to the peace of nations. Sometimes honor is a mere expression of vanity and under this guise leaders may act imprudently and hastily. But to discourage honor as a virtue because of pique or other malpractices would be to give up the deepest beliefs and the highest values which we hold,and upon which our democratic government rests.

President Lyndon B. Johnson has frequently and rightly referred to our national honor as a reason for continuing the conflict against the Viet Cong in South Vietnam. "We just cannot now dishonor our word," he said in July 1965, "or abandon our commitment. . . ." [30] It is evident that "national honor" continues to be a very real cause of war.

To be honorable it is not necessary, of course, for one to act with such candor as to disclose the secrets of his country. One can be quiet, keep his mouth shut, and still be honorable. However, when the military man *must* speak to a friend he should be as honest and as straightforward as reasonably possible. Should human discourse ignore this rule, the civilized world would slip back to the law of the jungle. Civilization rests on honesty. Honesty is the crux of mutual confidence. And without confidence in our fellow man neither business nor self-government could survive.

NINETEENTH CENTURY DIPLOMATS

Recently there have been a growing number of soldiers assigned to diplomatic posts. Napoleon was the first chief of state in modern history to use soldiers widely in diplomatic positions. In some cases, he used this as a means to banish troublesome generals. One such assignment resulted in a new dynasty being formed, that of Bernadotte in Sweden.

Napoleon's adversaries fought him with a strict division of labor between civilian diplomats and military commanders. Since the Allied armies were newly raised, they could not readily spare officers for nonmilitary purposes. In July 1814, however, General Wellington accepted the first postwar British ambassadorship to Paris. "He proved definitely the most diplomatic and the least militaristic general, helping the returned Bourbons in their struggle for recognition at home and abroad." [31] Nevertheless Wellington was criticized for not earlier recognizing the French disposition which would permit Napoleon to make his spectacular return from Elba. Wellington thought Napoleon would be destroyed quickly by Louis XVIII, just as everyone else did. No one at that time conceived of Napoleon's ability to make such a comeback.

Wellington was later sent to Vienna as Castelreagh's successor (January 1815) where he served as a conservative statesman in uniform. Following the second peace of Paris, he became commander of the Inter-Allied Forces occupying France. Although the occupation was to last five years, Wellington recommended an early termination. This was agreed to at the Aachen Congress by the Allies in 1818.[32] It is interesting to note that these generous terms were proposed by the victorious general.

Following the Congress of Vienna, military influence in affairs of state fell off rapidly throughout Europe. August Compte writing in 1841 was moved to prophesy that the new "diplomatic class" was everywhere robbing the military of "their political attributions...." [33]

But after the American Civil War and the European wars of the mid-19th Century, military consideration again took on importance. Bismarck made considerable use of military men in politics, yet he distrusted them in diplomatic posts because their *esprit de corps* was "too strong." His remark, "once a general always a general," is typical, particularly in the United States, of the imagined taint that the uniform inflicts on its wearers. Some generals themselves have contributed to this unsavory attitude as did General Marquis de Gallifet when he was France's Minister of War. He objected to being called "Mr. Minister" because, he said, he would be a minister only "a few days" and a general all his life.[34] There is a tendency even today in America to give priority to the title "general" over transient civilian titles. General Eisenhower, for example, is no longer "President" Eisenhower, whereas "Ex-President" is not a title. So he is again most often referred to as "general." This can be accounted for largely by the problem in semantics. Because of the aversion held by our forefathers for titles, military and professional titles are the only ones which have a lasting quality.

In 1869 Bismarck sent as ambassador to Russia General von Schweinitz who reported that he could not lie to Alexander II. Bismarck replied, "Then you cannot be ambassador at all,"[35] but he still kept the general on. Apparently even Bismarck realized that there was a useful place for honesty in diplomacy. But the growing antimilitary bias caught up with General von Schweinitz himself and when he retired in 1892 he advised against sending more generals to St. Petersburg.

During the same period another Bismarck appointee, General Count Carl von Wedel, was sent as ambassador to Vienna. He also served with success, but Bismarck nonetheless reduced the number of his military diplomats after 1890. None was appointed to the big embassies.

Civilians were everywhere in the ascendancy as "British morality" began to spread. This "morality" taught not only that it was evil to prepare for war but that any military activity whatever contributed to war and hence the uniform should be kept in the background. The military departments were increasingly isolated from other functions of government and the civilianized foreign ministries again took on the full business of diplomacy.[36]

There was one exception to the new civilianization of diplomacy in the late 19th and early 20th centuries. Since diplomats avoided military issues it was considered proper for military cooperation between friendly countries to take the form of general staff visits. But being held in a diplomatic vacuum such exchanges were irregular and often unrealistic.

Germany reasoned that because England and France had had so few general staff exchanges prior to 1914 military coordination would leave something to be desired. This proved correct.

The French had fewer military diplomats than did the Germans during Bismarck's era. France had undergone another popular revolution in which the military, representing the forces of reaction, had been decisively beaten at "the barricades." Nevertheless, a series of generals were sent as ambassadors to Russia. General Le Flô was one. He had been the first war minister of the new Republic and became "the darling of St. Petersburg society." [37] But after sending a series of emissaries with military backgrounds, France, too, reverted to civilian diplomats toward the end of the century. There was, according to Vagts, a "kind of international craft unionism agreement . . . among civilian diplomats" [38] to keep out the military types by passing the word of civilian superiority in the diplomatic field. The uniform, or the absence of it, was and still is a symbolic figure of the times, however, indicating the importance put by governments on military matters. The appointment of General Maxwell D. Taylor to South Vietnam is a modern-day case in point.

MILITARY ADMINISTRATORS

During the Napoleonic wars there was some discussion in England about putting more military men into diplomatic and administrative posts. It seemed to some observers at the time that France with her military diplomats was making more political progress than were her opponents with civilian negotiators. The Roman system was considered, with politics and generalship mixed so thoroughly as not to be considered separate trades. However, the early 19th Century civil control policies of England were too ingrained to do more than debate the merging of foreign service and the military services. There was concern, too, about maintaining conservatism against the revolutionary spirit which was raging on the Continent and it was felt that imitation of Napoleon's measures might lead to revolutionary activities.

Most parliamentary systems of government attempted to maintain a civilian dominance over the military. Civilians headed not only offices of diplomacy and foreign affairs but defense departments as well. In those countries where there was less parliamentary rule, the military exercised greater political influence and ministries of defense were often occupied by generals or admirals. Professional military men headed the military ministries in France up to 1871 and in Russia to 1917; in Prussia and German federal states up to 1918; and in Austria also to 1918.

There are too many examples in Europe of military men serving as administrators of conquered territories, both in parliamentary and nonparliamentary governments, to mention all here. But one might be mentioned because it reveals that generals, even Prussian generals, might possess a "social consciousness." Bismarck appointed Field Marshall Edwin von Manteuffel governor of Alsace-Lorraine in 1879 where he "won the hearts of the French people."[39] His administration was marked by kindness, wisdom and good government. Later Manteuffel declined an appointment to Paris as ambassador.

The concept of civilian control of the military has always been considerably stronger in Britain than in other European countries. Bismarck achieved some civilian dominance over the German military in the latter part of the 19th Century and established a strong feeling of the necessity for separating civilian and military matters in affairs of state. The foreign service became a civilian preserve. The services of generals after 1890 were seldom sought for diplomatic roles. However, this development of civilianizing the German foreign service and reducing the number of general diplomats did not deter the ignition of the First World War.[40]

Vagts says that ". . . a readiness for war as the supreme consideration" dominates military men in civil positions. Does he mean "willingness" for war? Or a "preparation" for war? The general tone of his remarks seems to be that generals are ready to "go" to war at any provocation and to solve any international problem. He seems to believe that most generals have a Napoleonic outlook and he even questions their loyalty to civilian superiors. This deep prejudice against the military paints the basic theme of his voluminous research. Certainly a rereading of the facts he has so thoroughly compiled leaves one with no such conclusions as his.

CONCLUSION

We have seen that the separation of military and political factors is not a contemporary phenomenon by any means. In modern history it is found more often in the democratic societies. Yet in all governments there is a clear association between the political policy which directs, and the military strategy which plans the execution of that policy. Military strategy, divorced from political policy becomes purposeless and incomprehensible, as for example, the allied occupation of Berlin.[41]

None of the great captains of history dreamed of partitioning the political and military features of statecraft. Alexander, Caesar, Cromwell, Gustavus Adolphus, Frederick the Great and Napoleon owe much of their success to the integration of these inseparable factors of effectual government.

Modern representative government emerged with the growth of mercantilism and the middle class. This class never has learned to cope with the military instrument of government and still regards it as an enemy to freedom and democracy. The traditional fear of the military may be self-defeating and itself dangerous to democracy. Certainly this is so if it leads to military defeat and political subjugation by a foreign power. The ancient Greek city states, the Roman Republic and the Swiss provide examples of a successful and safe employment of the military within governments by the people. But perhaps an entirely new rationale is called for to fit the nuclear age.

CHAPTER 8

THE MILITARY PROFESSION IN AMERICA

The American military profession antedated the Declaration of Independence. Our colonial forebears had a long history of warfare and although no standing armies were created in the colonies there was enough fighting to keep some citizens quite busy at the avocation of war. George Washington was one of these as were many others who fought the Revolutionary War to a victorious conclusion.

As Walter Lippmann has pointed out in *U.S. Foreign Policy: Shield of the Republic,*[1] the English began settling in North America about a century after Columbus discovered the new world. This corresponded to British ascendancy over the Spanish after defeating the Armada in 1588, thus permitting safer transportation across the Atlantic. A century later a series of wars between Britain and France kept the American colonists continually embroiled.[2] These wars bore different names to the colonists than to the Europeans. The long War of the League of Augsburg (1688-1697) was called King William's War in America. The War of the Spanish Succession (1740-1748) was called Queen Anne's War here. The Seven Years' War (1756-1763) was known as the French and Indian Wars. Early Americans had been hardened by their experiences in protecting themselves against the aborigine Indians. They had also been liberally recruited to assist the mother country in her dynastic and commercial struggles, which was another important factor shaping their attitude toward political affairs.

THE REVOLUTION

Thanks to these earlier experiences, American colonies were not entirely without military talent when the shot at Lexington was fired on April 19, 1775. They could never have fought a successful war had not there been available a number of experienced leaders.

Of the thirteen generals appointed by the Continental Congress all but two had served under fire and eight held grades of lieutenant colonel or higher. Four officers had served in the British regular army: Charles Lee, Horatio Gates, William Alexander, and Richard Montgomery. Many others like Artemus Ward, John Hancock, Israel Putnam, Philip Schuyler and Ethan Allen had seen combat service in the Seven Years' War just ended.[3]

This local talent was leavened with the teachings of Friedrich von Steuben from Prussia, of Thaddeus Kosciusko and Casimir Pulaski from Poland, and of other sympathetic soldiers of fortune who introduced conceptions of formal order and discipline. The Marquis de Lafayette, Jean de Kalb, and Francois L. de Fleury also contributed but were in a somewhat different class considering France's open alliance with the United States. All of these great soldiers evinced a deep sympathy for the American cause of liberty.

Eight long years of rough campaigning molded a body of true professional soldiers, inured to hardship, knowledgeable in tactics and strategy, skilled in discipline and command. The crucible of war had forged a fine alloy of professionalism which was to inspire the American regular soldier from then on. The examples of courage and fortitude of Washington at Valley Forge in the bitter winter of 1777-78 when, of 11,000 troops he had "no less than 2,898 unfit for duty because they are barefooted or otherwise naked,"[4] were to mean more to future Americans than all the proud military victories before or since. Not only were Washington's men suffering starvation, sickness and exposure, but he, himself, was under a personal attack by Horatio Gates, the hero of Saratoga, who aspired to Washington's post as Commander-in-Chief.

Gates had been pandering to Congress. He had sent Congress a report of his victory over Burgoyne at Saratoga, but had sent no report at all to Washington, his commander. Then Congress had made Gates president of the Board of War, a post which might be compared with the present Secretary of Defense. In this position Gates assumed that he was superior to the Commander-in-Chief, a pattern which has been followed to the present day.[5] It is indeed a wonder that Washington did not resign in disgust at this point, since there was evidence that Quartermaster Thomas Miffin, also a member of the Board of War and a friend of Gates, was responsible for many of the supply shortages at Valley Forge.[6] Washington's forbearance and self-control in the face of these slanders and inefficiencies at the seat of government set a behavioral pattern for all American regular soldiers to emulate.

In defense of Congress it must be said that its authority to prosecute a war was extremely circumscribed. It could vote money but levy no taxes. Congress was dependent on the willingness of the separate states to raise money and grant it to the Confederation treasury. Although Congress could in theory provide for an army it had to rely on each state to contribute voluntarily the actual fighting troops. Congress could make treaties with other countries but the states were legally able to ignore the terms. Congress could not regulate commerce or establish a common currency. Things got so bad after the end of the war that Congress could hardly finance its own existence let alone run a new government with countless pressing problems.[7]

The Congress of 1780 came near to repeating the history of the Long Parliament before Pride's Purge. As with the Long Parliament, the American Congress failed to pay, supply or even feed many of the colonial troops. Pay was as much as five months late and then sometimes no more than worthless scrip. Some troops were existing on half rations. And we seemed to be losing the war. Mutinies broke out on May 25, 1780 at Morristown when two regiments of the Connecticut Line paraded with drums beating, proclaiming their intention to hunt for food at bayonet point. This outburst was quelled, but on New Year's Day, 1781, a more serious disturbance occurred.

Soldiers of the Pennsylvania Line announced that their three-year enlistments had expired and demanded their discharges, which were refused. Several men were killed in the ensuing riots. Six regiments marched out of camp bound for Philadelphia and Congress to get their pay and discharges. They camped at Princeton the first night and were met there by Joseph Reed, the president of the Congress. He met the soldiers' demands. Most of the mutineers reenlisted and returned to the colors.[8]

But this event started a chain reaction among other troops and three New Jersey regiments attempted the same strategem. From West Point Washington sent Major General Robert Howe with a New England detachment. The detachment surrounded and captured the mutineers, then hanged two of them. This sobered the unhappy soldiers for the time being.

These mutinies looked like an opportunity to Sir Henry Clinton, who was in command of the British forces. He sent emissaries to Princeton to offer pardons and payment of all back pay. But the mutineers hanged the Tory emissaries as spies. The mutineers were not about to turn their coats but they did insist on fair treatment.[9]

THE NEWBURGH AFFAIR

After the victory at Yorktown the United States army inactively and impatiently awaited the peace settlement. Most of the forces were encamped outside Newburgh, New York. In December 1782, a group of officers formulated the Revolutionary Army's many legitimate grievances in a petition and sent it to Congress. When Congress failed to act, mutiny flared again and the "Newburgh Address" was circulated. Colonel Lewis Nicola suggested to General Washington that he accept a crown. A stern admonition from the Commander-in-Chief quelled the disturbance and thereby established one of the principal precedents for civil control of the military as well as for the military code: uniformed organizations do not collectively participate in political activity. Yet Congress understandably "continued to conjure up visions of military despotism when the greatest need was to prevent the Continental Army from melting away."[10]

The men of the army at Newburgh were acting like average American citizens, willing to fight for their country but expecting to be recognized for their services. When they thought they were being abused, they were not adverse to taking the initiative. Any society which preaches that the ultimate authority of government rests with the will of its people has a difficult time convincing certain minority groups that this noble precept does not apply to them —that a citizen is only he who wears civilian clothes (or who is white, or Protestant) and in no way risks his life for his country. The status of second class citizen is not acceptable to any American whatever his profession.

As Baron von Steuben discerned and wrote in a letter to a friend, "The genius of this nation is not in the least to be compared with that of the Prussian, Austrian or French. You say to a soldier, 'Do this," and he doeth it; but I am obliged to say, 'This is the reason why you ought to do that,' and then he does it."[11] The rough-hewn individualism of the American soldier established some unique patterns of behavior and a system of values that does not respond docilely to dogmatism or injustice. The American soldier insists on fair, honest and purposeful treatment even from his civil superiors. Writing on military morale in 1933 General Douglas MacArthur said, "Though it can survive and develop in adversities that come as an inescapable incident of service, it will quickly wither and die if soldiers come to believe themselves the victims of indifference or injustice on the part of their government. . . ."[12]

The timorous Continental Congress had fled Philadelphia in panic during the Revolutionary War, running not only from the British Redcoats but in fear of mutinous colonial troops and the traditional specter of a Cromwellian eviction by bayonet point. It is little wonder that as soon as it was able to do so Congress disbanded the Continental Army. Unlike Cromwell's Roundheads, the Americans dispersed quietly but all of them did not remain peaceful.

SOCIETY OF THE CINCINNATI

In an effort to show some minor appreciation by the new American nation for outstanding individual service in the army, General Washington provided a Badge of Military Merit as a decoration. This act was looked upon with such disfavor by Congress and the civilian public that the decoration had to be withdrawn. Next an attempt was made on the recommendation of Baron von Steuben and Major General Henry Knox to form the order of the Cincinnati, an association of ex-officers of the Continental Army. But this, too, was looked upon as an effort at worst to establish an hereditary aristocracy and at best to perpetuate rank and caste by commemorating only the officers. The spirit of egalitarianism was widespread. A pamphleteer, Aedanus Burke, warned that officers were "in their hearts aristocrats and enemies to the popular equality of a republic."[13] The common man was worshipped as opposed to the uncommon man who had been so much responsible for winning the American independence and forging a new nation.

Opponents of the Cincinnati included the two Adamses, Elbridge Gerry, John Jay and Thomas Jefferson, all civilian leaders of the Revolution. Jefferson wrote to Washington that he believed the order would emphasize the military as a separate caste so that "a distinction is kept up between the civil and military which it is for the happiness of both to obliterate."[14]

It is interesting to note that the modern idea of civil control of the military is the antithesis of what Jefferson proposed—that there be *no* distinction between the military and the civil. Washington accepted Jefferson's recommendation. When he presided over the first general meeting of the Society of the Cincinnati in 1784 at Philadelphia, he suggested changes which reduced the society to impotence. Thus no veterans' organization grew out of the Revolutionary War [15] and the "officers only" categorization was properly discredited.

EARLY PROFESSIONALISM

In the spirit of those times it is not surprising that no military profession developed. As Samuel P. Huntington wrote in his excellent study, *The Soldier and the State*,[16] military professionalism "lacked institutional manifestation. Prior to the Civil War no significant military institutions existed in the United States." Washington and Hamilton were the two champions of the army. But with the failure of Federalism, which they personified, and the Federalist doctrine, which related to the military ethic and the chain of command, there was no chance left for a military profession to develop.

The small school at West Point established in 1802 was little more than a drill camp and a prep school until the second war with England revealed the need for regular officers. Hamilton had recommended five military schools: Fundamental, Artillery, Cavalry, Infantry and Naval. When Jefferson finally established West Point its principal object was to produce engineers to fulfill the needs of the emerging industrial revolution. Its first superintendent, Jonathan Williams, had no military experience whatever.[17] This kind of technical training led away from the military arts and ideals and left a stamp on the military which is evident today. Military academies still stress technical study over military study, which is pursued only as a necessary but secondary sideline, usually on an after-hours basis.

"The traditional civilian attitude toward a professional military class," wrote Harold Sprout, "and the ideas such a class was traditionally assumed to represent, is one of avowed distrust."[18] In this atmosphere Congress was not about to establish a military academy unless it could be pointed at a nonmilitary objective such as science and technology.

THE CONSTITUTIONAL CONVENTION

The divisive policies pursued by a Congress which not only had inadequate authority but little incentive to go to the root of any problem, put the young Republic close to the brink of disaster following the ratification of the Treaty of Paris on April 15, 1783. Anarchy was in the air and the union was rapidly breaking up. The answer was obvious. A strong central government was necessary. Only Washington's genius and vast popularity led the disorganized country in this unpopular direction. As early as 1783, he had circulated a letter urging a more powerful government. Backing this move was Alexander Hamilton who repeatedly denounced the Articles of Confederation and promoted a new convention to draft a constitution based on an entirely new principle of centralized authority.

When a convention assembled at Annapolis to discuss collective taxation matters, Hamilton parlayed this meeting into the Constitutional Convention which met at Philadelphia on May 12th with fifty-five representatives present. Here the uncommon man took over from the helpless and bickering Congress, with giants in attendance like Washington, Franklin, Hamilton, and Monroe. Eight had been signers of the Declaration of Independence, and nearly all had been active in the Revolution in one way or another. Conspicuously absent was Thomas Jefferson, then minister to France. Neither was John Hancock there, nor Patrick Henry, who said he "smelled a rat."[19]

The majority of those assembled were quick to agree that the Articles of Confederation should be cancelled and that an entirely new beginning should be made. This was a bold stroke. Lesser men would have attempted to modify the 10-year-old Articles of Confederation which had been "battle proved." The model for the new government, of course, was the government of Great Britain, with a President resembling the King (he was given even more power than Britain's hereditary monarch) and with two legislative houses, the Senate and the House of Representatives, resembling the House of Lords and the House of Commons.

THE CONSTITUTION

As with the British King, the President was made "Commander-in-Chief of the Army and Navy of the United States and of the militia of the several States when called into the actual service of the United States." [20] Nothing is said in the Constitution about the President being a "civilian" as authorities on civil-military relations often imply. The only qualification necessary for the office of President is that he be a "natural born citizen" who has "attained to the age of thirty-five years and been fourteen years a resident within the United States."[21] It would have been anomalous indeed for the Founding Fathers of the Constitutional Convention to write antimilitary conditions in the Constitution while the presiding officer was the first soldier of the land. In fact the President was empowered to "commission all the officers of the United States,"[22] which demonstrated great trust and faith in the man they no doubt expected to become the first incumbent of that high office. And the *purpose* of the convention, one must remember, was to provide a strong central government which meant, of course, a powerful executive office.

The checks on the President were not "civilian" but organizational. Congress, like Parliament, was to have the purse strings "to raise and support armies. . . ."[23] Nothing was said furthermore about Congress being "civilian," the only qualification being that a member "shall have attained the age of twenty-five years and been seven years a citizen" and who shall "when elected be an inhabitant of that state in which he shall be chosen."[24] The basic qualifications for senator were similar.[25]

There was more of an anti-Federalist sentiment in America in 1787 than an antimilitary one. It is indeed remarkable that the Constitution was ever ratified. The fact that it was is a tribute to the political acumen of its instigators. Military policies were affected by and related to this fear of Federalism and of the aristocracy that a hierarchical system of government might bring." [26] As time went on other issues coincided with antimilitarism such as individual and states' rights, imperialism and overseas entanglements, taxes, and governmental regimentation. As Ekrich wrote, "Leadership in this opposition has been provided by a strange mixture of bedfellows, including conservatives as well as liberals, isolationists, pacifists, labor unionists and socialists." [27]

Champions of the military have been few and far between in peacetime. In fact, "militarism" has been associated with almost everything dangerous, onerous and undemocratic in our society. It has been termed arbitrary, authoritarian, imperialistic, antiliberal, reactionary, coercive, dogmatic, ignorant and violent. The new United States needed land power even less than Great Britain, and thus the mother country's antimilitary tradition could take root and flourish in the new world. Madison wrote that ". . . there was not a member in the Federal Convention who did not feel indignation at such an institution [as a standing army]."[28]

The Declaration of Independence had objected to the King keeping standing armies in the colonies "without the consent of our legislature." But this seemed to refer more to jurisdiction and legality than to an objection to standing armies *per se*. Similarly, the complaint that the King "has affected to render the military independent of and superior to the Civil Power," referred to the usurpation of the power of local colonial government by the distant power of a crown and a parliament in which the colonists were not represented. It had nothing to do with the status of colonial military forces. One is hard pressed to relate this grievance against the King's military forces in the colonies to the civil control doctrine now practiced. The colonists were understandably annoyed at having to quarter the Redcoats in their homes and at being subjected to British martial law during the long occupations of Boston, New York, and Philadelphia. When independence was achieved, most states included in their constitutions a prohibition against billeting troops in private homes as well as resolutions opposing standing armies in times of peace. The prohibition against quartering troops in private homes was repeated in Article III of the Bill of Rights to the Constitution.

No American attitude thrived better over the years than this early antimilitary tradition. Fresh adherents were found among the thousands of immigrants who rushed to America in the 19th century to escape the wars and conscription in European countries. Toward the end of the 19th Century this aversion to the military as an institution began to take on the form of a vendetta against professional military men. A law was passed in 1870 prohibiting them from holding public office except with specific Congressional approval.[29]

THE MILITARY IN PUBLIC OFFICE

During the first years of the Republic there had never been opposition toward military men holding public office. Washington and Hamilton moved in and out of civil and military life with ease. Major General Henry Knox became the first Secretary of War, and Major General John Armstrong, as Secretary of War in 1812, took command of armies in the field against Canada. President Andrew Jackson typified the military leader turned politician and became the darling of the backwoods liberals of his day.

Public opposition to standing armies persisted, however, in the early years. It was believed the state militias could provide adequately for defense. But the professional military man himself was highly respected. General William Henry Harrison, the victor of the Battle of Tippecanoe, was elected president by a landslide in 1841. General Zachary Taylor, a forty-year professional soldier of Mexican War fame, became the twelfth president in 1849. General Winfield Scott ran against Franklin Pierce in the campaign of 1852 and lost by a popular margin of less than 50,000 votes. Pierce himself had reached general officer rank in the Mexican War but was never considered a professional soldier. In the next Presidential election (1856) General John C. Frémont was defeated by James Buchanan, and General George B. McClellan ran against Lincoln in 1864. Frémont later was elected to the Senate and McClellan became governor of New Jersey. When, after the war, General Ulysses S. Grant was elected no one seemed concerned about the possibility of a military dictatorship.

During this period of our national life the right of an officer to speak out and to engage in politics was no different from that of any other citizen.[30] In fact it was rather expected that he behave like a public figure. The attitude of Jefferson that the distinction between the civil and military should be obliterated[31] was rather universal. The conception of civil control of the military as we know it today and the apolitical officer code was unknown. The possibility of dictatorship in the United States was suggested during Jackson's administration but the fear was minor and unrelated to the military. Nor did any of the military Presidents or public officials provide one single justification for any charge of Caesarism, which was sometimes heard when the modern conception of civil control began to take shape toward the end of the century.[32]

PROFESSIONALS VERSUS SECRETARIES OF WAR

The change in heart against the military politician began to reveal itself concurrently with the rise of Socialist doctrines. The military, being the guardian of the state, was regarded by the Socialists as the bulwark of the forces of capitalism. As such the military had to be discredited and the best target apparently was the professional himself. This phenomenon will be discussed in subsequent chapters. It happened that this new attitude toward the military man himself also appeared about the time of the hesitant birth of a military profession.[33]

The War of 1812 had demonstrated the need for military education. Winfield Scott and Jacob Brown began to write manuals and to put life and purpose into military duty. West Point had been "militarized" to some extent under Sylvanus Thayer and educated career officers were beginning to be found in the active service. A naval academy was established at Annapolis and a professional navy began to take shape.

In 1821 Secretary of War John C. Calhoun reorganized the War Department into technical bureaus which were to report directly to him (medical, quartermaster, engineers, pay, subsistence, etc.). A military commanding general responsible for operations only, was given semi-autonomous authority over the troops of the line. When General Jackson succeeded to the presidency the commanding general became entirely independent of the Secretary of War as might be expected. A similar arrangement obtained under Franklin D. Roosevelt during World War II, with Secretary of War Henry L. Stimson and Secretary of the Navy Frank Knox taking back seats to Admiral Leahy and General Marshall. As with Stimson and Knox, the Secretary of War under Jackson was limited to handling political, fiscal and housekeeping matters, with the exception that the supervision of technical bureaus was integrated in the General Staff of General Marshall. Jackson's Secretary of War endorsed the system which left the military commander of the army independently in charge of troops. This dual control was formally written into Army Regulations in 1836:

> The military establishment is placed under the order of the Major General Commander-in-Chief, in all that regards its discipline and military control. Its fiscal arrangements properly belong to the administrative departments of the staff, and to the Treasury Department under the direction of the Secretary of War.[34]

The kind of military organization in which the professional Commander-in-Chief reported directly to the President remained in force with few exceptions until 1903 when Secretary of War Elihu Root created the General Staff system. Root's so-called reforms put a layer of civilian supervision between the senior professional soldier and the President which was to be multiplied by the National Security Act of 1947 and fortified by repeated amendments to that act.[35]

The feature of civilian control *within* the defense establishment itself is therefore only as old as the 20th Century. It has nothing whatever to do with Constitutional principle or traditional practice before 1903.

It was inevitable that clashes would occur between the Commanding General and the Secretary of War because of the overlapping responsibility and authority implicit in the dual arrangement. In 1855 General Scott and Secretary Davis tangled in a bitter dispute. General McClellan fought with Secretary Stanton during the Civil War, General Sherman with Secretary Belknap after the war, General Sheridan with Secretary Endicott, and General Miles with Secretary Alger during the Spanish-American War. Even so, authors and authorities on military subjects hailed this dual military system as an enlightened and efficient defense arrangement. President James A. Garfield announced that "the General of the Army is second in command to the President"[36] but some of the Secretaries held other views. It is interesting to note that Great Britain employed a similar dual system between 1795 and 1870.[37] Never was the charge heard that the commander of the army wielded too much power for one man or that he threatened to establish a military dictatorship. The Root reforms were made to better *coordinate* the various activities of the army, not to subjugate the commander of the army to more civilian control.

Since the Civil War there have been almost no appointments of military men to the President's Cabinet. General William T. Sherman served temporarily as Secretary of War in 1869 but not until the appointment of General George C. Marshall in 1950 as Secretary of Defense was there another military man in this traditionally civilian post. Marshall had also served as Secretary of State from 1947 to 1949. Under his administration there was never a threat to the ultimate civilian control of the military through the President and Congress.

MILITARY DIPLOMATS

The Anglo-Saxon countries were the leaders in the antimilitary tradition at the turn of this century and they were most reluctant to use military men in diplomatic posts. President Theodore R. Roosevelt, who himself admired the military way, broke this tradition by appointing General James C. Smith as ambassador to Tokyo in 1906. General Smith had been governor of the Philippines and Roosevelt believed those islands were threatened by growing Japanese militarism.

Vagts suggests that an earlier appointment of General Horace Porter to Paris (1897-1907) was a military incursion into the civilian province but this stretches the point. Although a West Pointer who had served in the Civil War as a general officer, Porter had been long retired and had accumulated a fortune in railroading which, by normal American standards, allowed him to fill the ambassadorial post. Porter had been adequately "civilianized."[38]

Following the First World War the aversion to things military continued to exclude soldiers from diplomacy with some minor exceptions such as John B. Jackson, a former naval officer sent to Berlin as chargé d'affaires, and Gilchrist B. Stockton, a retired rear admiral sent to Vienna as minister plenipotentiary in 1930.[39] Generally speaking, however, it took the Second World War to cause another swing in the pendulum in favor of military diplomats.

Because Marshal Petain was made the puppet chief of state of defeated France at Vichy, it was decided by President Franklin D. Roosevelt to send a military ambassador. General John J. Pershing was nominated but declined for reasons of health and Admiral William D. Leahy was appointed instead. German domination of the Vichy government led to Leahy's recall in 1942 and he served out the war in the unconventional post of Chief of Staff to the Commander in Chief and Presiding Officer of the JCS. No one worried that the Admiral in this powerful position might become a military dictator, but there was much concern that Roosevelt might—if indeed, he wasn't that already.

During and just after World War II the United States followed the precedent set much earlier by Germany and France in sending military ambassadors to Russia. It was felt that hard-talking, strong-minded men might have more success with the rough Soviet leaders. Admiral William H. Standley was sent in 1942 but resigned after announcing that the Soviets were keeping their people ignorant of American Lend Lease aid.[40] Lieutenant General Walter Bedell Smith was sent to Moscow after the war and was authorized by Congress to retain his military rank. The thought was that this might revive some of the military understanding between the U.S. and the U.S.S.R. which was experienced during the war. It didn't. Stalin had no particular respect for military people.[41] Admiral Alan G. Kirk followed General Smith in Moscow with no more success, although it has never been charged that their failures had anything to do with the fact that they were military professionals.

Major General Patrick Hurley, a politician and sometime soldier was sent to China in 1944 after General Stilwell was relieved, and Generals George C. Marshall and Alfred C. Wedemeyer were sent later in unsuccessful efforts to check a rapidly deteriorating military and political situation. Wedemeyer's recommendations were neither published nor adopted.[42]

Following the Second World War a veritable campaign was run by the Department of State to eliminate military influence from foreign affairs and diplomacy which State considered to be its exclusive province. Since mid-century, except for minor setbacks, and even with a military man in the White House, this effort has been largely successful. One exception can be found when the friendship between President John F. Kennedy and retired General James M. Gavin led to his appointment to the ambassadorial post in Paris. It was argued that Gavin might be better able to deal with General Charles de Gaulle than would a civilian. But when Ambassador Gavin took up the cause of General de Gaulle for help in developing France's nuclear *force de frappe,* Gavin was soon replaced. The appointment of former Chief of Naval Operations Admiral George W. Anderson as Ambassador to Portugal provided an opportunity to "kick him upstairs" after he disagreed with the Secretary of Defense. Also, the losing brushfire war in South Vietnam led to the appointment of General Maxwell D. Taylor to the ambassadorial post at Saigon. But for these and a few other exceptions, State has been able to hold the line.

CONCLUSION

Throughout the history of the United States, civil control of the military has meant many things, but only in this century has it meant a denigration of the military profession and the subordination of professional military men to layer upon layer of civil superiors, bureaucracy and civilian domination. American military men have served honorably and faithfully in almost every public office, always behaving according to the best traditions of American democracy while exercising the highest ethical standards. It is indeed a strange phenomenon of our age that the profession of arms has become, in the name of civil control of the military, the whipping boy for all and sundry.

The many myths about military authoritarianism, caste-consciousness, arbitrariness and incapability in civil positions are seldom supported by the facts of history, unless one wishes to select and distort those facts to fit a preconceived conclusion. The professional soldier in America has behaved much like any other professional man in public life and has never been a danger to Constitutional and representative government.

If this interpretation of the American military man's performance is correct, why then is he so constantly vilified? As has been noted, militarism has been confused with many other controversial issues such as Federalism, states' rights, imperialism, war and taxes. Militarism, too, was alleged to have been a major cause of World War I and the rise of Hitler. Much of this blame for militarism has been hung on the neck of the Prussian (or German) General Staff. The condemnation of the German staff system has probably been inspired to some extent by Communist, Socialist and far-left propaganda.[43] But the cause goes much deeper and is widely reflected in honest interpretations of modern history.

The German General Staff has become a particular villain, held up as the invidious example of what will come should military policymakers ever be permitted to reorganize our defense establishment along general staff lines. What validity is there in the popular analyses of the German General Staff? Or in viewing every attempt to improve the American staff system as a step toward the abyss of German militarism?

To get at the roots of these questions we must turn again to history and reexamine the development of our doctrine. The dogma of general staff evils has spread like crabgrass through our culture. Has it been motivated by fear or foresight? Desires to weaken America or to preserve democratic government? Is it libel and slander or justified interpretation?

The next six chapters will focus upon German military history in a further effort to identify more specifically the reasons why the American military man has become such an apparent threat to the American civilian in the last few generations.

PART III

THE GERMAN GENERAL STAFF

CHAPTER 9

ORIGINS OF THE GERMAN GENERAL STAFF

Walter Millis has written that for "two generations of Americans the German General Staff has stood as an object of hatred, fear and revulsion."[1] In two world wars, the amateur American military establishment, hastily raised and trained, came face-to-face with the well-drilled and highly organized German counterpart. On the battlefield there was hatred and fear, no doubt, but also respect. The revulsion came as a civilian afterthought when the need for a scapegoat was felt. The "German General Staff," with little relationship to the actual organized leadership of the German army, became one of the whipping boys to assuage the guilt and remorse caused by the cruel war.

Nonetheless, as Millis truthfully notes, much of the thinking and many of the codes of the German General Staff provided the pattern for modern military organization. In fact, the strict military code and practices of civilian control of the military can be traced as much to the German military ethic as to the American heritage.[2] "The traditions of almost monkish divorcement of military policy from political affairs . . . of corporate anonymity in planning and command . . . of selfless devotion to the sovereign and state . . ."[3] are features of our own military system derived to some degree from the German General Staff. These and other German traditions give life and endurance to the principle of civilian control as exercised in our democratic society, although the code failed to retain the military-civilian divorce in the unstable German environment of the 20th century. Had the United States suffered two major defeats in one generation as did Germany, one can question how much civilian control would have persisted in America.

EARLY BEGINNINGS

As Barton Leach has noted, the German General Staff was more of a military caste than it was a military organization, and a caste with its own traditions, recruiting system, and homogeneous characteristics.[4] "Without the Junkers of East Elbia, without the Prussian aristocracy of sword and service which for two centuries supplied it with most of its officers, the Prussian army is inconceivable, and this applies with even greater force to the Prussian General Staff."[5] A comparatively small number of noble families comprised the Junkers which filled the General Staff ranks. Living on poor farms, yet comparatively tax-free, the younger sons were expected to pursue military or public careers. The term *Generalstabsdienst*, or "General Staff Service" came into being as early as 1640 with the Prusso-Brandenburgian Army.[6] Unswerving loyalty and devotion to the Emperor became the central moral foundation of this service and persisted until its violent demise under Hitler. The popular impression of blind unthinking obedience as a part of this system is not altogether warranted, as illustrated by the story told by Goerlitz of von Seydlitz when, at the battle of Zorndorf in 1758, Frederick the Great ordered him to attack the formidable Russian infantry. He replied, "Tell His Majesty that my head will be at his disposal after the battle, but that as long as the battle lasts I intend to use it in his service."[7]

The renown of the Prussian army was enhanced by the masterful maneuvers of Frederick the Great. His most famous "war" was that of the Bavarian Succession which he waged in 1778 to prevent the union of Austria and Bavaria. No battles were fought and an outcome favorable to Frederick was decided by diplomacy. This antedated by over half a century the violent war doctrine of von Clausewitz, although the Turks had been waging wars of extermination against the House of Hapsburg in the Balkans for some centuries.[8]

GNEISENAU'S CONTRIBUTION

The actual *modus operandi* of the General Staff didn't become stylized before the early 19th century, when Gneisenau developed the concept of a duel responsibility for the chief of staff of any military organization. The chief of staff became responsible not only to the commander of his own organization, at whatever level, but to the General Staff headquarters. This double chain of command was unique to the German army and persisted as a sort of secondary organization superimposed upon the normal military structure.[9] A General Staff officer eventually came to have two channels of communication and command—one through regular and obvious command channels, and another through less formal routes to other General Staff officers in the higher headquarters and finally to the Emperor.[10] This system obviously led to the accumulation of power in the hands of the General Staff officer and resembles somewhat the dual command relationship of the Commissar system of political leadership which is now practiced in Russia. The principle difference, of course, is that the General Staff officers reported to a military headquarters whereas the Commissars report to a political office.

Rivalry between staff and command seems inherent in such an organization of dual authority, but this was overcome to some degree by refinements which put commanders on the same General Staff team. In Germany, principal commanders were selected from the General Staff ranks.

Gneisenau further established the idea of the staff corporate body, which provides team solutions to the commander and thus exerts considerable pressure to utilize "war council" decisions.

Other less laudable conceptions of warfare were fostered by Gneisenau and have persisted to the present day. It was he who counseled the military annihilation of Napoleon, an early advocacy of total war. This meant the occupation of France and Paris, with surrender of the capital in 1814. At the Treaty of Paris the Napoleonic regime was completely destroyed. Had Gneisenau had his way, Napoleon would have been shot, never to have lived to make his dramatic one hundred-day comeback from Elba. In this abortive coup, Gneiseau, as Blucher's Chief of Staff, was largely responsible for the victory at Waterloo. It was he, in the absence of Blucher, who ordered the badly mauled Prussian army to take the road which led to a union with Wellington, thus defeating Napoleon's strategic design of separating the Prussians and the English.

REFORMS OF BOYEN AND GROLMAN

Prussia was the first to recognize the effect of emerging technology on the conduct of war. Mass armies were appearing and national conscription was the inevitable consequence. A universal service law was passed in September 1814 over the Junkers' fears of democratic revolution. Major General von Boyen as war minister was largely responsible for this law, and even went so far in this new thinking as to suggest that the war minister was not primarily responsible to the King but rather owed first allegiance to the nation.[11] This idea of ultimate loyalty to the nation at large grew roots in the democracies but failed to flourish in Germany.

An influential protege of Boyen was Karl Wilhelm von Grolman, who became Chief of the General Staff. It was he who pressed for officer education in the new sciences and set standards which the impoverished Junker families complained of. To break up the strong caste system, Grolman introduced periodic exchanges between duty assignment on the General Staff and regimental duty. This policy of frequent transfer between staff and line was adopted in the American army at the turn of the century and persists today with excellent results. Staffs are prevented from becoming ingrown and bureaucratic while staff officers are kept alert to problems in the field.

Under Grolman, Department II of the General Staff began to take on the function of Intelligence. It was split into three "Theaters of War" to acquire data concerning the armies of neighboring states, and a fourth section of military history. Today the efficacy of military history as an element of military planning has been shoved into the background by the American armed forces. Radically new weapon systems have led planners to feel that past experience has minor bearing on the future. Only time and more experience can test the validity of this assumption.

METTERNICH'S REACTIONARY INFLUENCE

The military liberalism of Boyen and Grolman was not to endure. Reaction, under pressures from Prince Metternich, a civilian diplomat of aristocratic extraction, caused these two exponents of democratic innovations for the military to resign. Policies of the Austrian Metternich influenced the Prussian Army to return to its absolutist disposition as an instrument of the monarch. But the enlightened General Staff concepts were not lost on the rest of the world where more liberal political systems provided fertile ground.

The Prussian General Staff reverted to the caste system it had known under Frederick the Great, self-perpetuating and hide-bound in its own existence. The oath of allegiance was sworn to the king, never to the constitution or the people. This reactionary pattern persisted until the end of the Second German Empire in 1918.

Many of the leading German generals came from unprofitable small estates as a sort of precondition to the military profession. Moltke, Waldersee, Hindenburg, Goltz and Seeckt, for example, were scions of land poor nobility who found a calling in the army. This practice was somewhat responsible for the Spartan ideals of the officer class, such as the spurning of personal gain, the disregard of pain and hardship, and the glory of death in battle. As Hindenburg wrote, the keynote was "wantlessness."

INFLUENCE OF CLAUSEWITZ

The character of the Prussian, and the succeeding German General Staff was no little influenced by the philosophy of war expounded by Karl von Clausewitz, whose classic work *On War*[12] stands today as the most influential treatise in all military literature. He, too, was a Prussian from an impoverished *petit nobilite,* who entered the military service at the age of twelve and later came under the influence of Scharnhorst, Boyen and Gneisenau. It was Clausewitz who legitimized the view that war was no longer an institution solely for despots, but rather was a vital concern of the people who must wage it for their own purposes. The entire power of a people must be brought to bear for victory in modern war, he wrote, and thus war became an integrated function of all national life. This concept of total war led the General Staff to some involvement in diplomacy and government, and to the making of plans for total mobilization.

Clausewitz preached ruthless and violent war in order to shorten the period of combat, bring swift victory, and thus, in the long run, save lives of all concerned. He advocated war waged against the opposing government, thus again bringing into focus a political aspect for General Staff consideration. His oft quoted phrase about war being an extension of politics waged by other means fogged the sharp distinction between government and the military which had been held during the age of Metternich. It was, as we have noted, Clausewitz who demanded that in time of war the military commander should be given a seat in the cabinet. He also taught that, in a desperate situation, the existence of the army became more important than that of the state itself, because it was the army which held the state together, or through which the state could be resurrected in case of defeat. This philosophy can be noted at work during the period following World War I, when an army was trained in violation of the Treaty of Versailles, and later during the Hitlerian period when the disapproving army played along with the hated dictator rather than risk complete destruction and substitution by irregular military bodies.[13]

Possibly the most revolutionary doctrine of Clausewitz was the belief in state supremacy as opposed to the popular will. He was opposed to democracy and believed that people derived their power from the state. This idea was common to Hegel, a contemporary philosopher, and is similar to the doctrine of Marx and Engels.

Unity of Germany, according to Clausewitz, could be realized only by the sword. So, too, with larger political amalgamations. The belief in German dominance of Europe by military means was born in Clausewitz' writings. Thus was established the background for Bismarck's policy and the theme for two World Wars.

The emerging age of science and the industrial revolution complemented the doctrine of Clausewitz, and after his death his writings took on increasing significance. However, successive individuals in the General Staff hierarchy itself continued to shape the pattern of that misunderstood institution, the Prussian and later the Imperial German Army.

VON MOLTKE, FATHER OF THE GENERAL STAFF

Perhaps the one who left the deepest mark on the General Staff was Helmuth von Moltke. Although born in Mecklenburg rather than Prussia, he fit the pattern by coming from an impoverished aristocracy. As a young subaltern he was so poor that he turned to writing as a means of earning a little money. His first important assignment was to Turkey to assist the Sultan in westernizing his army. The Sultan was searching for a substitute for the recently disbanded Janissaries who had dominated Turkey for over four hundred years. During the Turkish adventure Moltke sharpened his literary skill with numerous descriptive accounts of his experiences. Unfortunately he contracted fevers during his long tour in the Middle East which left him completely without hair. In a day when most men wore beards, Moltke was bare-faced, and he wore a black skull cap indoors to cover his bald pate.[14]

The revolution of 1848 found Moltke a staff officer on the Rhine. He objected to the liberal movement as inconsistent with the General Staff credo for the dominance of the state and the rule of law. Although Moltke believed in the unification of Germany he also believed, like Clausewitz, that union could only be properly achieved through military action under established authority. Consequently, he enthusiastically supported the crushing of the insurrection with Prussian troops.

After a tour as adjutant to Prince Frederick, where he broadened his view of politico-military affairs, Moltke was appointed Chief of the Prussian General Staff in 1858. Applying Clausewitz' principles to the industrial revolution, Moltke reorganized and rearmed the army along modern lines. Yet the most far-reaching of his innovations was apparent only to the sophisticated observer. This was Moltke's doctrine of delegated authority.

Paradoxical as a doctrine of delegated authority may be to the popular conception of Prussian blind obedience, it is true that under Moltke this doctrine achieved its original impetus as a military *modus operandi*. Moltke preached the necessity for independent decision by subordinate commanders. Given the objectives and the general plan of campaign, the subordinate commanders were expected to proceed with initiative and confidence. They were trained to think and act on their own. Conversely, the commander was taught not to try to do it all himself. Continued personal intervention was discouraged as an illusory advantage. The commander should not engage in tasks which he could properly delegate to others. Fundamental to this philosophy was a confidence in others, a quality which Moltke held to a high degree. It was enhanced by high moral standards and trustworthiness as General Staff credos, combined with a Spartan simplicity of life.[15]

There was no moral compunction, however, about meddling in affairs of state. It was felt perfectly moral to reverse an unsatisfactory political development with military intervention. So long as the king did not object, even a *coup d'état* was deemed morally acceptable. Such an event occurred in 1861 when Field Marshal Wrangel was selected to lead an expedition into Berlin to overthrow the Diet. The King himself had signed the secret orders for the coup. It is interesting to note that the King later lost his nerve and wished to abdicate, but Wrangel talked him out of it by warning that the officers involved might be court-martialed without the King's protection. Only the appearance of Otto von Bismarck on the political scene a few years later saved Prussia from chaos after this adventure. In addition, the likelihood of a war with France turned the General Staff attention to external rather than internal affairs. As early as 1860 Moltke recognized as a real danger the possible encirclement of Prussia by a union of France and Russia. For a time, he recommended preventive war until dissuaded by Bismarck. Fortunately Moltke recognized the superiority of the political leadership under Bismarck and submitted himself to the Chancellor's direction. His subordination may have been a consequence more of Bismarck's evident political sagacity than of any belief in civil control of the military.

WAR WITH AUSTRIA

Moltke's military genius, however, asserted itself in the war against Austria in 1866. Bismarck at one point attempted to retain forces to protect the Rhine Provinces, but Moltke gained royal sanction for his operational plan of an all-out attack in the Clausewitzian manner. The great General Staff came into its own when the cabinet, at the King's direction, authorized the Chief of the General Staff to issue orders on its own authority. Up to this point the General Staff had been concerned only with plans.[16]

The war with Austria was a resounding success. The Austrian muzzleloaders were no match for the new Prussian needle guns, nor for the revolutionary military organization and tactics developed by the General Staff. The impersonality of the General Staff was illustrated by the fact that, as the battle of Sadowa flamed to a resounding triumph, a Prussian divisional commander asked, "Who on earth is this General von Moltke?" The war was concluded in the astonishingly short time of seven weeks.

But the Peace of Nickolsburg saw the end of Moltke's anonymity. Now a national hero, he was rewarded by the King of Prussia with sizeable monetary gifts which ended his poverty once and for all. As a landed gentleman with an estate, he now entered the Federal Assembly as a member for Memel-Heydedrug. Obviously there was no conception here of separating the military from political office. But even more famed than Moltke became the Prussian General Staff, and all modern states began to study this new phenomenon of military organization.

WAR WITH FRANCE

France was not happy with the Prussian successes and the formation of the potentially powerful North German Federation, as a consequence of the war. Under Napoleon III, France found excuses to declare war in 1870. Again, with full authority to act, Prussian mobilization under the General Staff ran like clockwork. Perhaps the skill of the General Staff can be attributed to the fact of its small size. Apart from Moltke, his two adjutants and three lieutenant colonels who ran the three army groups, the General Staff consisted of only ten officers: three majors, six captains, and one lieutenant.

The siege of Metz and the encirclement of the French at Sedan ended the Franco-Prussian war with a spectacular finality comparable to the war against Austria four years before. The concepts of Clausewitz and the doctrines of the General Staff were doubly vindicated. Moltke and his General Staff were called demigods by the German Army. But friction between Moltke and Bismarck began to show. The civil-military conflict was accentuated by debates over the proposed bombardment of Paris to which Moltke objected. It must be noted that it was the civilian statesman who recommended the merciless attack on the population of Paris in order to end the war formally before Austria might attack. Bismarck professed to see personal motives in Moltke's decision not to bombard Paris and accused Moltke of being under English influence through his English wife. But Moltke withstood this and other efforts of Bismarck to sully his reputation.

COMPOSITION OF THE 19TH CENTURY GENERAL STAFF

Many legends surrounding the Prussian General Staff were spawned during this decade of the 1860's when Prussian invincibility went unquestioned. Yet there were surprisingly few officers assigned to the General Staff, and more surprisingly, these few now came from rather diverse backgrounds. As Goerlitz notes:

> In 1857 Moltke had found 64 General Staff officers at his disposal. In 1871 there were 135. When he resigned in 1888 the number had risen to 239, of which 197 belonged to the Prussian Army, 25 to the Bavarian General Staff, ten to that of Saxony, and seven to that of Wurttemburg. The General Staff mirrored the extent to which the officer corps was being invaded by bourgeois elements. In 1872, roughly one-third of all German General Staff officers were untitled. One was even a Jew.[17]

This reveals considerable broadening of the Prussian military sytsem and an invasion of commoners into the Junker officer caste. One century earlier, at the death of Frederick the Great in 1786, all of his 100-odd generals and colonels were noblemen, although

43 were noble foreigners, while there were just three non-nobles of the 200 lieutenant colonels and majors.[18] Also the character of the Prussian army had changed radically with the development of the General Staff system. By the end of the 19th Century the German officer corps had achieved a true professional nature, led by the exacting example of the General Staff itself.

THE 19TH CENTURY GENERAL STAFF

Education and examinations became central requirements for advancement. Professional military schools had been established, and the pursuit of science and engineering achieved respectability. Comprehensive theories and doctrines provided a *raison d'etre* while the strict and Spartan officer codes of conduct knit the leaders together into a dedicated whole.

Under von Moltke the General Staff system was brought to full maturity and provided the successes which gave it a worldwide reputation. It was the scholarly Moltke who, more than anyone else, caused the German officer corps to look upon soldiering as a profession. Under King William I, Moltke and the General Staff were regarded with such confidence that he was granted virtual supreme command, a prerogative that had heretofore been retained by the sovereign.

It was no less through the efforts of Moltke and the General Staff than through the political acumen of Bismarck, that it became possible to reconstitute the German Empire in 1871 at Versailles. But a far greater legacy than this political success was the professionalism and the prestige which General von Moltke gave to the German army through the General Staff system. Its power for good or evil remained of primary concern to the western world until Hitler managed to destroy it utterly.

When William I died in 1888, von Moltke, his ever-loyal servant, resigned. Two years later Bismarck was forced to retire. With all their great teamwork, Bismarck and Moltke never got along well. Moltke had felt slighted by Bismarck when the Chancellor had ignored the General in making military proposals to the Austrians. Later, Moltke was insulted by Bismarck's wife Johanna at a diplomatic dinner and left in a huff. On his ninetieth birthday the old General received no more than a congratulatory note from Bismarck. But this quiet feud was kept private.[19]

Thus came to an end a glorious period of development for the

German army, a period which has never been matched before or since. Although the German General Staff deteriorated from this high point and expired ignominiously under Hitler in 1937, it was still castigated in America after World War II and blamed for Germany's defeat.[20] Seldom in history has so misunderstood a villain been created to rationalize events that were too complicated and too horrible to cope with in any true perspective.

CHAPTER 10

FROM MOLTKE ON

Under "the man of silence," Helmuth von Moltke, the German General Staff reached its fullest flower. With Bismarck it had united Germany and created a strong state in the heart of Europe that killed the dream of a revived Holy Roman Empire. This Protestant victory seemed a praiseworthy achievement to the Americans. At that time the militarism most feared by England was that of France or of France and Spain.[1]

The reputation of the German General Staff was well deserved as the source of scientific and objective war planning, as a repository and center for the soldierly virtues, and for unswerving loyalty to the chief of state. High on the list of these virtues were the anonymity of General Staff members when dealing with affairs of defense, the practice of Spartan simplicity and economy, and the dedication to absolute integrity and honesty. Moreover, the resounding successes of Düppel, Sadowa and Sedan left no doubt anywhere in the world that this military system, if not the resulting army, was anything but the best ever. The German General Staff gained such eminence that within the next quarter century every major army in the world was to adopt modifications of the German plan.

The spread of the German General staff system was in no small measure a result of the work of Spencer Wilkinson, an English scholar of the art of war, who published *The Brain of an Army* in 1890.[2] This far-reaching work advocated the staff system which had become legendary. Few books on military subjects have had such immeasurable influence. Sir Charles Dilke used it to advocate the formation of a general staff in Britain,[3] and Secretary of War Elihu Root studied it carefully before reorganizing the United States Army.[4] A companion volume, *The Brain of a Navy*, was used at the United States Naval War College.[5] In a letter to Wilkinson dated October 15, 1919, Root observed:

> . . . Plainly, it would have been impossible both for England and for America to play the roles they have in saving us from German domination but for the existence of the General Staffs whose business it was to think and plan and secure information.
> I do not forget . . . what a great part your little book played. . . .

General von Moltke was no warmonger, nor did he leave any warlike tradition with the German General Staff. Once he remarked that any war, even a victorious one, was a misfortune for the nation concerned. However, he believed that war was an inevitable condition of life and "a link in God's ordering of the world."[6] Hence he had little patience with the beginnings of the ideas of peace through international law or with international peace organizations: ideas which were then being debated at Heidelberg. It was his most optimistic hope that civilization would cause war to become less frequent. As with most great military men, his principal guide and motto was, *si vis pacem, para bellum,* a remark also attributed to Julius Caesar[7] and George Washington. This actually was the major mission of the German General Staff—to prepare for war in time of peace by developing thorough and complete war plans. These plans directed against any possible enemy, whether France or Russia, were kept up to date with continual modification.

THE WALDERSEE PERIOD

After von Moltke, the German General Staff was never fully able to live up to its shining reputation. A great blow came at once with the selection of von Moltke's successor, Alfred Count von Waldersee. He was everything that von Moltke was not. A political general with aspirations of becoming Chancellor, he was selfishly ambitious and set an example which began unwholesomely to penetrate the staff and the army itself. Arrogance and self-interest began to replace the former code of modesty and dedicated service.[8]

Waldersee's career had been spotted with adjutant jobs to powerful princes. He gained an enviable reputation as military attaché to Paris where his accurate dispatches just before the outbreak of the Franco-Prussian War caught the eyes of Bismarck and the Kaiser. Even von Moltke considered Waldersee a man of talent. But where von Moltke had dealt with the Emperor through the War Ministry, the channel irked Waldersee and he managed to have the War Minister replaced by General Paul von Schellendorf, a former General Staff officer who had pressed for emancipation of the General Staff from the War Ministry.

As a major, incidentally, von Schellendorf had written the first authentic description of the German General Staff.[9] This was to become a guide for Spencer Wilkinson[10] in England and subsequently for Elihu Root[11] in America in their efforts to reform the British and American armies.

Waldersee fitted the popular stereotype of the military warmonger. Not content with making plans for war, he actively advocated war with Russia and dealt clandestinely with England, Austria, Italy, and Turkey as possible allies in this project. He was somewhat responsible for failing to renew the Reinsurance Treaty with Russia which had been the cornerstone of Bismarck's foreign policy and guaranteed each country against attack by the other if either should go to war with a third power. This had protected Prussia's rear in her three swift wars. It seemed that now Germany wished to assist Austria in the Balkans. The foundation was laid for World War I.[12]

In 1886 Waldersee took the step that was to end for him as a tour-de-force: he attacked the policies of Bismarck and suggested that the old Chancellor was running out of steam. Upon learning that Crown Prince Frederick was suffering from cancer, chances seemed good for young Prince William, Waldersee's friend and mentor, to ascend the throne. So the General redoubled his efforts in political affairs, taking part in conservative party activity.

The in-fighting with Bismarck grew hotter when the old Emperor, William I, died and Moltke retired. Waldersee then assumed the post of Chief of the General Staff and pandered to the whims of the new Emperor, William II, the Kaiser of World War I, who he thought would lead Germany into war. But Waldersee misread the young Emperor's attitude and, after two years, the General lost royal favor although retaining his post. When the inevitable showdown came with Bismarck and Bismarck was relieved, Waldersee told the Emperor that he hoped he would choose the right man for the chancellorship, meaning himself. But the Emperor crushed Waldersee's ambitions with the remark, "Oh, I think we'll manage. Good hunting!"[13]

Because of the strained international situation, the Emperor appointed a general of infantry, Georg Leo von Caprivi, to the chancellorship and Caprivi opposed many of Waldersee's policies.

The new Chancellor caused, for example, the military attachés to report through diplomatic channels, thus denying Waldersee his direct channel in foreign affairs. Caprivi also managed to achieve a rapprochement with Russia and to reduce the term of military service, both contrary to Waldersee's advice. Eventually (1891) the Emperor decorated Waldersee and reassigned him to limbo as commander of an army corps. Alfred von Schlieffen, later to author the famous "Plan" for the conquest of France, succeeded to Chief of the General Staff. This firing of Waldersee from the General Staff was a move generally approved by the officer corps which had been embarrassed by Waldersee's political machinations.

Before he expired into oblivion in 1904 Waldersee's name came into prominence once again. He was selected to command the allied armies to relieve Peking during the Boxer Rebellion of 1900. But even here failure dogged his steps. Before he arrived in China, the Europeans in Peking had been liberated.

SCHLIEFFEN OF "THE PLAN"

The tour of General von Schlieffen as Chief of the General Staff was marked by an increasing fear of war on two fronts and the development of a plan to cope with such a nightmarish eventuality. The "Great Plan" thus evolved, to attack France first with overwhelming force from the north through Belgium, and then to turn on Russia. This plan was religiously defended by the General Staff against many influential doubters; each year it was reworked and exercised in maneuvers until near mechanical perfection was achieved. But in 1905, the aging von Schlieffen was kicked by a horse and forced to retire. His successor was von Moltke's nephew, also named Helmuth von Moltke. Although younger and handsomer, he enjoyed few of the intellectual talents of his illustrious namesake.

COMPOSITION AND CODE OF THE GENERAL STAFF

By 1905 the General Staff had changed little from what it was under the first von Moltke. It was still a small organization, with but 106 officers, although the Chief had acquired a deputy called the Quartermaster-General, who managed the activities of the four *oberquartermasters* heading the four staff divisions. Almost half of the officers now came from commoner stock. Moreover only about one-quarter of their number had been educated at cadet schools, while one-half had been educated in the public *gymnasiums*.

Under von Schlieffen soldierly principles had returned to the

German General Staff and the army. The Chief of Staff and its members refrained from political activities, even political discussion. The Great Plan was in reality a simple tactical maneuver with no room for diplomacy or statecraft. Germany's encirclement was accepted as an accomplished fact without hope for a political détente on either front with France, Russia or England. Because of this technical perfection and political blindness, German diplomacy entered a decline.

VON MOLTKE THE YOUNGER

Under the rather desultory guidance of the younger Helmuth von Moltke, the Schlieffen Plan was revised and watered down even though von Schlieffen still exerted some influence from retirement with his extensive historical and theoretical studies. He died in 1913 with the final warning: "See you keep this right wing strong!"

By that time the younger Moltke was in ill health too and a new personality had manifested itself in the General Staff. This was Erich Ludendorff, a commoner and a real Clausewitzian who believed in mass attack with every soldier Germany could muster. Where Schlieffen preached flexibility and maneuver, Ludendorff advocated violent shock action and total war. This required a revision of Germany's conscription laws and so the General Staff again became involved in civil activities.

AUTHORITY OF THE GENERAL STAFF

Let us take a moment here to trace the development of the German unified (army-navy) command. The General Staff up to this point, at the beginning of the First World War, was entirely an army war planning headquarters which acted as an operational staff for the Emperor in time of hostilities, the Emperor being the "Supreme War Lord." In terms of requiring the army to carry out its plans, the General Staff had considerable political influence, although, except for the Waldersee period, this influence was exerted through other governmental agencies.

Over the General Staff was the War Ministry which reported directly to the Emperor and the *Reichstag*. This organization, at cabinet level, was responsible for weapons development and industrial mobilization. It administered the army: housed, uniformed, and paid the troops. Usually a general staff officer was appointed war minister, but this did not mean that the ministry was in any subtle way subservient to the inferior General Staff. In fact there often was considerable friction between the administering political ministry and the planning, "purely military," General Staff.

The Emperor's personal military staff was called the Military Cabinet and had minor influence over the army either in peace or war. When the independent navy was authorized by the *Reichstag* in 1889, a Naval Cabinet was formed and integrated with the Military Cabinet. This combination eventually was called the Imperial Headquarters. There was some talk of the Imperial Headquarters becoming a separate general staff but this never materialized. Waldersee discouraged any effective unification which might have reduced his power. Even though the General Staff developed the plans which built the army, the General Staff was not the supreme military authority by any means, nor did it control the navy in any way. But, since Germany was essentially a land power, the army overwhelmed the navy in importance.

In 1912 Ludendorff pressed hard for three new corps but was turned down cold by the War Ministry. To shut him up he was removed from his post and transferred to a regiment. He was a mere lieutenant colonel at the time. This incident serves to show that despite the great reputation of the German General Staff it was far from omnipotent, even when the country was on the threshold of war.

It is interesting to note that Ludendorff's failure to get the three new corps is used by Telford Taylor in his remarkable book *Sword and Swastika*[14] as evidence of the anachronistic character of the German military system. He remarked that although Germany could well afford the increase in manpower for the army, and that the three corps probably would have spelled success for the Schlieffen Plan, still the "old guard" acting through the War Minister defeated the proposal. Their reasoning, according to Taylor, was that there was not enough "officer class" material remaining to lead the proposed corps, and they did not want officers coming from bourgeois sources. No doubt opponents of the plan used this reason to sow dissension within the officer corps, but considering the composition of the General Staff itself, with half of its officers of commoner stock, the argument must have been a hollow one to those officers and civil leaders alike who really understood the situation. The reasoning that only aristocrats could command was about as invalid then as is the reasoning today that any improvement in the Joint Chiefs of Staff system in the United States would be bad because of similarity to the German General Staff system. But playing on biases is a standard tactic for winning political arguments.

There are reactionary elements in any institution and it can only be said that in this case the reactionary element prevailed over the "young Turks" in the General Staff led by Ludendorff. Such a course of events, at least, can hardly be used to cast discredit upon the General Staff. If anything, the political War Ministry, a system we embrace today in the United States, was responsible for the wrong military decision.

THE GERMAN NAVY

As noted earlier, the General Staff had no authority over the rapidly growing naval command. Indeed, there was so little co-ordination that the General Staff was not able even to get an exchange of intelligence reports. The upstart German Navy, with neither tradition nor an hereditary officer corps, was able to maintain its independence and to operate on the pattern laid out by the United States Navy's Alfred Thayer Mahan. Such was the power of the commercial interests which had sponsored the High Seas Fleet, as opposed to the military authority of the General Staff. To suggest that there was any army-navy unification under the German General Staff is to misread the facts.

WORLD WAR I

On June 28, 1914, the assassination of the Austrian Archduke by a Serb was the spark which lit the tinder for World War I. Austria-Hungary's harsh ultimatum to Serbia was not completely accepted by the little country and the Austrians marched. When Russia began to mobilize in order to fulfill her treaty obligations, the Germans feared the worst and, unable to induce the Russians to hold up, set the Great Plan into motion. Contrary to the popular impression, however, Germany began her mobilization well after Russian mobilization orders had been issued and fifteen minutes after France had taken a similar measure.[15]

There can be no doubt that the Kaiser, the Chancellor, and other political leaders knew full well of the Plan's purpose to march through Belgium. To blame the General Staff for this invasion of a neutral country is to credit the staff with considerably more author-ity than it enjoyed. There apparently had been no debate between civil and military elements over the question of violating Belgian neutrality.

In the offensive through Belgium Ludendorff again came into prominence. He had by chance been assigned as a liaison officer to the army which was to take the fortress of Liege. This was an operation he had personally planned when he had been with the General Staff. With unlimited self-confidence, he all but usurped command. His advice assured a complete success. Such was the prestige of General Staff officers among the rank and file of the army. Ludendorff was still a lieutenant colonel at this time.

Neither Emperor William II nor the second von Moltke had much confidence in his own ability to direct the conduct of the war. Moltke had tampered with the Schlieffen Plan before war broke out. Now, with the issue still in doubt, he grew overly concerned with the Russian threat to Prussia and detached two corps from the west for movement east. These corps never arrived in time to participate in the great victories of Tannenberg and Masurian Lakes, which the genius of Ludendorff (as chief of staff to the aged Paul von Hindenburg) had engineered.

But the two missing corps contributed much to the stalling of Germany's western offensive, even though a stronger hand than von Moltke's might still have carried out the plan. It became obvious to the Kaiser that von Moltke had to go. He was replaced by Erich von Falkenhayn, then the war minister. Now the two posts of War Minister and Chief of Staff were combined in one man and the power of the General Staff took on new dimensions. This did not come about by General Staff ambitions for more authority. In fact the new governmental and political responsibilities were thrust upon it by the emergencies of war. Other sources of authority had proved incapable of acting.

The move was something like that made in the United States when General George C. Marshall was made Secretary of Defense during the Korean emergency. To make this possible Congress had to permit a one-time exception to the National Security Act, which prohibited the appointment of a Secretary of Defense who had "within ten years been on active duty as a commissioned officer in a Regular component of the armed services. . . ." [16]

Where Germany in World War I moved a war minister to chief of staff, the United States in 1950 made a former chief of staff the war minister (Secretary of Defense). Both changes were made politically with no military pressure whatever because the national danger was such as to demand the best man in a position of authority. The United States, however, fared somewhat better than Germany did because von Falkenhayn did not measure up to the job.

With the Schlieffen Plan gone down the drain the new German War Minister/Chief of Staff seemed out of ideas. Ludendorff and Hindenburg urged a concentration in the east to force Russia out of the war, which seemed reasonable considering the eastern victories, but Falkenhayn never gave up his fixation on the western front.

STRENGTHENING OF THE GENERAL STAFF

With von Falkenhayn's indecisive leadership, the separate heads of departments in the General Staff assumed greater authority than ever. Tappen, for example, chief of the Operations Department, was obsessed with holding all territorial gains, and Falkenhayn. acceded to his policies. The young and able chiefs of staff of various commands, such as Ludendorff and Seeckt, began to carry more weight with their direct channels to the General Staff. Groener, head of the railway section, and new department chiefs in the War Ministry dealing with production and labor, ushered in a sort of "war socialism." [17]

The General Staff was untrained and unprepared to assume such broad powers of government. One can marvel only at how close it came to success. The point to remember, however, is that the General Staff in no way usurped the civil powers. As Germany found herself besieged on all fronts in the "paralyzing embrace of her enemies," only the General Staff was able to function as a directing head of a war which had become almost total.

There is another American parallel here which might be made. Great authority was thrust upon the United States Joint Chiefs of Staff during World War II. None of this authority was sought, yet, when directed to do so, the Joint Chiefs of Staff assumed whatever responsibilities seemed necessary for military success. Never was a thought entertained of holding the reins of power after the fighting had ended. Nor did the German General Staff of World War I aspire to overthrow civil control, even in defeat.[18]

Falkenhayn approved Tappen's strange strategy of attacking the French where they were strongest, at Verdun. Over a quarter of a million soldiers were lost on each side in this mass slaughter, with no significant result except to further weaken Germany. This ended

Falkenhayn's career. He was induced to resign, being replaced by the popular and successful team of Hindenburg (as chief) and Ludendorff (as first quartermaster-general).

About this time there was talk of creating a military dictatorship but Ludendorff rejected the idea. Nevertheless, because of the economic mobilizaton necessary to propagate the war, there existed a sort of military economic dictatorship, and the term "war socialism" was heard more often. But, so long as the mild Bethmann-Hollweg was Chancellor, the full mobilizaton of the country for total war could not be realized. By threatening resignation, however, the Hindenburg-Ludendorff team managed to get Bethmann-Hollweg replaced by Dr. Michaelis, the food minister. Using the same tactics the General Staff leaders secured the downfall of Foreign Minister Kuhlmann. But no effort was made by Ludendorff actually to assume these civilian powers. Chancellor Michaelis also proved incompetent, and the General Staff took no action when Count Hettling was selected to replace him. Moreover, both Hindenburg and Ludendorff took a back seat at the Brest-Litovsk negotiations after Russia's collapse.[19]

COLLAPSE OF GERMANY

Although the defeat of Russia released many troops to the western front, Germany was already bled white and headed down the slippery slope to collapse. Ludendorff staged huge offensive after huge offensive to break loose from the iron grip of trench warfare, but to no avail. Social outbreaks on the home front presaged Germany's ultimate distintegration. In 1917 crews of the idle High Seas Fleet revolted, and some German prisoners of war returning from Russia mutinied. Desertions increased. The Austrian Empire petitioned for peace, as did Bulgaria. German armies were steadily retreating before the Franco-American offensive in 1918 when Ludendorff finally requested an armistice. At the last moment he considered the terms offered by President Wilson to be unacceptable and in an imbroglio with the new Chancellor, Prince von Baden, Ludendorff resigned.

But Hindenburg retained his position as Chief of the General Staff, and Groener, "the first convinced democrat who had ever held a leading position on the General Staff"[20] became the new quartermaster-general.

Thus closed a dramatic but not too auspicious chapter of the German General Staff. Certainly no luster was added to its reputation, yet much criticism of its wartime activity is unjustified. It is unfair to criticize an institution for failing to do well what it was never designed or expected to do in the first place. The German General Staff failed in diplomacy, in statecraft, in politics, and in economics. The best that can be said of it is that it never intended to usurp any of these functions of government. These functions fell to the General Staff by default because of the inability of the civil agencies and leaders to function in the wartime environment. Nor did the German General Staff have any post-war political aspirations other than to preserve the army.

CHAPTER 11

AFTER WORLD WAR I

There is puzzling inconsistency running through many texts about the German army and General Staff: It was too political before Hitler, while during Hitler's rule it was not political enough. Several books have been written describing the "state within a state" [1] which the German army was supposed to represent, about its independence from civil control, about the military dictatorship of Erich Ludendorff during World War I, and about the various other manifestations of its political nature, all implying that such political activity by an army was intrinsically dangerous and evil.[2] Yet when the Nazis finally wrested power from the German army and subdued it completely to civilian control in 1934 by requiring its members to take a solemn oath to Hitler, the detractors blamed the army for succumbing to this new state authority. John W. Wheeler-Bennett in *The Nemesis of Power* [3] describes with painstaking detail the weaknesses and ineptitudes of the German army for not overcoming the hierarchy of civilian control as represented by Hitler and the Nazi party. A review of the literature seems to indicate that the Germany army has had few apologists and was condemned out of hand no matter what position it took. This anomaly leads one to suspect that there may be considerable emotional bias at work among Western authors. Nor should this be surprising considering the suffering brought about in the last half-century at the hands of the German army. The German army is possibly too handy and too identifiable a target to escape the vituperation of all its former enemies on whatever charge is at hand. Moreover, it is safe and fashionable to run with the pack of critics.

Nevertheless, the German army has demonstrated a surprising resilience after defeat. The reforms of Scharnhorst and Gneisenau after Napoleon's resounding victory at Jena provided a rebirth which restored the army's earlier luster, whereas the amazing success of Hans von Seeckt after World War I overcame the futile attempt of the Allies to reduce the German army to insignificance.

UNIQUE CHARACTERISTICS OF THE GERMAN ARMY

There were some fundamental customs and attitudes in Germany toward its army which differed widely from the military practices in other Western countries. Pre-World War I German soldiers had not been subject to civil law as were British, French and American servicemen. Allegiance was sworn to the Emperor only, not to parliament or to an abstract constitution. No civil court could touch them, all discipline being handled within the army according to a code somewhat at variance with the civil laws.

As autocratic and independent as the German army appeared to be, it was governed in some ways which might have appealed to those guided by democratic principles. For example, the formula evolved by Scharnhorst in 1808, which broke down the aristocratic character of the officer corps, persisted to modern times. Promotion by merit was established: by knowledge and study in time of peace and courage and military success in time of war. This did not eliminate the obvious preference for Prussian officers with a military background, but even they had to live up to the mark by demonstrated merit.

Another democratic feature was the doctrine of selfless dedication to the state, spurning wealth or fame for the cause of defending the country. Still another was the nonpolitical doctrine which although it may not always have been followed, nevertheless kept the military clear of the rising popular institutions of government such as the *Reichstag.*

Esprit de corps became so high in the German army with its closed system of life, its Court of Honor, its firm organization, and its single loyalty to the Kaiser, that it tended to become a caste whose members considered themselves the knightly servants of the ruler rather than of the nation. Condemnation by the Court of Honor, which might eject an officer from the service, was considered such a severe punishment as to warrant suicide

THE ARMY SAVES GERMANY FROM CHAOS

But it was fortunate for Germany after defeat in the first World War that her army was so well disciplined and so well organized as to survive. Allied military leaders have frequently remarked that it was a mistake to agree to the Armistice of 1918 before the German army had been soundly trounced, as the Allies had been fully capable of doing considering the state of economic collapse of the German nation. But the German army was allowed to march home from foreign soil relatively undefeated in combat and to remain intact as the last manifestation of order and authority in the country. It stands to reason that such a disciplined body would assume political significance and help to stabilize the newly emerging civil government.

Ludendorff was dismissed in October 1918 just before the Armistice when Germany decided to accept President Wilson's Fourteen Points. One of the stipulations of the President was that the Allies must negotiate with German political leaders rather than with military or Imperial authorities. In other words, a popular government had to be formed out of the chaos of defeated Germany. Any such government would logically have had to gain the support of the army, the only vestige of authority remaining.

Wilhelm Groener, an expert in railway logistics and son of a noncommissioned officer, succeeded Ludendorff as the first quartermaster general. Groener threw his weight behind Fritz Ebert, the leader of a shaky coalition of Independents and Majority Socialists which was in a death struggle with the Communist-inspired Spartakist movement, embracing extremists of both parties.

On November 9th Germany was miraculously saved from violent revolution and possible Bolshevism when the radical forces were about to wrest power from the provisional government. A telephone call from Groener to Ebert resulted in an understanding that the government would side with the army to suppress Bolshevism and restore order, if the High Command would agree to maintain discipline in the army and bring it home from the front.

THE PACT OF SPA

This Pact of Spa (Spa being the headquarters of the army) is reputed to be the event which permitted the formation of the Weimar Republic and bolstered its power. Some authors [4] deplore this pact which preserved the German army from dissolution and caused the government to recognize the army's quasi-independent status. But as Groener said in 1925, the aim of his alliance with Ebert was to combat the revolution then brewing as a consequence of the militant Spartakist movement and of the agitation within the army by the Soliders' Councils, elected bodies attempting to abolish rank and discipline. The Pact of Spa was designed "to re-establish lawful goverment, to lend the government armed support and to convene a National Assembly." [5] It is hard for one to find much fault with these legitimate aims.

To carry out his part of the bargain, Groener met with representatives of the Soldiers' Council and parried their demands for communizing the army by pointing out the technical difficulties of returning troops from the front and asking if anyone chose to assume this task. Finding no takers he cleverly invited the council delegates to act as advisors to the Supreme Command and to assist in maintaining order in the army. The resultant withdrawal of troops from France and Belgium proceeded with such smoothness that some morale was restored.

THE STAB IN THE BACK LEGEND

After a parade of the returning troops up the Unter den Linden in Berlin, Ebert created the "stab in the back" legend by remarking that they returned as "unvanquished on the field of battle."

It may be noteworthy that the fiction of the German army being undefeated was instigated by the civilian chief of state and not by the officer corps or the General Staff, even though Hindenburg repeated the statement in his testimony before the Commission of Enquiry investigating war crimes later that year. Ironically, it was Ebert who thought he could discredit the army by the Commission of Enquiry and thus placate the Allies.[6] This effort backfired and army prestige grew. Hitler, of course, in his National-Socialist movement was to make much of this "stab in the back" legend and use it as a reason for enforcing rigid discipline upon the German nation as a whole, a discipline of the civilian population far beyond the dreams of any previous dictator.

NEAR SUCCESS OF THE COMMUNISTS

But the Soldiers' Councils of 1918 were not easily subdued. The first Soviet Congress of Germany assembled in Berlin before the year was out and demanded an end to the officer corps, the abolition of cadet schools, the transfer of supreme command to the Council's Control Committee, the abolition of all insignia of rank, and prohibition against carrying arms when off duty. These measures were modeled on the infamous "Order No. 1" which took authority from the Russian officers not quite two years earlier. But the steel-nerved

Groener solved the problem by adamantly refusing to recognize the ruling of the Soviet Congress and telegraphed all field commanders not to change their regulations. The Provisional Government also ignored the resolutions and the army was saved. A subsequent effort by the irregular "Peoples Marine Division" to kidnap Ebert was also thwarted by Groener and the army.

ARMY OF THE WEIMAR REPUBLIC

By the time the National Assembly met in February 1919, the Spartakists had been crushed. The new constitution subjected the army to parliamentary control, with the President of the Republic as the supreme commander, similar to the arrangement in the United States, and the oath was taken to the constitution. The army became even more unified by the transfer of all legislative authority from the separate German states to the Reich, and by the institution of a single Minister of Defense and a single commander.

Interestingly enough, the position of Minister of Defense under the new constitution could not be held by a military personage.[7] It appears that great efforts were made to achieve civilian control of the military in the Anglo-American pattern. Could this have been one of the reasons why the German army was so helpless in curbing the later Nazi excesses?

It appeared that the German army was well on the way to restoration under the new Weimar Republic. By May 1919 some 400,000 volunteers were available. But at that moment the Allies presented the conditions of peace: conditions derived at Versailles where the Germans themselves were not permitted to negotiate in any way. This was a low blow. The army was to be reduced to 100,000 men, each with a twelve year tour to prevent the building up of a reserve force by rapid turnover as Scharnhorst and Gneisenau had done with the *Kruemper* system a century earlier.[8] No aircraft, tanks or offensive weapons were authorized and the Great German General Staff was to be dissolved and "not [to] be reconstructed in any form." [9] These and other harsh stipulations were designed to reduce the German army to impotence.

The Germans had no choice. Government and army leaders realized that resistance would cause greater dismemberment of the country and that in all probability Bolshevism would gain dominance. So the treaty was signed on June 28, 1919.

GENERAL VON SEECKT

A new military organization was established, "The Preparatory Commission of the Peace Army," with General Hans von Seeckt as its president. Von Seeckt was to save the German army from extinction by a series of stratagems which have become classic examples of disarmament evasion.

In the reorganization of the *Reichswehr,* von Seeckt pursued a fundamental policy to keep the military out of politics. On the other hand, Dr. Wolfgang Kapp, a reactionary politician, with the assistance of several disillusioned generals, was leading segments of the army into political waters. Great resentment had been generated as a consequence of Allied demands for the surrender of "war criminals," the list of which represented Germany's most illustrious patriots, including Hindenburg and Ludendorff. A mood was created which was ripe for reactionary revolution.

KAPP PUTSCH

General Freihern Watther von Luettwitz was the leading revolutionary figure in the *Reichswehr* but his support was limited. Von Seeckt vehemently opposed any *coup* which might cause German soldiers to shoot each other, and repeatedly preached army unity. Although he approved the reopening of hostilities if necessary to oppose the Allied demands, he shunned revolution and earnestly disapproved any such participation. When in early 1920 von Luettwitz triggered a march on Berlin with two irregular *Freikorps* brigades, von Seeckt would have nothing to do with the revolt one way or another. After a council of war with Ebert, von Seeckt went on an indefinite leave of absence to avoid involvement. From this it was apparent that army loyalty to the new Republic was somewhat conditional.

President Ebert and his cabinet fled the city and the Kapp-Luettwitz forces took over, the latter only to flee, themselves, within a few days because of the lack of army support and a debilitating general strike called by the President. Thus ended the Kapp *Putsch* which served as an example of mistakes *not* to be made by the Nazis in later years. It was evident that no *coup d'état* would be possible without either popular or army support.

DISGUISED GENERAL STAFF

The army had been reorganized in 1920 to conform with the

Allied terms for eliminating the General Staff. A troop staff, the *Truppenamt,* had been established with von Seeckt in charge. This small office of sixty-odd officers inherited what was left of the General Staff system and traditions. The principles of direct access to the head of state, as well as the doctrine of co-responsibility of the chief of staff with his commander, lost emphasis under this new arrangement. The *Truppenamt* was just one of many staff sections under the Chief of the Army Command, or *Chef der Heeresleitung,* who reported to the Minister of Defense instead of to the chief of state as formerly. By this time Groener had retired and the number one military spot had been given to General Walter Reinhardt, an officer of no particular military distinction. But it was believed that Reinhardt's South German background would put him more in sympathy with the new state.[10] Civilian control was being exercised here to induce political action by the commander rather than to shun it.

After the abortive Kapp *Putsch* Reinhardt resigned and von Seeckt was appointed Chief of the Army Command in his place. This position in itself was a violation of the Treaty of Versailles which forbade a general in chief. Under the Treaty command was to be vested in the civilian parliamentary Minister of Defense with *two* subordinate generals of equal rank reporting to him.[11] The Weimar Republic never got around to creating this odd organization. In his position of principal authority, Seeckt began to build, in miniature, the new German army.

The Kapp *Putsch* also ushered in a period of relative national stability, and it was possible for the army to enter a new phase of unity and loyalty toward a government of some substance. The army had been searching for a substitute for the Emperor as an object to which it could pledge its allegiance and was beginning to find it in the legitimate Weimar Republic.

THE ARMY OF LEADERS

Seeckt determined that the new 100,000 man *Reichswehr* was to become an army of leaders. Since quantity was denied by the terms of the treaty, the accent was to be on quality. Intensive drill and study marked the order of the day within the military garrisons, regardless of the closing of war academies. Strict examinations were administered for officers who aspired to the new general staff, now called the Leader Staff, who wore the traditional red trouser stripes as in earlier times.[12]

The surprising Treaty of Rapallo signed with the Soviet Union in April 1922 provided opportunities for training Germans in Russia in the use of arms which had been forbidden by the Treaty of Versailles. Moreover, clandestine plans were made to manufacture aircraft, artillery, and poison gas. This unusual collaboration continued until the Treaty of Versailles was formally abrogated in 1936.[13] It was a marriage of convenience and one must not discount the possibility of its happening again if similar situations should prevail. Current policies to deny nuclear weapons to the Federal Republic may contain similar hidden dangers.

The most striking lesson to be learned during this dramatic postwar period is that the German people are not easily discouraged and are masters at the "comeback." Today we see a prosperous West Germany arising from the rubble of widespread strategic bombings. The pervasive and inestimable drive of the German people and their army is still the dominant characteristic of that race. They seem capable of surmounting any adversity, no mattter how devastating.

CHAPTER 12

CAPTURED BY HITLER

Short of war itself, the German nation went through increasing hardships during the next few years following the Armistice. Galloping currency inflation became chaotic after France invaded the Ruhr to exact reparations payments. An undeclared war on the French forces of the Ruhr threatened to expand and although chief of the *Truppenamt,* General von Seeckt, disapproved, the government was obliged to support this popular resistance. Weak and disorganized as the country was, the army took steps again to prepare for war by developing mobilization plans and further encouraging irregular military bodies.

HITLER APPEARS

The danger of war appeared so threatening that von Seeckt held a conference with Adolf Hitler, the leader of the growing National Socialist party and of an efficient private army, the *Sturmabteilungen* or S.A., in an effort to secure Hitler's support for a passive resistance scheme. The meeting took place in Munich on March 11, 1923. Strangely, Hitler did not agree to collaborate with von Seeckt. It was rumored that French money had bought off the National Socialist leaders who were always struggling for funds.[1]

THE BEER HALL PUTSCH

A short time later, on November 8, 1923, Hitler made his first unsuccessful bid for power. This first National Socialist "Beer Hall *Putsch*" presented a national crisis and was put down by Seeckt and the army. Although the revolt had no support from the active military establishment as represented by von Seeckt and the *Truppenamt,* some prominent inactive officers participated, including the illustrious former Quartermaster-General, Ludendorff, and at least

142

one active officer, the infamous Captain Ernst Roehm who was later dismissed from the service for this political activity.

Telford Taylor implies that there was some sort of army assistance by mentioning that the Hitler revolt "would never have been attempted but for the promised collaboration of the *Wehrkreis* commander, General von Lossow. . . ." [2] But General von Lossow had been dismissed from his command of the Reich troops in Bavaria the month before on October 20th. This action had been taken by President Ebert on the advice of von Seeckt because of Lossow's continued activity in Bavarian politics.[3]

Lossow supported a revolutionary faction which rivaled Hitler's National Socialists. The major difference in their aims was that the Lossow faction promoted a separation of Bavaria from the Reich while Hitler's group preached pan-Germanism. Each needed the other to achieve a successful revolt and so they attempted collaboration, as Taylor noted. But after at least two previous Lossow doublecrosses Hitler's march was stopped by Bavarian police led by Lossow's friends. Contrary to Taylor's implication, however, there seems to be no evidence that von Seeckt, the *Truppenamt* or the *Reichswehr* in any way assisted this Beer Hall *Putsch*. In fact, the German army did everything possible to defeat the revolution and was eminently successful in doing so. Ludendorff was so annoyed at army opposition that he swore never again to don his uniform.

The actual revolt ended in a march on the *Feldherrnhalle* in Munich led by Ludendorff and Hitler and supported by the mutinous Infantry School. A detachment of about one hundred state police opened fire on the three thousand S.A. Storm Troopers and the *putsch* evaporated. Mopping up throughout the country was performed with precision by von Seeckt who had been given extraordinary powers by the President. All the young officers who had taken part in the revolt were dismissed and the Infantry School was moved to Dresden. Adolf Hitler was sent to jail where he wrote his highly prophetic autobiography, *Mein Kampf*. Hitler's first bid for power had been foiled by the German army and General Staff.

HIGH POINT OF THE WEIMAR REPUBLIC

There followed a short period of recovery and readjustment in Germany. For a time it looked as if the Weimar Republic might survive. Currency reforms were undertaken and with the American-inspired Dawes plan the problems of reparations were settled. Resistance in the Ruhr was terminated and a "policy of understanding" took its place. Even the Allied Control Commission for disarmament inspection was revived, although with this measure von Seeckt found little favor. Most significant was his voluntary relinquishment of the extraordinary powers that had been conferred upon him to put down Hitler's *putsch.* This surely was impressive evidence that the German army at this time had no wish to govern.

In February 1925 President Ebert died and the seventy-nine-year-old Hindenburg was elected in his place. This strengthened the army and assured its loyalty to the Republic. The threatening Nazi movement steadily lost strength and appeared to be headed for oblivion. Although Hitler was released from prison after only nine months, he was unable to recharge popular enthusiasm for his cause. The postwar turmoil upon which the movement had thrived was settling down. The way was being paved for Locarno, where Germany would be accepted into the League of Nations and again become a respected member of the family of nations.[4]

As Germany prospered with allied loans totaling over seven billion dollars between 1924 and 1930, Hitler's fortunes continued to ebb, but he never gave up. In the election of May 20, 1928, the Nazi party polled only 810,000 votes out of a total of 31,000,000 cast. Party membership was only 108,000. Nevertheless membership was slowly growing, having reached the nadir of 27,000 in 1925.[5]

THE NAZI PARTY

Hitler intended the Nazi party to be much more than an ordinary political organization. It was designed not only to attack and undermine the government, but to be a total government in itself, a state within a state. The army of this shadow state was the S.A., brown shirted Storm Troopers *(Sturmabteilungen)* organized at first to protect party meetings, but later to conduct armed brigandry and insurrection. It was generally anticipated within the party that this irregular military body would eventually supplant the regular German army.

For his personal protection Hitler organized still another military body, the S.S., or *Schutzstaffeln,* which grew from a few hundred black-uniformed fanatics to army strength by World War II. Its leader Heinrich Himmler, originally a chicken farmer, managed to retain his position throughout the rise of Hitler and to become the most powerful military leader in Germany.[6]

The architect of Germany's recovery in the late 1920's was Gustav Stresemann, the great foreign minister who, through loans and diplomacy, had restored defeated Germany to the ranks of the great powers and reduced the war debt to manageable proportions. Exhausted by his labors, Stresemann died in 1929. A few weeks later the Wall Street market crashed. As loans dried up, Germany was again plunged into hard times. Hitler had been waiting in the wings for just this opportunity. In the elections of September 1930, the Nazi party polled 6,409,600 votes and gained 107 seats in the *Reichstag*. It became the second largest party in Germany.[7]

The regular army had successfully resisted the blandishments of the Nazi party during the twenties. No Nazis were allowed in the 100,000-man *Reichswehr*. In fact, no Nazi civilians were employed. But with the resurgence of National Socialism in 1930 as a legitimate and powerful political party, Nazi propaganda began to get through to the army, particularly to the younger officers. Not only was Hitler's intense nationalism an attraction but he promised to restore the army to its old glory.

Noting this tendency, General Groener, the Minister of War, issued a warning. The Nazis were greedy for power, he said, and "they therefore woo the *Reichswehr*." He cautioned all personnel to refrain from politics and to serve the state aloof from party strife.

Not long after this warning three junior officers who had been disseminating Nazi propaganda were tried for high treason before the Supreme Court at Leipzig.[8] In testifying at this trial Hitler exploited the opportunity to reassure Germany and the army that he had no designs to take over except by legitimate and constitutional means and that when this occurred he had no plan to supplant the army with the S.A. but rather to strengthen and restore the regular forces. He was perfectly sincere in making both statements as subsequent events revealed.

This assurance meant much to the army leaders. Thus began the period of political blindness of the German military establishment. The Nazi movement itself was considerably more threatening to Germany, and to the *Reichswehr*, than the danger of substituting the S.A. for the army. The Nazi movement portended a complete revolution of the German ethos, a one-way street to total war, and the ultimate crushing defeat and dismemberment.

GERMANY IS TAKEN IN BY HITLER

But the generals were not the only segment of Germany to be taken in. So were the captains of industry who believed that, by backing Hitler, he would become beholden to them. They also were attracted by the Nazi opposition to trade unions and Communism. Fritz Thyssen, head of a steel trust, and Emil Kirdorf, the Ruhr coal king, contributed generously.[9]

It took no small sum to support the Nazi private army, the S.A., which had grown larger than the *Reichswehr*, numbering over 400,-000 men. Captain Ernst Roehm, the S.A. chief, had mobilized that many Brown Shirts at the time of the presidential elections in 1932 and he was prepared to seize all power had Hitler been elected.[10]

It is important to note, however, that this coup did not take place, nor did Hitler permit any illegal seizure of power but persisted in gaining strength through legitimate processes and free elections. Nevertheless, the Germany army was in real danger of being supplanted by Roehm's S.A. irregulars. Even though Hitler had no intention of this, Roehm had other ambitions.

Unfortunately the incorruptible von Seeckt had been discharged just eighteen months after Hindenburg's election as President in 1925. Von Seeckt had never been on good terms with the old Field Marshal, while an unscrupulous subordinate, Kurt von Schleicher, had assiduously cultivated Hindenburg through his weak son, Oscar. Von Schleicher finally found a means to replace von Seeckt. Von Seeckt committed the unpardonable error of permitting the eldest son of the Crown Prince to take part in the autumn military maneuvers. Not only was this a violation of the Treaty of Versailles but it suggested to Hitler a reinstatement of royal power. Pressure from Hitler and Schleicher ended the illustrious career of one of Germany's greatest generals.

THE ARMY BECOMES POLITICAL

The nonpolitical nature of the *Reichswehr* which von Seeckt had so earnestly cultivated came to an end with his dismissal. Not only was his successor as army spokesman, von Schleicher, inordinately ambitious, but he was a political schemer of the first magnitude. One must keep in mind, however, that during this period Germany was a caldron of seething politics and divided loyalties. It is only a wonder that the unhappy country could have produced a von Seeckt at all. This fact spoke well for the underlying nonpolitical doctrines of the *Reichswehr*.

In opening his political campaign in Munich in 1929, Hitler urged the army to forsake its pledge of loyalty to the state and to cooperate with the Nazi movement in order that the Nazis could gain political control. He asserted that the army owed its loyalty to the

German people, not to the "lazy and decayed" Weimar Republic.[11] When the Nazi party gained about 6,500,000 votes in 1930 it appeared that the people were indeed behind the revolutionary movement. Von Seeckt's successor, General von Schleicher, then began to intrigue with Roehm, which sealed the *Reichswehr's* fate. From that time on the army became an active political influence in contradiction to its ancient traditions. The disease had finally infected the army. The trials of the three junior officers for passing Nazi propaganda had revealed a disturbing conflict of loyalties. The steadying influence of von Seeckt was lost after only a few years of political scheming under Schleicher.

Although von Schleicher did not succeed von Seeckt as *Chef der Heeresleitung* (Chief of the Army Command) he assumed the leadership of the army in his new assignment as political advisor to the Minister of War. At this ministerial level he had more opportunities to act as kingmaker. It was not long before General Wilhelm Groener was appointed Minister of War with Schleicher's help, and by 1929 Schleicher was established as Deputy Minister of War with the rank of major general. In the following year Schleicher was able to establish his intimate friend, Kurt von Hammerstein, as *Chef der Heeresleitung*. Thus did the German army come under the complete influence of Schleicher: Hindenburg, Groener and Hammerstein were all subject to his charm.[12]

Schleicher's meteoric rise to power was soon to clash head-on with the even superior ambitions of a former Bavarian corporal and to come to a gory end from the pistols of Hitler's assassins. It was a dangerous game.

HITLER TRIUMPHS LEGALLY

When old President Hindenburg stood for reëlection in 1932, Hitler was his opponent. For the Nazis it was a no-holds-barred campaign conducted with furious energy. The party staged three thousand meetings a day while Hitler made scores of addresses. Hindenburg spoke only once, yet he took 49.6 percent of the vote as opposed to Hitler's 30.1 per cent. Because a majority was not achieved, the election had to be run again. In a sense this was a victory for the Nazis, as was the surprising number of 11,339,446 votes polled for Hitler.

In the final reëlection one month later Hitler gained another two million votes for 36.8 per cent of those cast, although a clear majority of 53 per cent was cast for the aged Hindenburg. Even so, the popular base for National Socialism had been well and legitimately established.

Seeing the specter of Hitler's ultimate power, General Groener attempted to force the dissolution of both the S.A. and the S.S. but was undercut by his own deputy, General Schleicher, who confidentially informed the district military commanders that the army opposed the move. Schleicher's next step was to instigate a smear campaign against his friend and mentor, Minister of War Groener. It was Schleicher himself who, after Groener had been viciously attacked in the *Reichstag*, told the Minister of War that he "no longer had the confidence of the army and must resign." [13]

Next in Schleicher's sights was Chancellor Heinrich Bruening who had secured the backing of the German majority for Hindenburg. Yet the near-senile President listened to the complaining Junkers who labelled Bruening a Bolshevist when he suggested that the government take over some bankrupt Junker estates. Soon Bruening's resignation was asked for and accepted. A new cabinet was formed with the incompetent and blundering Franz von Papen as Chancellor, while Schleicher was made Minister of War. Then Papen dissolved the *Reichstag*, lifted the ban on Hitler's S.A. and called for new elections. A wave of political violence and murder followed. Over 460 street battles are recorded for the first twenty days of June, 1932, largely between Nazis and Communists, while the Papen government sat on its hands.

The *Reichstag* elections on July 31 were the third national elections to be held within five months, but the Nazis entered the contest with more zeal than ever. Although Hitler had told Hindenburg that he would support Papen's cabinet, he told the Chancellor that he considered Papen's government as only a "temporary solution" and that Hitler himself would soon assume the office.

The Nazis won a resounding victory at the polls with 13,745,000 votes giving them 230 seats in the *Reichstag*. They became the largest party in a house of 608 members. The second party, the Social Democrats, gained 133 seats, while the Communists were third with 89.

Yet the Nazis had gained only 37 per cent of the total vote and did not by any means control the country. Hitler demanded the chancellorship but Papen would not give it up nor would Schleicher agree to the substitution. Confronting Hindenburg, Hitler was denied his wish because his party was "intolerant, noisy and undisciplined." Von Papen remained chancellor but could not form a government with the Nazi party in control of the *Reichstag*.

When the *Reichstag* convened, Hermann Goering, one of Hitler's chief lieutenants, was elected President of that body. Chancellor Papen took steps to execute a dissolution order which old President Hindenburg had granted him. Papen intended then to govern by decree. This ploy was easily parried by Goering who simply failed to recognize Papen when he tried to present Hindenburg's dissolution authority. Goering then called for an immediate vote to bring down the Papen government. By the time Goering recognized Papen the Papen government had been voted out of office, 513 to 32. Again national elections were called for, to be held on November 6, 1932.

This time the Nazis fared badly, losing two million votes and 34 seats, although they retained a large plurality with 196 deputies. Urged on by the ambitious Schleicher who predicted civil war if Papen remained in office, Papen resigned and Hindenburg sent for Hitler who was offered the chancellorship if he could secure a *Reichstag* majority. When Hitler proved unable to do so General Schleicher made his own bid for the chancellorship.[14] Minister of War Schleicher's pitch was that only he, as leader of the *Reichswehr*, could restore order. Hindenburg agreed. So on December 2, 1932, General Schleicher became Chancellor, the first general to hold that post since Caprivi in 1890.

"I stayed in power only fifty-seven days," said Schleicher later, "and on each and every one of them I was betrayed fifty-seven times. Don't ever speak to me of 'German loyalty'!"[15] This was the pot calling the kettle black. Schleicher's strategy was to split the Nazi party by offering Hitler's chief lieutenant, Gregor Strasser, the vice chancellorship. This had its intended effect, creating friction and animosity in the Nazi hierarchy. The move also was intended to withdraw Strasser's following from Hitler. Having suffered heavy losses at the polls in Thuringia, and burdened with mounting debts, the party was at a low ebb. But the political acumen of Hitler showed up best in adversity. Upon Strasser's resignation from the Nazi party, Hitler managed to take over Strasser's political organization and close the party's ranks.

To soften the aged President's hostility toward him, Hitler was able to reach some sort of accord with the President's son, Oscar von Hindenburg, who habitually acted as his old father's most trusted aide. Some months after Hitler's meeting with Oscar, with Hitler firmly in power, five thousand tax-free acres were added to the

Hindenburg estate and, by August 1934 Oscar was jumped from colonel to major general.[16]

When Schleicher found himself unable to form a government, and yet unable to convince Hindenburg that he should govern by decree, he submitted his resignation on January 28, 1933. There followed a grim political charade ending with a strong Hitler-Papen coalition. An incipient army revolt sponsored by Schleicher, the last chance to keep Hitler from ruling, was smothered by Hindenburg's timely appointment of General Werner von Blomberg, a Nazi sympathizer, as new Minister of War. Blomberg had been hurriedly summoned from Geneva where he had been representing Germany at the Disarmament Conference. Being the popular whipping boy, it is often charged that the German army, because it failed to revolt at this time, permitted Hitler to take over.

Thus, on January 30, 1933, Adolf Hitler was appointed Chancellor and the Weimar Republic soon came to an end. With all the deals and the juggling for power, it is important to note that Hitler assumed power legally and in accordance with democratic processes. As Shirer says, "No class or group or party in Germany could escape its share of responsibility for the abandonment of the democratic Republic and the advent of Adolph Hitler." [17] Although the Nazis had never obtained more than 37 per cent of the vote, the remainder was so divided as to be ineffectual. "The Germans imposed the Nazi tyranny on themselves." [18] The strongest resistance to Hitler came from the German army.

HITLER BECOMES A DICTATOR

Within a few weeks Hitler used the *Reichstag* fire as a pretext to request the Enabling Law which passed 441 to 94. By this act the *Reichstag* voted itself out of office, permitting Hitler to govern by decree for the next four years. This occurred in March and no time was lost by the Nazis in taking a tight grip on all the reins of government from the economy to the communications media.

During these fateful days the *Reichswehr* under Hammerstein played doggie, even though the general was an outspoken anti-Nazi. Not only was Hammerstein naturally apathetic, but being under police supervision he was virtually powerless. Within a year Hammerstein was retired and replaced by Lieutenant General Werner von Fritsch, another officer of the old school yet somewhat more discreet than his predecessor. About this time Ludwig Beck became *Chef der Truppenamt*, the then equivalent of Chief of the General

Staff. This fine officer was to become the leader of the anti-Nazi conspirators in the German army.[19]

Hitler set out right away to woo the high military brass by staging a dedication of the new *Reichstag* at the Garrison Church in Potsdam by the tomb of Frederick the Great. Von Seeckt showed up in full uniform, as did von Mackensen, von Hindenburg, von Blomberg, von Hammerstein, Admiral Raeder, and the former Crown Prince of the Kaiser's Reich. The union of Hitler and the *Reichswehr* seemed assured with Hitler and the senile Hindenburg shaking hands for photographers.

The *Reichswehr* was the name for the German army under the Versailles Treaty. Hitler quickly restored the old title, *Wehrmacht,* which established a traditional link with the past.[20]

THE BLOOD PURGE

By June 1934 Hitler, egged on by Himmler and Goering, felt constrained to purge the Nazi party of his rivals who he believed were threatening a *putsch* against him. He caused his assistant and S.A. leader Ernst Roehm, to be murdered in cold blood together with Gregor Strasser and hundreds of others. Nor did the German army escape this blood bath. Schleicher was shot down in his Berlin home, as was his wife. General Kurt von Bredow was another to die at the hands of Hitler's S.S. executioners. This "Blood Purge" not only assured Hitler's dominance over the S.A., now two and a half million strong, but it eliminated the S.A. as a rival to the *Wehrmacht.* Roehm, it will be recalled, was the one who had wanted to replace the German army with his irregular Storm Troopers. Now he and his principal backers were dead. The *Wehrmacht* officers drew a sigh of relief over this development but other concerns quickly materialized.

The status of the officer corps, for example, was seriously threatened by the murder of two of its senior members although many felt that General Schleicher had had it coming to him for his nefarious intrigues as well as for his abandonment of the officers' apolitical code.[21]

UNIFICATION AND ORGANIZATION OF THE GENERAL STAFF, 1934

The successor of the German General Staff, the *Truppenamt,* was already subordinated successively to the *Chef der Heeresleitung* (Fritsch) and the Minister of War (Blomberg). Additionally, the

War Minister's office had a staff. This latter *Ministeramt* was headed by Walther von Reichenau, Blomberg's former Chief of Staff and another pro-Nazi. General Ludwig Beck who capably headed the *Truppenamt* was submerged by three levels of Nazi authority. When one understands this subordination it becomes unreasonable to blame "The German General Staff" for Hitler's rise and control of the military establishment.

Hitler later attempted to encompass all three services, army, navy, and air force into one supreme staff and the War Minister's authority was expanded with the *Wehrmachtamt*. This apparently unified organization caused many subsequent detractors of the German General Staff to argue that a unified or supreme general staff is the hallmark of military failure. In point of fact Hitler never had a true unified general staff. His effort to achieve this never materialized. Although the *Wehrmachtamt* gathered more and more government functions unto itself, it was only nominally superior to the new *Luftwaffe* whose leader, Goering, was in practice superior to the War Minister at cabinet level. Even more troublesome to the *Wehrmachtamt* was the independent nature of the S.A. and the S.S. The Blood Purge may have halted the effort of the S.A. to take over the army but considerable political authority remained, while Himmler's S.S., now Hitler's own elite corps, was entirely independent and closest to the throne of any of the armed forces.

The *Wehrmachtamt* might be compared to the present United States Office of the Secretary of Defense. Rather than a true military general staff, it was a number of politically oriented bureaucratic offices competing for power with other offices such as Goering's Air Ministry, Himmler's S.S. and the weakened S.A. In Washington today, OSD must deal with State, CIA, AEC, NASA, ACDA, BOB and several other independent agencies. In fact the *Wehrmacht* Law of May 21, 1935, is similar to the U.S. National Security Act of 1947 in that the Commander-in-Chief of the German army was specified as the chief of state, with the minister of defense (or war) exercising command under the chief executive's orders.[22] In United States law the word "control" [23] is used instead of "command" but recent practice of the Department of Defense has made any distinction between the terms almost imperceptible.

Despite the difficulties, General Beck conscientiously tried to retain what was left of the German General Staff and its officer code. As Wheeler-Bennett wrote:

> Like many of his fellow generals he did not regard war as the primary role of the soldier, but believed that Germany's armaments should be of such a degree that they would lessen rather than increase the danger of war by making it impossible for Germany to be attacked or gainsaid with impunity.[24]

RESIDUE OF THE GENERAL STAFF CODE

A true professional, Beck regarded war as the last resort in the power struggle, with peace as the fundamental aim. But Hitler, the civilian leader, had a completely opposite view. War was a tool of politics to be used as a threat to achieve his international aims, or to be actually initiated if necessary to satisfy his ambitions. This fundamental difference in philosophy led to Beck's recommendation against the occupation of the Rhineland in 1936, an exercise which risked war with France and England. His advice was ignored.

As commander of the army, von Fritsch was able assiduously to devote his attention to rearmament without becoming involved in Nazi politics. Strangely those within the army felt that von Fritsch could be depended upon to rid the country of Nazi tyranny and replace it with a respectable government. But this kind of authority had long since slipped from the army.[25] Fritsch was a political cipher.

THE ARMY OPENLY CAPITULATES

Hitler, however, through blandishments, concessions, pressures, firings and appointments was able to reorient the purpose of the army. In return for Hitler's sacrificing the hated S.A., the senior officers consented to Hitler's becoming the political replacement for the ailing Hindenburg upon the old general's demise. Von Fritsch then issued a new version of "The Duties of the German Soldier," the theme of which was that "military service is a service of honor toward the German people." The implication here was that loyalty to the Nazi party was competitive with loyalty to the President. This put the army squarely in the political arena, with Nazi swastika emblems on the army uniforms.

The degeneration of the German General Staff tradition was perhaps best demonstrated by the minor nature of its reaction to the S.S. murder of General Schleicher and Bredow. Only retired General Hammerstein and Field Marshal von Mackensen objected. War

Minister von Blomberg, on the other hand, congratulated Hitler for wiping out the "mutineers and traitors." His further statement that "the *Wehrmacht* as the sole bearer of arms within the Reich, remains aloof from internal political conflict but pledges anew its devotion and its fidelity" had a hollow sound of insincerity. The fact that the army could turn its head while two of its senior members were unceremoniously shot and branded traitors left a stain on the army that it could never eradicate.[26] A resolution passed by the Schlieffen Society of which von Mackensen was president where about 400 officers were in attendance, declared that Schleicher and Bredow had fallen on the field of honor, but the press was not allowed to carry this story.[27]

FINAL MILITARY ORGANIZATION

By 1935 the new German military organization was settling down into the pattern which would last throughout the Second World War. The *Chef der Heeresleitung* was retitled the *Oberbefehlshaber des Heeres* (Supreme Commander of the Army), and *Heeresleitung* changed to *Oberkommando des Heeves* (O.K.H.). The *Truppenamt* finally took on its original title of General Staff of the Army.[28] It consisted of 190 officers, about fifty of whom were titled as opposed to a proportion of ten per cent titled officers in the army as a whole.

It is interesting to note the Goerlitz observation that Hitler viewed the General Staff as "just a club of intellectuals," and studiously ignored it.[29] During the whole period of his office (1934-1938) Beck had only one short conversation with Hitler. Beck's isolation and that of the German General Staff was complete. As with the current U.S. Army Staff, the German Army Staff's dealings were with the Department of Defense in the resolution of command and organizational matters.

Hitler progressively removed the German army from its position of authority. It ceased to be a political factor and as Hitler gained more control he gradually assumed the army's military direction as well. The generals were reduced to the status of technicians, divorced from strategic decisions and military policy, to respond only when questioned, something like what has been done by the Secretary of Defense in the Pentagon today. Hitler's military, as with the present day United States military, exercised a minimal influence on affairs of state and national defense.[30]

IMPOTENCE OF THE GERMAN GENERALS
AGAINST HITLER

The German generals had fought Hitler's warlike policies at every turn, only to be repeatedly defeated. They opposed withdrawal from the League of Nations, the declaration of rearmament, and the remilitarization of the Rhineland. It is true that they approved of Germany's *actual* rearmament after having lived under the restriction of a 100,000-man army since the Treaties of Versailles and Locarno, but the generals had no wish or intention to assume an aggressive attitude. Not so Hitler, who considered this reluctance of his generals to be a sign of weakness. For Hitler his armies existed "for triumphant exertion in war," not to preserve the peace.[31]

As might be expected, the Nazi party instituted a smear campaign against the army in order to undermine military prestige and authority. By Himmler's reports Hitler was led to believe that von Fritsch and his generals were plotting a *putsch* to restore the Kaiser. Modern fiction, such as *Seven Days in May* and other efforts to degrade the prestige of the United States military establishment are having much the same effect in this country today. The military voice is either disregarded or suspected of ulterior motives.

Many of these antimilitary rumor mongers in the Third Reich were people who had been discharged from military service for dealing in politics or for more serious reasons and then had risen to high rank in either the S.A. or the S.S. One such person was Reinhardt Heydrich, Himmler's deputy and the number two man of the S.S. who was charged with security (the Gestapo) and with Hitler's safety. Heydrich had been dismissed from the navy for "conduct unbecoming an officer and a gentleman." His animosity for the German military establishment can be compared to that demonstrated by some of today's "defense intellectuals" in America who resented their low rank and regimented treatment at the hands of the military services in the second World War. Scratch a "defense intellectual" and you often find a frustrated wartime soldier.

The effort to achieve a supreme general staff superior to the army, navy and air force staffs made some progress with the replacement of Reichenau by Wilhelm Keitel, an ardent Nazi and close friend of Blomberg. Then Alfred Jodl was brought in to head another kind of general staff—the operational department of the War Ministry. Beck opposed this move by every means in his power, but failed to make his point. It resulted in Beck being given planning responsibility without power of command. Blomberg retained that power for himself although Hitler never permitted its execution.[32]

When Hindenberg died on August 2, 1934, Hitler consolidated the offices of President and Chancellor and assumed the new post of Fuehrer of the German Reich. He had all members of the armed forces swear allegiance to him personally just as had been done formerly under the Kaiser. In fact, one source reports that directly upon the old Field Marshal's demise Hitler had his senior generals awakened in the night to recite this personal oath:

> I swear by God this sacred oath, that I will render unconditional obedience to Adolf Hitler, the Fuehrer of the German Reich and people, Supreme Commander of the Armed Forces, and will be ready as a brave soldier to risk my life at any time for this oath.[33]

TRIUMPH OF CIVIL CONTROL OF THE MILITARY

The take-over of military authority in Germany was complete. Civil control of the military in the Third Reich was almost absolute, yet Generals Beck and Fritsch still had the audacity to argue against the remilitarization of the Rhineland in 1936. Not only would action by Germany violate the Versailles and Locarno treaties, but the Germany army was in no condition to hazard such a gamble which might lead to war. Hitler, however, was adamant and went ahead with the military plans without further consulting Beck or Fritsch. In fact, these top army leaders were notified just one day before the actual operation.

This reminds one in many ways of the Bay of Pigs operation in 1961, the principal exception being that in remilitarizing the Rhineland, Hitler succeeded. The Western allies in 1936 were too timid to push the Germans out even though this could have been accomplished easily in view of Hitler's military weakness at the time.

The Bay of Pigs failed through want of a modicum of military direction, through the caution of the President, and the audacity of Castro. It would have been instantly obvious to an experienced military planner that the Cuban T-33 jet trainers could be quickly converted to fighters and achieve an air superiority over rebel B-25s. Even when this was belatedly discovered, had a few carrier air strikes been made, the fortunes of Cuba would have again turned toward freedom and self-government. But the operation had one thing in common with the Rhineland remilitarization: military leadership was missing from the planning and execution.

With the Rhineland operation Hitler prevailed in one of his first great bluffs. Only one German division was employed. Even Blomberg lost his nerve and recommended withdrawal when he learned that the French were mobilizing thirteen divisions on the border and alerting the Maginot Line fortifications.[34] But the thirteen never moved against Hitler's one. This German tactical victory ultimately led to exactly what Beck and Fritsch had warned of: war, with defeat for Germany.

Having thus demonstrated his superior military judgment with the Rhineland success, Hitler summoned his senior generals on November 5, 1937, to brief them on his future plans. He said that by 1943 Germany was to be fully rearmed and ready for total war. In the meantime he intended to improve Germany's geographical position. Austria and Czechoslovakia must be annexed. Also, alliance with Japan would alleviate Russian pressure. In effect Hitler had established a timetable for war against England and France.

The generals were shocked at this outright announcement for aggressive war. Both Fritsch and Blomberg strongly voiced their disapproval.[35] By opposing Hitler they were soon to suffer not only dismissal but disgrace. The manner in which Hitler got rid of his two highest generals, his Minister of Defense and Army Commander, is a story stranger than fiction. It is indicative of the unscrupulous leadership which held no regard for codes of conduct, laws, fair play or human decency.

FRAMING GENERALS FRITSCH AND BLOMBERG

From the time of Hitler's briefing General Fritsch was tailed by the Gestapo of Himmler and Heydrich, Fritsch's worst enemies. When Fritsch and Beck disapproved "Case Green," the plan to capture Czechoslovakia, Hitler became convinced that the last thing the General Staff wanted was a war. He concluded that he himself must assume direct command of all military forces.[36] But first he must dump the two senior generals who objected.

The fantastic framing of Fritsch and Blomberg began at Ludendorff's funeral in December, 1937, when Blomberg confided to Hitler that he planned to marry his secretary, Fraulein Erna Gruhn. Although the general mentioned that his intended had "a past," Hitler gave his blessings to the union, and both Hitler and Goering attended the wedding the following month.

The next act was by Goering, who had ambitions of being appointed Minister of Defense. He presented to the Berlin police a list of alleged indiscretions by Blomberg's bride. Rumors and anonymous telephone calls about Frau von Blomberg's "past" grew apace and within two weeks after the wedding Goering took the damaging evidence to Hitler himself.

At about the same time a fabrication of "evidence" was built up to accuse Fritsch of homosexuality. The Gestapo used a professional blackmailer to accuse the general in front of Hitler.

These two very dirty attempts to discredit the leadership of the German army proved highly successful. Within two days of Goering's visit to Hitler with the "evidence" Blomberg was dismissed. Hitler solved the problem of finding a successor by appointing himself to the post of Minister of Defense.

The slander perpetrated on Fritsch was devastating to his reputation. Moreover he was less capable than von Blomberg of holding up under the scandal. The former War Minister went on an extended honeymoon to Italy with the object of his downfall and refused to consider a demand by his arrogant young adjutant that he either divorce his wife or commit suicide.

But the more sensitive von Fritsch suffered a gradual disintegration of personality. Chief of the General Staff Beck urged Fritsch to stage a *coup* and clean the stench of Nazi tyranny from Germany. But instead von Fritsch humbly resigned from his post as Commanding General of the Army, unable in the final anaylsis to assume the initiative of breaking the von Seeckt tradition of an apolitical army and thus overthrowing a wicked government.

DEGRADATION OF THE GERMAN ARMY

There followed a struggle between the army and the Gestapo to determine which would try von Fritsch. Obviously Hitler and Goering preferred to have Himmler's Gestapo conduct the trial although in theory Fritsch was subject only to the criminal jurisdiction of the army and deserved a court martial. But the power of the Gestapo had grown so forbidding and the knowledge of its extra-legal capabilities was so vivid (as when the S.S. men shot down Generals Schleicher and Bredow), that Fritsch humbly answered a summons to appear at Gestapo headquarters.[37] Nor did the army raise a hand when Gestapo agents combed army barracks looking for men who had served on Fritsch's personal staff. In fact, the same policemen had charge of this task as had organized the execution squads for Schleicher and Bredow.

The impotence of the German army at the time of the Fritsch trial is best explained by Goerlitz:

The fact is that now the generals had a huge amalgamation of power ranged against them, and though most of the commanding generals still belonged to the old school, they could no longer be certain of the army's obedience. The Navy, on the other hand, was at best neutral, while the *Luftwaffe*, with which all A.A. units were incorporated, stood directly under Goering. In addition to these, there was the mighty apparatus of the Party with all its interlocking organizations, there was the police and there was the Gestapo. The Dictatorship was, moreover, master of the whole network of communications, including press and radio. There was thus no way for the generals to make their case known to the public. . . .[38]

Hitler had effectively captured and subdued the German army. His was the ultimate example of civilian over-control of the military. Stripped of its honor, unable to exercise the soldierly virtues, the army was rapidly becoming little more than a state police similar to its arch rival the S.S.

DEMISE OF THE GERMAN GENERAL STAFF, 1938

With the sacking of von Blomberg and von Fritsch, the death of the German General Staff and the officer corps was assured. Hitler lost what respect he had for the army, and its judgments on state affairs were largely disregarded. Civilian control of the military was approaching its ultimate goal. Military authorities were thoroughly demoralized by four years of Hitler's rule. The honor of the officer code had been so often compromised that this final humiliation of its leaders caused no effective military resistance.

Over the radio on February 4, 1938, Hitler announced a change of command along with the resignation of von Blomberg and von Fritsch. Walter von Brauchitsch was the new army commander but Hitler himself assumed the post of War Minister. "Henceforth," he pronounced, "I exercise personally the immediate command over the whole armed forces. The former *Wehrmacht* office in the War Ministry becomes the High Command of the Armed Forces (O.K.W.), and comes immediately under my command as my military staff. At the head of the staff of the High Command stands the former chief of the *Wehrmacht office*." This was Wilhelm Keitel, a devoted Nazi general who served throughout the war as Hitler's aide and mouthpiece. Goering, who aspired to the post of War Minister was promoted to Field Marshal, which was a rank senior to that of Colonel General, bestowed on von Brauchitsch.[40]

Hitler had set out to destroy the power and influence of the General Staff and make the army entirely responsive to his will. He succeeded in every sense. Through murder, blackmail, slander, forced resignations, and trials he was able to peel the good men off the top until he found stooges like Keitel, Jodl and Brauchitsch to do his bidding.

The measure of Keitel, now the first soldier of the land, can best be understood by noting that at one time he had been in a position to destroy the damning dossier on Frau Blomberg but instead he passed it on to Goering, Blomberg's enemy. And Keitel was Blomberg's own son-in-law!

Beck was still chief of the traditional Army General Staff but not for long. Hitler could not countenance any military leaders of integrity around him. As a matter of fact, his personal entourage included no generals whatever, not even the weak ones he had established in responsible posts. His adjutant, Colonel Hossbach, was the point of contact for all military matters. Goering, of course, was an intimate and thus managed to have his way in commanding the new and quite independent *Luftwaffe*. Himmler, too, who gradually gained increasing power with his S.S. and Gestapo, was a member of the inner council, but never Beck or even Brauchitsch. So the unity of command that seemed complete under the High Command (OKW) was mostly window dressing.

SOME MODERN PARALLELS IN THE UNITED STATES

Can historians who regard the German General Staff as a villain of modern history look upon the collapse of this institution with approval? Is it desirable for a country to subjugate its military establishment so completely to the political will? Most Western military establishments prize order, law, and constituted authority. They provide a check to the illegal usurpation of power, either from within or without. When the military fails to perform these functions, dictatorship and rule by personality is the almost certain result.

It might be interesting to note here that American military officers take a solemn oath upon each appointment "to uphold the Constitution of the United States against all enemies, foreign or domestic. . . ." If some people prefer that the military be relegated to that of a blind and docile government servant for "the management of violence" rather than a thinking, responsible arm of government designed to preserve and defend the sacred institutions of the country, then this oath had better be changed.

One can point to other tendencies in the modern American scene which similarly are undermining the integrity and the honor of our own military profession. With the formation of a super inspector general department under the Assistant Secretary of Defense for Administration, a post created in 1964, the civilian administrators in the Office of the Secretary of Defense have assumed what is tantamount to criminal jurisdiction and investigative authority over the Joint Chiefs of Staff and the uniformed services.

Similarly, all public relations services have been concentrated in the Office of the Secretary of Defense and there is "no way for the generals to make their case known."[39]

Moreover, the "amalgamation of power ranged against them" is formidable. An independent intelligence agency, CIA, reports directly to the President and the National Security Council. The major military ordnance and much of the military motive power is produced by another powerful independent agency, the Atomic Energy Commission. The military has been denied the medium of space for national defense while another independent agency, NASA, is provided billions of dollars to race to the moon. Even an Arms Control and Disarmament Agency (ACDA) has been established which, under the banner of "arms control," threatens the very security measures achieved by the military.

But most frightening of all, the burgeoning Office of the Secretary of Defense, led by men who are often unsympathetic to military traditions and ethics, has equated civilian control with civilian command and, when emergencies arise, actually orders about military units and equipment as if they were pawns on a chess board. This was done at the Bay of Pigs, again during the Cuban Crisis of 1962, during the Gulf of Tonkin affair of 1964, and during the Vietnam air operations of 1965 and 1966. Military channels and the chain of command are too frequently disregarded. These civilian officials arrogantly believe that only they, themselves, are capable of handling military force in this nuclear age in such a way as not to cause the escalation of a crisis to war.

CHAPTER 13

BURIAL OF THE GERMAN GENERAL STAFF

As noted earlier, General Blomberg obsequiously recommended that Hitler himself assume the position of Minister of War from which Blomberg had just been fired and Hitler readily accepted this flattering proposal. The *Wehrmachtamt* was renamed the *Oberkommando der Wehrmacht* (Supreme Command of the Armed Forces) or the OKW. Keitel, of course, became its Chief of Staff. This personal staff of the German dictator was composed of officers better known for their loyalty to Hitler and the Nazi party than for their military skill. It was anything but a supreme general staff.

General von Brauchitsch, Fritsch's successor as commander of the army, was a man of considerable talent but little intellectual honesty or moral courage. He rationalized this command duty and deceived himself into believing that by continuing to serve he could somehow influence Germany's return to sanity. He did not appreciate that the army's authority was dead and when his chief of staff, Beck, urged him to take a stand against Hitler, von Brauchitsch equivocated. When Beck finally resigned in protest (August 18, 1938) von Brauchitsch would not follow suit. He considered such resignations to be mutinous—the military ethic blinding him against the need to act against the obvious evils of the civil administration.

PURGE OF THE GENERALS

When on February 4, 1938, the German public was informed that Blomberg and Fritsch had retired on grounds of "health," they were not the only ones to go. Sixteen other senior generals, almost every one of whom espoused the nonpolitical Seecktian tradition, were given their walking papers. Hitler invited the remaining leading generals to the Chancellery where he told them of the misdeeds of Fritsch and Blomberg. There was no comment. Perhaps they

162

were stunned by the shocking story, not knowing what to believe. Later that day Hitler told his S.A. friends that he now knew every general to be either a coward or a fool.[1] The Party had feared a mass resignation of general officers. But the strength of the military oath to Hitler held them to their posts. Nor could they come to believe that Hitler had finally stripped them of every vestige of military honor.

The wily Hitler delayed the trial of von Fritsch while he was smeared and convicted by the public press which was fed the desired "news" by the Nazi authorities. Even so, the Gestapo tried to murder the general and fake it as a suicide but a group of young officers gave him protection.[2] Finally Hitler did authorize a military court of honor at which Goering presided along with the army and navy commanders, von Brauchitsch and Raeder. When the court at last convened on March 10, it was suspended before the day was over because Goering and von Brauchitsch were needed for the invasion of Austria.[3] By the time the trial was resumed a week later Austria had ceased to exist and Hitler had become a great national hero. The chances of upsetting him by the scandal which might have been revealed in the Fritsch trial had vanished. In fact, the Fritsch case had become old hat. Management of the news by the National Socialists had proved highly successful. To top this off, the trial was held in secret and the public got no word of the criminal methods used by the Hitler regime to ruin the once-proud general. The trial was an anticlimax.

Von Fritsch was "proven not guilty as charged and acquitted." The professional blackmailer who had accused him of homosexuality broke down in court and revealed that the Gestapo had threatened his life to implicate Fritsch. The Gestapo took revenge for this confession by killing the blackmailer a few days later, but at least history got the word of Fritsch's innocence. Strangely, Fritsch made no attempt to expose the Gestapo, although he did attempt to challenge Himmler to a duel. For some unknown reason the challenge was never delivered by the intermediary, von Brauchitsch. The world next heard of Fritsch when he was killed by a Polish machine gun before Warsaw on September 22, 1939. As a colonel in charge of his old regiment, it appeared that he had sought death.

MUNICH

No study of civil-military relations could be complete without an examination of the Munich crisis of 1938. Hitler, the constituted civilian chief of state of Germany, was determined to employ his armed might against Czechoslovakia, even at the risk of a world war for which he was militarily unprepared. His army commander in chief, von Brauchitsch, advised strongly against this military adventure, as did the Chief of the Army General Staff, Beck. General Beck eventually resigned in protest, although no publicity was permitted of this act.

Franz Halder, Beck's replacement, was equally opposed to the planned military invasion of neighboring Czechoslovakia, and Halder went so far as to join and lead a cabal designed to depose Hitler if he should order such a military adventure. The principal confederates in this plot were another General Staff officer, Karl von Stuelpnagel, and the retired former Chief of Staff, Hammerstein, who helped mobilize civilian support. Also among these conspirators were the Chief of the Berlin police and the former Minister of Economics, Hjalmar Schacht. The army commander in chief, von Brauchitsch, was aware of this plan but not an active participant. At least he kept his counsel and gave the plan his tacit approval.[4]

PROBLEMS OF CONSCIENCE

At the Nuremberg trials after the war Halder testified that there were three conditions necessary in 1938 for a successful *coup*: leadership, popular support, and the right timing. Leadership under the clandestine wing of the General Staff was available, although there was some understandable reluctance by the army commander, von Brauchitsch, and others who could not quite reconcile themselves to this outright treasonous behavior. They were also bothered by the oath of loyalty they had taken to Hitler, and by the fact that the National Socialist administration was entirely legal and popularly supported. It was Beck, however, who did much to clear the air before his retirement. He insisted that a state and society ruled by law must be restored and that if necessary the generals should mutiny (although the word was never used) to prevent Hitler from starting another world war. Beck had suggested to von Brauchitsch that an ultimatum be sent to Hitler listing the following conditions for reform: ". . . against war, against boss rule, peace with the Church, free expression of opinion, an end to the Cheka terror, restoration of justice. . . ."[5] Although von Brauchitsch never passed this to Hitler, the memorandum was widely circulated and discussed among the officers and did much to justify the work of the plotters. The memorandum also included these courageous words:

> In order to safeguard our position before history and to keep the repute of the Supreme Command of the Army unstained, I hereby place on record that I have refused to approve any warlike adventures of the National Socialists.[6]

HITLER'S POPULARITY

The appropriate timing for the *coup* was to be when Hitler ordered the military movement into Czechoslovakia which, the generals were thoroughly convinced, would bring on a world war. It was the question of public support that concerned them most. Hitler was extremely popular, having pulled off the bloodless conquest of Austria in February of that year, 1938, and having brought a booming prosperity to the country with the rearmament industry. Whereas Hitler's National Socialists had polled only 37 per cent of the vote in 1933, they had, a year later, after Hitler became Chancellor and the supreme commander of the armed forces, polled a resounding 95 percent of the vote. Now, after three years of rule, with factories humming, public works and roads mushrooming, and with Germany again a world power to be reckoned with, Hitler's prestige could hardly have been higher. General Halder and the others believed that the *putsch* could only be pulled off in the face of war because the people had given so many indications that they were in no mood for another world conflict.

GENERAL STAFF EFFORTS TO DEAL WITH THE BRITISH

If, however, Britain and France should knuckle under to Hitler's threats and sacrifice Czechoslovakia as they had Austria, the generals would have neither any justifiable excuse nor popular support to make their dangerous revolt. It appeared to be necessary for them to get word to the British government that Hitler did indeed intend to march on the Czechs by the end of September and that if a military *coup* were to work the British should stand firmly against this German aggression and support the Czechs. The fears of the General Staff officers that Britain would again appease Hitler were well founded in that the British Ambassador in Berlin, Sir Neville Henderson, seemed anxious to give Hitler whatever he wanted.

It was decided, therefore, to send agents to London in order to get the word directly to the British Government. Ewald von Kleist was the first emissary selected for this purpose but Henderson knew about the effort and undercut the mission by advising the British Foreign Office that it "would be unwise" for Kleist to be received officially. Kleist, however, talked to Sir Robert Vansittart, chief diplomatic advisor to the Foreign Secretary, as he did to Winston Churchill who gave Kleist a letter of encouragement for his associates. This letter was shown to Beck, Halder, Hammerstein and others in the plot, but the British Government failed to provide similar encouragement.

Vansittart's report did get to Chamberlain, however, and Ambassador Henderson was recalled to London for consultations. It was decided at first that Henderson would convey a sober warning to Hitler but, according to his own story, Henderson persuaded the Prime Minister to drop this forthright warning. Thus did the General Staff's first effort to collaborate with the British in the cause of peace and the overthrow of Hitler end in failure.[7]

But the conspirators did not give up here. They attempted to work through military channels and informed the British military attaché in Berlin of Hitler's intention to attack Czechoslovakia, noting: "If by firm action abroad Hitler can be forced at the eleventh hour to renounce his present intentions, he will be unable to survive the blow." Nothing could have been clearer. But Ambassador Henderson forwarded the report with the remarks that it was biased and "largely propaganda." The Ambassador had lost touch with reality.[8]

A final desperate effort was made to reach the British through a counselor of the German embassy in London, Theodor Kordt, who managed to talk directly with the British Foreign Secretary, Lord Halifax, telling him bluntly that the German army was ready to arrest Hitler if the British and French held firm against Hitler's intended attack. Two days later the London *Times* hinted that Britain should abandon Czechoslovakia to the Germans and it appeared that the third General Staff contact would also end in failure.[9] Appeasement was in the air. This was September 7, and the invasion was scheduled for October 1.

APPEASEMENT LANDSLIDE

Hitler delivered a bellicose speech at Nuremberg on September 12 and the next day the French cabinet met. Prime Minister Daladier sent a frantic message to Chamberlain that night urging the British to make the best bargain they could with Hitler. There was no help from that quarter. The "responsible" powers of Europe seemed determined to sell Czechoslovakia down the river and to

disregard their solemn treaties of alliance and protection in order
to avoid taking prudent military action. There is not a reputable
historian today who will not admit that this spineless sell-out led
directly to the war it was designed to avoid.

ORDER OF BATTLE, 1938

And what was the European battle order at this time? Could
Britain and France have prevailed over Germany if they had taken
a firm stand? Germany had less than 55 divisions, many of which
were in the formative stages of training and development. The
Czechs were not to be sneezed at. They had 45 divisions on April
1st and a strongly fortified line. But German fifth column activity
had undermined the Sudetenland provinces, predominantly popu-
lated with Germans. And with Austria in German hands the Czechs
were surrounded on three sides. Nevertheless, the German General
Staff believed that Germany had no chance if France and Britain
attacked. The French could put over 40 divisions into the Maginot
Line while the Germans had less than 12 for the West Wall. Had
British and French statesmen known a little more about the military situation perhaps they would not have been bluffed so easily by
Hitler. Instead, they put their tails between their legs and panicked.

THE SELL-OUT

Chamberlain made three trips to Germany with his umbrella
which became a symbol of appeasement. Each time he gave in a
little more to Hitler, who never once budged from his intention to
consume Czechoslovakia no later than October 1, 1938. The last trip
to Munich on September 29 was for a four-power conference of
Germany, Britain, France and Italy. The victim to be dismembered
was not even invited. By now Hitler was able to write his own ticket
and on October 1 his armies moved "peacefully" into the Czech
Sudetenland. Five months later they converged on Prague while
Britain looked the other way. Czechoslovakia was no more. Naturally the Halder plot evaporated with this capitulation by Britain
and France. Hitler was now more popular than ever and the army
never could have gained support for arresting him.

ANALYSIS OF "THE PAUSE"

Here is an example of the "pause" at work. There is a time when
negotiations serve no purpose but that of the blackmailer. There

is a time when the threat of force can only be countered by a larger threat of force. This is the time when the military echelon of government must be called in for advice. Had this been done in England and France it might have become evident to the statesmen and the diplomats that those opposed to Hitler had little to fear. On three occasions the German General Staff itself had sought to tell the British of its sentiments and reveal that Germany had *no* chance of surviving a world war. The sub-rosa General Staff was, in effect, on the side of the British but the British could not see beyond their antimilitary prejudice to believe what they heard. As a consequence Hitler's appetite for aggression was further whetted. His confidence that Britain would never stand up to him was confirmed.

A year later Hitler marched into Poland, but this time the British stiffened. By then, however, Germany was much better prepared to wage a world war. The political weakness of Britain and France in the face of Germany's illegal occupation of the Rhineland in 1936 with just one division, of Germany's conquest of Austria in March 1938, and of Czechoslovakia in October of that year, set the stage for the world war that was to come.

CONSEQUENCES OF TOO MUCH
CIVIL CONTROL OF THE MILITARY

Civil control of the military had triumphed completely in Germany. Although various groups of officers plotted to assassinate Hitler from the time of Munich on (arrest was no longer a possibility) the General Staff itself was never again able to undertake such a venture. Anti-Hitler generals were usually identified and either put out to pasture or removed to concentration camps. General Halder managed to avoid this latter fate until the final unsuccessful *coup* of 1944.

Civil control of the military in Britain and France had left their statesmen and diplomats in such ignorance of the true state of military affairs in Europe that appeasement seemed to be the only solution to Hitler's demands. There is more to this than a simple understanding of the forces involved and pure military intelligence. Military analysis by professionals was needed. A frank rapport between the military and other government agencies, particularly the Foreign Offices was tragically lacking. Frequent contact by statesmen and diplomats with military leaders and military inclusion in the higher councils of government would have led to more realistic estimates of the situation and to less likelihood of gross overestimations of Hitler's power. Civilian over-control of the military was a real contributor to the causes of World War II.

Contrary to common belief today, the German General Staff was the one element in the German society which undertook an organized effort to curb Hitler's warlike ambitions and even at great danger to its members, to overthrow the dictator. When the German General Staff became fully subjected to civilian control under Hitler its effectiveness as a force for justice, peace and good government came to an end.

THE GENERAL STAFF IS BURIED

From 1939 on to the end of the war Hitler managed to submerge, to circumvent and to counter the dwindling residual power of the traditional army General Staff with his personal War Ministry Staff under Keitel (the OKW) ; with the independent S.S. and Gestapo under Himmler; and with the independent Air Force under Deputy Fuehrer Hermann Goering. There was no such thing as a unified General Staff which supervised the conduct of war. Hitler himself provided the only unity.[10]

The extent of Hitler's dominance over his military leaders is vividly illustrated in a telephone conversation between Halder and Field Marshal Wilhelm von Leeb. Leeb wished to retreat from an untenable position in Russia where Hitler had left orders to hold at all cost. Hitler's decision to hold every foot of territory he had conquered was militarily stupid but resistance to his decision by the generals was useless. This is the conversation as reported by Goerlitz: [11]

> Leeb: Do you know, Halder, that one can lose an army corps this way?
> Halder: Yes.
> Leeb: Do you know that one can lose a whole army this way?
> Halder: Yes.
> Leeb: Do you know that one can lose a war this way?
> Halder: Yes, but you know how it is, Herr Feldmarschall. Nothing that you and I have had to learn counts for anything today.

SUMMARY

The last five chapters have traced the course of the German army, its organization, doctrine and effect on government from the reforms of Gneisenau to its destruction by Hitler. The facts of history explode many myths which have had so much to do with determining the turn which America has taken in its effort to organize for defense. Let us review some of the exploded myths.

First, the myth of the political army: Vice Admiral Kurt Assmann of the German navy has thoroughly refuted the myth of the political *Wehrmacht.*[12] As he noted, the primary task of the German army was to support the government in power, and thus when Hitler assumed control of the Reich the army was essentially loyal to the legally established civilian government. The Admiral does not imply that the officer corps was unhappy with the new order, but the support it lent in the beginning was passive rather than active. Later on, the professional military element provided the only organized opposition to Hitler.

Second, the myth of an illegitimate Third Reich: It must be remembered that Hitler gained dictatorial powers through due process of law under the terms of the constitution of the Weimar Republic, however devious were his political maneuvers to achieve this legitimate facade. In the *Reichstag* elections of March, 1933, Hitler's National Socialist Party polled 43.9 percent of the votes which amounted to a wide plurality and subsequent control. He has been accused of burning the *Reichstag* building for a twofold purpose: first to focus attention on the Communist menace which he charged with the crime, and, second, to begin his regime dramatically as the legatee of the old Prussian tradition. When the new *Reichstag* was assembled in Potsdam at the Garrison Church the pews were filled with marshals, generals and admirals of the old and new *Wehrmacht.* The chair of the former Kaiser was left vacant while directly behind it sat the Crown Prince of the Kaiser's *Reich* in full uniform.

Again, through legal processes, the Enabling Law was passed by a two-thirds majority of the *Reichstag* (441 to 94) authorizing Hitler to change the constitution and pass laws for four years without *Reichstag* concurrence. It must be remembered that there was nothing illegal in this whole process, however dire the consequences, and the German nonpolitical military was bound by its creed to support the legal government in power. Hitler, the leader of the strongest *Reichstag* party, was legally handed the reins of government by the President, von Hindenburg.

When von Hindenburg died a little more than a year later, the Reich government passed a law to combine the offices of Reich President and Reich Chancellor. This was put to a popular vote and was approved by an overwhelming majority of 88 percent, Hitler's position of *der Führer* was established by the will of the German people and in the army there was no question about going along with this convincing mandate.

Third, the myth that the military put Hitler in power: The force that had wielded the real political power in this maneuver was Hitler's private army, the Storm Troopers, two and a half million strong, topped by the elite SS Special Guard of a quarter of a million. There was no love lost between the regular German army on these uniformed mobsters who were essentially an internal political force.

Fourth, the myth that the military caused the war: It was not the German professional army that promoted war. In fact, the army counseled peace. In 1937 when Hitler revealed his warlike intentions to his military chiefs, they argued strongly against such a policy. Three months later none of these objectors remained in office. Hitler then assumed command of the *Wehrmacht.*

Fifth, the myth that the army kept Hitler in power: When General von Fritsch, former army commander in chief, was relieved summarily for presenting his honest convictions, the German officer corps felt its first doubts about Hitler. Their honor had been sullied and suggestions of rebellion were cautiously broached. Von Fritsch, himself, quieted such agitation as unworthy of the officer' code. A short time later two abortive plans to seize Hitler were considered, first by von Beck, Chief of the Army General Staff, and next by his successor, Franz Halder. Such an action was so contrary to the basic beliefs of the officer corps that they never materialized, although an army plot on Hitler's life late in the war almost succeeded.

Sixth, the myth that generals want war: It is interesting to note that these same German professional soldiers believed that war on Poland could not be localized. Hitler, however, believed that England and France would stay out of it. Present day proponents of the limited war philosophy should take good note of this. Germany's limited war against Poland refused to stay limited, and *not* because any of the powers concerned wanted all-out war.

Even Hitler was a victim of the popular conception that all generals are itching for war. When his military advisors resisted his war plans, he cried, "What kind of generals are they anyway, that the Chief of State may perhaps have to drive them to war! If things were as they should be, I should be hardpressed against the urgings of my generals for war." It was the professional military of Germany, above any other segment of its society, that cautioned against war and resisted the Nazi dictator. The civilian Hitler risked the war.

Seventh, that civil control of the military is always desirable: Admiral Assmann reports that during Hitler's regime, 50 percent of 92 senior generals were dismissed in disgrace for disagreeing with him. Ten of seventeen field marshals were relieved, and only one retained his command to the end of the war. Of 36 four-star-generals, 26 were relieved and only three survived the war in their positions.[13] These figures speak for themselves. No regular military service has ever suffered more condemnation by civilian control, and the results were disastrous not only to Germany but to the world.

The seven exploded myths above, however, have not by any means been eradicated from American thought. The next chapter will demonstrate their emotional hold on the United States Congress and upon the laws which have governed national defense in our country.

CHAPTER 14

SPECTER OF THE
GERMAN GENERAL STAFF

The reader may question why this study has examined the history of the German army and General Staff in such detail. The answer is that it has been the specter of the German General Staff, not what it was but what it was thought to be, that has most frightened Americans, particularly American lawmakers, whenever any suggestion has arisen for reorganizing the American military establishment.[1] The probable cause for this pathological fear of a "Prussian type of high command" has been discussed elsewhere in this study, but it remains to be shown how deep, how pervasive and how distorted this attitude has become.

TYPICAL SENATORIAL REACTION

A review of the diatribes condemning the German General Staff could fill a library, but this typical bias can be adequately and vividly revealed in a speech delivered on the floor of the United States Senate on July 23, 1956, by the late Senator Styles Bridges of New Hampshire.[2] This two hour address was occasioned by a suggested Department of Defense and Joint Chiefs of Staff reorganization plan which had been published in the *New York Times*. It was alleged by James Reston that the published plan was one prepared by the army general staff.[3]

Assuming this to be the harbinger of another move by the Pentagon to seek unification legislation, Senator Bridges was moved to attack the plan vehemently with almost every cliché, bogy and prejudice that had ever been voiced about the "Prussian" general staff, the system to which he compared the proposed reorganization plan. He used the word "Prussia" or "Prussian" no less than forty-three times in his harangue and the word "German" at least eleven times. As Col. John L. Sutton said, in his analysis of the German General staff, "Both civilian and military spokesmen have used the German—or Prussian—General Staff as a pejorative term and have sought to identify with this organization measures or ideas of which they did not approve." [4] There was little in the proposed reorganization plan that was related to any German staff system which had ever existed since the time of Frederick the Great. But this does not alter the fact that the Senator and his colleagues *thought* there was a similarity, and that any reorganization of the Department of Defense which might lead to a more efficient line-type organization was considered "Prussian."

It is because such an extreme emphasis has been placed on the German army and the German staff system, and on its presumed wickedness, that so comprehensive a survey has been made here. In this survey it soon became evident that the facts were at considerable variance with the legends. Having reviewed the German General Staff system from its inception to its demise in previous chapters, it is hoped that the reader is now in a better position to judge objectively the not atypical outburst of Senator Bridges, excerpts of which will be given here, along with brief analyses.

AMBIVALENCE OF CONGRESS

In his introduction, Senator Bridges said:

> In 1946 we defeated the Collins plan—so named after its sponsor, General J. Lawton Collins—for a single chief of staff and a supreme general staff after the Prussian pattern.[5]
>
> Congress rejected the same idea when we amended the National Security Act of 1949.
>
> So stubborn and persistent were the advocates of a Prussian-type high command that Congress wrote into the National Security Act the most pointed and specific prohibition against a single chief of staff and a supreme general staff.

This is true, but Congress also revealed a surprising ambivalence in this regard because the same "Declaration of Policy" noted the intent to provide "integrated policies and procedures . . . authoritative coordination and unified direction under civilian control of the Secretary of Defense . . . [armed forces] operation under unified control and for their integration into an effective team of land, naval, and air forces but *not to establish a single Chief of Staff over the armed forces nor an armed forces general staff. . . .*"*

---

* *National Security Act of 1947,* Nov. 1956, *op cit.,* p. 1. Italics added.

From this it appears that Congress was intent on having its cake and eating it too. It wanted unity, integration and teamwork but it did not want a single military boss or a common staff to achieve this short of the civilian Secretary of Defense. No doubt it appeared perfectly safe to place a civilian in over-all control of the armed services, but dangerous for a military man to assume such a position, even as a direct subordinate to the civilian head.

As Colonels Archie J. Knight and Allen F. Herzberg pointed out in their study of national defense organization,[6] "It is difficult to know what exactly was meant by 'no general staff' for we certainly have a sort of one today in our Joint Staff. The present Joint Staff is hedged about by size, composition, and tenure restrictions, but it functions in the position where a general staff is called for. It is even organized along general staff lines today."[7]

These authors recognized the incompatibility of the restrictions established by Congress with the goals likewise established by Congress and noted that the Rockefeller panel of 1958 recommended that the Chairman of the Joint Chiefs of Staff be made the principal military advisor to the Secretary of Defense and the President.[8]

The principles established by Congress enjoy approval by friends and foes of armed forces unification. Everyone wants teamwork but the means of achieving this teamwork is something else again.

FEAR OF A "MASTER PLAN"

Further along Senator Bridges observed:

> I am convinced that a new drive is on to enforce the adoption of a supreme general staff. I have already detected the same old arguments that we must discard our JCS system and adopt the supreme general staff in the interest of economy, ending controversy, getting true unification, streamlining our defense organization, and obtaining more military efficiency.
>
> These are no new claims. Each one has been carefully considered in the past. In each instance it has been clearly evident that a supreme general staff would not only fail to provide improvements, but rather it would actually weaken and undermine every vital aspect of our national security.
>
> I know of no proposal which, if adopted, would place our national security and form of government in greater jeopardy.
>
> * * * * *
>
> This campaign to establish a supreme high command, to destroy civilian control, is no mere matter of imagination. The master plan has been prepared. It actually exists. I invite attention to the *New York Times* of Sunday, June 24, 1956, which printed extensive excerpts of an Army general staff plan for changes in our defense organization.

Why did Senator Bridges see the alleged "master plan" to be the embodiment of evil, diabolically designed to usurp civilian control? It is indeed strange that such an innocent proposal with no official standing whatsoever could have raised so much heat.[9]

A RETIRED OFFICER AS CHIEF OF STAFF

To go on with the Senator's remarks:

> This document is nothing but a blue-print for imposing the supreme general staff system on our Nation. The advocates of the supreme general staff system now try to disguise their Prussian product.
>
> What is the present camouflage? This time it is proposed that the military officer designated as the super chief of staff be retired prior to assuming power. We are expected to believe that by changing one person's clothes that the basic character of the entire proposed supreme general staff system would be changed.

No doubt the plan's proposal to designate as the "super" chief of staff a retired officer was an attempt to allay the fear that a military man is dangerous to the peace of the land. True, changing a person's clothes will not change the "basic character" of a system or a man, but neither does the fact that the Secretary of Defense is a civilian assure us that he, himself, might not be dangerous to peace—or, more likely, quite dangerous and inept in time of war.

When General Dwight D. Eisenhower ran for President of the United States he resigned his five-star commission. No one was deceived that this act changed his character, but it might have dispelled some of the unreasoning and unfounded fear that an American in uniform is intrinsically warlike and opposed to democratic principles. The records of the several generals who have honorably served as President of the United States have not seemed to clarify this distorted image of the American military man.[10]

UNIFIED STAFF BELIEVED STEP TO DICTATORSHIP

The core of Senator Bridges' argument boils down to this:

> What we are confronted with today is a continuation of this unfortunate but stubborn effort to induce Congress and the country to accept the system which has been the trademark of Prussian and German Nazi dictatorship.
>
> Let there be no misunderstanding about this. What is being proposed is nothing other than the Prussian-German supreme general staff system which has, as history shows, destroyed the democratic institutions of every government in which it has existed and has ultimately proved to be militarily inferior, making major contributions to the defeat of whatever nation has adopted and placed its faith in it.

Note that the hallmark of dictatorship is assumed to be a unified staff system. There can be no doubt that the legend of this relationship between a general staff and dictatorship is real but, as we have seen, a review of the appropriate history provides meager evidence to support this contention. Of course, a dictator seizes all of the elements of power into his own hands, including military power; so there is bound to be unity of command and centralized direction of some sort in any dictatorship. But this kind of military unity is a *consequence* of dictatorship, not the other way around.

WAS PRUSSIAN GENERAL STAFF INFERIOR?

As to the military inferiority of a unified general staff of the "Prussian" variety, we must note its phenomenal success in the three wars against Denmark, Austria and France in the mid-nineteenth century, and its near success in the first few months of World War I. Even a good staff system cannot overcome the individual incompetence of commanders like the younger von Moltke or overwhelming power allied against it. As for World War II, we have seen that the "Prussian" staff system had been emasculated and dismembered by Adolf Hitler by the time fighting began.[11]

General James M. Gavin reported in his book [12] that when he appeared before the Vinson House Armed Services Committee in the spring of 1958 he was asked a question by a member of the Committee that contained the implication that the United States surely did not want the kind of staff that Germany had when she lost the war.

> . . . I pointed out [said General Gavin] that Hitler did not have a general staff. This seemed to fluster him for a moment; however, he quickly recovered. His attitude is shared by many. Nevertheless, the fact is that in the last two world wars Germany did not have a German general staff. In World War I the German Army and Navy were completely independent and no staff existed to coordinate their efforts. In World War II, the failure of Germany to achieve a quick victory has been attributed to its failure to coordinate its Army and Navy efforts.[13]

As Gavin noted, one of the strongest indictments made against the uncoordinated German military staff direction was by General Bodo Zimmerman of the German army. General Zimmerman remarked that it was ironical that Eisenhower, the leader of a coalition of democracies, was given power over all three services, while under the dictatorship of Hitler each of the armed services fought its own separate battles. "Neither Rundstedt nor Rummel, try as they might, succeeded in changing this state of affairs in creating a unified command." [14]

Continuing with the speech of Senator Bridges:

> What, in essence, is this proposal for a single chief of staff and a national general staff? The basic ingredients of the Prussian system are a top-level, or "joint" staff and one military person who directs the staff and is the sole or principal advisor to the nominal civilian superiors. This chief of staff may be an active or retired officer, he may have full legal grant of power over the military forces, or he may legally have only the status of head of the over-all staff and advisor to the Secretary of Defense and President. The details of format have little significance. All that is necessary is to abandon or bypass our joint chiefs of staff system by setting up one man assisted by an over-all staff and we will have a supreme general staff, after the pattern of Scharnhorst, von Moltke, Ludendorff, and the militaristic lackeys of Hitler.
>
> * * * * *
>
> Furthermore, it is antithetical to every hallowed tradition of our government and way of life. There is good reason for labelling this single Chief of Staff—supreme general staff as the "Prussian system." It was the method by which the Prussian and later the German chiefs of staff controlled military and political policy, enslaved their nation, and goose-stepped their people along the road of militarism to national disaster.

There appear to be some inconsistencies, if not inaccuracies, in the foregoing statement. Since the National Security Act of 1947, as amended, authorized a Chairman of the Joint Chiefs of Staff to "preside over the Joint Chiefs of Staff," to "provide agenda" [15] and, for all practical purposes, to act as the go-between and the only major channel of communication between the JCS and the Secretary of Defense, this "format" seems quite similar to the one the Senator deplored. Yet it has little similarity to any of the staff systems of "Scharnhorst, von Moltke and the military lackeys of Hitler." In fact as we have seen, even the staff systems of these German leaders varied widely. We begin to suspect that not only did Senator Bridges misunderstand the DOD-JCS system then in operation, but that his references to German military history were grossly uninformed. Thus we find two systems being contrasted without a clear understanding of either system. Confusion and misunderstanding compound.

The theme that the "Prussian system . . . goose-stepped their people along the road to militarism and national disaster" recurs throughout Senator Bridges' speech. One would assume from this that the system was a poor one for managing military forces. If this were so, why was such a system feared? Since the United States fought against German forces in two world wars, it would seem that we could only fear a system of military management if it were a good system—one that required all our skills to overcome.

Walter Millis pays tribute to the effectiveness of the German General Staff during the second world war by mentioning that they were "managing still greater armies, launching them with still greater precision and more deadly effect. . . ." [16] Discounting the moral aspect, one must concede that the prostrate and dismembered Germany of 1919 made a magnificent comeback in a period of twenty years. By 1939 she was ready to challenge her conquerors and wage a war for six long years, albeit unsuccessfully. In any event, it was a good try. Without the German General Staff which had rearmed Germany in record time it is probable that Germany would have succumbed much earlier.

This general staff system was at its peak during the age of Bismarck (as we have seen in earlier chapters) when, in a period of seven weeks the German army defeated Austria, and in five weeks humbled France in comparatively benign wars. In fact, these successes raised the prestige of the general staff system to such heights that the system was generally adopted by England and, in 1903, by the United States Army. The United States fought World War I with a general staff system. Considering the country's abysmal state of unpreparedness, America performed rather well. Had the army been organized with semi-autonomous bureaus, as during the Spanish-American War, the result would probably have been disastrous. Germany possibly could have been the victor in 1918.

So whatever one says about the general staff system, it was not an inefficient one for managing war. In fact, no better system for this purpose has ever been developed.

PRUSSIAN SYSTEM ADOPTED BY OTHER COUNTRIES

Let us read further from Senator Bridges' speech:

> But it would be wrong to contend that this supreme general staff system has been limited only to Prussia and Germany. Yes, this Prussian concept has been adopted by other nations. Wherever freedom has died, wherever conquest and oppression have been rampant, there will be found a variation of the Prussian-type supreme general staff.
>
> It directed the malignant militarism of the Germany under both Kaiser and Hitler.

It was the organizational device by which Tojo and his militaristic clique ruled Japan and brought on the disaster that engulfed her.

It provided the basic military pattern supporting Mussolini's Fascist dictatorship.

It is the system in substance adopted by the Kremlin for making military power the tool of Red dictatorship within Russia and the evil militaristic brain for directing the world conquest of communism.

This Prussian system has not found this acceptance in such unsavory circumstances because of the superiority in the military sense. Actually, it is an inferior system of high command, for it has gross military inadequacies that impede instead of enhancing its nation's war effort. Rather, it has helped make dictators and in turn has been adopted by them because its inherent militarism and necessity for one man domination makes it the handmaiden of dictatorship in all of its evil forms.

While it is historically accurate to designate the single chief of staff —supreme general staff—as the Prussian or German system, it would also be correct, in the context of current events, to term it the Communist system.

It is indeed a phenomenon of our age how so many otherwise well-educated, prominent and respected people in our society can attribute so many of the major ills of modern history in every land to "the Prussian-type supreme general staff," no matter how far fetched and disproven these attributions might be. The simplistic approach to complicated problems is to seek the one key that opens all doors, the panacea for all ills, the one dogma for all philosophy. To a large extent the "Prussian General Staff" has become one such unified solution. History reveals little evidence that the military *systems* of Germany, Japan, Italy or Russia had either much in common or much to do with establishing the political dictatorships referred to above. Yet the "Prussian general staff" whipping boy is a most handy target.[17]

A STAFF SYSTEM IS A SAFE TARGET

As wars recede into history and it becomes necessary to deal peacefully with our former enemies, we begin to find excuses for their conduct during the war. We begin to apologize for them. Theirs was not a political decision to go to war, it was caused by the wicked machination of a supreme general staff system. A country composed of millions of people cannot be all wrong, we rightfully conclude. It was the way they were organized that was at fault. Eventually we have the villain established—not a person or a group, nothing human at all, but a very safe "system" upon which we can vent our emotions and our hatred with good conscience. For although we have consciously decided to deal peacefully with our former enemies and even to like them, we cannot as easily decide to purge ourselves of the animosity we felt for them when we were locked in mortal combat.

Nor will any amount of intellectual probing of history change this phenomenon. The hatred will remain at the subconscious level, finding its safety valve in inanimate targets like the "supreme general staff system." This study, therefore, is not intended to sway those steeped in the antimilitary bias who use such bias to assuage their subliminal feeling of guilt and hate. But new generations come along. Perhaps the facts of history will tend to overcome the false legends. And, although hatred is passed on from our elders along with the legends it is usually attenuated. Lacking new cause to hate, our descendents may have a better chance to digest the truth.

COMMANDER VERSUS COMMITTEE

But let us continue with excerpts from the speech of Senator Bridges in order to reveal the extent of the antimilitary bias:

> At this time I would like to review some of the more frequent assertions made by the advocates of a single chief of staff and a supreme general staff—which is the Prussian-type system—and at the same time also review the pertinent findings on these points by the Hoover Commission task force on national security.[18]
>
> One of the contentions advanced by advocates of the Prussian system is that because a single military commander is placed over combat units there should likewise be a single military commander over all the nation's armed forces.
>
> . . . Mr. Eberstadt[19] amplified this thought by later testifying that:
>
> "The choice in the strategic planning area lies between an organization headed by one man and a joint organization such as our joint chiefs of staff. The first type of organization insures speedy action, but at the cost of a marked increase in the probability of fatal mistakes. A deliberate approach is acceptable in the military planning in contrast with execution of plans where prompt action is the primary requisite."
>
> Also the proponents of the Prussian system claim that their system will end argument and differences of opinion in the armed forces. I cannot accept the proposition that the absence of controversy and differences of opinion are virtues. If we are to avoid having the rubber-stamp type of civilian secretary over the military, it is essential that he have access to all the various opinions within his department.
>
> Actually, it is in the resolving of military controversy where the civilian secretary performs his most vital function. This concept of

civilian control was stated precisely in the Hoover Commission task
force report as follows:

"If a 'split decision' occurs, it would, normally, imply that the issue
is beyond solution by the resource of military technology and experience, and is, therefore, within the competence of civilian judgment
and authority."

The report properly concludes that: "Modern war cannot be left
solely to the generals."

Our country *has* a single commander of the armed forces, the
President of the United States. It was found after the Revolutionary
War that the committee system of organization exercised by the
colonial states under the Articles of Confederation was highly inefficient. Washington was not in fact the commander in chief of
the Continental armies. He was only, from time to time, a combat
commander depending upon the temper of his troops. Each contingent of militia could march off the field since primary allegiance
was owed to its colonial state government. Washington was not
infrequently stirred to indignation by this committee system which
was instrumental in losing battle after battle. On two occasions in
the face of a military crisis Congress yielded him power of full
command, but even Congress had meager authority to do this. At
other times Congress itself attempted to exercise direct command
in terms of organization, supply and administration. A board of
war was appointed in 1776 composed of Congressmen. The next
year the board was composed of five who were not members of
Congress. By 1778 the board included both Congressmen and non-
Congressmen. Finally, in 1781 a single secretary of war was
appointed.

The boards of war were not known for their effectiveness. Their
members were often incompetent, with the dubious exception of
Gates who is credited with the victory over Burgoyne. But the selection of Benjamin Lincoln, a man of no stature, as secretary of war,
nullified the forward step of replacing the board with an individual. [20]

True, we won our independence under the committee system of
government, so one could say that the Articles of Confederation
were tried and true, battle-tested in victory. But perhaps we looked
at life more frankly and honestly in the days of our national beginnings. The Founding Fathers saw clearly that we could not afford
to continue to make the same kind of mistakes in war or even in
peace that we had made under the Articles of Confederation. Taxes
went uncollected, troops were not paid, Congressional promises

were not and could not be kept or enforced, and the economy was in chaos.

So the Constitution was written and approved to provide a federal line-type organization for our new government. Wisely included were checks and balances, to guard against dictatorship, to assure the people's rights, and to keep accession to the presidency in the hands of the electorate. Yet these checks did not alter the fact that a true line-type organization was established for the United States Government.

When General Eisenhower testified before the 80th Congress in 1946 on the matter of a single chief of staff, he said:

> There is weakness in a council running a war. That is true of any council. I don't care whether it is composed of the best men in the world. . . . In war, you must have decision. A bum decision is better than none. And the trouble is that when you get three, you finally get none.[21]

Just home from a war which had been won largely through his great leadership, General Eisenhower was speaking from vivid experience. But his advice went unheeded in the subsequent legislation. The chiefs of the armed services remained a council.

POWERS OF THE PRESIDENT

Save for the Civil War (when the Southern states challenged the federal system) there has since been little question of the President's supreme authority over the armed forces and over the general management of our government. It is seldom recognized, however, that the President has *all* the reins of ultimate military power in his hands. The single military check, that of the state militia, has evaporated since the Civil War. No state or group of states would now dare attempt to challenge the armed authority of the Federal government commanded exclusively by the President.

It must be kept in mind also that the President collects taxes and spends what he collects. If income from taxes is not enough (and it usually is not) he borrows and resorts to "deficit spending." No coercive power of Congress exists to assure that the President will abide by the budget. We must bear in mind, too, that he enforces the Federal laws with his own Department of Justice and its Federal Marshals and FBI, and that he administers the Federal prisons. The laws of Congress or the decisions of the courts are only meaningful if enforced and this is the province of the President. Neither Congress nor the Supreme Court has any militant or police power capable of opposing the President should he decide to assume extra-legal authorities, such as arbitrary arrest or abridgment of freedom of speech or press. True, the Senate can impeach the President, but an unscrupulous President bent on dictatorship might easily see to it that the one hundred Senators never met to vote on the issue. A strong President might find many more subtle ways to avoid impeachment. It would be quite difficult for a Senate to prove "treason, bribery or other high crimes and misdemeanors." [22] The point is that the President now has all the powers necessary for despotism if he were so disposed. The Founding Fathers did not tie his hands but provided him with a line-type organization and trusted that American traditions would induce him to honor the Constitution.

But with all this power there have been presidents, such as Truman and Eisenhower, and others who have served in high positions in the Executive Department, who claim that the President does not have adequate control over the armed services and that his control would be improved by creating some sort of a unified military staff system.[23] This would in no way abridge the authority of Congress under the Constitution "to raise and support armies," but it might provide the President with more direct and responsive control over the various instruments of national defense. In the nuclear age, with the timeliness of decision and response becoming more and more critical, such recommendations demand sober consideration. It is not a question of enlarging the President's power and authority, which are more than ample, but of providing him with a more positive and accurate military instrument.

THE TRUE CHECKS AND BALANCES

This speculation has all been intended to show that the presidency of the United States is indeed a powerful post of central authority, more so in fact than that of any prime minister whose authority rests on the will of a parliament. What keeps the United States from falling into dictatorship is probably not so much the vaunted checks and balances of the Constitution (which are unenforceable except at the will of the President) but the ingrained reverence for the American system of freedom and democracy in the President himself, in those around him, in the other officials of government, in the armed forces, and in the populace at large. In other words, it is not the *system* that keeps America free. (The Soviets, too, have a fine constitution.) It is the will and determination of all

Americans to remain free and to honor the Constitution and the precepts of our forefathers. "The basic safeguard is the people themselves and their national character." [24]

If, then, our national philosophy approves of a strong federal government, why is it that people like Mr. Eberstadt, when he testified before the first Hoover Commission, suggest that a federal system of central authority for our military establishment might cause "a marked increase in the probability of fatal mistakes?" This is in some contrast to a statement by Bernard M. Baruch who said, "Our peril today still is not militarism but civilian indecision." [25] There is as much evidence that a committee system makes mistakes by being deliberate as that a federal system errs by being hasty. Vacillation is a common ailment of committee action where responsibility cannot be identified.

BLENDING OF LINE AND STAFF

Most American organizational systems, public and private, incorporate *both* federal and committee activities by using policy staffs, boards and the like but headed by responsible authorities— chiefs of staff or chairmen. The boards of directors in business, the trustees of foundations and universities, provide these policy formulating bodies, but they do not supplant the federal-style line organization necessary for purposeful and smooth day-to-day operations. Businesses have presidents, vice presidents and staff who abide by the policies and regulations laid down by the boards of directors. Similarly, foundations and educational institutions have their presidents, chancellors and operating heads.

Why is it that the military profession, upon which rests such vital matters of ultimate survival, must suffer with a patently inefficient and truly un-American committee or confederate system of organization? The answer cannot possibly be that it is a "better" system as Eberstadt would have us believe. This is simply too far-fetched to be credible. It must lie in ulterior considerations such as the desire to keep an independent Navy or Marine Corps, or the fear that a too-efficient system might produce a "man on horseback" from the military leadership, or that too many existing bureaucratic offices formed by Parkinson's Law would be eliminated.

A line-type organization will not end argument, as Senator Bridges feared, but it *will* make possible a decision when one is needed. "It will resolve the conflict between those who fear too much concentration of power at the top levels and those who fear the absence of ability to make intelligent decisions quickly." [26] Committee systems, with no authoritative leader, can argue interminably without ever reaching a conclusion and this has happened too often within the Joint Chiefs of Staff. No one will assert that this practice is good for anything other than the sharpening of intellectual debate.

SECRETARY OF DEFENSE'S CONTROL

There need be no fear that a Secretary of Defense would become a rubber stamp by having a military chief of staff as his assistant unless the Secretary of Defense himself so desired such a relationship. Why would a Secretary of Defense be any more of a rubber stamp than would the President? No one has suggested that the President is a rubber stamp simply because he has a single Secretary of Defense reporting to him. Nor does there appear to be any reason why a Secretary of Defense with a military chief might be denied "access" to all the various opinions within his department. With a hierarchical line-type organization controlled by a chief of staff reporting directly to him, the Secretary would have complete access to and maximum control over his department. This "access" argument seems to be another strawman.

When Elihu Root was striving for a general staff for the United States army at the beginning of this century, one argument he used to defend his stand was that such a system would *enhance* the Secretary of War's control. In other words, civilian control would improve under a general staff system. The title of *Chief of Staff* (as opposed to that of *Commanding General* which then existed) "denoted a duty to advise, inform, assist and represent a superior officer." [27] The Chief of Staff would follow the secretary's policies and see that his commands were executed. Secretary Root noted further that the duties of the general staff could be circumscribed by law as Congress pleased.

RESOLUTION OF MILITARY CONTROVERSY

Senator Bridges believed it to be the role of the civilian secretary to resolve military controversy. There are parallels in civilian life which might raise some question regarding this presumed responsibility. No one would suggest, for example, that it might be the role of a hospital administrator to resolve medical controversy among consulting surgeons. Nor would a city mayor attempt to judge litigation when judges trained in the law are available for such decisions. Why should not military controversy too be resolved by military professionals themselves? There is no profession without controversy, but few would suggest that resolutions should be sought outside the profession on purely professional matters.

A "split" decision of the Joint Chiefs of Staff simply indicates that the military profession, as with all other professions, does not represent an exact science and requires considerable judgment. Whenever judgment is exercised, differences of opinion occur and someone in authority must, as a rule, decide. It hardly follows that the judge must be one who is unfamiliar with the problem as might be someone outside the profession in question. The magistrate, for example, does not arrive at his high position by avoiding the profession of law. His career has prepared him to judge with wisdom.

Senator Bridges believed that the Secretary of Defense had to be a judge and arbiter in order to administrate:

> It must be remembered that the one real, meaningful manner by which a Secretary of Defense and the President exercise control of the military is through the function of resolving interservice differences of opinion.
>
> Give that function to a chief of staff and civilian control over the military would cease.
>
> Nor would the situation be changed by saying that the chief of staff's function was "advisory" only. What secretary of defense would, or could, repeatedly overrule the advice of a single chief of staff? As a practical matter, it just could not be done.

When the military decision to be made has political overtones it is most certainly the responsibility of the Secretary of Defense to modify that decision as he sees fit. In fact, as Secretary of Defense McNamara has so frequently demonstrated, it is within the province and the authority of the Secretary of Defense to reverse *any* decision, political, military or otherwise, sent to him by his Service Chiefs. The TFX issue is a vivid case in point in which Secretary McNamara overruled the unanimous professional judgment of no less than three joint Air Force-Navy boards together with the Chief of Staff of the Air Force and the Chief of Naval Operations.[28] It would be far *less* difficult to overrule a single chief of staff than to overrule the unanimous judgment of the Joint Chiefs of Staff, yet this latter action has been taken repeatedly by Secretary of Defense McNamara.[29] Since rulings by the Secretary of Defense in opposition to the JCS are seldom publicized because of the classified nature of most of the issues involved, the public is not aware of how often or under what circumstances this occurs. In any event the course of events has proved Senator Bridges' fear of a rubber-stamp Secretary of Defense to be entirely groundless.

COMPETITION BETWEEN MILITARY SERVICES

Senator Bridges said further:

> Another argument advanced by proponents of the single chief of staff is that it will eliminate competition by the military services. With reference to this, the Hoover Commission Task Force states, "The appointment of a single military chief of staff as commander of our three military services might lead to a military party line with static concepts and ensuing mental unification. The dangers of one-man military control of the armed forces of a nation are illustrated by history. The case of the Third Reich is a recent example of the hazards of unilateral strategy. When military differences completely disappear military progress will cease."
>
> This, I believe, is a most fundamental observation, for it is based upon the clear historical fact that wherever the single chief of staff system has existed it has intensified rather than reduced inter-service conflict.

As we have seen the Third Reich had little military unity, although under Hitler it did have a unified strategy. History can hardly attribute this strategy to the German military leadership. There can be no doubt that interservice conflict under the Third Reich was rife, as with the Army versus the S.A. versus the S.S. versus the Luftwaffe versus the Navy. But this conflict was more likely accentuated by the lack of military unity.

DANGERS OF A PARTY LINE

From Senator Bridges:

> This comment by the Hoover Commission Task Force points up another fundamental danger of the Prussian concept. I completely concur with the fears of the Hoover Task Force that a single chief of staff system would well result in a military party line which, in effect, would be a Maginot-line type of thinking within the Armed Forces.
>
> A single chief of staff would have the authority to impose his will on the military services. If that single chief of staff's decisions were wrong it would mean disaster for this nation.

Today one need only insert above the term "Secretary of Defense" in place of "single chief of staff" to appreciate what has happened with a strong civilian leader who has enforced his will upon the military services in almost every instance. "Maginot-line type of thinking within the Armed Forces" is an accomplished fact simply because only that strategy established by the Secretary is acceptable. Deterrence, behind a "wall" of ICBM's and Polaris missiles, is the "military party line" established by OSD and no other concept of strategic defense will be tolerated. Not even a single chief of staff could overcome this imprisonment of military thought. It is not the *system* which creates a party line, it is the *leadership* and how inflexible the leaders might be when confronting new ideas. As Senator Bridges said, a wrong decision "would mean disaster to the nation."

As military attaché to Berlin during the early days of Hitler's regime, General Albert C. Wedemeyer observed how party-line thinking had affected the German army. When Hitler declared to General Beck that "The Armed Forces are an instrument of politics . . . the army has to fulfill its assigned tasks and is not to argue whether it is right or wrong," Beck responded: "This is a point of view which I cannot accept. As Chief of the General Staff, I am not prepared to take the responsibility for orders which I do not approve." [30] It was the German political leadership that eventually imposed party-line policies, not the military organization.

To allay the fear that unification will suppress service views it might be well to point out here that the Marine Corps, even though it is fully administered by the Navy, has consistently taken its views to Congress and to the public in its opposition to cuts in its own strength. Congress has repeatedly specified that service chiefs are legally bound to express their independent views, even if in opposition to the views of the Secretary of Defense and the Administration. This privilege has been frequently exercised as recent testimony on the nuclear powered aircraft carrier and the B-70 bomber amply demonstrates.

DEPRECIATION OF AIR POWER THINKING

Pursuing the Senator's speech:

> As one who is an advocate and believer in the utter necessity of air power second to none I have the most profound fear for the future of our country if a single chief of staff—national general staff system in any form should be adopted. Under such a system there is the strong possibility that our Air Force would be eventually subjected to ground-power thinking, the same type of military thought that for so long stifled and throttled the efforts of our pioneer airmen to give our country the air power it needed in the 20th century.

American air power is rapidly decreasing under the leadership of a strong Secretary of Defense who considers military bombers to be "provocative" and "de-stabilizing" influences in international relations.* [31] Again, this de-emphasis of certain weapons systems will result more from doctrinal trends at the political level of government than at the military level, regardless of how the military itself might be organized.

COMBINING OPERATIONS AND PLANS

Somewhat further on in his speech Senator Bridges said:

> Another contention of those who advocate the single chief of staff—supreme general staff system is that it would be an improvement on our present Joint Chiefs of Staff in which the military service chiefs who do the top level military planning are also responsible for executing those plans.
>
> In reply to this argument the Hoover Commission Task Force is most forceful in its belief that the Joint Chiefs of Staff should remain under the law "the highest responsible source of military advice within the national security organization." Particular emphasis is placed on the advantages of the joint chiefs of staff system in which those who plan our military operations are responsible, in their role of chiefs of the military services, for the actual execution of those plans.

There seems no reason why the single chief of staff as proposed in the "army" paper under question could not likewise be responsible for the *operations* of the armed forces. This ought to obviate the Senator's objection to having planners divorced from operations. In point of fact, JCS plans are now sometimes modified by the Chairman of the JCS as well as by the Office of the Secretary of Defense. The latter office is taking unto itself more and more operating responsibility—a fact which should concern Americans, for when bureaucrats usurp military authority, military ethics are superseded by political expediency. Dangers of dictatorship are accordingly enhanced.

It might be noted further that "the highest responsible source of military advice" is now the advice of the civilian Secretary of Defense. The JCS, individually and collectively, understandably hesitate to go over the Secretary's head to the President. And since no chief sits on the National Security Council, the chiefs rarely have an opportunity to see the President.

DISTINCTION BETWEEN TERMS "COMMANDER" AND "CHIEF OF STAFF"

The Senator quoted extensively from the first Hoover Commission task force, which concludes:

> The committee (task force) does not believe that a chief of staff—
> a commander over all armed services—is needed. The Secretary of
> Defense, and constitutionally, the President, occupy this role. This
> tremendous authority should not be transferred from civilian to mili-
> tary hands, with consequent danger to our democratic institutions.
> There has been much loose criticism of the war efforts of the Joint
> Chiefs of Staff as constituting "command by committee"; yet there
> can be no doubt whatsoever that in the broad field of grand strategy
> a meeting of several minds is far safer—and in the end more sound
> —than the dictates of one. The responsibilities for strategic planning
> and the conduct of war are soundly placed by the National Security
> Act upon the shoulders of the Joint Chiefs of Staff who, in turn, are
> under the authority, and subject to the control of, the President and
> the Secretary of Defense. There should be no change in this concept.

From this it is obvious that the Hoover Commission task force
was vague about the distinction between a "commander" and a
"chief of staff." The chief of staff traditionally exercises his
authority *in the name of* the Secretary. He is not, in his own right,
a commander, and his advice can be accepted or rejected as the
Secretary chooses.[31] Assuming for the moment that "a meeting of
several minds is far safer," if the JCS resolved all agenda items
with unanimous decisions there would be no need for a single chief
of staff. The single chief's purpose would be to resolve the *differences* when the time for decision became imperative. Nothing in
this would in any way negate or detract from the authority of the
Secretary of Defense or the President nor for a "meeting of several
minds" whenever that were possible.

The implicit assumption that a chief of staff's decision is a
decision by one man is a contradiction in terms. Any such decision
would have been thoroughly studied, coordinated and "staffed" by
the general staff itself. Even the Hoover Commission could raise
a strawman, although there was a contrary minority report.

THE JOINT CHIEFS OF STAFF IN WAR

Further on in his speech Senator Bridges praised the JCS:

> Among those views of James Forrestal will be found a ringing
> endorsement of our Joint Chiefs of Staff system and therein also will
> be found a most vigorous and intelligent condemnation of the supreme
> general staff concept. While he said much upon this subject I would
> like to read a few brief quotations by James Forrrestal. With respect
> to the Joint Chiefs of Staff, he stated:
> "The conception of the Joint Chiefs of Staff has proved successful.
> It has been one of the great developments of the war and I think no
> one can gainsay the fact after a look at the captured documents of

the German *Wehrmacht* that the Chiefs of Staff functioned more effectively."

No one who has studied the history of the second world war and the staff work of both sides will disagree with the statement above of Secretary Forrestal. The point is that the various staff systems proposed for the American military have no semblance to the staff system of the German *Wehrmacht*. Again, the strawman.

TOO MUCH AUTHORITY FOR ONE MAN

Toward the end of his speech, Senator Bridges concluded:

> In these perilous times one basic miscalculation in defense policy could mean the defeat and destruction of our Nation. For example, a mistaken judgment on development of missiles, a wrong decision as to the importance of long-ranged jet bombers, a failure to understand our peculiar need for large aircraft carriers, a lack of faith in ground forces, or an inability to appreciate our need for an amphibious force in readiness, could result in an irretrievable and fatal strategic error.
>
> The fate of America will rest on the correctness of such decisions. No one man—no superchief of staff—should be given the authority to decide such vital matters. No one man should have so much power— direct or indirect—to destroy America by his own miscalculation.
>
> When our Nation's existence is at stake, our Nation deserves the mature and collective judgment of its responsible military leaders, the heads of the military services who comprise the time-tested, war-proven Joint Chiefs of Staff.

One can only ask, who decides these issues now? Not the Joint Chiefs of Staff, even when they are unanimous in their advice. So a single chief of staff would fare no better. These are "perilous times," to be sure, and a civilian Secretary of Defense, principally advised by other civilians, is making the major strategic decisions. If "the fate of America will rest on the correctness of such decisions," the American public should ask itself: Are these decisions better made with or without a thorough understanding achieved through a lifetime of training, study and experience in the military profession?

It is true, as often charged, that no one man is sufficiently wise to supervise personally such a vast organization as the Department of Defense. This is the precise reason for having a general staff— the "brain of the army" in the words of Spenser Wilkinson.[32] As size, complexity and technology grow, whether it be in business, public administration or national defense organization, more and better organic system is required; more specialized knowledge, advice and assistance are mandatory. Because the job is unquestionably too much for one man, a general staff carries the burden.

CONCLUSION

In conclusion, it has been blindly assumed that the German General Staff system is at the root of the evil which forced Germany in the past to seek war. Therefore it is reasoned that any similar staff system adopted by the United States will breed evil in America, leading to war, military failure, loss of democracy and dictatorship. This study of the history of the German General Staff finds little basis in fact for believing in the diabolical nature of a particular kind of staff system. In fact, we have seen that throughout its history the German General Staff has been many kinds of systems, often contributing materially to democracy, good government and national defense. Nevertheless, the ghost of what the Prussian General Staff is imagined to be continues to haunt the halls of Congress.

It has been further assumed in an oversimplified way that any reorganization of the American military departments which might lead to more unity of command at the top would resemble the German Staff system. This widespread and inaccurate belief has deterred many well-meant efforts to improve on the American military organization. Military staff systems are so complicated, so variable and so difficult to understand that debates often depart from the specifics and dwell upon the shibboleth of the imaginary Prussian General Staff. Enlightenment in military organization will never come until the specter of the Prussian General Staff is buried.

PART IV

PROFESSIONALISM

CHAPTER 15

THE PROFESSION OF ARMS

A profession is defined in dictionaries as an occupation or calling requiring advanced training in some liberal art or science, and especially involving mental rather than manual work, as teaching or engineering. The "learned" professions usually refer to medicine, law and theology which antedate the liberal art or scientific professions. Few modern dictionaries mention the military profession at all although older volumes allude to "the profession of arms." In the Middle Ages, however, the three professions of repute were the military, the legal, and the clerical. Medicine had not yet achieved much stature, and although some authors include the teaching profession as one of the early "great callings," [1] teaching did not materialize in America as a separate and distinct profession from the clergy until the 19th century.[2]

A common man in the Middle Ages could seldom aspire to a high place without pursuing one of the three major callings of arms, clergy or law. The profit motive was ostensibly of secondary consideration in these professions. The concept of service to society, the state, or to God provided the professional with a noble aura which set him apart from those who pursued commercial or agricultural endeavors. Thus these latter occupations were denied the professional stamp because, rationally at least, they sought personal gain as opposed to a higher service.[3]

As we have seen, there was no such thing as a profession of public service, statecraft or diplomacy in early times. Most states were ruled either by hereditary dynasties or by individuals who had gained power through one of the three major professions. Therefore the three major professions—clerical, military and legal— were all intimately associated with statecraft, and the body of knowledge which they absorbed and pursued was an approach to government from different routes. The clerical profession approached the governing of men through the religious precepts of the various faiths; the military profession regarded government as a feature of conflict and force; while the legal profession regarded government as a function of law and jurisprudence established by state authority.

Commerce, agriculture and the crafts had been historically associated with the work of slaves, serfs and the lowest classes of free men. The prestige of these callings was so low that they seldom produced leaders or statesmen.[4] Craftsmen and tradesmen eventually formed guilds which gradually gained some political influence, and, in a few isolated cases, dominated city states such as Venice and Amsterdam. After the Renaissance, people who worked with their hands were looked upon with somewhat more favor, and as states became industrial and more dependent upon commerce, the prestige of the nonprofessional grew. By the 19th century some individuals who had amassed great wealth through banking and commerce, such as Baron Rothschild and Benjamin Disraeli, actually penetrated to governing positions. But these, too, were exceptions. More often the wealthy tradesmen exercised their power through third party professionals who had prestige but no wealth.

With the Renaissance a new craft developed which was to revolutionize the world—the mechanical craft. Although the roots of this new craft can be traced to the construction of weapons, castles and fortifications, the age of enlightenment impelled the mechanical craft into prominence.[5] The steady advances in mechanics led to the Industrial Revolution and to the complex scientific and commercial society in which we now live. The mechanical craft, associated with the liberal arts and sciences, rapidly expanded its fund of knowledge in the 18th and 19th centuries while the military profession too often ignored the new order except for a narrow interest in fortifications and ordnance. Military prestige suffered accordingly. As a feature of national thought and in the conduct of government the military profession tended to stagnate. This was related to the rise of commercialism and anti-military liberalism, but it was also influenced by the tendency to isolate the military profession from the mainstream of national life in most of the western democracies.[6]

It might further be said that the clerical profession suffered a setback especially in America with the separation of church and state by the Founding Fathers. This split excluded the clergy, as an institution, from direct participation in government. However, the clerical decline in the western world is also evident even in those countries where the government supported a particular religious doctrine. The ideological conflict of the churches with rising science has never been fully resolved and the profession of the clergy has suffered accordingly.[7]

Medicine is usually considered the prototype of the professions.[8] The secret of the phenomenal advance of the medical profession can be found in its comprehensive self-organization. With minor exceptions, all kinds of medical expertise in America were incorporated into one comprehensive and well-disciplined professional society which included many subsocieties of various specialties. Thus the parent medical society, the American Medical Association (AMA), achieved a control over all medical thought and practice. It compelled the layman and even government to take notice and approve.[9] Foundations have generously contributed to the improvement of medical education. A report by Abraham Flexner for the Carnegie Foundation in 1910 had a great impetus on the development of the modern medical profession. This was followed by an influx of money from the Rockefeller Foundation and many other private sources under the supervision of the Council on Medical Education and Hospitals of the AMA.[10]

The aims of the medical societies were altruistic and beneficial to mankind. Nevertheless one suspects that an accompanying purpose in organizing was to raise the prestige of the profession itself which was indeed low on the social scale in earlier centuries, the surgeon ranking along with the barber. With higher prestige the profession could raise its internal standards, enforce a more rigid code, and allow admittance to the profession for only those who could meet the higher standards. It could also, of course, establish fees more in line with the investment in learning required of its members.

This has all happened in relatively recent times with the realization that the *practice* of medicine was the true center for the *learning* of medicine, and with the laboratory discoveries of Louis Pasteur and Joseph Lister which were applied to surgery and the treatment of illness. Within the last hundred years as a consequence of this enlightenment the medical profession has surged to the top in prestige and influence. For some inexplicable reason the profession never attempted to gain a foothold in the practice of government but has kept within its own field except where government seemed to encroach upon its expertise. Perhaps because its professional concern has been of man as an individual, rather than man as a collective body, there has been little reason for a carryover into politics. With the increasing interest which the medical profession is now assuming in psychiatry, social psychology, and sociology, this non-political aspect of the profession may not prevail indefinitely.

Other budding professions in the new age of commerce and industry were quick to recognize the success of the medical profession and they largely adopted the same pattern of organization.[11] Few, however, were as spectacularly successful simply because of their inability to organize into comprehensive and integrated societies. Professional fractionation took place among scientists and engineers. Social scientists and physical scientists each developed numerous amorphous and poorly organized societies which often fought bitterly with one another, while engineering was looked down upon as too manual and commercial. Competing societies sprang up within the same fields as did independent societies of minor specialties with no higher affiliations. The same was largely true with the efforts of education, business, agriculture, and a number of other callings which sought professional standing. Nevertheless most such new professions achieved some real success along these lines in the 20th Century [12] and many surpassed the relatively dormant military and clerical fields.

LEGACY FROM ANCIENT PROFESSIONS

The modern professions cannot escape from the historical value judgments placed upon human occupations. Stated or not, they apply in the modern age simply because they have been so long ingrained into human culture. It is still, for example, not quite as respectable to work with one's hands as with one's head.[13] Even though much head work is required to build a great bridge, because it requires some manual work the task is not quite as highly regarded as that of developing a new formula for the propagation of radio waves.

Also, there is a certain element of profit in the construction of a bridge which is not so evident in the development of a propagation formula. Even though commercialism has become a central feature of modern life, and even though commercialism provides the major motivation behind many great contributions to the advancement of mankind, the simple search for and acquisition of knowledge regardless of its usefulness, still gets the nod of prestige. Thus the ancient brain-work-over-hand-work conception of a profession continues to have some validity in terms of prestige, while dedication to a higher cause than that of personal gain is also influential in determining the status of a profession. Most will agree that law still ranks ahead of medicine, chemistry over agriculture, and diplomacy over the military.

With the modern revival of learning, comprehensive bodies of knowledge were accumulated and recorded in texts of all sorts. It soon became necessary for aspirants to attend school for many years to digest this broad body of knowledge. For this purpose, among others, schools and academies were established to teach particular areas of professional knowledge. Sometimes schools would gain assistance from government, as when West Point was established to teach, essentially, military engineering (which included the later "civil" engineering), or when Jefferson's University of Virginia took up the teaching of law. Other times the professions managed to have their own specialized schools endowed, such as Johns Hopkins Medical School, Rensselaer Polytechnic Institute, Massachusetts Institute of Technology, Stevens Institute and Case School. Stephen van Rensselaer established his school in 1824 for the purpose of ". . . affording an opportunity to the farmer, the mechanic, the clergyman, the lawyer, the physician, merchant and in short, to the man of business." [14] Of course, the professional societies largely determined what would be taught in the schools which they fostered. When state universities were established with schools such as law, medicine, business, agriculture and engineering, it was again the appropriate professional society which largely dictated what should be taught and what standards would be set.[15]

PROFESSIONAL ASSOCIATIONS

The corporate nature and the cohesion of the professions was assured by the professional associations. Learned societies provided the cement which bound each profession into a common whole. The associations published journals and passed judgment on the results of research. They established procedures and practices, ethics and codes of behavior, standards and examinations. Certificates of admission to the profession and accomplishment within the profession were granted and withdrawn by these professional societies. We find the disbarment procedure in the legal profession, for example, to enforce the internal standards.[16] In many instances, as in law, medicine and engineering, associations succeeded in having laws passed for licensing practitioners to help enforce their standards.[17]

To develop consistency and to exchange ideas and knowledge, frequent meetings, conventions, seminars and conferences were held where the business of the associations was conducted.

The very heart of the modern profession is its professional association. And modern professions succeed and advance in direct proportion to the success of these guiding professional societies. Professions which have slipped, such as the military and the clergy, may have dropped behind because of their inability to organize cohesive and comprehensive professional associations which are devoted to general professional advancement.

It is true that both the military and the clergy can point to numerous professional societies. But these societies are generally devoted to promoting one particular kind of doctrine, sect, or expertise in contrast to another, i.e., Catholicism versus Protestantism, army versus navy, air versus ground warfare. Such competition is self-destructive to a professional organization. Few efforts have been made to organize a military society which will encompass *all* concepts of warfare with a particular devotion to no single one of them.[18] Where is the military association dedicated to general professional progress as a whole? In order to develop a successful profession, it is necessary for rival factions to bury the hatchet long enough to agree that wide professional improvement must supersede internal differences. As Colonel Robert N. Ginsburgh put it, "To meet satisfactorily the challenge to its professionalism, the military must first of all become more professionally expert . . . by developing an expertise which transcends that of the individual service." [19] Neither the military nor the clergy has been able to arrive at this internal meeting of the minds.

DEFINITION OF THE MILITARY PROFESSION

What is the military profession, and what should it be? In his comprehensive study, *The Soldier and The State,* Samuel P. Huntington of Harvard attempted to define the profession and to present his conception of what it ought to be.[20] The first characteristic of any learned profession, he wrote, is expertise in an identifiable field of endeavor. This includes a unique body of knowledge, schools to teach it and means to acquire and catalogue new knowledge. The second characteristic is responsibility to society which involves a dedication to human progress through learning. Under this is included Huntington's major thesis that the principal criterion for military professionalism is the rejection of any political activity in the affairs of government. This concept of military professionalism, although characteristic of the American scene, is unique to definitions of the profession of arms and will be examined at some length in this study. The third characteristic of professionalism to which Huntington referred is corporateness which provides a common bond of loyalty and establishes standards of behavior and accomplishment.[21]

Military officership fits these three criteria but the third criterion of corporateness limits the military profession to the active regular as opposed to the National Guardsman or the reservist. This also excludes the many civilians and the "defense intellectuals" who devote their lives to the military profession in fields such as administration, scientific research, or military history.

Although Huntington's definition of a profession seems generally adequate, the cart gets before the horse when he confines the military profession to regulars in order to find a group which best fits his definition. By considering the nonpolitical code to be a fundamental criterion for the profession of arms only the regular can be considered a professional.

It is difficult to compare the military profession with civilian professions because it departs from the pattern in so many particulars. Perhaps the military profession would be better off if it were modeled along the lines of other professions, but this has rarely been attempted. The principal reason for the military singularity is that other professions are free to develop and establish their own standards and codes, whereas the military profession is a servant of the government first and foremost and receives its highest orders from nonprofessional and political sources. "The officer corps," wrote Huntington, "is not only a professional body; it is also a bureaucratic hierarchy." [22] Perhaps the order of these two features should have been reversed. It is the peculiar nature of the bureaucratic hierarchy which handicaps the development of a true military profession.

Recently some military leaders have analyzed the military profession. General Bernard A. Schriever [23] listed eight distinguishing marks of a modern profession: First, a history of accomplishment; second, standards for entrance and practice; third, a large body of specialized knowledge; fourth, provisions for specialized practices; fifth, resources for producing new knowledge; sixth, resources and time for continued formal education; seventh, a strong sense of cohesion; and eighth, a strong sense of public service. In Schriever's analysis, the nonpolitical military code was not mentioned as an underlying criterion of the military profession.

Nor was mention made of the military nonpolitical code, which Huntington stressed, in another address dealing with the military profession. Speaking at West Point, General Maxwell D. Taylor said,

> As a nation we are still the prey of clichés about men on horseback and of the dangers of the military to democracy. . . . We must perhaps progress further toward maturity before there will be wholehearted acceptance at home of the continuing need for a large and respected military profession in the United States in the same way as there is a need for a class of businessmen, professional men, scientists, clergymen, and scholars.[24]

Still another address dealing with the military profession failed to mention the non-political code as a distinguishing feature. This was a talk on "Professionalism in the Air Force," given before the American Ordnance Association by General Curtis E. LeMay.[25] It would seem that Huntington's criterion is not shared by those within the military as a distinguishing characteristic of professionalism although this does not imply that the nonpolitical code is absent.

Unfortunately Huntington oversimplifies the "central skill" of the military profession by repeating the pejorative phrase invented by Lasswell: "the management of violence."[26] Speaking before the Senate Committee on Government Operations, Colonel George A. Lincoln, Professor of Social Sciences at the United States Military Academy, remarked that he preferred a definition used by Robert Lovett: "The function of the profession of arms is the ordered application of force to the resolution of a social problem."[27] Lincoln, however, would substitute "military resources" in place of "force" because, as he said, resources can be used for deterrence and peacekeeping as well as violence.[28]

In the latter definition, the term "social problem" might raise some eyebrows. Few military men would agree that their purpose is to solve social problems although "problems of government and international relations" would find wide favor. It might better be said that *war* is what the military man is trained to manage, and *war*, even if it, too, is a loaded word today, is not always violent. Frederick the Great demonstrated how a war could be won without fighting. The very best management of war is its avoidance, and this seems to be the most central skill of the military profession, particularly in time of peace. Certainly it is not "the management of violence." In fact, a cardinal principle of hot war is to achieve objectives with a *minimum* of violence ("economy of force"). The military man is, however, the only professional who openly concedes that violence is a bona fide last-ditch tactic in the pursuit of national objectives.

Perhaps in narrowing his definitions of the military profession to the craft of organized violence, Huntington gets off the track and draws the implicit assumption that military men do not have the capability of assuming the strategy-policy role at high level. Or perhaps he accepts the popular belief that military men are dangerous influences when outside the military service. Certainly he must hold one or the other or both of these views in order to advocate a still stronger cap of "objective" civilian control over the professional military than now obtains.[29]

Some obvious questions were neither raised nor answered in his book. Why are military men so objectionable in nonmilitary posts of government? Why are they considered less qualified than lawyers or businessmen in posts which deal largely with national defense? Do military men truly present dangers in these traditionally "civilian" posts? In analyzing the military professionals who have reached high places, Huntington implies that they were deviates to the professional nonpolitical ideal and that they somehow became liberalized (i.e., civilianized) and thus were no longer dangerous. This rather laborious reasoning might profit by further analysis. So many exceptions to the ideal may be reason to suggest that the ideal itself is misconceived.[30]

Another oversimplification comes with the classification of all people into categories of "conservative" or "liberal." Huntington aligns the military with the conservative, and explains antimilitary attitudes as a feature of the conservative contra liberal clash of ideals. It is inconceivable to him that a true military man can believe in and foster liberal ideals, as for example, Generals Andrew Jackson and Dwight Eisenhower. He explains such inconsistencies by saying that military liberals have forsaken the military code.[31]

With these few shortcomings, *The Soldier and the State* is still the most insightful study ever made of the military profession. Many antimilitary prejudices were refuted by exhaustive research and keen analysis. This is the first book of its kind which has been mainly sympathetic toward the military profession and Huntington is one of the few scholars who has taken the time to see that the military profession is more often than not an antiwar influence in government.

One feature of Huntington's definition which seems rather parochial is his treatment of the civil supremacy ethic. The civil supremacy principle is certainly evident in the United States but may be missing entirely in other countries. Huntington writes that only "A highly professional corps stands ready to carry out the wishes of any civilian group which secures legitimate authority. . . ." [32] This would eliminate many highly professional officer corps that *have* intervened in politics such as the German and Japanese, the Soviet and Turkish, the French, the Brazilian and Pakistani.[33] The concept of political sterility as a universal criterion for military professionalism may even lead to civil-military strife in that the military may regard its loyalty to the abstract "state" as superior to its loyalty to the particular government in power.[34] This was demonstrated in Brazil in 1964, although with a benefit to representative government. General von Seeckt said that "the army should become . . . the purest image of the State" [35] which obviously alludes to an ideal allegiance.

Absolute observance of the nonpolitical ideal may contain some hidden dangers. A less than sincere loyalty to the government in power is one such danger, but a still greater hazard is the blind acceptance and support of a patently evil government such as Hitler's Third *Reich*. Military officers are still people, still citizens, still heads of families, still live under the laws and edicts of their country. They do not resign from the human race when they join the military profession. They, too, have as much concern over the *kind* of government which employs them and under which they must live as do lawyers, businessmen, or teachers. "The soldier cannot surrender to the civilian his right to make ultimate moral judgments." [36] Nor is the legitimacy of the government in power the final arbiter for military loyalty. Hitler's Third *Reich* was legitimate. So were George III's colonies in America.

THE MILITARY IN POLITICS

The nonpolitical feature of the military code today is vaguely understood and poorly applied. With the mixing of military and civilian thought it is gradually diminishing as, for example, with the encouragement of the military vote. The boundaries between military and nonmilitary matters are becoming increasingly obscure, just as are the boundaries between peace and war.[37] Political influence can also be recognized at the Joint Chiefs of Staff level with the endorsement of a Korean stalemate in 1953, and of the limited nuclear test ban in 1963. Although some deplore this trend without explaining why, it may not be altogether bad. If the military becomes more active politically, perhaps national defense legislation will become more realistic and the standards imposed by the government on the military more truly professional and equitable. In other words, the military profession might approach the standards of other professions.

One would be hard pressed to make a case of the apolitical nature of either Generals Eisenhower or MacArthur, two of the most illustrious military leaders of our age. The fact that Eisenhower resigned his commission as General of the Armies in order actively to run for President revealed a *pro forma* effort to abide by the military ethic. His commission was restored by act of Congress when he left the White House. MacArthur, on the other hand, did not achieve Eisenhower's political success and never resigned his active five-star rank (which holds no retired status). As keynote speaker at a Republican National Convention, MacArthur was obviously available to become his party's standard bearer.[38]

The ancient fear that the military might use armed force to gain political ends is real enough from an historical standpoint but baseless in this country. The political tradition of America that no organization will gain power except through due process of law is as strong within the military as within any other segment of the American society. There is a strong moral barrier in almost all military professions against military rule and lack of legitimacy but it is nowhere so marked as in the United States.[39] In fact, United States military forces are scrupulously careful to act only when they have received legitimate orders from constituted national authority. If anything, this is the most strictly held tenet of the American military code. In the words of Alfred Thayer Mahan, "the rule of obedience is simply the expression of that one among the military virtues upon which all the others depend. . . ."[40] The officer takes his oath to uphold the Constitution as the supreme law of the land. In this respect he differs from officers of many other countries, where loyalty to a military or political superior—the chain of command—is sometimes paramount to national loyalty.

As long as the fundamental allegiance of the American officer is to the Constitution he can serve any President or any political party without a serious conflict of loyalties. This does not mean that the military man must be a political neuter any more than any other government official who serves the President. In the Civil Service, for example, it is not uncommon for Democrats to serve under Republicans and vice versa. The Hatch Act constrains all members of the Executive Branch except certain high officials [41] from actively engaging in politics and there seems to be no purpose in applying this law more strictly to the military.

As we have seen, barring regular military officers from politics is a relatively recent manifestation of America's civil-military relations and it would be enlightening to learn what influences brought this about. Knowing this it might be possible to evaluate the separate causes.[42] There never have been objections raised to National Guard or reserve officers participating in politics even when such officers have spent full careers in the military service. For some reason only the regulars have suffered unusual discrimination, not only with respect to political participation but in every other area, from pay to retirement benefits and employment opportunities. To paraphrase Huntington, no matter what the issue, the professionals "are always on the other side" and left out in the cold.[43]

One possible cause for this general unpopularity of the regular officer is the false image of him which has been foisted on the American public by three generations of antimilitary writers who identify the regular with reactionary conservatism, opposition to social progress and the management of violent total war. Huntington has slain these dragons, one after another, but for each Huntington there are dozens of other authors who enlarge on the false and ugly image. The term "militarism," for example, has been made out by Walter Millis and Alfred Vagts to represent almost everything evil.

> Militarism is thus not the opposite of pacifism; its true counterpart is civilianism. Love of war, bellicosity, is the counterpart of the love of peace, pacifism; but militarism is more, and sometimes less, than the love of war. It covers every system of thinking and valuing and every complex of feelings which rank military institutions and ways above the ways of civilian life, carrying military mentality and modes of acting and decision into the civilian sphere.[44]

Walter Millis, in his study of the Spanish-American War [45] first painted this image of "militarism," and although it was not intended to be applied to the regular officer, that is where it has come to rest. Once a profession becomes so caricatured with no literary means available to erase or alter the image, it soon becomes indelible and unquestioned.

SEPARATION OF THE MILITARY PROFESSION

Clemenceau's oft-quoted remark that "war is too complicated to be entrusted to the generals" applies only as long as the military are reduced to the status of technicians and craftsmen or "managers of violence." This has happened in many societies at various stages of history, and was most noticeable in this country during the latter half of the 19th Century. During this period the military profession isolated itself from society and atrophied into narrow, unrealistic channels. This was likewise the period when the other modern professions were born in the general form we now recognize and in which they flourished into national prominence.

These tendencies of the latter 19th Century formed the civilian professions as we know them today, but not the military profession. There was some rebirth of learning in the military—the civilian example was infectious—but hardly enough to keep pace with the expanding civilian professions. Some professional military schools were established, but few in comparison to the mushrooming educational effort found in the other professions. During this period of military separation from American life the officer corps took on alienating standards of behavior. Social customs as practiced by the financial elite of the period, "the four hundred," were adopted and snobbishly stressed as "customs of the service." Social beliefs, attitudes, and mores followed these same unpopular lines, with birth and social standing assuming more importance than the expansion of knowledge through organized learning and painstaking research —the standards which were then being adopted by the civilian professions.

There was a distinguishable military profession being molded during this period but it can hardly be compared to the civilian professions then in development. And it was during this professionalizing period that the military missed the boat. The military produced a profession, but not a learned profession in the pattern of law or medicine. With the one exception of the Military Service Institution of the United States between 1880 and 1917, it developed no unifying professional societies. With few exceptions, its members remained craftsmen and its knowledge stagnated into parroted doctrine. The nonpolitical ideal became a fetish which led to political ignorance and naiveté. Clemenceau was right not to rely too heavily on advice from professionals with such a narrow background.

Although the military profession has made much progress since 1900, particularly with the reforms of Emory Upton, Elihu Root,

Tasker H. Bliss, Alfred Thayer Mahan, and the establishment of the Army and Navy War Colleges, the military profession has never overtaken its lag in self-development behind other professions. Educational standards, codes of conduct, zealous research, expanding knowledge, improved skills, courses of instruction and specialized schools, although existing in every particular, do not compare with similar aspects of the civilian professions either in scope or depth. As Edward L. Katzenbach has so clearly put it, the curricula lack context and provide a sort of intellectual smorgasbord with ". . . breadth of view as an educational objective so overriding that it virtually precludes depth of view on any subject included in the syllabus." [46] Why is it that the military fell behind other professions in this direction of professional development?

ECONOMIC MOTIVATION

Perhaps one reason for its backwardness is that there is little profit motive in the military profession. Although all definitions advanced for learned professions stress their altruistic nature—a motivating force of service to society—every other profession nevertheless has a strong economic attraction underpinning the service motive. A pre-legal student visualizes the fat fees of a successful attorney and a pre-med student is not likely to spend an expensive nine years in training to serve mankind on a pittance. Nor are college professors content with meager salaries. The able ones are paid for research, hire out as consultants, and write textbooks that are sold to the students. Without economic motivation, it is highly doubtful that knowledge would be acquired and spread so rapidly as it is today. Huge sums are spent for military hardware but military pay is given little attention. Because salaries are held so low and because military men are discouraged from extra-curricular endeavors, there is meager economic incentive in the military profession.

For decades, advancement in the military was based on seniority. Since World War II seniority has been given less consideration but it still holds a major place among the criteria for promotion. Steady, reliable, loyal and *untroubled* service are the factors which gain most favorable consideration. These are typical bureaucratic standards rather than professional ones. One poor effectiveness report may ruin an officer's career, and it will certainly excite more attention than one "outstanding" report. Trouble is to be avoided in the bureaucratic society for it embarrasses superiors. And any progress without risking trouble by questioning established beliefs or traditional practices is hardly possible. Change and progress become threatening. Therefore a thirst for new knowledge, which is characteristic of civilian professions, is not marked in the military profession unless such knowledge deals with non-controversial hardware—military weapons and equipment.

There is even some potential economic benefit in the hardware end of military endeavor. As long as expensive weapons are required by the military from commercial sources, military experts will be recruited for jobs with arms industries. But this is the exception rather than the rule. In general, there is little economic or professional reward for in-service research and education: activities which provide the life-blood and the basic framework of other professions.

ETHICAL STANDARDS AND CONTROL BY GOVERNMENT

The military profession differs from civilian professions in another major particular and that is in its ability to establish its own professional ethics and to police itself with respect to those self-generated ethics. It is true that an internal military code does exist —duty, honor, country. Honesty, trustworthiness, punctuality, cleanliness, thoroughness, justice. Samuel Finer mentions "bravery, discipline, obedience, self-abnegation, poverty [and] patriotism. . . ."[47] The list could go on and on. It is a description of virtue versus evil, although modern soldiers would take issue with the virtue of "poverty." But beyond the broad and glittering generalities, there is little to help the officer who runs up against a mandatory choice between two of those noble precepts which may be conflicting. How does he behave, for example, if he must make the choice of killing his prisoners in order to avoid the capture of his own unit? (A German officer had to make this decision in the Huertgen Forest.) How should he behave if given a legal order from established authority to shoot civilians who were wilfully blocking a vital road? (Some of our own officers were faced with this decision in Korea.) Should he blind himself to a political despot? Should he hold the military virtues of obedience and duty above traditional American political concepts such as "life, liberty, and the pursuit of happiness"? It is unlikely that any consistency could be found among officers asked such questions. The limits of duty, where it runs contrary to honor or honesty or civil law are not clearly defined because the military profession is neither free to debate such issues nor to establish more precise codes which will help it solve these dilemmas.

International civil law, to which the United States contributed, condemned the murder of prisoners in the Huertgen Forest as well as the execution of civilian prisoners in German concentration camps. Justifiable as this legal action might have been, what happened to the military code of duty and obedience? The post-World War II war crimes trials at Nuremberg declared illegal the military principle of "superior orders." The military have of necessity remained mute. In short, military ethics extend more generally from non-military legislation and legal judgments than from internal development and control. And such wholly civilian-inspired ethics may be difficult to apply in the heat of war.

ORIGIN OF THE APOLITICAL CODE

The concept adopted by the military in the latter 19th Century which eschewed political activity may have been acquired by the military not for any reasons of self-betterment or of national safety, but rather to satisfy the popular conception that the military threatened democratic and liberal principles. And indeed, with the military adopting the aristocratic social standards of the captains of industry in opposition to the growing middle-class trend of democracy and individuality, there may have been some justification in keeping the military out of politics at that time. Certainly the regular officers were not then as representative of the American people as they are now.

"The United States Constitution," wrote Huntington, "despite the widespread belief to the contrary, does *not* provide for civilian control." [48] Huntington has clearly shown that the Founding Fathers had no conception of a nonpolitical military service, and that until the Civil War there was no question raised about military men engaging in politics. In fact participation in politics by officers was considered a normal exercise of individual rights. It was held that in a free state the citizen did not cease to be a citizen when he became a soldier. Not until the latter part of the century, when the military on a steadily decreasing budget withdrew from society, did the tenet emerge regarding the nonpolitical behavior of the military. This no doubt was re-enforced by emulating the apolitical codes of the German and British armies of the times.

It is human nature, of course, for those in authority to keep qualifications so narrowed as to admit only those of their own stamp to the high positions. Civilian civil servants, lawyers and businessmen have the field of executive government pretty well in hand, albeit with much vigorous competition among themselves. One thing they would all agree upon, however, is the desirability of keeping the military out of the running. And this principle is always justified with the unassailable "civilian control of the military" argument which, upon analysis, makes little sense at all in this context. Going one step further, civil control of the military is usually justified on the mythical concepts of the bellicosity, authoritarianism or rigidity of the "military mind."

Since the military is the servant of the state, it is to the advantage of the government in power to gain political support from a sympathetic military profession, or at least assure that an unsympathetic profession is a political neuter. Extreme political activity was noticeable in the armed services during the wartime election of 1944 because incumbent President Franklin D. Roosevelt was obviously popular with the GI's. Every effort was made to "get out the vote" even overseas and in combat theaters in order to permit each soldier to exercise his constitutional rights as a citizen. This enthusiasm for the soldier vote was not as evident during the election of 1964 possibly because of some unsympathetic attitudes of the servicemen with the defense policies of the Administration. Nor were there as many potential military voters.

Several noteworthy lectures and talks were given during this time about the importance of an apolitical military code. The then Secretary of the Air Force Eugene M. Zuckert stressed this feature of the professional military ethic in a speech at the Air War College.[49] This panegyric to Secretary of Defense Robert S. McNamara, who was antagonizing many military professionals with his detailed and decisive strategic direction of the services, was an obvious effort to gain support for policies of the Administration, or if not support, at least acquiescence by virtue of the apolitical tradition. Thus does the apolitical military code continue to be shaped by influences outside the military.

There are certain segments of the military which are highly political, such as the National Guard and the reserves although the regulars would be the first to deny that these branches are truly professional because they usually work only part time at the military business. The extensive political influence wielded by the Guard and the reserves has never threatened civil government. Yet the political success of these military organizations has resulted in their perpetuation whether or not there may be merit to their existence from the standpoint of national defense. Not even within states have the National Guard organizations attempted to use military force to seize political power. From this it hardly seems justified to fear that the active regular force would be less likely to follow the American tradition if it were to take a greater interest in politics.

CONCLUSION

Elihu Root challenged army critics in 1899 to point out a single act of disloyalty by the regular army. He stated that "No one ever knew of the American army seeking to make itself a political agent. No one ever knew of the American army seeking to make itself a Praetorian Guard to set up a president or an emperor. No one ever knew of the American army seeking to throw off . . . civil control. . . ." [50] It might be further noted that no civilian administrator or official group has ever attempted, like Louis-Napoleon, to subvert the American army to his personal ambition. What way would the American army go if its Commander-in-Chief, the President of the United States, ordered it to use force against American citizens in some obviously illegal way? This question has not been subject to much debate. Does the army's loyalty rest ultimately with the President? The Congress? Or the people? Can we Americans be smug because we, unlike many other peoples, have not for a hundred years had to make such hard choices?

The American military man has much to be thankful for. Not only have broad oceans protected the country for almost two centuries, but the deep reverence for American principles held by civilian officials and military men alike has created a situation with very few conflicting loyalties or questions of ultimate moral values. Seldom has it been necessary for the military officer to question his code.

The American military man until recently has been able to isolate himself from the political life of the nation. He is still encouraged to do this whenever it appears he may be out of sympathy with the Administration and it is to the advantage of all civilian administrators to keep him from competing for civil positions in government. This aspect of "civil control of the military" may not be in the best interests of the country and it certainly handicaps the military man.

The American military profession suffers because of its bureau-

cratic and hierarchical nature but this might be mitigated if a true
service-wide professional organization were established as has been
established in all other modern professions of significance. Higher
standards, clearer codes, greater learning and more status and prestige would undoubtedly follow.

CHAPTER 16

THE MILITARY
PROFESSION CHALLENGED

If every citizen is a part-time soldier, goes the ancient reasoning, a state need not fear military despotism from a professional army. Even should a small professional army be necessary, "citizen-soldiers have been regarded as a means of curbing any excesses the small professional army might be tempted to inflict on the civil population." [1] This hoary doctrine harks back to classical times and is about as applicable today as foretelling the future by reading chicken entrails. A far more sensible doctrine, recommended by Plato in his *Republic,* is that soldiers should be educated to be loyal to the laws and customs of their country.[2] This doctrine is embedded in the education of American professional soldiers with the motto of ' Duty, Honor, Country." Yet the sincerity of this motto continues to be questioned. General of the Army Douglas MacArthur in an address at West Point noted that "the unbeliever will say they are but words, but a slogan, but a flamboyant phrase. Every pedant, every demagogue, every cynic, every hypocrite, every troublemaker, and, I am sorry to say, some others of an entirely different character, will try to downgrade them even to the extent of mockery and ridicule." [3]

To the extent the motto "Duty, Honor, Country" is believed and observed not only by the professional military man but by the country at large in its conception of itself and its permanent military establishment, to that extent the country is secure from military usurpation. Should the cynicism and hypocrisy which General MacArthur mentioned be allowed to creep into the hearts of the military themselves, the country is in deep danger. If ultimate loyalty to the legitimately constituted government of the United States were ever shaken, the professional military establishment could well become a political instrument little different from that of several of our Latin American neighbors.

The national constitutions of several Latin American republics resemble our own, yet we are all too familiar with the military dominance of government and with the political *caudillo*. Obviously, the words on a piece of paper are not what keep a country free. It is the sincerity, the conviction and the honesty of its people and of its armed men. An effective constitution must be written in the hearts of *all* the people. A citizen army or any other organizational panacea will not create or hold this spirit which assures a free nation an orderly government under a living constitution. A body of traditional values resting on the high ideals of individual freedom is the surest pattern for lasting democracy.

Yet the ancient conception of a "safe" citizen army continues to be advanced. Not only is a part-time citizen army incapable of mastering the innumerable skills necessary to achieve a modern defense but it has been demonstrated repeatedly in history that a citizen army can be, and usually is, more dangerous to the constituted government than is a professional army. The examples of Cromwell's Roundheads, of our own Revolutionary War, of Napoleon's seizure of power, of Mussolini's and Hitler's usurpations, should be enough to alert us to the volatile nature of citizen armies. Yet we persist in regarding the citizen army as guardians of democracy and the regulars as potentially dangerous and unreliable.

ORIGINS OF THE AMERICAN CITIZEN ARMY

Our colonial forefathers were steeped in the British tradition derived from the Great Rebellion in England over a century earlier that standing armies were a threat to liberty. One must recognize the difference here between a threat to liberty and a threat to government. Standing armies usually uphold government against revolutionary armies. Thus citizen armies are a more likely tool for revolt and a dubious instrument for peacetime defense. This distinction was not appreciated by our Founding Fathers. To "provide for the common defense," therefore, the Militia Act was passed in 1792 which charged each state with the responsibility of training all able-bodied young men. This law remained on the books for over a century, a complete failure. States did not feel compelled to train good troops and each war found the United States so unprepared it was forced to raise and train new levies from scratch.

The conception of a nation-in-arms, with every able-bodied man liable to military service originated during the Napoleonic wars. The organizing genius and logistical skill of the Little Corporal created the largest armies ever assembled. He marched almost 500,000 into Russia in 1812 only to suffer his worst defeat.

This doctrine of mass armies amplified the citizen army thesis but the idea did not achieve fruition until the Industrial Revolution provided the railroads which made mass mobilization possible along with logistic capabilities to supply the great armies. The American Civil War disclosed the use that could be made of railroads to assemble, move and supply large forces. The doctrine reached its zenith in 1914 when Germany was able to hurl four million soldiers against its enemies just nine days after ordering mobilization.[4]

But mass armies were soon to give way to armor, mobile artillery, automatic weapons, tactical aviation and all the other technical inventions of modern land warfare. In the second world war, instead of huge quantities of manpower (the "cannon fodder" in the first world war), generals began to ask for more modern weapons and more highly trained men to operate the complicated equipment. The pendulum began to swing toward machines and quality manpower. The professional again became the key to military success.

MODERN APPLICATION OF THE CITIZEN ARMY

With the advent of the Cold War and the necessity of maintaining a peacetime military establishment numbering over two and a half million strong, it was found that military service with its meager emoluments and low prestige failed to attract enough volunteers to fill out the ranks. The draft was reinstituted and is now the major coercive force behind recruitment. Here again, is the citizen army at work although its purpose is far from that conceived by our forefathers. Today almost everyone prefers an army of volunteer regulars, but adequate numbers of volunteers (other than those who take the Air Force, Navy or Marine choice to avoid conscription into the Army) are just not to be had.

The traditional citizen military establishment is the National Guard and reserve forces which today number just over a million men.[5] It is no longer contemplated that these reservists will protect the country against an unlikely political usurpation by the two and one-half million regular forces. The inactive National Guard and reserves are simply a reserve pool of partially trained manpower available for an emergency such as Korea in 1950 and Berlin in 1961.

It appears that the day is past when every male citizen needs to be drilled as a soldier as Thomas Jefferson envisioned when he said "We must train and classify the whole of our male citizens. . . ." But so that all citizens become aware of the vital military aspects of national life, and to create greater affinity and empathy between citizen and soldier, it might still be wise, as Jefferson recommended, "to make military instruction a regular part of collegiate education." [6] The American public has shown little studious interest in military affairs and discounts the necessity of the military role in national life even though maintaining over one percent of its population in uniform. Other than its interest in foreign affairs, the public pushes the military features of life out of its consciousness as one of the less pleasant and abnormal burdens of an otherwise orderly existence. By not attending to the disease of war in our educational institutions we will scarcely learn how to control and cure it.

To conquer war or to maintain our liberty and freedoms, it will take more than taxes for military budgets and more than acquiescence to the temporary slavery of our young men to stand guard in uniform. The complicated business of the disease of war permeates every vein of human existence and requires the application of our finest minds. Demosthenes recognized this when he pleaded with the free Athenians to awaken to the dangers of the ambitious Macedonians: "I only call upon you, Athenians, to perform on your own account those duties for which you honor strangers [he spoke] and not to surrender that part of dignity which you won through many glorious dangers. . . ." [7] The eloquence of Demosthenes could not arouse the citizens of Athens or its citizen army and the proud city succumbed to the professional phalanxes of Philip of Macedonia.

Many writers have extolled the citizen army of Switzerland and held it up as a model which not only has provided adequate protection to the country but which has been entirely subject to civilian control. Fredrick Martin Stern [8] is one of the more recent exponents of this system of national defense. Arguments of this sort begin with the implicit assumption that a professional army is *not* composed of citizens. The usual assertion is also made, of course, that a professional army is unreliable and dangerous to democratic institutions. Seldom are distinctions made between professional armies in differing countries and eras, and all regular forces are suspected of aspiring to overthrow government. Histories of the French Republic, of the German Weimar Republic, of Spain, Argentina, Egypt, and other countries are offered as examples of behind-the-scenes intrigues and overt actions by which armies have influenced the political events of a country.

One major fallacy in this argument, as pointed out previously, is that all professional armies cannot be equated simply because they are professional. Each professional army has its own unique code of conduct. The professional army of the United States, for example, has been one of the greatest bulwarks against tyranny and dictatorship in the American society, not because it was apolitical but because it *believed* in American traditions. The military profession steadfastly upholds the democratic principles of our government as established by the Constitution. It is generally agreed and historically demonstrated that our armed forces are as loyal to those principles as any other organized group of citizens in the land.

The professional army of the United States as represented by Washington's Continentals was the most reliable and effective segment of our Revolutionary forces, if not of the body politic. Without it, we would not have gained our independence in the first place. Time and again throughout the history of the United States it has been the professional force which has saved the Republic. To assume that the United States military professional Army, Navy and Air Force are in any way untrustworthy institutions, hostile or unsympathetic to democracy, is completely false.

On the title page of *The Citizen Army* there is a quotation by George Washington: "When we assume the soldier, we do not lay aside the citizen." It seems likely that Washington, who loved his Continentals and spoke rather disparagingly of his short-term militia, had a professional force in mind when he made that statement. Professional soldiers were also citizens. In Washington's "Sentiment on a Peace Establishment" which he submitted to Congress after the war, his first recommendation was for a "regular and standing force." [9] It seems strange that Stern missed this salient implication.

THE REGULAR IS A CITIZEN

The members of the regular forces of the United States *are* citizens of the United States. They have the same ideals and aspirations as the grocery clerks and the college professors. They are subject to civil law. The regulars pay income tax, property tax and sales tax. They usually live with their families in a house off Main Street. Their neighbors are businessmen, firemen and newspaper correspondents. Their parents are schoolteachers, farmers, shoe clerks. These professional military men vote in national, state and local elections. So do their families. Their children go to the public schools. The professional military men attend P.T.A., contribute to the Community Chest, participate in neighborhood meetings to urge the city government to improve the sewage system. Considering this typical all-American background of military professionals it seems strange indeed that they should be treated like sub-citizens. What is at the root of the discrimination and segregation of the military professional?

HOW "DANGEROUS" IS THE REGULAR?

As we have seen, Stern echoed the American prejudice that the United States must be protected from some potentially sinister political activity of the regular forces. Only an army of amateurs, composed of part-time soldiers, is safe, he believed. In his view only such an army is a citizen army. He failed to trace the histories of irregular military bodies or review their not inconsiderable record of revolution and usurpation of authority. Nor did he note how seldom was a regular army the central force in these revolutions. Once new governments are formed, the regular armies of necessity support them. But so does every other institution of the society. A regular army is indeed a poor revolutionary force. Regular armies are also poor counter-revolutionary instruments, as witness the many abortive efforts of the *Wehrmacht* to eliminate Hitler. The great modern dictatorships of Italy, Germany and Russia were established by politicians supported by irregulars of their own choosing, whose ideals were those of the politicians and not of the established governments.

This is not to presume that a regular force cannot become a revolutionary instrument. Regular forces which reject the ideals of democracy and have no regard for a system which aspires to government by popular law may well become tools of strong men. Certainly we have seen many examples of this in the Latin American republics, not to mention General Francisco Franco's dictatorship in Spain. Less frequently do we read about the military strong men who established representative governments. Mustafa Kemal Ataturk, a professional soldier, deposed the Ottoman Sultan and Caliph in 1923 and 1924 and set up a civilian parliamentary government. His successor, Ismet Inonu, also a military professional, carried out the "will" of Ataturk by instituting a multiparty political system.[10]

In Japan, the Emperor Meiji (1868-1912), with the backing of the military, overthrew the dictatorial Tokugawa Shogunate and restored the dynasty to temporal rule, with constitutional and parliamentary civil government. In our time, General MacArthur restored civil government in Japan and abolished the military establishment entirely.

We also have seen, in more recent times, regular forces supporting Gamal Abdel Nasser overthrow the blatantly corrupt King Farouk in Egypt. And Ayub Khan in Pakistan who, backed by regulars, deposed the corrupt tyrant Iskander Mírza and restored democratic government. Freedom-loving people throughout the world in 1964 applauded the military overthrow of Communist leader Joao Goulart in Brazil to re-establish representative government. On the other hand Fidel Castro wrested his power in Cuba with the rawest kind of irregulars. The point is that regulars as often as not support good government and it is a mistake to categorize them or compare them unfavorably with reserves.

Only a superficial analysis such as the foregoing is necessary to reveal that various regular forces display different characteristics: different codes, different ideals, different traditions, different political predispositions. They cannot be packaged and weighed with generalities. They represent what their particular and distinctive customs ánd traditions have taught them. For example, in the Egyptian regular forces, the officers' clubs were and probably still are political organizations. In the United States, the officers' clubs are and always have been purely social organizations similar to community country clubs. One of the most flexible codes in the military system of the United States is that military hierarchy and social groups will not be used as an organized political force. Such would be anathema to the ideals of the American officer. Even though the military individual votes and participates in civilian activities which may have quasi-political implications, he does not use his military organization as a political tool. This was a fundamental feature of the American officer code long before it was legalized by statute.

VARIED CONCEPTIONS OF THE MILITARY

Autre pays, autre moeurs. The military has been many things to many people, from villains to heroes, from slaves to saviors, from criminals to policemen, from citizens to mercenaries. Some regard the military as a guardian class apart rather than a strong right arm corporately joined to the body politic and sharing its every function. This separation of the military from the rest of society, as we have seen, has manifested itself more often than not in modern history. But it is not necessarily the "natural" condition for armies. The Greeks, and Romans of the Republic, could not conceive of a citizen who was not a warrior for this was the *sine qua non* of citizenship. And his political rights were contingent upon his good deportment in combat. The United States' Founding Fathers had this in mind when they specified in the second amendment to the Constitution that "the right of the people to keep and bear arms shall not be infringed."

Certainly it was not expected that the American soldier become a social eunuch as many writers today recommend in the name of "professionalism." On becoming an officer a man does not and need not renounce any part of his fundamental character as an American citizen in order to become professional.[11] He simply takes on more responsibilities and subjects himself to stricter laws and standards of conduct.

As Walter Millis put it, "the United States was born in an act of violence." [12] And the Founding Fathers—Washington, Hamilton, Jefferson, Madison, Monroe—being fully conscious of this "did not regard peace as more important than national security." [13] Nevertheless, the anti-aristocratic and equalitarian temper of the times which had been fired by the pen of Thomas Paine and other pamphleteers soon drove the military officers into the background so that what residue of professionalism remained after 1783 was virtually lost by 1812 when a British general at Detroit turned loose the untrained American soldiers he had captured and let them go home because they were not dangerous.[14] The stagnation and stigma of the military profession caused a series of similar catastrophes throughout our history: At Bladensburg when 1,500 British defeated 5,400 untrained Americans,[15] resulting in the capture and burning of Washington, D. C.; at Bull Run in 1861 where Union forces retreated with casualties of only 2.7 percent whereas by the end of the war sixty-six regiments had sustained losses of over 50 percent in one battle;[16] and in Florida and Cuba where poor sanitation and a bungled supply system contributed to the great yellow fever epidemic. In the First World War neglect of the military profession delayed the United States from putting organized troops into combat until fifteen months after the declaration of war, and during the Second World War neglect of the military required us to train new troops with wooden guns.

August Comte was convinced in 1850 that war was losing out to peace and that military activity was being subordinated to commerce. The French Revolution of 1848, he concluded, was only an aberration which interrupted the final trend of the "inevitable final decadence" of war.[17] President Woodrow Wilson also believed that war was on its way out. When President Wilson heard that officers of the new Army War College were working on war plans against Germany in 1915 he heatedly directed that this activity cease at once and all officers responsible be transferred immediately from Washington. This attitude did not enhance the budding professionalism which had been encouraged by Elihu Root. Nor was professionalism advanced by the exclusion of military leaders from active participation in the negotiations at Versailles following the war when Clemenceau fulfilled his famous remark that war was too important to be left to soldiers. Clemenceau, "The Tiger," could hardly have been proud of his work at Versailles, since he later told the military in 1919 to "Be without uneasiness as regards your career—the peace we have made guarantees you ten years of conflict in Central Europe." [18] Events proved him a good prophet on this score, at least, and the peace treaty deliberations which excluded military participation became the infection for a new war.

General Pershing wanted unconditional surrender and predicted a recurrence of the war if the German army were not decisively defeated. His prediction, too, was fulfilled, and led to President Roosevelt's decision at Casablanca in 1942 for unconditional surrender of the Axis powers. The consequent decisive defeat in 1945 may account for the fact that Germany has so far revealed no significant *revanchist* tendencies. Who, then, was right in 1918—Wilson with his reasonable Fourteen Points for a negotiated peace, or Pershing with his unconditional surrender?

With the coming of nuclear warfare the conceptions of unconditional surrender and of victory have been disparaged and ridiculed with the idea that total war will bring near total destruction and death to vanquished and victor alike. This may well be, and professional soldiers have no more desire to commit suicide than do civilians, but when the chips are down there may be no choice left for either politician or soldier. One feature of war which is often overlooked by the modern "defense intellectual" is the behavior of the enemy over which our side may have little or no control. No matter how we may counsel peace and pledge that we shall never initiate nuclear war, a nuclear Pearl Harbor is a distinct possibility. Should the terrible day ever come when nuclear weapons are employed it would be better to leave the fighting and the control of war to those who understand it best. They may find means of limiting the intensity of the conflict or of ending it before all is lost. There is nothing in the military profession justifying the belief held by many that the military seek violence and total war for its own sake. This mad-dog reaction to conflict is more often associated with the unreasoning hate and revenge found in nonprofessionals who regard the enemy as the embodiment of all evil.

SOCIAL ACCOMPLISHMENTS OF THE MILITARY

Some people regard the military establishment as a wholly destructive feature of national life, a drain on the taxpayer and a drag to social progress. One could say as much for many other institutions of our society, such as fire departments, police departments and insurance companies, all of which hedge against undesirable, unplanned and unfortunate circumstances inherent to life on earth. Although the first mission of a soldier is to prepare for war in such a way as to win it in the manner desired by his country, there are many by-products of the military profession which actually contribute to social progress and well-being. We have discussed the matter of military virtues which hold to ultimate moral values, irrespective of political considerations or expediencies. A segment of society so oriented provides a rudder and a conscience to the body politic. An example of discipline is a steadying influence in an uncertain and fearful world. So, too, are examples of courage, dedication, duty and honor.

War was raging on the Western Front in Europe in 1915 when Chief of Staff Leonard Wood of the United States Army was attempting to awaken America to its need for preparedness. "In the sudden onrush of modern war," he wrote, "undeveloped military resources are of no more use than an undeveloped gold mine in Alaska would be in a panic on Wall Street," [19] He recognized the prejudices which underpinned the belief that large standing armies were a menace to civil liberties, but he was able, with the help of many enlightened citizens, such as President John Grier Hibben of Princeton University, to get the "Plattsburg movement" started. This volunteer training program was conducted by several contributing universities. In sponsoring this program Wood removed some of the onus from the military profession by reciting the many great discoveries in medicine and sanitation that had sprung from the martial field.[20]

In Puerto Rico, army doctor Bailey K. Ashford cured tropical anemia or hookworm. The lives thus saved exceeded the total killed in the war with Spain. Major Walter Reed in Cuba with associates Carrol and Lezear discovered the yellow fever mosquito. In the Philippines, army sanitation eliminated beriberi and controlled malaria. The Panama Canal was built by General Goethals after General Gorgas had made it possible with sanitary measures which dramatically cut the death rate from tropical disease. Successful military governments in Puerto Rico, Cuba and the Philippines were undertaken by the army during the most trying periods and the governments were turned over to civil leadership with well-filled treasuries.[21]

Brigadier General Adolphus W. Greely, an arctic explorer, was made Chief of the Signal Corps following the war with Spain and, assisted by Billy Mitchell of later aviation fame, built a telegraph system which linked Washington to Alaska. From the exploration of the West, to the Erie Canal, to the railroads, to electrical communications, to aviation, the military has spearheaded the way. It is the nature of military preparedness to rush ahead with social and technical developments. Not always does the profit element of business produce the necessary motivation. The adventure, romance, pride and acclaim associated with this breathtaking technical and social advance which has typified so much professional military activity in America is now being drawn off by nonmilitary activities such as NASA, CIA, and AEC. This tendency, unfortunately, is aided and abetted by the civilian superiors of the military who more often than not take the traditional view of the incompetent and "dangerous" uniformed professional.

Not all officials of government accept the remarks made by Ivan A. Getting, President of Aerospace Corporation:

> ... we need to restate the historical peacetime military role of sharing in exploring the frontiers ... now in space ... and that this sharing be on a basis of both cooperation and also some healthy competition. Let us clearly recognize that we are all Americans equally patriotic and all working for peace.[22]

The natural provinces of military activity should be restored if the
dignity and health of the profession are to be maintained.

SEARCH FOR PEACE

Rather than the management of violence, the ultimate goal of the
military is the search for peace. The approach is not through
protestations, breast beatings, toothless proclamations, fragile
treaties, appeasement or graduated surrender, although no approach
is ruled out completely, even by the military. The military approach
is, of course, circumscribed by the bounds of national sovereignty
and honor, and it specializes in the areas of national health and
strength: economic, social, spiritual, political—and military.

It is inconceivable that an American military professional could
become a member of an international military body which might
be called upon to take up arms against the United States. Central
to the American military profession is the dedication to country
which transcends any other loyalty. Without this basic dedication
the uniform is quickly stripped from its wearer. The word treason
is so ignoble as not to be uttered.

Thus does the search for peace remain in the framework of the
American society and traditions. International organization is not
ruled out, by any means. It was largely military thinking which led
to the great coalitions of the two World Wars and to the grand
alliance of the North Atlantic Treaty Organization.

Even the United Nations holds promise in military eyes as a
forum for discussing world problems and for increasing international understanding—provided member nations are sincere in these
purposes. But when international organizations are subverted to
propaganda bodies for narrow nationalistic aims, the military
regards them as unhealthy and weakening influences upon the United
States. The conception of such an international body acting as a
world government with a military force superior to any of its
member states is abhorrent to the military man. Association with
such a scheme would be organized treason by any definition of the
term. Nevertheless, I have been a witness to repeated sober discussions among senior civilian officials of a world "peace force."

Military men do not conceive of strength for its own sake but
as a guard against foreign threats to national survival. International cooperation, understanding and amity reduce such threats
and consequently the need for raw military strength. National
health and strength are of course relatively enhanced through inter-

national cooperation and amity. True military professionals seek such amicable international relations no less than do diplomats. A friendly international climate is simply the other side of the coin of national strength. But this cooperation must be bona fide and sincere. Rival countries must also seek friendly, cooperative means of international behavior. And a true world government becomes possible only when all nations willingly subscribe to the same basic philosophies of life and political organization. For Americans with their highly developed social and political cultures, this means every fundamental doctrine, from freedom of speech and press, to freely elected government by the people, to Anglo-Saxon jurisprudence, to the morality of Judo-Christian religions— and so on. These concepts must be adopted by member nations. This appears to be a long way off.

People cannot be forced to live in peace with one another by imposing upon them an all-powerful government. The different factions would soon be at one another's throats as with the bloody Moslem-Hindu civil strife in post-war India and the Jewish-Arabic conflict in the Middle East. Forcing people to climb into bed with one another is not a sure formula for peace. Marriage strife and divorce continue regardless of propinquity. The best predictor for marital bliss whether it be associated with individuals or nations, is a common pattern of ideals, customs and values. This seldom is achieved by edict and coercion.

A ruthless police state can achieve a certain kind of slavish conformity and zombi-like tranquility but this fate hardly seems preferable to nuclear war. At least in war there is a chance for victory and freedom for the few survivors.

THE GREAT CALLINGS

The three great dedicated callings of our time have been identified by Frank H. Bowles as the religious, the military and the educational.[23] These three great callings depart from other professions in that each is hierarchical in form and highly disciplined. Each has its symbols and titles of rank, each has distinctive uniforms, each has a ladder system of promotion through study and service. Material rewards are meager and advancement offers "increasing responsibilities and ever-deepening dedication." [24] Frugality and poverty seem to be endemic to these callings. Satisfaction in being "an instrument for the introduction of some new ideas or elements into the social structure," [25] according to Bowles, provides the major inspiration.

> Thus, the religious calling has introduced such great concepts as the stability of the family, the responsibility of the individual for social behavior, and the community of man in the sight of God; the military calling has introduced the idea of group responsibility for security, and as a product of military art, had developed the great profession of engineering on which so much of our contemporary society depends; while the teacher has, over generations, worked unceasingly to affirm man's insight into knowledge. . . .

Bowles noted that each of these callings has been indispensable to the development of nations and that through their discipline, altruism and organization, they have provided what stability and political order mankind enjoys today. The idea that the state is the servant of its people stems from these three callings.

The nuclear age places awful yet magnificent challenges before the military. Every aspect of professionalism must be strengthened and improved in order to accept these challenges and prevail. Security which seems so tenuous today must be regained. Every route must be travelled, every clue scrutinized, every idea studied. But since the great danger to mankind has been caused by the material development of nuclear energy it would seem logical to presume that further material development may just as likely harness the atom.

Nothing is gained by throwing up our hands and crying, "We have loosed the genie! All is lost!" It is a military responsibility to put him back in the bottle. Is the military up to this challenge?

And the American military profession must stand up to many other challenges. It must somehow achieve the same public faith and confidence that is enjoyed by the non-regular military establishments. Members of the regular profession must be restored to bona fide citizenship. The "dangerous" image must be corrected. The regulars must not step back from the pioneering of former days and from the social accomplishments which have done so much to improve their reputation. And finally, the professionals must set the standards for "Duty, Honor, Country."

CHAPTER 17

MODERN MILITARY PROFESSIONALS

Considering that the officer corps of the military is recruited from all walks of life, from almost every secondary school and college in the country, as well as from the enlisted ranks, one would reasonably surmise that military officers represent a cross section of American society. Competitive examinations in every state result in the selection of students to service academies and flying schools. Most officers come from ROTC programs conducted at state universities. It is inconceivable that the military profession could become an inbred self-perpetuating corps under these methods of selection. In fact Congress has always been particularly alert to prevent an "hereditary" or "aristocratic" officer corps from ever materializing. Since the officer corps is as representative of middle-class Americans as bacon and eggs, it stands to reason there is nothing in the background of the military officer which would tend to endanger democracy.

Janowitz wrote that "the military has never been fully at ease with this self-image of its representativeness. . . . They have also come to believe that in some respects, they are superior to the bulk of the population. More secretly than publicly, they held the self-conception of standard bearer." [1] He concluded that there must have been something in the professional soldier's social heritage to cause this. His hypothesis is supported by the study of the historian, C. S. Brown, who examined the social background of 465 generals from 1898 to 1940. [2] This study found that American generals had backgrounds similar to the business and political elite of the period. [3]

In effect, typical generals of the period under study (1898-1940) largely came from native-born, Anglo-Saxon parents of the upper middle class. But one must keep in mind that this selectivity came about over many years of service since Brown studied generals, not second lieutenants. These were the people who gradually rose to the top, just as people with somewhat similar backgrounds rose to the top in other professions. One can see nothing un-American about this phenomenon.

Moreover the officer corps would be a poor institution indeed if it did not feel itself to be superior to the general population in areas of its military expertness. Do not physicians, lawyers or educators feel superior in their own areas of specialization? One does not compete again and again in examinations of every description, win, and then feel "average." The mere fact of being selected to the officer corps after undergoing numerous competitive experiences, both academic and physical, would reasonably lead one to believe that he is somewhat superior to those who failed. If not, why go through the exercise?

The schooling which follows for an officer is vigorous and demanding. One out of four or five fall by the wayside. Even after being commissioned, schooling continues with 12 percent of the officer's career spent in formal military training. Is it any wonder that an officer feels better prepared than the average citizen to solve problems of national defense? This is his special field of endeavor, the heart of his profession for which he prepares himself with a lifetime of study.

One concern of those who are particularly antimilitary is that the uniformed men might develop a self-perpetuating elite by recruiting an excessive number of sons of professionals. Brown's study suggests that these fears are groundless. The amount of self-recruitment in the Army was 11 percent in 1950. For the Navy, 7 percent, and for the Air Force, 5 percent.[4] Since self-recruitment at West Point for 1960 (25 percent) compares with self-recruiting in the medical profession (20 percent) [5] it might be assumed that self-recruitment in the military is about the same as that for other professions.

In a sample of 113 officers Janowitz found that more than 80 percent would not choose the military profession if they had it to do over again.[6] The fact that about 72 percent of these same officers would like their sons to follow a military career does not necessarily belie their fundamental dissatisfaction with a military career (as it is and as it has been) but rather suggests some hope for improvement in the future.

Janowitz made some interesting comparisons on self-recruiting from records of the German *Wehrmacht*. Among senior German generals from 1911 to 1945, self-recruitment ranged from 50 to 30 percent, with the lower figure standing when the *Wehrmacht* was destroyed in 1945. This supports the theory of a self-perpetuating general staff corps throughout the *Wehrmacht* and demonstrates the measure of Hitler's success in destroying it. Certainly nothing like this self-perpetuating heritage has ever occurred in the American military services.

In summary, Janowitz finds that the American military elite has been drawn from "an old-family Anglo-Saxon, Protestant, rural, upper middle-class professional background." [7] There seems to be nothing frightening in this background picture of the average American general. It is doubtful that any other profession could come so close to representing the American norm.

LOW PRESTIGE OF THE REGULARS

Perhaps the very average background of American military leaders to some degree causes the military profession to be regarded as a poor career choice. Seldom do teachers and professors urge their students to pursue a military life, whereas law, medicine and business enjoy high prestige and young people everywhere are enthusiastically encouraged into these fields.

Janowitz suggests that the liberal ideology which holds war to be evil and superficially associates the profession with war contributes to the low prestige of the military as a career choice. The best minds, goes this twisted reasoning, are attracted to constructive rather than destructive professions.[8] One does not spend thirty years in the military profession without coming into contact with numerous manifestations of this "liberal" philosophy. Teachers and professors seem to be the ringleaders in holding the military profession in low repute, and their influence is widespread and self-perpetuating. A little reflection might cause them to see that associating the military with the causes of war may be little more justified than associating physicians with the causes of disease, or lawyers with the causes of crime.

The general impression persists, moreover, that the intellectual level of the military profession is somewhat lower than that of other professions. Recent comparisons, however, which have been made between service academy students and students at civilian institutions of higher education, fail to support this impression. The average intelligence quotients of military students have been found to be significantly higher than the average of students at the same grade level in civilian colleges.[9]

The military professional himself is not immune to the low esteem in which his profession is held by the American public, particularly now that he is mingling more intimately with civilians. Perhaps this is one reason why resignations are rising in the military. In the interim between World Wars I and II resignations of West Point graduates increased 2.4 percent (from 12.5 to 14.9). More recently resignations of officers, five years after graduation, ran between 20 and 25 percent.[10]

For the new Air Force Academy, losses of first year cadets rose from 14.1 percent in 1955 to 20.8 percent in 1961.[11] Not only does this heavy attrition waste public funds, but the objective of providing professional officers for defense suffers.

INDOCTRINATION OF CIVIL SUPREMACY

Janowitz noted that military academy education has been marked by the inculcation of the acceptance of civilian supremacy and that the cadets are thus led away from the political dimension of warfare. He concludes that this narrow emphasis on military history as opposed to political history has produced a political indifference, if not conservatism.[12] The conclusion of conservatism seems rather loosely drawn; however, it is well established that no group is more firmly dedicated to the concept of civilian supremacy over the military than is the military itself.

Civilian supremacy is regarded by the military as a political supremacy, not a tactical, technical or professional supremacy. For instance, it has always been regarded as improper, if not illegal, for civilians to command military units. But when civil administrators are given such sweeping authorities over military forces that traditional prerogatives of military command are usurped then it is conceivable that civilian supremacy has exceeded its traditional bounds and instead has become improper military command by amateurs who are neither subject to the military code nor to military justice. Thus civilian "commanders" can hide behind their civilian status and not be held accountable for their actions. The intervening military officer, powerless to decide, becomes no more than a fall guy when the civilian's plans go wrong.

A vivid illustration of this usurpation of military command by civilian direction from Washington, and the dire consequences, can be found in the Viet Cong victory at Bien Hoa Air Base on November 1, 1964. A small guerrilla mortar unit succeeded in destroying twenty-seven United States and South Vietnamese aircraft, killing four Americans and wounding thirty-one, all in a space of less than thirty minutes. After the Gulf of Tonkin crisis in August of 1964 about forty B-57 jet bombers had been flown into South Vietnam. Since the B-57's had never been used, but instead were left jammed together on crowded and inadequately protected airfields, one can surmise with some confidence that this move was a "signal" to Hanoi from Washington and a movement of military forces by civil administrators in the Pentagon. Certainly no military leader in his right mind would have left B-57's so exposed month after month when their range of operation would have permitted them to be based well out of the danger zone. Of twenty B-57's at Bien Hoa, five were destroyed, and the American public was mollified by being told that the jets would be "immediately replaced." Since the B-57 bombers had never been used, replacement was hardly the issue. And the "signal" had *not* been received loud and clear by Hanoi.[13]

It is further noted by Janowitz, and correctly so, that cadets have not been indoctrinated with the concept that civilian administrative supervision of the military establishment is fitting and proper.[14] The military services had traditionally administered their own departments until the creation of the Department of Defense in 1947. Moreover the self-administration of the military had been at least as efficient as that of other departments in the Executive Branch. Political and policy supervision by the service Secretaries provided an adequate expression of civilian control, and the civilian superiority under this former system had never been threatened.

With the creation of the Office of the Secretary of Defense, however, increasing direct administrative supervision was imposed upon the uniformed services. The true and announced purpose of this was to achieve more coordination between the separate services rather than to achieve, for its own sake, more firm civilian control. But the original purpose has been forgotten by many analysts such as Janowitz who regard the reason for this strong civilian administration as an extension of the civilian control premise.

POLITICAL INFLUENCE OF REGULARS

Janowitz also suggests incorrectly that the military profession is a pressure group "on its own behalf for more appropriations." [15] The common definition of a pressure group is a body which is politically organized in such a way as to have some influence over elections. Thus a lobbyist for a pressure group can exert influence on the elected representatives of those who are involved with the issues in question. Even appointed officials must pay attention to pressure groups which have propaganda outlets and powerful political connections.

The regular military meets none of these criteria which define a pressure group. Of course its members have the franchise from the various states where they claim residence, but public discussion on political matters, political talks, political clubs or any other form of political activity is strictly taboo. As we have noted earlier, political activity in the military is not only contrary to the military code, it is illegal. Rarely, moreover, is the kind of subrosa political activity sometimes found among government civilian employees (where such activity is equally illegal) practiced in the military.

Budget requests of the military are computed by the various service headquarters after careful study of strategic and force level requirements. These requests, after being grouped in various weapon system "program packages" by the Joint Staff, are passed to the Office of the Secretary of Defense who in recent years has made numerous alterations before forwarding the requests to Congress. It is natural and proper for the respective services to object to cuts which they feel will endanger national security and it is reasonable to assume that the professional military judgment of the requirements for certain weapon systems is sound. But there is no "pressure" being brought to bear on anyone when service leaders speak out unless it is the pressure applied by Defense administrators on the military spokesmen themselves. Usually the military spokesmen are asked for their opinions by Congressional committees and other proper authority; military men seldom volunteer their candid views in opposition to civil authority. When unclassified, budget figures and requests for various weapon systems are freely debated in the press. This can sometimes bring pressure on civil administrators as with the TFX debates but the process can hardly be called a military lobby.

Such legislative activity is nowhere similar to that of the organized pressure groups. It is simply the democratic process in action. Should the decision in Congress go against the desires of a particular service, no pressure whatsoever could be brought to bear by that service on the Congressmen involved.

No doubt the regular military services would be better represented in Congress, be accorded a higher place in the political scene, and be listened to more intently if they were organized in such a way as to exert some political pressures, although this idea is anathema, if not repugnant, to the military ethos. The regular services have long held in low regard the political activities of the reserves and the National Guard, but through their political efforts the reserve components have achieved much favorable legislation: legislation from which the regular establishments often have been excluded. Regulars grouse about the superior emoluments and benefits of the reserve components and of the civil servants but seldom move to correct these inequities. Sulking and complaining that they are not appreciated is hardly a substitute for positive political action which is the approach taken by every other element of our government and our society.

At first blush it might seem that a politically oriented regular military establishment could become such a powerful force, controlling up to two and a half million votes, as to threaten the very existence of democratic government. One must keep in mind that the military services are highly disciplined institutions and conceivably could mobilize a block of votes great enough to swing a national election. The specter of a *Praetorian Guard* determining the elected head of our country would take on more substance, although it might be difficult to compare military men voting as citizens with an all powerful palace guard. Moreover, at most, military votes would amount to less than two percent of those cast.

But the possibility of military rule is not one we can throw aside lightly. However its materialization is more likely to come from another quarter altogether. It is not inconceivable that, with continued degradation of the military profession and continued tightening of the so-called civilian control, the national defense posture of this country would fall into such a deplorable state as to cause a violent foreign, if not domestic, reaction. Postulating a time of great danger, it would not seem unlikely that ambitious or frightened civilian leaders would push disillusioned military men into high positions of government. Not since the dark days of the Revolution when Congress granted Washington dictatorial power has the United States truly faced imminent disaster with its back against the wall. In fear of such a national disaster and with dire concern over second-rate weapons which are believed incapable of defending the country, customary civilian government might be set aside. A politico-military state would thus be born. This is a pattern which has been followed all too frequently by other countries and we would be short-sighted if not supercilious to suggest that the United States is above such a response to national crisis. Recently we have seen this happen in the United Arab Republic, the Sudan, Pakistan, Iraq, Turkey, Korea, Burma, Thailand, South Vietnam, France and Brazil.

PAY OF THE MILITARY

In the United States the military is made to look and feel like a class apart because of the substandard pay given to all ranks. This was not as evident in the past when the military was relatively isolated on posts and bases where the disparity between military salaries and those of private life was not so noticeable. But today, with the military largely mixed with the civilian society, even with civil servants working alongside, over and under uniformed men, the pay differential is embarrassingly painful to the men in uniform.

Military salaries are far below the national norms and the gap is growing progressively greater each year. Military professionals have thus become second-class citizens. Pride is destroyed, volunteers fail to materialize and spaces must be filled more and more with the coercive draft. Simply in order to exist military professionals are faced with the necessity of moonlighting with extra civilian-type jobs, from teaching night school to driving taxis. The incomprehensibly expensive and complicated modern military weapons and equipment are being manned by men who understand their jobs only partially because of the high turnover. Soldiers are growing less motivated to study and learn unless it is for the purpose of getting a job on the outside at much higher salary.

A major effort to adjust military pay with pay in other sectors of the national economy was attempted in 1958 as a result of the Cordiner Committee studies.[16] Neither the Secretary of Defense nor the Congress came up to the marks recommended by the Cordiner Committee and the military services remained underpaid, maintained by forced conscription.

Not until 1963 was there further military pay legislation and by then the military pay had dropped much further below the national averages for similar work in civilian life. Quarters allowances were increased in January 1963 but were based upon 1960 Federal Housing Administration statistics which were out of date even then and now bear little relation to reality in our expanding economy. The base pay increases authorized in October of 1963 failed to approach the national norms, while the 2.5 percent increase in September 1964 was no more than a token raise, particularly after a civilian pay bill was passed in August of that year granting a 5 percent increase to 1.8 million federal employees whose salaries already far exceeded those of the military for comparable jobs.

Thanks to the persistence of Representative L. Mendel Rivers, Chairman of the House Armed Services Committee, who introduced a bill which gave servicemen an average raise of 10 per cent as opposed to a Department of Defense bill which recommended less than half as much, an improvement in the military pay structure was made in September, 1965. But servicemen still have a long way to go to reach parity with civilians.

In the United States the standard of living is rising about three times as fast as the Consumers Price Index. Since the computation of the 1958 pay rates, the Consumer Price Index has risen 9.5 percent. For the same period the Bureau of Census and Bureau of Labor Statistics surveys of salaries in industry reveal a standard of living increase of 28 percent. On top of this, so-called fringe benefits in private enterprise were moving up at the rate of one percent each year while the comparable benefits for military men were whittled away. Yet military pay has failed to keep pace even with the cost of living as measured by the Consumer Price Index, let alone keep up with the increasing standard of living. In sum, military people not only are not sharing in the rising standard of living, their net take-home pay is steadily diminishing from an already substandard level.

Let us look at some examples: A second lieutenant in early 1965 made an annual salary of $2,892, base pay, when he first donned his uniform. Quarters and subsistence allowances brought this up to $4,790. Civilians with Bachelor's degrees in engineering and no experience commanded Civil Service salaries of from $5,990 to $7,050. On the outside the average starting salary was $6,925. The Rivers Bill passed in August 1965 raised the second lieutenant's salary $53.40 per month [17] but he still makes much less than his civilian counterpart.

In the upper income bracket the disparity is even greater. It is difficult to comprehend how the annual salaries of upper-career Federal employees could be increased as much as $9,000 while military grades were increased only $1,500 in the six years before passage of the Rivers Bill. This was the disparity between Brigadier General and GS-16. Civil Service salaries through GS-15 averaged

17.6 percent over military salaries, but this did not include the superior civilian fringe benefits such as retirement, overtime, etc., nor the lack of restrictions which a military man suffers because of his special legal status, and the vital importance and danger of his daily work. If these features of the two government services were considered from the standpoint of justice, the military man's salary should be considerably higher. Yet the opposite holds true. Is this because civil servants are more active politically? Because they have a union? [18]

Let us look at a comparison of fringe benefits revealed as a consequence of the submarine Thresher tragedy. A widow of a GS-14 who perished on board received a total of $40,000 plus $525 per month. The widow of the commanding officer, a lieutenant commander with twelve years' service, received only $3,000 death gratuity, plus between $178 and $432 per month depending on children's and mother's ages. Is this justice? Which man's job was more dangerous? More demanding? More exacting?

Continuation of these short-sighted and profligate military pay policies is destroying military morale. Military careerists are becoming embittered at the obvious injustices. The injury to the country is not only reflected in the large numbers who are resigning and failing to reenlist, or even in the reduced effectiveness of our armed forces, but a large section of our population is growing cynical of the good faith of a once great and just country.[19] Foreign aid to pay allied military men, and military hardware, receive a higher priority than pay for our own men.

MILITARY STANDARD OF LIVING

National neglect of the military profession is starkly reflected in the steady decrease of the standard of living within the services as compared to the country's norms. Janowitz wrote, "There is a widespread belief among military professionals that their standard of living has not been adequately maintained since the end of World War II. They are beset by a sense of subjective deprivation, and feel that the material welfare of the rest of society is somehow advancing more rapidly than is their own." [20] This is more than a "belief" as Janowitz so condescendingly puts it. As we have noted above, it is a hard, cold statistical fact and has been pointed up with figures in one pay study after another. An Air Force study of this sort[21] noted, among many other startling pay discrepancies between military and civilian, that 8,000 airmen were qualified in the theoretical poverty level as defined by the President's Council of Economic Advisers, and that 71,000 heads of families were supplementing pay with off-duty employment. Other services were, of course, equally affected.

As a new second lieutenant in 1935 I was assigned to Hamilton Field, California, a beautiful community which had just been built. Quarters of Spanish design were completely modern, spacious and attractive. Although my salary was barely $200 per month including flying pay (50 percent of a month's base pay which was $125), at least the well-built and attractively landscaped quarters were a source of pride.

Twenty-six years, two wars and 5,000 flying hours later I was assigned to Stewart AFB, N.Y., this time as a major general in command of an air division. Again, new quarters were assigned— the best set of quarters in a large Capehart on-base housing development. Congressional restrictions on the amount that could be spent for each set of quarters ($16,000), together with numerous other restrictive regulations, specifications and contracting procedures resulted in houses of a quality that will result in their becoming veritable slum dwellings within a few years. The house assigned to me—the senior officer present—was grossly inferior to the quarters which I had been assigned at Hamilton Field twenty-six years earlier as a second lieutenant. When the opportunity presented itself to inspect my old quarters on Hamilton Air Force Base I found that this old dwelling was still far superior to the new general's set at Stewart Air Force Base. This is presented as another concrete example of how the military standard of living has deteriorated.

Degradation of the living standards is hardly something which will instill pride in military service, particularly when the standards in civilian life have taken the opposite, upward turn. The spreading gap between the military standard of living and the affluent civilian society presents an invidious comparison. The net result has been a growing pessimism within the military, increased resignations, low reenlistment rates and an exorbitantly costly turnover of personnel.

The following table showing percentages of reenlistments illustrates this point:

| | Fiscal Years [23] | | | |
	1962	1963	1964	1965
Army	52	51	50	46
Navy	49	46	41	36
Air Force	69	67	63	61
Marine Corps	43	35	30	29

So-called compensations in social prestige of the military have not been demonstrated. As the services grew during World War II and remained large during the extended Cold War, the public regard for men in uniform has lessened. The post-World War II military has lost much of its exclusiveness, its autonomy, its glamour, its adventure and its excitement. The profession has become more like a big busines or trade. Huntington makes professionals shudder by calling it a "craft."

It is no secret that in the United States membership in the upper class is based upon wealth rather than upon public service, and the military profession provides no path to wealth. In our capitalistic society prestige and affluence go hand in hand. Perhaps it is for this reason that the more powerful appointive positions in the Department of Defense are reserved for civilians regardless of their knowledge or skill in the specialty of defense. With few exceptions, only civilians acquire the wealth which places them in the upper class—the "power elite," as it has sometimes been dubbed.

PROFESSIONALS VERSUS AMATEURS

Battles have been won and lost by all manner of soldiers: from raw levies to seasoned professionals, from unpaid mobs to handsomely remunerated veterans, from unorganized rabble to highly disciplined troops. It is difficult to generalize on the relative merits of the amateur and the professional soldier by simply tabulating won and lost battles. Each has prevailed at various times in history. Moreover, there are always degrees of amateurism and professionalism and all armies usually have had a mixture of each in their ranks. The truth is, warfare presents so many variables that one must subjectively attempt to hold "all other things equal" in order to speculate on the value of professionalism in arms.

But the first step in analyzing military history is to reject the myths which color our judgment. War is a violently emotional phenomenon and tends to leave in its wake innumerable highly charged beliefs which often bear little resemblance to the objective conclusions which might be drawn from the military facts.

Not much time is devoted in our schools to Middle Eastern history, for example, and little respect has thus been paid to ancient Turkish military prowess. This could be due to the fact that the Ottoman Turk repeatedly subdued his Christian neighbors and, except for his inadequate logistical system, he very likely could have subjugated all Christendom. The terror generated by knowledge of the Turk's capacity extended over several centuries, and became a part of Christian folklore. Turks were despised. The word "Janissary" was used as an epithet. It was not until the first world war, when the Turks were decisively defeated, that the phrase "fought like a Turk" took on a respectable meaning. This belated recognition of Turkish military ability added prestige to the Christian victors, whereas earlier defeats were probably alibied on the basis of the Turk's unfairness or un-Christian methods.

The facts are that the Janissaries were one of the greatest bodies of professional soldiers in history and the four-century dominance of Turkey in the Middle East was largely the result of her well-disciplined Janissary *Ortas*. True, the Janissary eventually degenerated into a rioting and corrupt palace guard which had to be destroyed in 1826. But it would be a mistake to judge this professional corps entirely by its despicable behavior in its dying years. It would be as erroneous to do this as it would be to judge Roman legions by their conduct during the 4th century A.D.[24]

The erroneous assessment of the Janissaries is just one more myth which has helped to amplify the Anglo-American objection to professional armies. Although historians usually conclude that professional forces present an internal political danger and are prone to gain control of the state, military history does not suggest this conclusion. Regardless of the oft-quoted examples of the Roman Praetorian Guard and the Janissaries, military history reveals that most of the truly professional armies seemed to have no political aspirations whatsoever.

Xenophon's Ten Thousand Greek professionals in the Persian pay, and Alexander the Great's professionals, never made a bid for political power. Innumerable mercenary forces of the period between 1300 to 1800 were rarely a threat to the states that hired them. The Italian *Condottieri*, the Swiss Guard (acknowledged champions of Europe), the German *Landsknechts*, and the Spanish phalanxes which under Charles V outdid Charlemagne in the extent of their conquests—none of these professional forces became a threat to royal power. In fact, the contrary was true. These professional troops strengthened the state of their origin and brought money to its coffers.

The marked preference in the United States for the amateur citizen-soldier is today demonstrated in the composition of our armed forces and in the Pentagon civilian headquarters. Strangely, this aversion to a regular establishment is still being justified on the basis of the potential danger of setting up a Praetorian Guard. The bogy of an all-powerful "military-industrial complex" is another fear although it is difficult to visualize why Department of Defense civilians, many more of whom have political and financial connections than do military leaders, would be less susceptible to the blandishments of big business.

CONSCRIPTION

The deep feeling against the military in America was influenced to some extent by the conscription system which began to appear in Europe during the 19th century. To escape compulsory service, Europeans migrated to America. Obviously, anything military became repulsive to these immigrants and to their descendants. Yet the nation-in-arms philosophy of war inaugurated by Napoleon, indoctrinated by von Clausewitz, and made increasingly possible by the Industrial Revolution which provided logistical feasibility to mass armies—this new doctrine of war made conscription a military necessity even in America. Immigrants unhappily learned the doctrine had jumped the Atlantic. The American Civil War found us in a domestic struggle and, by military necessity, reluctantly getting into step with the mass doctrine of war. The South soon adopted conscription, while in 1863 the North followed suit. The unpopularity of this measure was demonstrated by the New York riots, the corruption of substitutions, the bought exemptions, and the murders of federal draft agents.

After the Civil War we reverted to our Indian Summer isolation (except for a brief naval war with Spain), until the harsh reality of the mass doctrine again struck us in 1914. But before we began to fight in 1917 we had time to write and pass a good draft law which obviated the evils of the Civil War draft. (It might be noted here that this law was a consequence of objective military study.) Great land armies were essential to victory on the Western Front. Thus America finally succumbed to the full consequences of the Napoleonic concept of the *levee en masse*. But it is wrong to suggest as many do that this Napoleonic doctrine was inspired by democratic ideals.

Blackstone called professional soldiering a species of slavery,[25] but he would have been more accurate to say that conscription which compels a man to serve regardless of his wishes is the very essence of slavery. To gain acceptance of conscription, the public was told again and again that it was a democratic measure. The

Swiss democracy with its conscription was held up as a shining example. And Americans were led to believe that the obligation of every citizen to serve his country as a soldier was established by the citizen-armies of the ancient Athenian republic.

The catch was that the Swiss and the Athenians *wanted* to serve in the military. They considered it no obligation, but a distinct privilege. Thus there was no coercion, no slavery. Swiss mercenaries had made military service so attractive that Swiss boys yearned to be trained as soldiers. And the classic Athenians served in the military to qualify as citizens. This was a high honor, for citizens were an elite minority. So in each example, the full picture was not given, and the comparison was somewhat erroneous.

Americans were not enthusiastic about conscription in the first world war. Over one-quarter of a million were draft dodgers. Military service was considered no privilege. Although patriotic fervor led to a million enlistments, there were few who wished to remain in the service on the completion of hostilities. And there is no way of knowing how many volunteered, as they do today, because they felt the draft was inevitable and by volunteering they might gain some special advantages.

Conscription (now called by the euphemistic term Selective Service) was introduced again in 1940 and has continued to this day with a sort of public resignation to the inevitable. Better administrative methods were adopted and more publicity on the "obligation" was disseminated, so that the system has been generally accepted as a necessity. Few regard the draft as an obligation of citizenship and the individual caught in its clutches seldom considers it an exercise in freedom and democracy.

The point is, that conscription has been less a democratic measure than it has been a military necessity to preserve an otherwise democratic society. And if nationwide conscription were considered democratic, it would follow that the obverse, a voluntary professional military, would be undemocratic. Thus one error in logic generates another. Today, now that the long-haul policy and complicated weapons place greater military emphasis on professionalism, people continue to regard professionalism as undemocratic.

But of vital moment to America is the increase of military effectiveness that would come from a wholly voluntary force. When the Athenian citizens grew tired of war after the long contest with Sparta, and their independent spirit turned against military service in the golden age of Pericles, the hardier Macedonians under Philip quickly subdued them. In this short struggle the admired human qualities of freedom, democracy and individuality held no military advantages for Athens. Could the United States be at this turning point in its own history? Certainly conscription, as opposed to enthusiastic volunteering, contributes to the deterioration of America's military profession and its defense posture. The double-think postulation that conscription is democratic may be even more harmful to our traditions of free citizenship.

It is vividly clear that our young conscripts have no taste for military service. Compulsion will not make them good soldiers in peacetime. In wartime, with the flags flying and the bands playing, they become inspired and willing, but they are still woefully short on training and thus subject to a hazardous life expectancy. But in peacetime, when their brothers are getting fat jobs in the civilian economy, our young conscripts look upon military service as purgatory, nothing less.

We cannot compare the conscript soldier of today with the Dutch amateurs under Maurice of Nassau who whipped the professional Spanish phalanx, nor with the American doughboys in the Argonne who cracked the Hindenburg line, nor with the Schwienfurt air crews. These were zealots fighting for a noble cause. We saw cynicism first demonstrated by defections among our men in Korean prison camps. Today the average American in service is uninspired. He is held in service by force of law and threat of punishment. He is no crusader. He is chained.

DISINTEGRATION OF PROFESSIONALS

There was a period in the history of France when the lot of the soldier sank to a very low level with disastrous consequences. Following the Thirty Years' War, as we have seen, princes fought to settle dynastic questions. Plunder and pillage were forbidden because conquest was for the purpose of acquiring productive land. The soldiers, deprived of this traditional bounty, could hardly live on their meager pay, and recruits were drawn from the lower strata of society. Armies filled up with the worst dregs of the countryside and towns. Such professional forces were easily defeated by the French mobs in the revolution of 1789. In this case an inadequate professional standing army was not only no threat to the state, but it failed to protect the state from mob uprisings.

Conscription, by its very nature, fosters a discontent *within* the armed forces. We have been lucky so far in experiencing no serious consequences of this discontent, although the not too honorable behavior of our Korean prisoners of war may be traced to this questioning attitude toward our military policy. True, professionals as well as conscripts broke down under Communist torture, but professionals are by no means immune to the attitudes which the conscription system causes. The high rates of professional retirements and resignations, and the phenomenally low reenlistment rates, all attest to this. Not until service life can be made attractive enough voluntarily to recruit able young men in necessary numbers, to provide fulfilling careers, and to instill pride in service will an adequate professional force become possible.

Present policies, therefore, are not likely to result in any marked broadening or deepening of the military profession. And it is seriously open to question whether our security interests are best served in this manner. Although all citizens should understand war to that degree necessary for judging the military policy which protects them, and all should be obliged to serve their country in some way according to the capacity of each, it is no longer necessary or desirable for every able-bodied man to become a soldier with a rifle. The *levee en masse* is a tactic of history. Conventional limited wars should require no general mobilization of manpower.

There can be no question but that professional forces are more skilled in the job of war, and in these modern days of complicated weaponry, skill is a salient consideration. Furthermore, professionals by virtue of voluntarily taking the "queen's shilling" tend to be more committed to and less critical of the military missions handed them by civil authorities. And as for the danger of professionals seizing civil power, this myth should be laid away with other old wives' tales.

FUTURE OF THE RESERVES

Modern war can provide innumerable critical assignments for the part-time soldier but few of these assignments are in the peacetime standing forces which must be ready and fully trained for instant action. On the other hand, the part-time soldier's assignments should not take him far from home, simply because the demands of modern war will be immediate and there should be many bona fide defense tasks to perform in his own neighborhood.

Every city, missile site, and airfield must have a close-in ground and air defense. Guerilla warfare and sabotage must be controlled. Guard and reserve units could be prepared to provide much of this local defense. Anti-aircraft and antimissile defenses must be manned along with interceptor fighters. Electronic early warning systems can best be operated by Guardsmen and reservists.

Every city must have an elaborate civil defense system ready to go into operation on a moment's notice. The local part-time soldier should assume this responsibility. He should not look upon civil defense as something beneath his dignity. It is hard to conceive of a more significant military task than that of saving thousands of lives at home.

CHAPTER 18

INVASION BY "DEFENSE INTELLECTUALS"

The greatest threat to the military profession occurred with the strategic revolution of 1961. For some reason which has yet to be adequately explained, a vast surge of military literature was produced in the decade of the 1950's by so-called "defense intellectuals." Almost none of these prophets of nuclear doom were of the military profession although a good number of them had been handsomely paid for research and development work by military contracts. The Air Force-financed RAND Corporation, for example, was an influential leader in this field. It is indeed ironical that the scientific research organization established to assist the Air Force in the solution of its post-war problems was instrumental in creating the greatest problem ever faced by the Air Force—that of its imminent extinction as a separate air arm.

Other think factories in a variety of shapes have blossomed throughout the land. Patterned after RAND, the Army established the Research Analysis Corporation (RAC), while the Navy sponsored the Operation Evaluation Group at MIT. The Weapon System Evaluation Group (WSEG) originally of the Joint Chiefs of Staff but later captured by the civilian office of the Director of Defense Research and Engineering (DDR and E) sponsored the contract think factory of the Institute for Defense Analysis (IDA). These rather famous groups are supplemented by a plethora of other organizations most of which have an interest in some aspect of national defense. There are some 350 nonprofit corporations, over 300 college research centers, at least 1,400 industrial companies, and a large variety of foundations and advisory bodies all involved in some way with military matters.[1]

This boom in the acquisition of military knowledge has been like a modern-day gold rush. With the overwhelming problems of nuclear war facing mankind, with the sanguine philosophy that this problem can be solved if enough effort and brainpower are applied to it, with a prosperous economy which can afford this vast stimulus of thought, with contracts requiring little investment or overhead, and with a product which cannot be checked against factual criteria, it is not hard to see why the think factories have been so successful. The situation was ready-made for charlatanism. The only way quackery could have been suppressed was, as other quackery has been controlled, through the efforts and standards provided by a bona fide profession. The military profession not only failed to provide this control, it fostered a flood of quackery.

I do not wish to imply that all the studies performed in the think factories are superficial or fallacious. Indeed, a great many of them have been real contributions to the military art and national defense. But far too many have been of no value, or even harmful. And military evaluation is either superficial or disregarded.

The defense intellectuals have had a free hand. Public speculation on the art of war or its consequences in the nuclear age has been denied the military professional because of the "civilian control" policies established in the Office of the Secretary of Defense regarding the clearance of manuscripts for publication or speeches. The military "gag" is and has been a real and effective policy regardless of how it may have been whitewashed.[2] Consequently many fallacious and amateurish military studies by the "intellectuals" more often than not go unchallenged in the public press.

RATIONALE OF THE DEFENSE INTELLECTUAL

The major premise of the defense intellectual is simply that nuclear war will be too devastating to engage in. That victory is impossible. That only a holocaust would result and the winner would suffer as much as the loser. Ergo, some alternative to nuclear war must be found.

This is the same premise used by pacifists throughout the ages except that now the cataclysmic drama of nuclear explosives and intercontinental ballistic missiles has made the proposition much more believable. The prophets of doom have convinced most of the modern world that nuclear war will write finis to civilization.

Because military men are not so quick to jump to this fashionable conclusion they are unmercifully branded by the defense intellectuals as simply too stupid to understand the problem. The vitriolic Raymond D. Senter put it this way:

Unless the military professional more quickly grasps the true meaning of the quantum jump in the gradient of warfare that has resulted from thermonuclear-tipped missiles and adapts to it, he is likely to become its victim rather than its beneficiary as he now imagines.[3]

Senter goes on to say that "top military leaders reveal clearly that they are unable to escape the rigidity of their traditional training and narrow service loyalties, as the dinosaur was unable to adapt to its new environment." Such remarks are typical views of the new defense intellectual who has invaded and all but captured the military profession. It is not strange that Senter chooses to use a pseudonym because few of his stamp are so indiscreet as to reveal their true feelings. Senter's arrogance is only exceeded by his obvious ignorance of military matters. For example, he writes that the reason Air Force pilots flew obsolete B-26's in South Vietnam was because the Air Force had not developed non-nuclear tactical aircraft. Since quite modern Air Force wings of F-100 and F-105 tactical fighter-bombers were stationed in the Philippines, Okinawa and Japan, there must have been another reason for using B-26's in South Vietnam. Senter would have known this if he had been alert to what was going on there and most certainly if he presumed to set himself up as a critic of national policy. As a matter of fact, the reason for using B-26's was entirely political. It was believed at that time by civilian leaders that Air Force jets would be provocative.

The defense intellectuals believe that the present period in history is so unique that experience and history provide an inadequate guide to prediction. As Huntington puts it, "Without rejecting the worth of historical interpretation [which they obviously do], they emphasize the total nature of potential destruction and the technological basis of modern armed services and thus justify not only the application of theoretical, as well as experimental, techniques of analysis and evaluation, but also the search for alternatives to conflict through systems of deterrence and arms control." [4] Reduced to the military man's vocabulary which Senter says is an indication of "the depth of his thinking," what Huntington means is that the problem of nuclear war is so difficult that we are better off in a dream world of speculation than in the factual world of experience. The defense intellectual may deceive himself and the public by this flight from reality but the military man must face the problem squarely. He is a man of responsibility who cannot indulge in the fantasies of intuition which seek new "alternatives" to a problem which the experience of history has shown to have a clear if difficult solution.

Colonel Ardant du Picq, the French military philosopher who was killed in combat near Metz in 1870, analyzed the defense intellectual of classical times: "The Greeks were," he wrote, "an intellectual civilization superior to the Romans. Consequently their tactics ought to have been more rational. Such was not the case. Greek tactics proceeded from mathematical reasoning—Roman tactics from a profound knowledge of men's hearts." [5]

DISPARAGEMENT OF MILITARY LEADERS

Senter criticizes former Chief of Staff of the Air Force Thomas D. White for "applying the traditional clichés of the past to the new gradient of warfare." The clichés he refers to are expressed in General White's sentence, "Should the United States be required to use its military forces, however, they must be strong enough to achieve victory." [6] The mere mention of "victory" in the concept of nuclear warfare strikes a sensitive nerve among the defense intellectuals for they conceive that nuclear warfare must never be fought, only deterred. This contradiction in terms, if not in logic, seems not to disturb them in the least. How deterrence can be dissociated from victory and defeat is an escape from reality that is seldom noted in serious literature. Senter arrogantly observes that in General White's subsequent writings for *Newsweek* magazine "there is no evidence that he has read, let alone grasped, the true implications of strategic warfare so ably set forth by Bernard Brodie in *Strategy for the Missile Age* [7] [who wrote that] 'Of future total wars we can say that winning is likely to be less ghastly than losing but whether it be by much or little we cannot know.'" Every human individual casualty, even in limited war, no doubt has the same thought. Granted as much tolerance as possible, Brodie's statement seems somewhat less than profound. But in harking on casualties, the common blind spot of the defense intellectual, both Senter and Brodie miss the central point. If there is any reason for fighting in the first place, one must win or surrender. And although winning need not necessarily imply the waging of an all out war, or even a hot war, the *objective to prevail over one's implacable enemies* is what "winning" truly means and it has little to do with the degree of suffering on one side or the other. Friction may become so heated that nuclear war bursts out, cruel as it may be. The decision may well be that of our enemy and in no way subject to our control. What do the Senters and Brodies then suggest? That we surrender in order to avoid the new "gradient of warfare" and the holocaust which it portends? One can hardly draw any other conclusion.

The charge of military myopia so commonly directed at the professionals by the defense intellectual seems to come through a red haze of fear. When fear becomes so intense that all principles can be forsaken and all the progress of Western man can be callously tossed aside, then it is time to die in any event for there is nothing much left to live for. If this be the route of progress by the "military scientist" (a flattering term used by Senter for those who are about as scientific in the military field as astrologists are in the cosmic field), then perhaps we should return to the simpler precepts of behavior preached by our forebears. Senter speaks of "blackshoe admirals" who could not grasp the value of aircraft carriers but overlooks the fact that the Navy fought the war in the Pacific to a resounding victory *with* carriers that hardly materialized out of whole cloth overnight. The long lead-time for constructing carriers would indicate that the "blackshoe admirals" had learned the lesson in time to build the fleets which could win. When Senter pontificates that the Germans were able to subdue France in 1940, because top Allied military leaders did not understand tank warfare, he overlooks the moral decay of the French army between the world wars. The French military had lost its fighting heart by succumbing to a Maginot strategy of defense, or surrender, if the going got too tough. The strategy now advocated by Senter and others sounds frighteningly familiar.

SENATOR FULBRIGHT'S VIEWS

The campaign to disparage the military received a big boost in the summer of 1961 when Senator J. W. Fulbright of Arkansas published an attack upon military officers who had been involved with anti-Communist activities for which, he declared, they were unqualified by "education, training or experience." The Senator identified the "military mind" with the far right and consigned the military profession to a status comparable to the hewers of wood and the drawers of water.[8] In the hearings which followed it was confirmed that the military were indeed attempting to educate the public on the menace of Communism through "cold war seminars" and speeches. The Special Preparedness Subcommittee of the Senate, however, concluded that "qualified military men, because of their experience and specialized knowledge, have a proper and legitimate function in this field." [9] It appears that the Preparedness Subcommittee had different views from Senator Fulbright but the harm had already been done to the military profession.

THE CLEARANCE PROBLEM

The hearings held by the Special Preparedness Subcommittee [10] during the first part of 1962 also investigated allegations that military leaders were being muzzled by censorship in the Pentagon. Many witnesses were called, both civilian and military, and the question of civil control of the military was thoroughly aired in the context of censorship by civil authority.[11]

An analysis by the subcommittee of speeches submitted to the Office of the Secretary of Defense for review seemed to indicate a certain pattern of deletions. Anti-Communist phrases were frequently cut out as were any references to the term "victory." Out of 167 speeches scrutinized by the committee, 128 had been "purified" by the Department of State, in addition to OSD censorship. It appeared that civil authorities, both in OSD and State, were exercising their prerogatives of review in order to press for a new strategy of accommodation with Communism, and that military leaders were not being permitted to voice their views even indirectly.[12] For example, in a manuscript submitted by Lt. Gen. Arthur G. Trudeau, an OSD reviewer had stricken "Sino-Soviet bloc" from this sentence: "We must make sure that our military strength is geared to cope with the *Sino-Soviet bloc* threat today and in the future." [13] In the same paper the reviewer deleted all the following: "*With Soviet infiltration menacing this nation and extending through the far corners of the globe, freedom of spirit and self stand in great jeopardy. The threat of catastrophic war again haunts the lover of liberty and the protagonist of peace. The Reds deliberately, fanatically, unceasingly, strive to destroy the shreds of stability remaining as we enter the new frontiers of the '60s. A tower of peace founded on anarchy and chaos cannot stand.*" [14]

Other typical deletions from military speeches were noted by the subcommittee as follows:

eventual victory in all phases of the cold war
and victories determined
emerge victorious
by the poisonous fumes of world communism
and to achieve victory.[15]

In testifying before this subcommittee General Eisenhower had urged that the military be permitted to speak. ". . . I question the desirability," he said "of requiring the topmost government officials, whether military or civilian to submit to censorship. . . ."[16] Although emphasizing that the military should abide by "properly established policies," the former President stressed that the military should be encouraged to speak out against Communism and help alert the country to danger.[17]

But the core of the matter was not Communism so much as the proper degree of civilian authority over the military. No senior officer who testified (all of the Joint Chiefs of Staff appeared) denied the right of civil authority to insist on conformity to national policy. But it appeared that this control was being exercised in a most stringent and belittling manner upon the topmost military leaders. They were (and are) obliged to submit any public statement to OSD for review like a callow schoolboy asking teacher to be excused. Since their statements are usually reviewed by individuals with considerably less experience, rank, or even political acumen than the military leaders themselves, the practice is to say the least, a debasement of military dignity.

Some editorials passed off this censorship as being more silly than sinister.[18] Such a superficial analysis reveals a striking naïveté of the movements afoot in America to alter our national strategy on the one hand, and to actively debase military prestige on the other. The purpose in the latter campaign is to assure that Congress and the public will disregard military advice contrary to the new strategy. Sanitizing military speeches is simply another manifestation of thought-control which is designed to mold public opinion into the new philosophy of national defense. General Eisenhower observed that military speechmakers should abide by "properly established policies," but the new strategy of parity, disarmament and accommodation with Communism are a long way from being "properly established." A properly established policy, it would seem, should have the support of the President, the Congress and the American public. Parity, disarmament, and accommodation with Communism might well represent an emerging policy being religiously plugged by many individuals within the Executive Branch of the government, but these controversial ideas have not yet become universally or authoritatively accepted. Because they are civilian and not military leaders it follows (by those who assert that civil control of the military is, like virtue, an unalloyed blessing) that these reviewers can modify military speeches to agree with the newly advocated (but less than authoritative) strategy. This is the way national military policies are born. The military are thus reduced to political eunuchs even in the area of their principal knowledge and experience.

This censorship can and does extend beyond the obviously political aspects of policy. Daniel Z. Henkin of the *Army Navy Air Force Journal and Register* [19] reported that an article submitted for clearance by Lieutenant General Garrison H. Davidson, one time West Point Superintendent, had been rejected. It might be mentioned here that for every one article cleared with deletions as discussed by the Stennis Committee, two to three articles are totally denied any clearance whatever.[20] General Davidson's article warned that "the ROAD concept reduces once proud organizations steeped in tradition, to meaningless entities." [21] The creation of the ROAD division had been pressed hard by the civilian Secretary of Defense, and General Davidson's article, which had been submitted to a professional military magazine, was deemed to be "criticism." General Davidson reflected the military code, if not the national ethic, by commenting, "I have always considered it a duty for any officer when he has constructive suggestions to make, to offer them." [22]

Similarly, a book entitled *Design for Survival* [23] by General Thomas S. Power, the former Commander of the Strategic Air Command (SAC), was denied clearance for publication in 1960.[24] Yet the civilian defense intellectuals, many of whom are employed by military contractors, were free to express their views in almost any forum by virtue of their civilian status.[25] By law, even the retired officer is not free to express his views without first subjecting his manuscript for policy clearance. Fortunately this law has never been enforced and therefore General Power's book finally has been published now that he has retired. Thus, too, was General Maxwell D. Taylor's controversial book, *The Uncertain Trumpet*,[26] published after his retirement.

Secretary of Defense McNamara said that "it is inappropriate for any member of the Defense Department to speak on subjects of foreign policy" and in May 1961 ordered all officials of the Department to "confine themselves to defense matters." [27] This edict has not seemed to apply to himself or to the senior civilians in OSD who manage the war in South Vietnam with minimal assistance from the Department of State. The policy does, however, put a tighter gag on those in the military echelon who might wish to discuss some of the tactics and strategy employed in Southeast Asia, for this comes under the headline of "foreign policy." In fact, there is seldom a military move anywhere in the world that cannot be construed as "foreign policy."

Mr. McNamara remarked before the Senate Armed Services Committee in 1961 that ". . . the military establishment is an instrument, *not a shaper,* of national policy." [28] Could any statement be more clear that the military profession is to be seen and not heard? To respond automatically to the signals of the civilian echelon on all matters whether they be related to strategy, tactics or weapons? Like the Light Brigade at Balaclava the Secretary must believe the modern soldier is not to question why. The Secretary went on to say that the military members, "as free Americans, are entitled to their views on the issues of the day, and they have every right to make their views effective through the ballot." [29] No one, I am sure, is deceived that the military men are either "free Americans," or that their views on complicated military issues can be made known through use of the ballot. How, for example, could one vote on the strategy for Berlin? Or South Vietnam? Yet few would argue with the statement of former Secretary of Defense Robert A. Lovett that "military professionals should be the *contributors* to and not the deciders of final national policies." [30] The present effort is obviously to prohibit military professionals even from making their logical contributions to national defense policies.

In 1950, before the military had lost so much status in national life, the then Secretary of the Air Force, Thomas K. Finletter, remarked:

> I must say that it seems to me that this reticence [of the military] to speak on military matters can be overdone. For there is a counter balancing right of the people, who make these military capabilities possible and who are so vitally affected by them to know the most that can be said which does not aid a possible enemy. [31]

From this it would seem that there is adequate restraint present in the military code to prevent encroachment by the military upon the policy preserves of the civilian leaders.

A STATE WITHIN A STATE

I do not wish to leave the impression that all civilians working in the Pentagon are defense intellectuals, as I have defined them, or even that they are antimilitary in outlook. Nor do I wish to imply that all of those working in the think factories can be so classified. The large majority of civilian leaders in OSD and in the defense industries are capable, sincere and effective public servants. Nevertheless, there is an elite and powerful circle which holds to the views so often found in the *Bulletin of the Atomic Scientists* and in Donald G. Brennan's famous anthology.[32] These people can be found not only in OSD but throughout the government although they naturally are attracted to agencies dealing in some way with national defense, such as the Arms Control and Disarmament Agency (ACDA), the Atomic Energy Commission (AEC), the Central Intelligence Agency (CIA), the Department of State, and the White House Staff. They speak with an uncommonly similar voice. It is not unusual to find that a proposal by a defense intellectual in one agency has been thoroughly discussed with his counterparts in other agencies so that the final government position paper has clear sailing in the coordination channel. Such informal coordination is salutory were it not that those involved use it as a tool to overcome opposition in their own departments. Thus does this government-wide circle of defense intellectuals become a sort of state within a state, attempting little by little to alter defense and foreign policy to meet their own philosophy of nuclear parity, disarmament and eventual world government.

PART V

CIVIL CONTROL

CHAPTER 19

REASONS FOR CIVIL CONTROL

We have discussed the military stereotype but the arguments usually advanced for controlling the military go somewhat deeper and are frequently referred to under the heading of the "military mind." Before getting too deeply into the matter of civil control it might be helpful to examine some of the common conceptions and misconceptions of the "military mind" which seem to be at the root of the civil (civilian) control premise.

Justice Oliver Wendell Holmes once remarked: "A man is bound to be parochial in his practice, and to give his life and, if necessary, his death for the place where he has his roots." [1]

BIASES OF OTHER PROFESSIONS

It should strike nobody as odd that Army, Navy, and Air Force officers cannot agree on the way a future war should be waged or how the Department of Defense should be organized. Members of all other professions tend to regard the world in the light of their professional learning and habits. Why should one expect military men to behave differently?

A doctor of medicine is devoted to curing illness with drugs, surgery, and other therapy. Does not he regard this as a high calling and does he not view most of mankind's problems through glasses colored with the hue of his medical knowledge and values? If any medical man should deviate from these views he would be ostracized from the profession as a quack. Because they have not concentrated on medicine and surgery it has taken decades for the psychologist and psychoanalyst to become respectable and they are still regarded with some reserve. The idea that illness might be caused by emotional disturbances ran counter to earlier medical beliefs that all illness was caused either by bacteria or by some

258

organic malfunction. Thus, to the orthodox, therapy took but two courses: drugs or surgery.

Today there are therapists who have had some success in curing defective vision with eye exercises. This deviation from respectable professional parameters, i.e., drugs, surgery, and later psychotherapy, is still regarded with some disdain by the profession.

So it goes in other professions. Let us look at business and industry. America's greatness is largely the product of the knowledge and habits acquired through the business profession. No businessman is likely to deny this statement. What businessman will not weigh the major ills of the world against business standards? Efficiency in government is judged as that administration which handles the tax dollars as would a successful corporation and promotes trade, commerce and industry. The first criterion of success is good management of government resources.

Does not the businessman attribute international problems largely to the inability of backward people to adopt American business practices? Is not a viable economy and a higher standard of living the goal of many of our foreign aid programs? This fosters business activity in accordance with American business standards.

Who would want to embrace communism if he benefitted by the high standards of living we enjoy in America? On the surface all of us are apt to agree because we, too, are guided by these same business standards. They have made a deep influence on our system of values. Few of us try to fit anomalous evidence into this pattern and there are many puzzling events which simply cannot be explained by the good-business philosophy. Why have some well-off intellectuals in our own country been influenced by communism? Gerhart Eisler, Alger Hiss, Harry Dexter White, Nathan Silvermaster and J. Robert Oppenheimer, to name a few. Why did relatively prosperous Czechoslovakia succumb to communism? And as for the depressions which are supposed to breed war, why did prosperous Nazi Germany embark upon war in 1939? And why did we and most of the world remain at peace after 1929, the year of worst depression?

Yes, there is a lot of evidence which sheds doubt on the higher-standard-of-living-through-American-business-practice panacea to the world's ills. Yet we tend to disregard this evidence because it does not fit our system of values and our habitual manner of regarding the world.

The lawyer will assert with complete conviction that universal

peace can only be achieved through due process of law. John Foster
Dulles spoke for the profession when he wrote, "World peace depends upon *world* law." [2] The jurist repeatedly speaks of a world
of law as opposed to a world of force. And since the majority of
our national leaders come from the ranks of the legal profession it
is small wonder that our national policies take up this theme. All
too often the force, the raw naked force, if you will, which makes
law possible even in the domestic sense is disregarded as an integral
and indispensable component of practical law.

The advertising expert will point out that people are swayed and
convinced not by law but by propaganda; that the legalistic approach to international politics is causing us to lose out to
communism.

What are the views held by the professional diplomat in regard
to world affairs? This professional has a rather broad and varied
background. He can often boast of legal training, but he may
come to diplomacy from the educational profession, from business,
or from other walks of life. There is even a chance that he has
served in the military. Nevertheless, the diplomat acquires a rather
common system of values with his brothers after long service in
the corps. The one word which seems to describe his highest ideal is
serenity: the art of making everything run smoothly, of preventing
or easing hurt feelings, of building prestige and respect.

Small wonder that the most significant international issues are
not always grasped. "Let the dust settle," we were advised about
China in 1947. When the dust settled communism had been well
established. "Don't rock the boat," applies to any situation that is
apparently serene, regardless of the boiling ferment beneath the
surface.

BIAS OF THE MILITARY MAN

Finally, is it any wonder that the military man regards the avail-
ability of force and its judicious application by threat and maneuver
as the prime ingredient for peace and national survival? And is it
any wonder that the military man of a certain school—Army, Navy
or Air Force—considers the major peace-keeping or war-winning
force to be that force which he understands best and which he
has been studying for most of his professional life? These differences of view are not hypocritical. They are sincerely and firmly
held; just as are the views of the physician, the businessman, the
lawyer, the advertiser and the diplomat.

There are, of course, certain professional attitudes which can sometimes be properly held up to ridicule. The apolitical one, for example, sometimes takes ridiculous extremes, as when General Peyton C. March, Chief of Staff during World War I, said that the "military profession frames entirely on its merit without any relation whatsoever to national or international politics." [3]

Much has been written of the "military mind" to justify the exclusion of military men from their just rights of citizenship and to suggest that a wholly natural military bias would somehow exclude military men from high civil posts and elected positions.[4] Justice William O. Douglas believes "the military mind is too narrow" and too highly specialized; [5] others feel that the tendency to use "the yardstick of physical power" is a pattern to be watched; still others believe the military mind views world affairs "solely in the perspective of preparedness for war and is opposed to public debate, dissent and disagreement." [6] C. L. Sulzberger recognizes "the popular suspicion of what is often referred to as 'the military mind'" and suggests that it involves formal, rigid thinking and limited knowledge of social behavior." [7] Arthur M. Schlesinger, Jr., listed an array of unwholesome characteristics of the military mind including "ignorance of ultimate moral and spiritual values." [8] One might speculate upon the consequences of such a vitriolic anti-military bias when its owner operated from the lofty eminence of the White House. And novelist John P. Marquand brands all professional soldiers with mental attitudes which must be overcome "in order to get on with the great mass of his fellow citizens." [9]

Somewhat before this widespread literary indictment of the military intellect, John J. McCloy came to the defense of the military mind in a *Harper's* article.[10] But in a conversation with me in 1961 it became obvious that Mr. McCloy, too, had succumbed to the widespread prejudice against the military intellect. In discussing the fantastic German development of the V-2 at Peenemunde during World War II, Mr. McCloy remarked that such an imaginative program would have been beyond the capacity of the military. The ballistic missile developments at Peenemunde were, in fact, military programs of the Ordnance Department of the German Army.

It might be noted here, in further defense of the military mind, that when it was decided to put the V-2 into operation the missile was known to be full of technical bugs and because of this the civilian scientists wanted to employ fixed launching sites. But the military insisted on mobile launching systems. A typical bureaucratic compromise was reached and both fixed and mobile systems were developed. According to Dr. von Braun in testimony before the United States Senate on December 17, 1957, the fixed sites were completely destroyed by allied bombing, but not one mobile launching system was hit.[11]

Seldom do military decisions which have proved correct appear in literature dealing with the "military mind" simply because most such writings are designed to stimulate the prejudice that military men are not to be trusted in positions of authority outside the highly circumscribed confines of the military establishment itself. Yet the general military sophistication engendered by the Second World War, which mobilized over ten million citizens of the United States and sent them to fight throughout the world, left a haunting suspicion, at least in the minds of most veterans, that something was wrong with this antimilitary tradition. And the military had been right about the dangers of war. They had warned of the conditions which found us in 1941 to be so grossly unprepared to cope with the real world.

It may have also surprised some opponents of the military that the uniformed professionals showed up quite well as civil administrators after the war. Military government of occupied areas was performed quietly, skillfully and, insofar as possible, in accordance with the best traditions of democracy. Generals Douglas MacArthur in Japan, Lucius B. Clay in Germany and Mark Clark in Austria were all successful administrators under most trying circumstances. The harsh, arbitrary and autocratic regulations, such as JCS 1067 which provided the initial guidance for governing our zone in Germany, originated in the civil leadership.

THE MILITARY MIND

New attacks on the military mind have been accompanied by the rise of the "defense intellectuals." Those highly confident scientists who have, in the past decade, worked on specialized military problems in the think factories, speculated learnedly in print, and sometimes graduated to high administrative posts in OSD, have somehow been threatened by the military professional and feel constrained to cut him down with ridicule. The unflattering military writings of Raymond D. Senter are typical. His enmity goes so far as to accuse uniformed services of "self-serving expansionist interests."[12]

Gene M. Lyons, director of the Public Affairs Center at Dartmouth College, who, with John W. Maseland, wrote *Education and Military Leadership*,[13] is another authority on the military mind. Lyons approves of such wildly imaginative and scurrilous attacks on the military as are found in novels like *Fail Safe*, and *Seven Days in May*. He notes that such books "picture the 'military mind' as a real threat to the democratic process and the exercise of a rational foreign policy." This conclusion is about as valid as saying that Frank Baum's *Wizard of Oz* reveals all scientists to be humbugs. Or that *Uncle Tom's Cabin* proved all slave owners to be Simon Legrees, although it *is* generally conceded that the inflammatory nature of *Uncle Tom's Cabin* did contribute to the Civil War. *Fail Safe* and *Seven Days in May* are even less responsible pieces of literature because the authors were well aware of how these novels would shake America's confidence in its military profession and its system of defense. If such authors have been "greatly disturbed by the military" as Lyons puts it they are scaring themselves and the public with ghost stories which they falsely imply are "based on fact."

A long-standing authority on the military mind and militarism, Walter Millis, continues to stimulate public fear of and animosity toward the military profession. Millis has become convinced that the military stereotype of a dictatorial, warlike, glory-mad swashbuckler is invalid.[14] Having thus found the military professional to be surprisingly like the average citizen, Millis then identifies him with the ultra-conservative radical right. The case of Maj. Gen. Edwin A. Walker is employed to prove this point, overlooking the many military liberals such as Eisenhower, Bradley, Gruenther, Taylor and Lemnitzer. Millis also argues that the military professional becomes conservative by virtue of his spending a career in "hierarchical services." The thought comes to mind that most careers in America are hierarchical, as in education and business. Nor does the point hold up that the standards of the service academies set the mold. Too small a percentage of officers are recruited from the academies to stamp all military professionals with a common character. Service academy graduates in the officer corps are a small minority. In 1964 approximately 600 new lieutenants from West Point joined over 16,000 commissioned by other means.[15] There is as much validity in asserting that Harvard Law School sets the standard for the "legal mind," although Harvard, like West Point, attempts to impart certain ethical standards to its students.

Millis speaks of a middle-class conservatism as if it were some-how unique to the military. In a country composed largely of middle-class citizens one might express a legitimate concern if the military *failed* to mirror the middle-class American. Millis' label of conservatism may well be valid considering the oath an officer must take to uphold the Constitution "against all enemies, foreign or domestic." This should not imply, however, that an officer is prone to support violent hate groups with which the "radical right" is usually identified.

In suggesting that the professional military man shows a certain naïveté toward politics, Millis has hit upon a valid difference. One cannot expect a class of people to be sophisticated about an activity from which they are denied participation, as the military are from domestic politics. This does not go so far, however, as to suppose that military men "show a certain naïveté in the major issues of national life and policy."[16] The opposite is more often so. The inti-mate association of most military men with the primary concerns of national life, from the strategy in Southeast Asia to the national budget at home, leave him with an insight into national life and policy seldom shared by his civilian contemporary. The man in uni-form may, however, be less well versed in local domestic issues.

Bernard Brodie has written that in the area of strategy it is a "basic fact" that "the soldier has been handed a problem that extends far beyond the expertise of his own profession."[17] In re-sponding to this dogmatism Colonel Robert N. Ginsburgh writing in *Foreign Affairs* [18] made the wry comment that originally the word "strategy," derived from the Greek *strategos*, meant the art of generalship. Brodie's "basic fact" is neither basic nor factual, but a fashionable tendency to belittle the military profession.

SIZE OF THE MILITARY PROFESSION

If one is to take Huntington's definition of the military profes-sion, a definition which includes a career commitment of those officers on active duty, the total number of professionals is not particularly impressive. Of approximately 343,000 officers on active duty in 1962 [19] Huntington considered half to fit his definition of a professional (80 percent regulars and 20 percent reserves) or 165,000. This professional corps would then be smaller than the medical profession (256,000 in 1960) or the legal profession (248,000 in 1960). Should this group of professionals vote as a block in any national election their influence would hardly be noticeable. Yet this is the group which remains nonpolitical, while the far more numerous inactive reserves, National Guardsmen, and retired components energetically engage in politics at all levels from local to national. One seldom hears of the dangers presented by this large voting population which runs into the millions. Could it be that the fears of military involvement in politics are inflated?

LOSS OF MILITARY CONTROL

The armed services today have never in their history been so impotent in the conduct of their own affairs. They have been captured and hogtied by the civilian "defense intellectuals." These "defense intellectuals" almost constitute a new profession in the national scene. As Huntington observed, "This constant decline in the power and influence of the military profession is the single most important trend in American civil-military relations during the past fifteen years." [20]

Secretary Robert S. McNamara has used the principle of civilian control of the military to wrest the last vestige of authority from military leaders, and with it a good deal of their pride and self-respect. By changing and creating new organizations, communications channels, disciplinary procedures; by penetrating the Joint Chiefs of Staff and reducing it to an advisory body which, for all practical purposes, can be overruled with impunity even by a civilian Deputy Assistant Secretary of Defense whose understanding of national defense and war has been limited to popular fiction and the press; by making a great show of statistical data, automation, cost analysis, program definition and other fashionable techniques of management as if they had never been understood or practiced before he came to the Pentagon; by setting himself up as the final judge and arbiter of military requirements as if his sole judgment of military weapons was superior to the collective experience and understanding of the country's greatest military leaders; by all this he has reduced senior generals and admirals to technicians and yes-men. The war in Vietnam is truly McNamara's War. As the *Washington Star* correspondent Richard Fryklund has noted, ". . . civilians are in complete control of the war in Vietnam. They dictate strategy and closely supervise tactics." [21]

According to Fryklund, guidelines include such instructions as "avoid hitting civilians; don't bomb when the weather is too poor to see the target clearly; confine yourself to military installations and transportation routes unless you have something particularly hot in a power or oil tank farm; don't get any closer to Hanoi until we tell you; and so forth." [22] But others have reported an even tighter control over air operations by the "defense intellectuals" of OSD. Not only have targets been dictated but the tactics to be used, the bomb load, the number and type of aircraft, and even the altitude to be flown. Nothing has been left to military decision on the theory that only civil leadership half way around the world can comprehend the delicate political circumstances involved and thus avoid escalation of the war.

It is strange indeed that these civil servants would arrogate such matters to themselves. Certainly neither their individual histories nor their records in planning the strategy for military operations in the past few years would warrant such unbounded self-confidence. When attempting to carry their newfound enlightenment on military strategy to Canada, a group of McNamara's bright young civilians were alleged to have been asked by a Canadian officer, "Gentlemen, what is your and McNamara's studied analysis of the Bay of Pigs? Up here, we've always wondered."

Prior to the McNamara regime it was customary for Secretaries of the Army, Navy and Air Force to act as civil champions of their particular services, as buffers between the uniformed men and the political attacks which are so often leveled at the military, and as advocates for service interests among the powerful civilians in the offices of the Secretary of Defense. But Secretary McNamara changed all this. His regime demanded loyalty to the Secretary of Defense regardless of service interests. A parade of service Secretaries in and out of office finally resulted in the clarification of this point.

The rapid turnover of service Secretaries was sometimes assisted by their questionable behavior in office. In 1963 *Aviation Week* noted that Fred Korth "resigned amid politically embarrassing disclosures that he had written letters while Navy secretary to get business for his Fort Worth, Texas, bank." [23] There was also some talk of his bank having been involved with the TFX controversy. It made a loan to General Dynamics, the contract winner by arbitrary decision of McNamara. Korth's replacement was Paul Henry Nitze who is considered to be a McNamara man.

Secretary of the Army Stephen Ailes resigned in 1965, after it was disclosed that he owned stock in a loan company for servicemen. His replacement, Stanley R. Resor, was the Army's third civilian chief in nineteen months.

The replacement of Air Force Secretary Eugene M. Zuckert with Dr. Harold Brown, the former director of the powerful office of Defense Research and Engineering, again strengthened McNamara's hand.

The decline of military influence, of course, has not come about with the consent of the military. The drumbeat of disparaging and frightening literature directed against the military in recent years, the vicious civilian-military in-fighting in bureaucratic offices where the military is at a distinct disadvantage, and the appointment of an extremely energetic and skillful Secretary of Defense, all combined to place the military profession at its historical nadir.

THE MILITARY-INDUSTRIAL COMPLEX

The stage was set for enhanced civilian dominance when President Eisenhower warned against the potential dangers of the "military-industrial complex." Having served forty-two years as a professional soldier, Eisenhower had no concern about the military getting out of hand as long as he held office. But Eisenhower was not unlike many others who envisioned a powerful association between the military and the burgeoning arms industry during the protracted cold war. It has been said that General Eisenhower has since come to regret this statement because the danger was actually to be found in another quarter altogether. Nevertheless, his remarks provided the opening wedge for the civilian "defense intellectual," rather than the military man, to move in and seize control of this vast industrial power.

All major military contracts are now negotiated by the omnipotent civilian agencies in OSD. The next step was for the civilian "defense intellectuals" to usurp other traditional military duties and responsibilities, such as command and control, strategic formulations, plans, tactics, weapons design and selection, and even, as we have seen, operational command. This was usually done under the guise of increasing civilian control of the military as if there were no limits to the virtues of this shibboleth. Military men particularly are loath to challenge any aspect of the civilian control principle. It has become a sacred cow, fraught with emotion and glittering with high principle.

On January 17, 1961, three days before leaving office, President Eisenhower made his oft-quoted "military-industrial complex" speech. His remarks first drew attention to the great American standing army and the industrial war machine.

> This conjunction of immense military establishment and a large
> arms industry is new in the American experience.
>
> We must guard against the acquisition of unwarranted influence,
> whether sought or unsought, by the military-industrial complex. The
> potential for the disastrous rise of misplaced power exists and will
> persist.
>
> We must never let the weight of this combination endanger our
> liberties or democratic processes. Only an alert and knowledgeable
> citizenry can compel the proper meshing of the huge industrial and
> military machinery of defense with our peaceful methods and goals.

No one can seriously question the justification of General Eisenhower's concern that potential danger exists in the annual spending of up to fifty billion dollars to maintain our military establishment. Such vast expenditures take on more political than financial
implications. With this in mind it would seem that those more politically inclined elements of the Department of Defense would be
expected to take advantage of the power potential offered by defense contracting. And that is exactly what happened, with the
civilian echelon of control taking over this traditionally military
function of weapons' requirements and procurement.

Perhaps the only level of supervision which could organize and
nurture a military-industrial complex is the politico-financial level.
Former military dealings with industry had been with separate
and competing corporations and the possibilities of some sort of
monopolistic association among these competing firms was remote
indeed. The vast military spending undertaken during two World
Wars and Korea was surprisingly free of scandal or self-interest.
However, at the level of high finance which may control a number
of competing corporations, a partner might be found in some high
political-administrative post of government. The multiple governmental and financial associations of such men as former Deputy
Secretary of Defense Roswell L. Gilpatric, particularly with respect
to the six billion dollar TFX contract, has been subject to much
speculation in the press. Certainly a defense administrator who
looks upon Pentagon duty as only a short sojourn from his principal
business interest is subject to considerably more temptation than
a career uniformed man.

It has been the military doctrine, religiously held, that the very
best weapons will be procured for the combat forces. In addition,
it need only be noted here that the officer code condemns any financial manipulations, kickbacks, or favors which might influence a
contract. Not being subjected to pressures of financial or political
influence, it has been generally possible for military procurement

officers to be guided by their code. Now that this function has largely been taken away from those in uniform, equivocation on performance of weapons in the name of "cost analysis" was the first standard to go. It is not unreasonable to suppose that other military standards will be sacrificed in this new civilian environment of OSD and that the military-industrial complex envisioned by General Eisenhower will become, instead, the "defense intellectual"-financial complex.

CHAPTER 20

DEVELOPMENT OF DEFENSE ORGANIZATION

All serious students of organization agree that there is no perfect organization which will lend itself to every situation and every personality. Human organization is first of all designed for a purpose, and it next must be adapted to the human beings as well as to the situations in which they work. Here we find three principal variables: purpose, people, environment. These variables make up the organization. The only constant is the conceptual organization itself, such as that conceived by the Constitution of the United States, or, in a lesser degree, by military regulations and organizational charts.

It is illusory, therefore, to seek a "perfect" organization fitting to all kinds of purposes, peoples and environments. Nevertheless, for any given purpose, people and environment, it is conceivable to arrive at an optimum kind of organization. But realizing that these essential features of an organization will change, another characteristic must be incorporated into the static conceptual (or written) organization if it is to continue as a valuable tool of progress. It must be given a certain degree of flexibility so that its character may change to accommodate the ever-changing ingredients of purpose, people, and environment. It is not meant to imply that such an organization be so loosely designed as to alter willy-nilly at the whim of any influential person. It should, of course, be adequately tough and rigid to withstand attacks by those with ulterior motives and by self-seeking individuals. And it should be resilient enough to weather radical environmental changes. Hasty and superficial decisions should be subject to careful evaluation by the organizational processes.

A certain stability and consistency is a strong socio-psychological asset contributing toward confidence and loyalty, and may often be preferable to a more clearly drawn and logically arrived at organization. Stability and consistency contribute to a sense of security and confidence so necessary to morale. *Esprit de corps* and morale are elusive features closely related to organization which are largely appreciated and fostered by human judgments and feelings. The analytical approaches to measuring or to creating these essential emotional aspects of organization have been found rather unproductive.

It is sometimes better to sacrifice the logical and analytical rather than to risk loss of the spirit and loyalty which may exist in an established organization. This is the argument frequently put forward by the Marine Corps when threatened by reduction or incorporation into the Army. It also applies to the Navy with its fear of losing institutional integrity in a straight-line type of unification. There is much to say for these arguments. A balance between institutional loyalty and logical organization must be met in order to achieve the optimum performance. Progress—consistent, enduring, and purposeful which fosters peace and the traditional American principles while at the same time preparing for the eventuality of successful war—is, after all, the ultimate criterion of good military organization.

It must be taken on faith that an optimum organization is possible. Unless this premise is accepted, we need go no further. The alternative is to believe that best organizations grow like Topsy and any analytical approach is a waste of time. Modern man, with his abundance of technical help, law and organization would probably have never materialized had he not accepted the rational and scientific approach to his problems. Although this approach has not created a world of peace and order as yet, and may never do so, it at least has demonstrated certain kinds of human progress. Rational man is healthier, freer, richer and better educated, we must admit.

Accepting the premise, then, that an optimum defense organization is possible, what is our conception of it? We must, of course, examine the present organization, its evolutions, its purposes, its people and its environment. Then we must assess its successes and its failures relative to these essential variables. Can we then, by adjustment, improve the organization against the measure of progress? Such an analysis must be entirely subjective. No pilot model, no controlled experiment, can ever approximate the condition of the vast Department of Defense. But at least we can examine its structure and its progress with as objective an approach as our intellectual integrity will permit, all the while recognizing and allowing for our natural biases and limited experience.

BEGINNINGS OF UNIFICATION

It became obvious during World War II that national policy and military capacity should be more in harmony; that there should be a melding of military and diplomatic thought; and that national policy should truly become politico-military in character. Thus, the National Security Council (NSC), a State-Defense body chaired by the President, was established to this end by the National Security Act of 1947.

But in the formulation of this legislation which so radically altered the Executive Branch of our government, the question of armed forces unification was paramount and dominated the debate. Unification was strongly supported by the Army Air Forces as a necessary step for achieving air force autonomy. If the Army and the Navy could not see eye to eye, it was reasoned, no legislator in his right mind would want to create a third independent force. Why compound the friction?

The dream of a single integrated military establishment had been held by numerous senior Army and Navy officers who had undergone one *tour de force* after another in attempting to achieve mutual cooperation and joint operations during the second world war. Among these was General Eisenhower whose great prestige was thrown behind the unification idea.[1]

Fighting the idea tooth and nail was the naval institution. By this is meant not only the active Navy but all those private activities which derive a large share of their sustenance from the Navy, such as the shipbuilding industry and the steel industry, as well as those organizations like the Navy League dedicated to perpetuating a strong United States Navy. Word had gone out that the proposed unification legislation, introduced by the Army, was a threat to the existence of the Navy and the Marine Corps. Several naval war leaders, such as Admirals Nimitz and Halsey, changed their earlier views in favor of unification and supported the new Navy line.[2] The Eberstadt plan was introduced into the proceedings by the Navy,[3] the plan being a very timid step toward the ideal, and the major features of it were eventually adopted. The result, of course, was no unification whatsoever short of a powerless civilian secretary of the "Military Establishment," as the unified organization was initially termed. Its first incumbent, James V. Forrestal, committed suicide. It was he who had sponsored the Eberstadt plan. Had Forrestal ultimately come to realize his error?

FORRESTAL'S CHANGING VIEWS

As the first Secretary of Defense, Forrestal was so highly dedicated to the service of his country that he literally worked himself to death. In 1949 he leaped from a window of the hospital where he had been undergoing treatment for severe mental depression brought on by his almost ceaseless efforts to solve the mostly insoluble problems of his job. His death was a tragic loss to national defense and to the progress of improved Pentagon organization.

Although a brilliant scholar who often studied half the night even when pressed with the manifold demands of high office, Forrestal could hardly be called a decisive man. Possibly because of his continued study, his opinions frequently changed. He was prone to see and learn the other side of every question. This was particularly so on matters of unification of the armed services—a subject with which he was completely identified.

Much can be learned about the early workings of the government with respect to national defense by studying the life of Forrestal, and we are fortunate in having one of the most revealing source books of its kind ever published in *The Forrestal Diaries*.[4] These diaries contain intimate thoughts and remarks on the major issues and personalities of the day, and are far more enlightening than the usual carefully edited autobiographies. There is an element of freshness in notations made directly after an event that discloses the depth of feeling and emotion as no account written years later could possibly recapture.

It is interesting to note that Forrestal, as Secretary of the Navy, started out opposing unification altogether; that he next came to believe that the Navy's strong opposition would bring on accusations of obstructionism and thus he proposed a modified and restrained form of unification based on cooperation and known as the Eberstadt plan; that through Forrestal's own diligent efforts, and his prestige with Congressional leaders and the administration, the Eberstadt plan was largely enacted into law in 1947, with Forrestal appointed to the new post of Secretary of Defense; but that on his resignation from that post in 1949 Forrestal recommended various measures to strengthen the office of the Secretary of Defense—measures which he initially had fought to keep out of the

legislation in 1947. This switch in Forrestal's conception of organizational philosophy only goes to demonstrate the truism that one's
view of an organization is largely dependent upon where one sits
in the organization itself. It became obvious to Forrestal that unification of our armed forces could not be had by cooperation alone,
skilled as was Forrestal himself at gaining sincere loyalty and
harmony.[5]

One remark often made by Forrestal and which he never altered
was that ninety-five percent of his work dealt with the removal of
human friction. Since the organization for national defense was so
unmanageable, it is not strange that so much human friction did
occur—friction beyond the ability of even a man as adept and
patient as Forrestal. In fact, if so much of the Secretary's time
was devoted to overcoming controversies, it would seem that the
organization itself was somehow wanting. For the essence of organization is purposeful orderliness with a minimum of human
friction. And conversely, the essence of anarchy is purposeless
chaos with people ever at each other's throats.

It seems that Forrestal himself began to see more virtue in a
straight-line organization for the Department of Defense, but this
revelation came too late to save his life. He exhausted himself to
the breaking point in a superhuman effort to gain harmonious cooperation under a system which was so loosely knit that bureaucratic
conflict of the bitterest sort was inevitable. In his final recommendations he asked, for example, that the word "general" be omitted
from the law which gave the Secretary of Defense "general" supervision over the military departments. He also asked for an Under
Secretary, as well as for a Chairman of the Joint Chiefs of Staff.
The Eberstadt report from which the act of 1947 was largely constructed had deemed that such strengthening of the unified office
was neither necessary nor desirable.

INITIAL CORRECTIVE EFFORTS, 1949

After the bitter Army-Navy-Air Force fight hit the public eye as
a consequence of the B-36 bomber investigation of 1949, an effort
was made to shore up the cumbersome and ineffectual legislation
of 1947. But since the Army, Navy and Air Force were now at
greater odds than they had ever been following the war, no sensible
proposals came from the armed services.[6]

The answer seemed to lie at the civilian control level. So in accordance with Forrestal's recommendation Congress broadened the

authority of the unified secretary. Whereas the 1947 Act established the new secretary as a coordinator between three Executive Departments—the Army, Navy and Air Force—the 1949 amendment gave him more direct authority. The three service secretaries had retained their full powers under the original legislation except for the authority ascribed to the Secretary of Defense, who, under the 1947 Act, had certain "general" responsibilities for coordinating budgets, expenditures, procurement, supply, transportation, storage, health and research.

To aid the Defense secretary in performing his coordination, the Act of 1947 had provided for only three "Special Assistants" and three agencies: the Joint Chiefs of Staff, the Research and Development Board, and the Munitions Board. In the amendment of 1949 the Special Assistants were upgraded to Assistant Secretaries of Defense while a Deputy Secretary of Defense was added as the number two in the hierarchy. A Chairman of the Joint Chiefs of Staff was also authorized with very circumscribed authority to guard against his becoming a supreme chief of staff; yet the size of the Joint Staff was increased from 100 to 210 officers. The amendment also called for uniform budgetary and fiscal procedures.[7]

As Forrestal had recommended, the word "general" was removed from the clauses "general direction, authority and control" concerning the authority of the Secretary of Defense over the military establishment[8] and it was stressed that the Secretary of Defense was to be the principal assistant to the President in all matters relating to the Department of Defense, leaving no doubt that he was in charge of the three service Secretaries.[9]

It is interesting to note, however, that the many restrictions in the Act designed to protect the integrity of the separate Services were retained. In fact, more sections in the Act specified what the Secretary of Defense could *not* do than what he could do, and should do. Although Congress aimed at providing him with more authority over the separate armed services, the legislators at the same time wished to retain the identity of each service. So the amendments of 1949 simply compounded the original ambiguity found in the Act of 1947.

By downgrading the service secretaries, however, and thereby placing more administrative authority in the hands of the Office of the Secretary of Defense (OSD) civilians, the net result was to strip the service military chiefs and other professionals of the authority necessary for them adequately to fulfill their responsibilities. Most of this authority was now lodged in the hands of appointed civilians who rarely had more than a smattering of military knowledge.

These people soon became the "military" representatives on the numerous National Security Council (NSC) study groups and other interagency boards and working groups. John Foster Dulles applauded this reduction of what he considered a "preponderance" of military influence.[10] The concept of politico-military thinking so urgently promoted by the Eberstadt plan was lost to politico-politico thinking. Let us turn for a moment to the organization of the NSC to illustrate this point.

PURPOSE AND STRUCTURE OF THE NSC

The National Security Council was a central feature of the Eberstadt plan designed to provide, in the words of Secretary Forrestal, "The immediate integration . . . of the War, Navy and State Departments" so that the United States could "act as a unit in terms of its diplomacy, its military policy, its use of scientific knowledge, and finally, of course, in its moral and political leadership of the world. . . ."[11] In the original plan this Council was to be composed of the Secretaries of State, War, Navy and Air and the Chairman of the National Security Resources Board.[12]

The amendment of August 10, 1949, to the National Security Act of 1947 eliminated the three Secretaries of the Army, Navy and Air Force from the NSC. The Council's composition now became: the President, the Vice President, the Secretary of State, the Secretary of Defense, the Director of Mutual Security, and the Chairman of the National Security Resources Board.[13] Reorganization Plan No. 6 of 1953 changed the title of Mutual Security (foreign aid) to Foreign Operations, and the National Security Resources Board became the Office of Defense Mobilization. It also abolished the Munitions Board and the Research and Development Board.

As simply stated in Section 101 (b) of the National Security Act of 1947 as amended, the NSC was designed "for the purpose of more effectively coordinating the policies and functions of the departments and agencies of the Government relating to national security . . . to assess and appraise the objectives, commitments and risks of the United States *in relation to our actual and potential military power.* . . ."[14] How well has this purpose been executed?

While not all national security policies are directly related to military affairs, the post-war years showed a growing reliance on military strength as the backbone of United States foreign policy. And the "massive retaliation" doctrine of the Eisenhower administration focused the spotlight on airpower as the prime ingredient of this military strength. Much was written and said at that time on the subject of air and space power; so much, in fact, that the country was led to believe that national security policies were predicated on a firm knowledge of the subject. This was a misconception. Not only was knowledge of air power largely missing at policy-making levels but, except for President Eisenhower himself, even military knowledge was sadly lacking. This was a trend which was to continue and lead to such fiascos as the loss of the space race, the Bay of Pigs, the South Vietnam involvement, and the close shave of the Cuban missile crisis.

The national security policies of the mid-1950's resulted from coordinated planning in two primary groups, the National Security Council and the subordinate NSC Planning Board. The Kennedy administration discontinued the NSC Planning Board but it held a prominent place under the Eisenhower leadership. Approximately twenty-five men from every interested department were involved in this planning process. Today this planning is accomplished by a coterie of Presidential advisors and ad hoc groups somewhat off the top of their heads and generally isolated from any regular contact with the military services.

During the mid-1950's I frequently sat with the NSC Planning Board as a nonparticipating observer for the Operations Coordinating Board and there deplored the fact that policies so intimately related to military and airpower matters were being promulgated with such little understanding of the subject. It is no wonder that the "massive retaliation" doctrine dimly conceived and awkwardly defended should soon give way to the "flexible response" doctrine hatched in Army circles. This new doctrine, spelled out in General Maxwell D. Taylor's book, *The Uncertain Trumpet*,[15] was far more understandable to the policy makers and has persisted until the present day, more strongly entrenched now than any politico-military doctrine since isolationism.

When President Kennedy moved into the White House in 1961 he all but abolished the NSC system which, with all its drawbacks, had been a step in the right direction. The Operations Coordinating Board and the NSC Planning Board were done away with while the statutory NSC itself met rarely and irregularly. The Special

Assistant for National Security Affairs, McGeorge Bundy, became a personal advisor to the President rather than the leader of a secretariat for managing the NSC. Thus the major (or at least the most immediate and confidential) military advice to the President came from someone who had no professional military background and no connection with or responsibility for the Department of Defense or the military services. If the politico-military policy planning system was faulty in 1955, it is much worse off today and a uniformed man might look with nostalgia to the days when the military profession had at least a weak voice in the formulation of national military policy at the NSC level.[16]

NATIONAL SECURITY ACT AMENDMENT, 1953 (REORGANIZATION PLAN NO. 6) [17]

The Korean War revealed glaring weaknesses in the Department of Defense structure. For example, the Munitions Board was unable, among other shortcomings, to provide an adequate supply of artillery shells. Nelson E. Rockefeller was asked by the new President Eisenhower to conduct a careful review of the department and Reorganization Plan No. 6 was the result.[18] This plan strengthened still more the hand of the Secretary of Defense, as we have already noted, by abolishing both the Munitions Board and the Research and Development Board and placing their functions under new Assistant Secretaries.

Six additional Assistant Secretaries were authorized together with a General Counsel of assistant secretary rank, bringing the total number of administrators of this rank to ten, which, with the Deputy Secretary of Defense, gave the Secretary of Defense eleven principal assistants appointed by the President.[19] The President mollified Congress by pointing out that those Assistant Secretaries would not reduce the authority of service secretaries, although practice has proved otherwise.

Was unification enhanced by these measures? Certainly the appearance of unification improved. The hierarchical civilian cap resting on top of the services gained immense authority. And the powerful Office of the Secretary of Defense, (OSD) began to suppress free expression of divergent service views with ruthless determination. Without Army Chief of Staff General Matthew B. Ridgway's disclosures [20] this condition would have probably gone unnoticed by the general public.

But statutory authority does not always permit the kind of authority envisioned, and it has not been easy for the senior civilian echelon of the Department of Defense to wrest policy and operating authority from the armed services. Decades of entrenched bureaucratic practices are not easily overcome by legislation, and the specialized knowledge of military professionals is often confusing to uninitiated civilians. Where a difference exists, the military argument can be made still more confusing by the common bureaucratic technique of "fuzzing up" the issue. This probably was not done consciously, but it was sometimes practiced.

The counter was obvious. Divide and conquer. Three armed services were at constant war with one another for budgets, equipment, manpower, perquisites, joint commands, jurisdiction and national prestige. The simple but effective strategy of divide and conquer did not go unnoticed by the civilians of OSD, although they seldom practiced it with malice and generally with pure national interests at heart. In the face of their complete fall from power the three military Services were still unable to close ranks. This internecine warfare did not abate until Secretary of Defense Robert S. McNamara wrested every last vestige of power from the service chiefs. Then it was too late.

During the struggle for control the Secretary of Defense and his assistants could usually find at least one service which would back an OSD-initiated project. The "new look" which curtailed Air Force expansion in 1952 was supported by the Navy, and naturally fought by the Air Force. "Massive retaliation" which restored Air Force cuts was supported by the Air Force and condemned by the Army and Navy. Of course, the Army backed the vast and unrealistic reserve program passed in 1955, while the Air Force and Navy resisted.

None of these activities, as presented, gained support from all three services, although as General Ridgway clearly indicated, pressure was put on the recalcitrant chiefs of staff to provide the lip service of harmony.

Secretary of Defense Charles E. Wilson from General Motors Corporation with his hatchet man, Deputy Secretary of Defense Roger Kyes, also from General Motors, proceeded to cut the uniformed services down to size. General Gavin wrote that "Wilson tended to deal with his Chiefs of Staff as though they were recalcitrant union bosses." [21] One Chief of Staff remarked ruefully that Wilson was not only uninformed about military matters but that he was "determined to remain so." [22]

This only reflected the continued drain of authority from the services into the growing omnipotence of the civilian OSD. It was ironical that in the hearings held on the 1953 reorganization, Congress became concerned not with the almost unlimited powers it had granted to the Secretary of Defense, but on the possibility of the JCS Chairman becoming a man on horseback.[23] This smokescreen continues to hide the repeated accretions of power by the OSD civilians.

THE REORGANIZATION OF 1958

On October 4, 1957, the Soviet Union put the first object into orbit about the earth and opened the space age. The flight of Sputnik I shocked America, not to mention the Department of Defense, which had been engaging in interminable shortsighted debates over the value of an earth satellite. Late in 1955, as we have noted, OSD had directed that Project Vanguard, as proposed by the Naval Research Laboratory, become the nation's approved satellite program, notwithstanding the fact that the Navy was unprepared for this effort while both the Air Force and the Army had made great strides in ballistic missiles and could have launched an earth satellite in a short time using rocket hardware then available.

> While Project Vanguard was the approved U. S. satellite program, we at Huntsville knew [wrote Werner von Braun] that our rocket technology was fully capable of satellite application and could quickly be implemented. All efforts to obtain permission to extend our technology into space were unsuccessful in Washington.[24]

The country was justifiably incensed that the great Department of Defense, lavishly supported with funds, should have allowed the Soviet Union to steal such a march on the United States. Public pressure finally forced the Secretary of Defense to unleash the Army which, in just eighty-four days, sent Explorer I into orbit on January 31, 1958. But America still suffered from the traumatic effect of this failure. Project Vanguard, which relied on a solid fuel third stage not yet developed when OSD authorized the program, did not fly a satellite until two years six months and eight days (March 17, 1958) after the start of the project.[25]

The military services might have said that excessive civilian control and policy direction by amateurs bungled the satellite program, and that had the problem been handed to JCS the United States would have been first into orbit. But the services cannot indulge in public discussions of policy. Only civilian leaders may do this. And they shirked responsibility by implying that the failure of America to win the space race was because, of all things, the Secretary of Defense was lacking in adequate authority. So another reorganization of the Department of Defense was recommended.

But to top this, in order to assure the world that America had no military designs in space (and also to keep the uniformed services from acquiring too much power?) the responsibility for space exploration was removed entirely from the Department of Defense. On October 1, 1958, the National Aeronautics and Space Administration (NASA) was created from the venerable research agency, the National Advisory Committee on Aeronautics (NACA).[26] America's space program has since managed to remain behind the Soviet effort in most particulars.

In the purely military field some laudable changes were made by the 1958 reorganization. The unified and specified commands throughout the world were to report not to separate military departments but to the JCS. Unified commanders in the field were to have full operational authority over combatant forces under them, of whatever service. An operational office (J-3) was authorized in JCS with an increase in JCS staff personnel (210 to 400) to man it. The Chairman, JCS, was provided with unmistakable authority to contral and manage the Joint Staff and its Director. General Nathan F. Twining, the Chairman, testified that the new organization would make of JCS a general staff insofar as operations were concerned.[27] "In total effect, the proposal approximates a single chief-of-staff system."[28] One wonders why Senator Bridges remained so quiet when he should have screamed in horror at the "Prussian General Staff." But in actuality the overall authority of the JCS continued to decrease vis-a-vis OSD.

One of the overriding features of the reorganization of 1958 was to give executive authority to all the Assistant Secretaries of Defense. Their revised charters published in 1959 gave them full authority to issue instructions and directives and to obtain reports and information.[29] The super office of the Director of Defense Research and Engineering was established with dictatorial control over research, engineering and weapon procurement. The number of Assistant Secretaries was reduced from nine to seven but by adding the new Director of Defense Research and Engineering of that rank the net reduction of senior administrators was but one. Thus ten remained.[30] But this reduction was not to last.

OSD IN 1965

When he took office in 1961, Secretary of Defense McNamara grasped every rein of power provided by the reorganization of 1958 and even added to the authority so liberally granted to his office by Congress. A great number of young and dynamic "defense intellectuals" moved in, each demonstrating an almost unlimited confidence to solve the most complicated military problems of the nuclear age. The JCS itself was reduced to another think factory, producing study after study for the new civilian teams, with few of these voluminous documents being approved by OSD. Studies from contract groups such as IDA and RAND achieved more attention and consideration than JCS studies and were sometimes published commercially [31] if the points were hard to sell within the Pentagon.

The first "military" operation in 1961 was the abortive Bay of Pigs invasion of Cuba, the planning and operation of which was run (on the approval of the Secretary of Defense) by CIA. When the operation failed, an abortive effort was made to blame JCS as a convenient fall-guy.

Later operations, which the JCS was charged with directing, dealt with the semi-blockade of Cuba in the crisis of November, 1962. Civilian officials in OSD usurped command authority and gave specific orders to ships at sea. When Admiral Geoerge W. Anderson, Chief of Naval Operations, protested this irregular flouting of the chain of command he was informed in effect that the issue was too delicate and dangerous to be handled by the military mind. The admiral's failure to understand this reason is reputed to have contributed to his fall from favor in 1963. Before leaving he voiced his obvious "great concern" at the over-centralization of civilian authority in the Pentagon, and of the overriding or ignoring of expert military judgment.

In a speech before the National Press Club, September 4, 1963, Admiral Anderson also mentioned the matter of weapons selection:

> I view any diminution of military recommendations on weapons procurement with grave alarm. Certainly the abrupt reversal of military recommendations without interim consultation, as was the case in the TFX and V/STOL [Tactical Fighter, Experimental and Vertical or Short Takeoff and Landing aircraft] contracts is fraught at a minimum with unpleasant developments, and potentially with grave dangers.[32]

Two years later similar sentiments were voiced by the Chairman of the Joint Chiefs of Staff, General Earl G. Wheeler, before an

Armed Forces Management Association meeting in Washington. He said:

> Our armed forces operate on a world-wide basis. Their operations have been successful in the past because commanders exercised command freely on the spot and not with their hands tied by bonds of management directives woven by theorists at higher headquarters.[33]

He went on to warn against the dangers of "overcontrol and overmanagement" at various levels of military authority in the Pentagon, and the dangers of equating the Department of Defense to a business.

> Finally, and most important [General Wheeler said], the manager must remember just what kind of support he is expected to give the commander—quality equipment and personnel, delivered on time to permit accomplishment of the mission concerned. This objective can only be attained to the degree that management goals are co-ordinated with operational plans. The managers do not make these plans, but the plans do "make" the managers if the management task is properly performed.

A RECOMMENDATION

It is not the purpose of this study to come up with a reorganization plan for the Department of Defense, but rather to identify the prejudiced thinking and misconceptions which have been most responsible for the Tower of Babel which the United States has created on the Potomac. We introduced this chapter with the premise that a rational optimum organization was possible, one which made the best use of people and their environment to achieve the national purposes. How then, can this be achieved?

To begin with, we must cease writing laws which, in effect, identify two classes of American citizens: good ones (civilians) and, if not bad, questionable ones (military men). The layer upon layer of multiple authority in the Pentagon has mushroomed for just one fundamental reason: to control the questionable military man. True, there may have been less acceptable, bureaucratic reasons involved, but civil control (or civilian control) of the military has always been held up as the one unassailable virtue to justify any act which strengthens or enlarges OSD and reduces the authorities of the uniformed contingents. Sometimes "business management" is used to justify this control on the basis, if we believe literature of the "defense intellectuals," that military men are incapable of sound business management.

Secretary of Defense Louis A. Johnson in 1949 began to "cut the fat" from the military services. A little over a year later we found ourselves at war in Korea, buying back the "fat" at exhorbitant markups from the junk dealers. Today, Mr. McNamara is proudly reporting his "savings" by adding up the billions "saved" by not building weapons systems which the JCS thought were necessary, from Dyna Soar to Nike Zeus. Mr. McNamara estimated that at least $1.2 billion was "wasted" on the B-70 bomber project.[34] It has been said in the Pentagon that, "Of course we'll lose the next war, but we'll lose it cheaply."

Making moral judgments of a whole class of people in uniform on the basis of an invalid stereotype leads to our relying upon amateur leadership of our most vital national interest—self-defense. This brings us to the second criterion for defense reorganization. *Rest qualification for office, no matter at what level, on proved ability, not upon whether a "regular" uniform is or has been worn by the individual under consideration.* It is time that regulars were looked upon in the same legal light as reserves or National Guardsmen, and given the same opportunities, privileges, citizenship rights and military benefits.

Once our laws are purged of the civilian-military dichotomy, the Department of Defense could be easily reorganized to reduce a good two-thirds of its personnel, establish clear lines of responsibility and authority, and gain better national defense at half the price.

But, one will say, the antimilitary attitude is part of the environment we must cope with. How can we expect to change it even if it is invalid? This leads us to the third criterion. *Let the military speak!* Let them defend themselves. Let them write, publish and have a professional organization as do other professions in our society. Given their voice, it is conceivable that the military could counter most attacks on their honor, capabilities and Americanism. As it is, the military man can seldom defend himself or present his case to the public in a positive way.

CONCLUSION

The continued accretion of power in the civilian Office of the Secretary of Defense should be cause for public alarm. Unheralded changes are still being made to add power to OSD. An Assistant Secretary of Defense for Administration was created in 1964, and an Assistant Secretary of Defense for Systems Analysis was added in 1965. The military professionals on the other hand have been increasingly ignored and undercut until now they are little more than technicians and puppets in the planning and management of national security. Civilian amateurs, unrestricted by a professional code of conduct or the Uniform Code of Military Justice, or by the countless laws and regulations which apply only to the man in uniform, have invaded every field of military professionalism: oper-development, weapons selection, and weapons procurement. If this trend is not reversed, not only will the military profession be reduced to errand-boy status, strutting in uniforms like doormen and ations, command, tactics, strategy, plans, organization, weapons ushers, but the United States will become so weak and unprepared as to be unable to resist aggression or prevail at the conference table.

A former Chief of Staff of the Air Force, General Thomas D. White, described the "impossible role" of the JCS in a *Newsweek* article.

> Our dynamic, management-conscious Secretary of Defense, Robert S. McNamara, has established agencies responsible directly to himself and has partially bypassed the Joint Chiefs. In effect, paralleling the JCS, there has been created a new general staff largely civilian and backed up by military underlings.
>
> No responsible military man in any of the services objects to civilian control; all recognize and accept this without question as a wise and fundamental concept of our way of life and government. But there are many young and temporary functionaries in the various departments who encourage the downgrading of military influence on purely military matters and would welcome further steps in this direction.[35]

One might remark that "this was a hell of a way to run a railroad." We don't have railroaders at the throttle, we have grocers and shoe clerks. And the trains run late and in every unprofitable direction. Although the grocers and shoe clerks no longer foster and excite factional struggles between the three railroad lines in order to gain and retain power, they have grown powerful and bold enough to dictate railroad policy to the railroaders.

The United States needs true armed services unification. No watered down Eberstadt Plan. No unification by means of an unskilled, unprofessional and dictatorial civilian cap. But unification of professional military leaders.

CHAPTER 21

THE ARMS CONTROL MOVEMENT

During World War II when he was inspecting a British head-quarters after a unit had performed very poorly, Winston Churchill had this to say to the officer commanding: "Young man, you are going down in history as one of the most stupid brigadiers ever to serve in the British Army. I know this. I am sure of it because I intend to write the history myself."

This anecdote may describe a phenomenon of today: a great movement of critical writing. The authors are not writing orthodox history by any means, but like Winston Churchill they are *making* history through their massive new body of literature. This is the literature of the arms control and disarmament school. Almost all of the "defense intellectuals" are members of this school. However we tag them, they are a large group of distinguished individuals, in and out of government, who have become experts on matters of military policy, strategy, tactics, weapons, disarmament and all related subjects. "Arms controllers" is another common term for them.

Ten years ago arms control was hardly a word. Today arms control has become a great national movement, even an international movement. Numerous international conferences have been held, official and unofficial, from Geneva to Pugwash. Foundations have opened their coffers to finance studies, publications, meetings, seminars. Many industries have taken an avid interest. A Department of Defense bibliography lists over three hundred significant books and articles in the field which have been published in the last four years.[1] Even the press and popular literature have been captivated by arms control ideas as witness the popular novels *On the Beach*, *Seven Days in May*, *Fail Safe*, and a parade of similar frightening tales. These themes have been adapted to several hit movies. The public is being indoctrinated and even the language is spotted with its jargon of "escalation," "proliferation," "second strike," "destabilizing" and what not.

THE INVERTED PROPOSITION

The former White House scientific advisor, Dr. Jerome B. Wiesner, is an avid arms controller who has written much on the subject. In a foreword to a basic arms control anthology Dr. Wiesner said, ". . . if the arms race is allowed to continue its accelerating pace, our country will have less security, not more, with each passing year. . . ." [2]

The President's former Special Assistant for National Security Affairs, McGeorge Bundy, reflected the same belief when he wrote ". . . the arms race itself is a new threat to national security." [3]

This same inverted thought, that with increased military preparedness our security will decrease, has been expressed by Walt Whitman Rostow, Chairman of the Policy Planning Council and a leader in the formulation of national strategy. He took the proposition a step further when he wrote that there is ". . . a legitimate American national objective to see removed from all nations—including the United States—the right to use substantial military force to pursue their own interests." [4]

A substantial government agency, the Arms Control and Disarmament Agency (ACDA), has been established by Congress and reports directly to the President. Its influential Director, William C. Foster, a former Deputy Secretary of Defense, testified before the Senate Committee on Foreign Relations on March 8, 1962, that ". . . the magnitude of the [arms] buildup will not contribute to security but could conceivably contribute to insecurity in view of the proliferation of weapons and in view of the massive nature of destruction which those weapons could inflict." Here again is the same upside-down approach to national security.

ARMS RACE ARGUMENTS

When he has been questioned about the danger of reducing our arms and not being assured that the Soviets, too, are reducing theirs, Foster has remarked: "Certainly there is a risk to disarmament. But the risk of the arms race is greater. The arms race will lead either to bankruptcy or to nuclear war." [5]

This is a belief widely and sincerely held. The question lies in how much risk we should take to gain disarmament, or as Foster says, to "turn down the arms race," and how the risk should be assessed.

There are several assumptions in the arms race reasoning which might require further analysis: First, that the arms race represents a dangerous competition for us. Our fifty billion inflated dollar defense budget doesn't compare with our eighty-one billion budget of 1945 when we were racing somewhat faster. As Foster himself noted in his testimony before the Senate Foreign Relations Committee on March 8, 1962, "The Soviets could afford [the arms race] with some sacrifices, and now they have found some difficulties. Mr. Khrushchev is going to find it difficult to find enough money to buy tractors to reorganize his agriculture, to completely streamline and readjust his total collective farm system while, at the same time, to maintain a substantial military establishment."

It would seem from this testimony that the arms race may present some possible advantages to us. Foster has refuted his own argument about the arms race being a dangerous competition and the comparative economic fortunes of the United States and the USSR today make the argument sound very hollow indeed. Implicit in the thought that we will lose in an arms race is a lack of faith in the American free society.

The second assumption in Foster's reasoning is that an arms race would lead to bankruptcy. History shows arms production correlating with prosperity rather than with depression. Yet the reverse is repeated like a litany in arms control literature.

The third assumption is that an arms race leads to war. As good a case can be made that disarmament leads to war. Again this idea is hard to find in current arms control writings.

There appear to be as many arguments for as against an arms race. The subject might warrant more objective study before we blindly rest our policy on arms elimination.

HAVEN FOR THE DEFENSE INTELLECTUAL

Arms control is even considered by many to be a new field of science. The American Association for the Advancement of Science recommended at its 1961 conference in Denver that there should be a new science—the Science of "Human Survival," as they called it.

Arms control already is providing new careers for many former physicists, chemists, and economists. These gentlemen turn out studies, lecture, and act as consultants to government and private research institutions. They are extremely influential and have not been without success in altering national military policy as expressed at the highest levels of government.

And where does the Office of the Secretary of Defense stand on this movement? Ostensibly, OSD resists many of the proposals of ACDA. Yet when the specific actions of OSD are measured against the common patterns of arms control, it becomes apparent that in a more practical and subtle sense, OSD is an ally of ACDA.

NUCLEAR WEAPONS PARITY

The aim of ACDA is to achieve nuclear parity with the Soviets as a major step in the disarmament program. This pattern can be clearly recognized in the United States proposal for General and Complete Disarmament which was submitted at the conference of the Eighteen Nation Committee on Disarmament at Geneva on April 18, 1962.[6]

Since the United States now has a distinct nuclear superiority over the Soviet Union, nuclear parity can be achieved unilaterally simply by reducing our own nuclear strength.

The notion of nuclear parity, of course, is based on the doublethink premise that the more we arm the less security we have. As far back as 1960 the Summer Study on Arms Control, sponsored by the American Academy of Arts and Sciences, worked out a comprehensive program for achieving parity and a world model designed to bottle the nuclear genie. An anthology of studies emanating from this effort was edited by Donald G. Brennan and published as *Arms Control, Disarmament and National Security*.[7] This work is the *Das Capital* and the *Mein Kampf* of arms controllers. The program is pretty much on schedule.

OSD POLICY ON PARITY

To judge whether Secretary of Defense Robert S. McNamara is an arms controller requires a detailed study of his statements and actions. His frequent speeches "quantifying" our nuclear superiority in missiles and bombers are apt to throw one off the track. But strong defense budgets do not necessarily reflect a strengthening capability for major war, and by letting our SAC air fleet grow obsolete we are gradually losing nuclear superiority. This has been noted by former Chief of the Air Force, General Curtis E. LeMay, in testimony before the Senate Preparedness Subcommittee and refuted publicly by Mr. McNamara. One wonders who is the better judge of our strategic nuclear strength.

In his famous Ann Arbor speech of June 16, 1962, McNamara announced his endorsement of the counterforce doctrine which doesn't jibe with the parity concept at all. Counterforce exponents conceive of a major nuclear war waged against purely military objectives such as opposing missile launching sites. To be successful, such a strategy would require a nuclear superiority because it takes more than one missile to destroy another one. A counterforce doctrine associated with parity would lead to no resolution whatever and very little deterrence. Parity, the arms controllers' proposal, conceives of targeting cities and this, they believe, provides a greater deterrence.

In a Saturday Evening Post article [8] Stewart Alsop praised McNamara for discovering counterforce. Counterforce had been an Air Force doctrine for years before this and our SAC forces had been so disposed. In fact, before McNamara's Ann Arbor announcement, OSD officials had been arguing rather strongly for the concept of parity. What could have caused the Secretary of Defense to suddenly accept the opposing military view for counterforce with its necessary nuclear superiority?

The answer to this can be found in the dialogue with Charles de Gaulle over the efficacy of France's small nuclear *force de frappe*. The United States has always discouraged an independent French nuclear force and one argument against it has been that a small nuclear force would be of little value, that only a large force such as ours is worthwhile. Since the parity argument calls for a small nuclear force, parity would hardly help our dialogue with de Gaulle. Moreover, the aim to reduce nuclear proliferation comes sooner on the arms controller's timetable than the aim of parity. For these reasons one might suspect that McNamara's counterforce statement was a tactical maneuver to be changed later.

Another reason for suspecting this is that so many other McNamara acts and statements are in accord with the arms control philosophy. The denouement of his strategic thinking appeared in the Stewart Alsop interview noted above. McNamara was asked if the Soviets might not achieve a "sure second-strike capability" similar to our hardened Minuteman and the surprising part was that his answer boiled down to "the sooner the better."

From this it would seem that McNamara had no faith in counterforce which would be more effective if the Soviet failed to harden their missile sites but rather left them soft and more easily destroyed. Most revealing, however, is the fact that this thought is the same one expressed by those arms controllers who promote parity.

In his syndicated column of January 13, 1963, General Ira C. Eaker ironically commented on Alsop's article. Eaker suggested that to assist Russia in becoming as strong as we are (a condition McNamara indicated he would be happy to see in the ICBM field), two courses of action are open to us. "One, under lend-lease, to give the Russians Minutemen and Polaris missiles. The other was to reduce our own armaments by progressive stages until we have military parity with the Russians. It now appears, according to this reasoning, that our leaders in the Pentagon have determined to adopt the latter course."

ARMS CONTROLLERS IN OSD

McNamara has surrounded himself with arms controllers. One was his immediate deputy, Roswell L. Gilpatric, who resigned early in 1964. The model second-strike military posture leading to nuclear parity was described by this former Deputy Secretary of Defense in the April 1964 issue of *Foreign Affairs*. Since the article appeared so soon after Gilpatric's retirement, it is inconceivable that McNamara was not only consulted in its preparation but was sympathetic to its conclusions.

Key OSD staff members attended or contributed to the famous 1960 Summer Study on Arms Control. Among them was Harold Brown who later held the powerful position of Director of Defense Research and Engineering, a position so high in the hierarchy that his deputy was an Assistant Secretary of Defense. Subsequently, Harold Brown was appointed Secretary of the Air Force. Brown assisted Arthur T. Hadley produce a layman's version of the Summer Study experience.[9]

Heading the powerful OSD office for International Security Affairs (ISA) is Assistant Secretary of Defense John T. McNaughton. Secretary McNaughton is perhaps the most unabashed and outspoken arms controller in the Pentagon. McNaughton began his meteoric rise by accepting the post of Deputy Assistant Secretary of Defense for Arms Control in 1961 and performing admirably by assisting Foster's new ACDA. Foster attended one of McNaughton's several promotion ceremonies and praised him highly for his cooperation.

The present incumbent of the OSD Arms Control post is Arthur Barber, another Summer Study man who wrote extensively on the need to de-nuclearize our NATO allies. Three others who participated in one way or another in the Summer Study were Henry Rowen, who works for McNaughton, Paul Nitze, the Secretary of the Navy, and Garry L. Quin who also works in OSD (ISA) and who edited the "Collected Papers" of the Summer Study. At the very least it must be concluded that the arms control influence in OSD is not insignificant.

BASIS FOR THE ARMS CONTROL MOVEMENT

The fundamental aims of arms control appeal to everyone. The desire to reduce the huge expenditure for armed forces and armaments is universal. Measures to reduce the risk of war or its destructive nature are crucial matters to all. Military men are no less concerned about this than are civilians. Of course, all concede that this must be done at no risk to our national security. Differences arise not so much with the ends but in the means to reach these ends and in the evaluation of the means in terms of national security.

Yet it is odd that very few historians, political scientists, or military men have been attracted to this new arms control calling. One would think that historians, political scientists, and military men would have the greatest competence in this area of study. But experts in the natural sciences have largely monopolized this field even though their training seems less fitting for the subject. What is behind this phenomenon? Why do physical scientists take up arms control with such consummate zeal?

Some scientists have suggested that there is a guilt complex at work. The physical scientists unleashed the horrible genie of nuclear energy and now they feel morally responsible for putting the genie back in the bottle. *The Bulletin of the Atomic Scientists* has beat this drum since 1947. A book by Robert Gilpin, *American Scientists and Nuclear Weapons Policy*,[10] indicates that the activists, initially led by Dr. J. Robert Oppenheimer (also a Summer Study participant), have set out to change the national ethos by making nuclear war so horrible to contemplate that national defense with nuclear weapons will be considered immoral and unthinkable. Oppenheimer expressed the motivation of the scientists when he said "the physicists have known sin, . . . and this is a knowledge they cannot lose."

This antinuclear movement is a highly charged, emotional "cause" which has attracted many other groups. The peace organizations have joined with enthusiasm. Yet so have some able and well-intentioned politicians, diplomats, and businessmen. Almost every walk of life is represented. These are all people with a crusading mission to bottle the nuclear genie and save us and the world from nuclear war.

Of course Communists and fellow travelers might find this movement fitting well with their aim for weakening America. When testifying at the hearings for the ACDA bill in 1961, former Secretary of Defense Robert A. Lovett warned that ACDA might become a haven for Reds and crackpots. Fortunately, this has not happened. ACDA pursues arms control and disarmament with the clear purpose of not reducing U. S. national security. Yet the questions remain: Which agency of government provides the most qualified advice regarding what constitutes good national security? And how does the OSD rectify the basic conflicts between defense and disarmament?

EFFECT OF ARMS CONTROL ON THE MILITARY POSTURE

Too many military men tend to look upon arms control as a civilian fad, a Utopian dream, which will never achieve reality. They point to the lack of agreement in the interminable negotiations with the Soviet Union. What these military people fail to see is that arms control doctrine is unilaterally affecting almost every feature of our military posture, from strategy to weapons. This influence is one of the most pervasive of all the forces at work today in directing our military policy. It is within the context of the arms control doctrine that we will find answers to many of the puzzling military decisions which have been made by the Secretary of Defense. And this movement partially explains the increased tempo and animosity found in antimilitary sentiments.

Most arms controllers believe that the risk of war can be reduced by making our forces nonprovocative. They conceive of this as a unilateral enterprise. The military establishment, they assert, should be made up of forces which can survive a first strike and react slowly and deliberately in retaliation. Hardened missiles and positive command and control arrangements stem from this doctrine. They want to deny nuclears to Nth countries, fearing that proliferation will increase the chances of war. Thus no MRBM's have been built for deployment in NATO countries while France has been denied United States assistance in developing her nuclear weapons capability. The new school of strategic thought considers bombers to be vulnerable weapons, only good for first strikes, and extremely provocative and de-stabilizing. Thus the B-70 construction was curtailed to two experimental aircraft. A stable world environment is implicitly considered to be the ultimate national objective.

Some arms controllers seem to want nuclear war to be as horrible as possible for then, it is reasoned, war will never occur. Thus we should target cities and avoid civil defense, even for ourselves. Also, they are against anti-ICBM developments, and the extension of the so-called arms race into space. The resulting strategic posture is sometimes referred to as the "balance of terror," an apt phrase indeed.

The ordinary citizen might find it hard to understand how the United States can pursue a strategy which will make general war not only more dangerous but also a strategy which places the United States in a position where it will be almost impossible to win. The average military man is equally perplexed by this inverted strategy. The answer is, of course, as the arms controllers explain it, that this posture of terror supposedly will better deter general war. Since there is no historical evidence to support this assertion, and an abundance of historical evidence to refute it, we rest our national security on the intuition of this new breed of defense intellectual.

If we unilaterally pursued these arms control avenues while the Soviets continued to arm without restraint of any kind, to develop anti-ICBM's, civil defense, and quick strike capabilities with Minuteman-type weapons as McNamara would have it, it is not inconceivable that our power position might become so weakened as to make agreement with Soviet disarmament terms our only means of survival. It is not suggested that this is an arms control aim, but without the leavening of professional military judgment applied to arms control measures, there is real danger of unwittingly falling into a second rate military posture which would leave no recourse other than to accept Soviet disarmament proposals, such as a treaty without adequate inspection provisions. We need only recall the uninspected test ban moratorium of 1958-1961 to see what might happen if we were caught in such a trap.

An editorial in the *Wall Street Journal* of January 28, 1965, recognized this danger:

> Although there is almost no likelihood of substantial disarmament in any near future, the state of mind surrounding much of the dis-

cussion is unhealthy—both as it may mislead public opinion and mis-
direct public policy. It is entirely conceivable that the U. S. could
become psychologically prepared to enter agreements that would put
the nation at a dangerous military disadvantage.

Arms controllers naturally want to reduce nuclear delivery weapons as a first step in disarmament. They have leveled their sights
on B-47's and B-52's because these bombers are considered provocative and destabilizing. Skybolt[11] cancellation perfectly fit the
new philosophy. So did Nike Zeus[12] cancellation and Dyna Soar.[13]

Many would like to see a nuclear parity with the Soviets involving perhaps a top limit of five hundred or less nuclear missiles on
each side as a "stable deterrent"[14] step in "General and Complete
Disarmament." This, they feel, would effectively cancel out the use
of nuclear weapons altogether. War could then be fought conven-
tionally. MRBM's, of course, will never be built because their employment in Europe is considered provocative. Remember that we
have removed Jupiters and Thors from Turkey, England, and Italy.

Have these new strategists overlooked the fact that even a conventional war cannot be won without air superiority? Has the
nuclear bomb or warhead taken on such overwhelming significance
in their thinking as to blank out other military considerations?
They conceive of nuclear weapons to be the greatest evil in the
world. This thought seems to cloud all judgment, all knowledge
and experience and sometimes all loyalties.

Strangely, many arms controllers believe that the United States
is as apt to cause nuclear war as the Soviet Union. This might
happen through "accident, miscalculation, or madness," and thus
arms controllers recommend measures to deter our own ability to
employ nuclear weapons. These measures are positive command
and control arrangements sometimes referred to as "permissive
action links," which will prevent the arming or launching of nuclear weapons without direct Presidential command.

Defense intellectuals are now engaging in still another bit of
inverted reasoning by claiming that military hardware has reached
a plateau of development and that future technological break-
throughs are unlikely. Hanson W. Baldwin incisively condemned
this attitude in his article "Slow-Down in the Pentagon."[15] He
ridiculed the belief that the technical revolution is over and criti-
cised the "simplistic viewpoint" that technological development
makes us less secure. The purpose behind this idea was revealed
by Drs. Jerome B. Wiesner and Herbert F. York in their *Scientific*

American article of October, 1964,[16] which was nicely timed for campaign literature. Misleading statements, ambiguous scientific terminology, and borderline classified information combined to give the impression that further technical development in the field of nuclear warfare would be fruitless and self-defeating. The wish is father to the thought that no further development is likely. "Both riders in the arms race," the authors wrote in a clear statement of the inverted proposition, "are thus confronted by the dilemma of steadily increasing military power and steadily decreasing national security." Then followed a statement which strikes one with a chilling shock when considering that it comes from two of the foremost scientists of our time, both of whom have served as White House advisors. The italics is in the original: *"It is our considered professional judgment that this dilemma has no technical solution."* Here is stark defeatism at the highest scientific level. One wonders if Benjamin Franklin or Alexander Graham Bell or Thomas Edison would have put their signatures to such a statement.

IMPETUS TO THE ANTI-MILITARY BIAS

Implicit in the fear of nuclear accident is the distrust of the military commander. Recent nuclear scare fiction and films reveal this all too clearly. The villain is often a military man who either goes insane or deliberately violates his orders and starts a war on his own initiative. Here again, the fact that there is no precedent for this in American history seems to be of minor concern to arms controllers. This paranoiac distrust of the military is another attitude which has been largely established by the arms control literature, and whatever its motivation, it is reducing the pride and effectiveness of the armed forces.

To the general public, and this includes many influential civilian leaders, the arms control arguments are quite plausible. And there can be little doubt that the large majority of arms controllers sincerely believe that their doctrine is the only way to save America. *Military* men are the naïve ones if they pooh-pooh what is now considered real political sophistication. It is up to them, and them alone, to bring military sanity to this growing movement. Arms control doctrine should not be regarded as military sophistry, but as a clear expression of the popular sentiment regarding armed forces and nuclear weapons.

The possibility of war being caused by military accident is harped on so much that the public may soon come to regard the military itself as a potential enemy. Can there truly be any other reason for such emphasis on positive controls and permissive action links over weapons than distrust of or at least lack of confidence in the military who handle these weapons? In prenuclear days, military forces were capable of starting war with gunpowder and TNT weapons but this fear was rarely expressed. What has occurred to cause us now to question the integrity and loyalty of our military commanders?

The accidental war concept was sensationally launched by the novel *Red Alert* by Peter Bryant,[17] a horror story describing a war started by a crazed SAC commander. It has become required reading for many arms controllers. Soon after the story was published in 1958, it was ordered that tactical pilots would be medically examined for possible mental abnormalities. The connection seems obvious.

Fail Safe by Burdick & Wheeler, as we have seen, is a later thriller of similar plot. This impossible yarn relates how a condenser blows in communications equipment and thus causes a bomber force to fly past its fail-safe point and attack Moscow. Such a ridiculously inaccurate story, deliberately twisting the whole concept of fail-safe which simply means that if any part of the system fails the system *is* safe, is passed off by the authors as an authentic possibility, even a probability. Say the authors, "it represents a competent estimate of the technical and scientific factors involved in the 'fail-safe' system." As to the chances of its happening, Burdick said "I believe it to be inevitable. . . . We interviewed scores of physicists and scientists with the AEC, the RAND Corporation, and the government. Almost all of them gave us the classical response: 'Of *course* war by accident not only could happen . . . *it* probably *will*.' " [18]

It may be interesting to note that military opinion on this assumed probability was evidently not sought.

CONCLUSION

The arms control movement gains new converts daily and is taking on the fervor of a religion. To question certain features of it one is branded out of hand as blind, unreasoning, stupid, and possibly evil, with little regard for life or humanity. Yet unless arms control doctrine is tempered with the practical political and military understanding of historians, politicians, diplomats, and military men, there is grave danger of our national policy taking a wrong turn. Given balanced inputs, some arms control schemes may become a means for improving our national security while at the same time decreasing military expenditures, although the present model as portrayed in the Summer Study anthology seems to be too far out to make much sense. One thing is sure, arms control today is weakening America's military posture and providing reasons for circumventing the professional military men who still believe in the doctrine of military superiority.

CHAPTER 22

THE MILITARY IN POLITICS

Speaking to the graduating class of the United States Naval Academy in 1961, President John F. Kennedy said, "I know that you are constantly warned during your days here not to mix, in your naval careers, in politics. I should point out, however, on the other side, that my rather rapid rise from a Reserve Lieutenant of uncertain standing to Commander in Chief has been because I did not follow that very good advice." [1]

This humorous anecdote of the late President reveals the wide gap between the military codes of the regular and the reserve, and the differing American attitudes towards these two categories of our military service. One of the two military men eschews politics by virtue of an internal code of behavior which warns that his participation would pose a "threat to democratic values and institutions." [2] The other military man holding to no such code, even when on active duty, actively engages in politics without restraint when off duty and never considers himself as threatening democracy by virtue of his military affiliations.

One will be quick to point out that the reserve does not engage in partisan politics while on active duty and thus does not use military connections to enhance his political ambitions. Nevertheless, he behaves considerably more freely in the political milieu than the regular, even when both are assigned to the same organization. The reserve obeys the Hatch Act as do civil servants and appointed officials of the government, but he rarely applies it to himself as strictly as does the regular officer.

RETIREMENT STATUS

When he retires, the reserve is not subject to the same legal re-

299

strictions as is the retired regular. The ex-reserve may take a government job, for example, without it affecting his retirement pay while the regular suffers a drastic cut of his retired pay for reasons of "dual compensation." The retired regular is denied employment which might require contacts with the military services for reasons of "conflict of interest." In other words he is prohibited from doing the kind of work he has been best educated to do. The reserve is under no such restrictions. The reserve may have served a long career on active duty yet nothing would prevent his appointment to the post of Secretary of Defense, or Deputy Secretary of Defense, for example, because the caveat against the military holding that office refers specifically to the "Regular component." [3] Nor could a retired regular be appointed to one of the many assistant secretaryships in the Department of Defense because they must be appointed "from civilian life" [4] and a retired regular, unlike a retired or inactive reserve, is *not* considered to be a civilian. The regular is constrained by the same special legal status, whether active or retired.

It is interesting to note that the first provision for reducing the pay of an officer who had been given the new status of "retired" was contained in the Act of August 3, 1861. Prior to that time an officer held his position and pay for life whether or not he had an active assignment. [5] Since 1861 pay deductions have been frequent yet the constraints of military status have remained constant. Hence a regular is not pensioned as are other veterans but rather "retired from active duty."

This discrimination against the regular extends into many other areas, from pay to dependents' benefits. Justification of this is sometimes attempted on the proposition that a regular presents a potential threat to democracy and hence must be kept at arm's length from the body politic, like a political leper of some sort, denied his rightful legacy of citizenship: freedom of speech, assembly, and even movement. He can, of course, avoid this discrimination by resigning and by giving up his retired pay and other benefits which he has earned through a long career of underpaid and often hazardous service. But now he is elderly, ill equipped for a civilian career, and often dependent upon his meager retirement stipend. No other retired Federal employee is so discriminated against; no other retired Federal employee must suffer such unfair restriction on his activities as the retired regular military man.

INDIVIDUAL REVOLTS

Periodically the injustice and irritation of the regular's segregation from society gets under his skin. A regular who thus loses his self-control then tends to justify all the antidemocratic stereotypes. Repeated frustrations have propelled certain officers into far-right political activities, as with Navy Captain Cromelin and Army Major General Edwin Walker. But their individual aberrations no more threaten the civil supremacy than would a similar aberration in civilian life, nor do they in any way suggest a possible military dictatorship. In fact, if America's political principles of a nation "of the people, by the people" are to be sincerely upheld, even those professing a far right doctrine should be respected as long as those proponents abide by the law.

Military dictatorship, if it is to be feared at all, is only possible when the military is used institutionally. A far more likely danger of military dictatorship might be suggested when the President employs regular troops to quell civil disorder. If this ultimate power is used habitually against citizens no corporal force is available to prevent its use against civil institutions of any sort and even against Congress itself in the Cromwellian manner. Only America's traditional principles of division of power and of checks and balances stand in the way of absolute Presidential power. Such traditions are more fundamental than the law and if the traditions are permitted to erode, the law is undermined.

EARLY TRADITIONS

As we have noted, in America's early history, there was little bias against and no political restrictions placed upon the military man as an *individual*, active or resigned. (There were no reserves except as state militia.) The antimilitary feature of early American customs and mores related to the military as an organized institution, not to the individual of that institution. Louis Smith lists five manifestations of this early antimilitary tradition, none of them mentioning political activities of individual men in uniform. In summary these antimilitary features were: (1) fear of standing armies, (2) supremacy of civil authority over military power, (3) preference for state militias over professional forces of the central government, (4) reliance on the navy as the first line of defense, and (5) a grant of "almost unlimited" powers to Congress to raise and support armies.[6]

These traditional antimilitary prejudices have been altered almost out of recognition through the subsequent changes brought about in American government and the nature of war. A standing army has been accepted as necessary in a dangerous world. Civil supremacy has been mistranslated into "civilian" supremacy as related to individuals, and to civilian participation and supervision of the military. We, somehow feel safer by keeping the "military mind" out of civil government. Militias (National Guards) are little more than an extension of the federal power and of the standing army. The Navy is one of three co-equal military institutions since we can no longer count on total protection from the oceanic waters girding our shores. And although Congress still votes the annual military budget, the Executive may or may not decide to use the funds authorized.

RISE OF THE APOLITICAL CODE

As the old antimilitary traditions have altered, new ones have been acquired, one of which is the apolitical tradition of the individual military man. This apolitical code manifested itself in law as late as 1870 when Congress enacted a statute prohibiting the military man on active duty from holding a public office in government, either by election or by appointment, without the express permission of Congress.[7] This was in contradiction to the constitutional theory of the Founding Fathers who did not wish to deny the soldier his citizenship rights.[8] As we have noted, General Scott was an active political leader, campaigning for the Presidency while commanding the army. So was General Jacob Brown a practicing politician. Huntington notes that the *Army and Navy Chronicle* of 1836 reported that most officers of the early Republic favored military participation in politics, arguing that the Founding Fathers had set the example and that every officer in the Revolutionary Army was a politician. "The feeling and the opinion that an officer should take no part in politics are conceived in the most servile spirit, and inculcated by heartless military aristocrats, whose interest it is to hold the minds of their subordinates in entire subjection to their domineering propensities."[9]

Was the law of 1870 which codified military avoidance of politics motivated to enhance civil supremacy after almost a century of government during which civil supremacy had never been challenged? Or was the law motivated to make more jobs available to the thousands of job-seeking veterans of the Grand Army? We might suspect the latter since today we experience political agitation from organized bodies of government employees whenever a traditionally civilian job within the Department of Defense is taken over by a man in uniform.

GENERALS IN THE WHITE HOUSE

The passage of the 1870 law barring military men from civil jobs marked a distinct change in the American attitude toward military leadership. After the Civil War, three ex-generals in succession had been elected to the presidency: Ulysses S. Grant, Rutherford B. Hayes, and James A. Garfield. President Chester A. Arthur, elected in the campaign of 1880, enjoyed no military distinction (although he had served in the Civil War), while Arthur's successor, Grover Cleveland, elected in 1884, had no military background whatever. Excepting for the 1888 election of Benjamin Harrison (when Cleveland's popular vote was the larger), who was the last Civil War general to serve in the White House, the civilian tradition was not broken until General Dwight D. Eisenhower succeeded to that high office in 1953.

SHERMAN'S ATTITUDE

The emerging apolitical tradition for military professionals was given further impetus by General William T. Sherman, who, next to Grant, was the most famous of post-war generals. Sherman was appointed Commander of the United States Army in 1869 and held that post for fifteen years, retiring on his own request in 1884. Repeatedly the powerful Grand Army of the Republic veterans placed Sherman's name in candidacy for President and just as repeatedly he firmly refused to run stating bluntly on one occasion, "I will not run if nominated or serve if elected." [10]

Sherman's violent aversion to politics, politicians and newsmen is legend and understandable. The Army Appropriation Act of July 15, 1870, drastically curtailed the authority of the Commander of the Army. The Secretary of War was assigned by law almost all of the former functions of the military leader, not unlike the more recent laws setting up the powers of OSD. General Sherman with a staff consisting of two aides moved to Cleveland in 1874 to escape "the mortification of being slighted by men in Washington who were using their temporary power for selfish ends." [11] Sherman returned to Washington two years later, however, after Secretary of War W. W. Belknap was forced to resign because of fraud. Belknap had collaborated with other politicians to curtail Sherman's power.[12]

Sherman was unbending in his belief that the military be divorced from politics. He also felt that it was "beneath a soldier's vocation" to engage in police work and that the army should always be "organized and governed on true military principles" so that it would be ready for war. Political neutrality, he believed, was essential to meet these objectives.

Sherman's anti-political attitude spread to those under his command. Several regulations were written supporting his doctrines. Thus was influenced the officer code of the United States Army. Sherman's attitude was in stark contrast to Winfield Scott's who thrice was a candidate and once was a nominee for the office of the President.

EVENTS IN FRANCE

Events in France were far overshadowed in America by the turmoil of the Civil War but as the United States settled into peaceful pursuits after the conflict the country began to take more notice of the outside world. The cause of liberty in France had been shattered in 1852 by the Second Empire of Napoleon III. Elected legitimately in 1848, Louis Napoleon, the Little Corporal's nephew, had used the French army to seize the throne of empire. His ambitions led to many adventures in foreign affairs, among them an abortive effort under Archduke Maximillian to take Mexico. Another, the disastrous Franco-Prussian War of 1870-71. A Third French Republic was proclaimed in 1871 after a bloodless revolution, with the goddess of liberty again restored.

The French army was left with a bad name for its support of the tyrant Napoleon and for its ignominious defeat at the hands of von Moltke's general staff. The lesson did not go unnoticed in America and it might have suggested that the best mode of behavior was for the United States Army to wash its hands of politics in any form, even for individual military leaders to avoid involvement.

GERMAN EXAMPLE

As we have seen, the code of the German General Staff was apolitical in the extreme. It was dedicated to serve the Emperor, and solely the Emperor, having no association whatever with the popular political elements of government. The inflated reputation of the German General Staff as a consequence of its three successive lightning victories over Denmark, Austria and France, influenced other armies, particularly those of Britain and the United States, to emulate Prussian military practices. Thus still another push was given to the growing apolitical military tradition in the United States.

As we have seen, Groener and von Seeckt translated loyalty to the Emperor into the "mystical concept of the Reich" and preached to the military "to serve the State far from all party politics." [13] Such warnings later went unheeded in the Third Reich because Hitler ruthlessly axed off the top men until he found those who would do his bidding. But the apolitical doctrine had already had its effect on the American army. Fortunately for America it has never had to endure a Hitler.

Speaking to the Massachusets legislature in 1951, General Douglas MacArthur revealed a similar attitude in the American army regarding a "higher" loyalty.

> I find in existence a new and heretofore unknown and dangerous concept that the members of our armed forces owe primary allegiance and loyalty to those who temporarily exercise the authority of the executive branch of government, rather than to the country and its Constitution which they are sworn to defend.
>
> No proposition could be more dangerous. None could cast greater doubt upon the integrity of the armed forces.
>
> For its application would at once convert them from their traditional constitutional role as the instrument for the defense of the Republic into something partaking of the nature of a praetorian guard, owing sole allegiance to the political master of the hour.[14]

MAN-ON-HORSEBACK IN FRANCE

Stories of the man on horseback continued to frighten the American public. In France, Marshal MacMahon was proclaimed "president of the republic" in 1875. He was regarded by the conservatives as a forerunner of a future monarch, although he represented the Republican factions.[15] In 1877 MacMahon attempted unsuccessfully to dissolve the chamber of deputies, and two years later he was defeated by a coalition of several leftist groups, "union des gauches," which had begun to dominate French politics. A Socialist Labor party was formed in 1879 which was to exert considerable influence in politics although its strength was largely in the cities.

By 1880 the Radical Republicans led by Georges Clemenceau managed to get a popular general, Georges Boulanger, appointed minister of war. Boulanger made himself popular by energetic reforms and by "republicanizing" the army. General Boulanger also stood for *revanche* against the Germans which was a popular cause in some circles. When a scandal broke around the French President whose son-in-law had been discovered selling decorations, Boulanger (who previously had been returned to a military command) was elected to Paris with much acclaim. There he attempted a *coup d'etat*. It failed and when the new Premier threatened to try Boulanger he fled to Brussels where he committed suicide.

This grand opera in France was soberly regarded in America. It provided further arguments for the American military to withdraw more and more from politics, as if in atonement for the ultrapolitical activities of military individuals in France.

Drama burst forth again in the volatile French Republic with the Dreyfus case of 1894-1906. Captain Alfred Dreyfus had been accused and convicted of selling military secrets to Germany but it was later revealed that much of the evidence against him had been falsely concocted or forged. The efforts to reopen his case and its retrial caused heated political debates. In this affair militarism had become linked with clericalism and Republicanism. Now the Radicals, who had been super patriots after the overthrow of Napoleon III and under the leadership of Gambetta, were antimilitary. So, too, were the Socialists who regarded the military as strike-breakers.

It is interesting to note that the French rightist parties which were antimilitary in the 1870's switched their attitude toward the military by the 20th Century while the reverse happened with the leftist parties. This provides a vivid illustration of the fallacy of stamping "left" or "right" on military institutions as innate characteristics. The military may be disposed in either direction depending, as a rule, upon its civil guidance. Certainly the Peoples Liberation Army (PLA) of Communist China is leftist, while the army of Franco's Spain is rightist. The United States Army was used in strikebreaking no less than 328 times between 1886 and 1895 [16] because it was ordered to do so by the civil authority, not because it had, as an institution, any antilabor tendencies.

Like the old German army, the post-World War II French army developed the notion that it stood above the government of the moment. Loyalty to *La Patrie* was ultimate. Therefore, following a series of bitter defeats from 1940 to 1958, it rationalized its right and duty to intervene in politics. The Algiers uprisings brought about the fall of the Republic and the re-emergence of Charles de

Gaulle. Once having broken the political ice, the army in Algeria later attempted to reverse de Gaulle's liberal policy there. An army *coup* failed in April 1961 and after several more years of strife de Gaulle finally gained the upper hand.

This praetorian activity shocked Americans who had regarded the French army as apolitical and who wondered, as a consequence, how truly apolitical might be the American army. It had been reasoned rather superficially that the theory of revolutionary warfare witnessed by the French army in Vietnam and Algeria had "transferred the battlefield of modern war from temporal terrain to the minds of men," [17] but this is hardly an excuse for the kind of political involvement practiced in Algeria. What more likely caused the French army's fall from grace was the complete bankruptcy of France's Fourth Republic which turned over governments so rapidly following World War II as to leave the country a morass of confusion, inefficiency and waste. Thousands of French soldiers fought and died in vain while Paris fiddled. The *coup* which restored de Gaulle, a *coup* staged by the army, seems in retrospect to have been a move in the right direction. France is now recovering her prestige, prosperity and stability. But the effect on America has been to argue for more complete civil control than ever before.

RECONSTRUCTION

Another influence on the military apolitical code was the unhappy experience of Southern Reconstruction following the Civil War. Vindictive individuals who gained control of the government after Lincoln's assassination were determined to teach the South a lesson. But first there was a pell-mell demobilization of Union volunteers at the end of the war, with the regular establishment reduced by 1866 to 54,600 enlisted men and 3,036 officers of the line. From this establishment came the occupation force of the Southern states which were divided into five districts, each headed by a military governor. The military governor was charged with registering voters and supervising the formation of new governments which might apply for readmission to the Union. This form of dictatorial military government continued in some form until as late as 1877 when the last troops were withdrawn from South Carolina and Louisiana.[18]

In the midst of this difficult occupation the strength of the army was cut still more. The Act of March 3, 1869, reduced enlisted strength to 37,000 and the officer corps to 2,227. Seven hundred and fifty regular officers were dismissed with a year's pay.[19]

Caught between a civil population in a South which despised them, and an ungrateful inept government in Washington dominated by get-rich-quick politicians, regular officers gained a bitter taste of politics. The army was obliged to carry out distasteful policies for reasons not altogether noble while carpet-baggers drained the last drops of blood from the prostrate Southern states. It is not surprising that the army took on an aversion to politics at this juncture.

INDIAN WARS

For the remainder of the 19th century the army was engaged in the vicious Indian Wars. Twelve major campaigns were fought between 1865 and 1898, with 943 engagements. Facing danger in lonely isolated posts, the small regular establishment, seldom with a strength greater than 25,000, became separated from the American society and largely forgotten. The "full bitterness of national indifference" [20] was experienced in 1876 when Congress failed to appropriate pay for the army. Troops had to live on what credit they could find. Interest rates ran about six percent. When pay was restored in November, 1877, Congress stubbornly refused to honor claims for the interest payments.

Janowitz refers to the "self-generated social isolation" of the soldier from the rest of the community,[21] yet this isolation was not exactly self-generated. The serviceman did not choose to live on the isolated frontiers. This was a military duty established by the government.

The obvious indifference of Congress and the isolation of the little fighting army in the West added still more emphasis to the apolitical tradition.

RISE OF PROFESSIONALISM

Some halting beginnings were made during this era toward a military profession and these professional movements tended to crystallize the apolitical code into military literature. General Winfield Scott Hancock, one of the last military politicians of the 19th century, experienced the changing temper by being defeated in a Presidential election. Realizing how military prestige was fading, he sponsored the creation of the Military Service Institution in 1878.[22] This society was dedicated to the advancement of the art of war, and modeled upon Britain's Royal United Services Institution, with a bimonthly journal and branch societies organized on posts throughout the army.[23] Emory Upton and Arthur L. Wagner, who were studying and reporting the Franco-Prussian War and the German General Staff, did much to advance this professional effort. The senior military School of Application was also established about this time at Fort Leavenworth, Kansas.

A far more successful professional society than the army's Military Service Institution was the United States Naval Institute. It had been organized five years earlier, in 1873, also along the lines of the Royal United Service Institution with the purpose of advancing the professional and scientific knowledge of the navy. Whereas the Military Service Institution folded for lack of funds in 1918, the U. S. Naval Institute continued to prosper, publishing its *Proceedings* for an ever-growing audience. Today its magazine is one of the most influential professional organs in the country. The army's failure with the Military Service Institution reflected the fragmentation of the army into specialties of Infantry, Artillery, Engineers, etc., each with its own professional journal.[24]

Although Huntington refers to the latter 19th Century as the golden age of military professionalism, the professional progress was halting and fractionated in comparison to the civilian professions of the same era. Moreover, both the Army and the Navy were so small as to leave but a slight impression on the culture, learning, or even the consciousness of the country.

RISE OF SOCIALISM

Socialism and the communist doctrines of Karl Marx and Friedrich Engels materialized in the mid-19th century as a concomitant of the industrial revolution. In the very beginning the military was identified as an implacable enemy of these new doctrines which preached the overthrow of capitalism by strikes and violence. The military, being a tool of government, dedicated to order and the protection of property, was again and again pitted against socialistically inspired uprisings. It was obvious to the socialists that their militant enemy must be weakened by whatever means. This had nothing to do with the philosophical disposition of the military itself, nothing to do with a "military mind," or with conservatism (although these tags were tied to the military), but simply with the fact that the military was the strong arm of government and had to be weakened if socialism and communism were to prosper.[25] As a consequence the "declared policy was one of enmity toward the

military machine, the military caste, and the military state. . . ." [26]
The philosophical conception of the communist millennium supported this attitude. The new order would bring absolute peace without government, a pure nirvana, although achievement of the ideal was to be accomplished through protracted class warfare and violence.

Communist doctrine called for class warfare at every level of human intercourse: economic, psychological and diplomatic. The technique of propaganda to win the minds of the people took on new meaning and achieved higher levels of persuasion. Value systems began to change. The credo of Marx was not just to interpret the world, but to change it. Capitalizing on all the other tendencies which were causing the isolation of the military and the crystallization of the apolitical military code, the socialist-communist antimilitary campaign achieved a phenomenal success. Had it not been for two world wars, one of which threatened the communist mecca, Moscow, when effective military force became a necessity, it is conceivable that the disparagement of the military would, by now, have been so complete as to have permitted a takeover of government by militant communism. Two successful wars allowed the western military establishments to recover their pride momentarily, but the antimilitary attack has continued.

Today the communist program supports the antimilitary bias in almost every particular. There are five basic targets toward which communist propaganda point with respect to the military of non-communist countries. First, it rejects the concept of "national" defense since ultimate loyalty must be bestowed on the socialist fatherland of the Soviet Union. Second, defeatism and the futility of military defense are emphasized, noting that the "real" enemy is within the existing government, such as the "far right" or "hate groups." As we have noted, nuclear weapons are also enemies, as are the "military minds." Third, in time of war it calls for revolutionary disintegration and fraternization between troops of belligerent forces. Fourth, it seeks to popularize the notion of "imperialist war" and encourages civil war. Fifth, all revolutionary war actions are supported as the road to a real "peace" which is possible only under the Soviet Union. [27]

"Revolutionary antimilitarism is an essential prerequisite for achieving Soviet power," wrote Robert Beerstecher in a monumental study of the problem. [28] The first step in seizing control of the civil power is to cause a disintegration of the existing military forces of the state. The armed forces, as in the October Revolution, are considered the decisive factor in revolution. Thus every means must be taken to shake the loyalty which the soldier holds toward the existing regime. Once the soldier becomes emotionally separated from his civilian authority he is ripe for revolutionary ideas and actions.[29] As the chief instrument of state power, the armed forces must be destroyed. This requires actual penetration of the military establishment, but might be achieved even more readily by penetrating its civilian leadership, particularly in a society where civilian leadership is so overwhelming.

CONCLUSION

A survey of military legislation reveals that the antimilitary bias, when directed at the *individual* military man as opposed to the "standing army," is a relatively recent phenomenon which materialized during the latter years of the 19th Century and has been growing ever since. Two world wars tended to check the growth of this bias momentarily but today it has become so ingrained in American culture as to go relatively unchallenged.

The Hatch Act [30] which makes it illegal for those in government to participate in partisan politics applies to civilians and military alike, but this law is interpreted much more strictly by those in uniform. Most of the military apolitical code is self-imposed as servicemen have come to believe that military participation in politics is dangerous to democracy because of the "military mind," whereas the restraints on civilians are justified more on the basis that an actively political bureaucracy could perpetuate itself in office. It would be unthinkable for a general to run for President without resigning although a senator or a cabinet member feels no necessity for taking such a step of dissociating himself from the office he has acquired through political means. As a matter of fact, the Hatch Act specifically does not apply to high level government posts, but does apply to all of those in uniform.[31] It is interesting to note, however, that before 1861 there was no retirement provision for the regular officer and, like a judge, he served for life. Consequently, when he ran for public office he remained an officer of the army. For example:

> Since the founding of the Republic officers of the uniformed services, remaining such for life, have drawn pay related to active duty pay (until 1963). For the first 70 years of the Republic officers of the regular uniformed services were continued on active duty at full pay during good behavior until their death, just as Federal judges have

been retained at full pay. There was no provision for retirement either for years of service or because of disability . . .[32]

Conflict of interest became a concern as early as 1838 for judges who were enjoined not to be employed as counsels or attorneys, and for military officers who were prohibited from engaging "in the services of an incorporated company." But this did not prohibit either kind of professional from holding public office.[33] On the contrary, it was expected that he continue his public service through the customary process of election.

The American citizen, including the uniformed professional, might take heed of a remark made by former President Eisenhower on the occasion of his receiving an honorary Doctor of Law degree at Messiah College, Grantham, Pa., in 1965: "Anyone who feels he is above politics as something dirty forgets the true meaning of the word . . . the affairs of man." [34]

It may be time for the regular military man to reexamine his apolitical code. Does it apply to the present milieu? The supersonic nuclear age? Is it, as Huntington asserts, a true criterion of professionalism? Or is it a habit of mind which has grown because of once valid reasons which no longer apply? Is it truly in the best interests of the country? Or does it eliminate a certain point of view which is essential to national survival?

CHAPTER 23

ARMED FORCES UNIFICATION

It has often been argued that unification would save billions for the government. But since the so-called Unification Act after World War II the cost of defense has steadily risen. Doesn't this demonstrate the fallacy of the economy argument?

Perhaps we have become confused by popular terms. The act referred to is properly titled the *National Security Act of 1947*. Nowhere does the act refer to "unification." "Coordination" is the key word and even that has been rather questionably accomplished among the armed services as a result of this legislation. To provide the appearance of unity and guard against the presumed dangers of military centralism, a civilian hierarchy was superimposed over all the armed services. This was the Office of the Secretary of Defense (OSD). Instead of reducing the overhead of the armed services, this legislation and subsequent amendments increased it many fold.

The civilian Office of the Secretary of Defense was entirely additive to the military establishment which then existed. At first the membership of the Office of the Secretary of Defense was held small by the statute, but as we have noted with each legislative revision the number of people in OSD has increased. The remedy for alleged ineffectiveness of the organization was generally considered to be an increase in authority for the Secretary of Defense, and with more authority went more office manpower. Almost all observers agree that OSD has become so large and unwieldy that this kind of "unification" has been both costly and counter-productive.

When Secretary of Defense McNamara came into office he declared his intention to pare down the size of OSD. Exactly the reverse took place. There were ten administrators with the rank of Assistant Secretary of Defense or higher in 1961 when he moved in. By 1965 there were still ten. There were some eleven Deputy Assistant Secretaries of Defense in 1961. By 1965 this number had been increased to thirty-five.[1]

Excerpts from the *Journal of the Armed Forces* of March 14, 1964, provide an eye-opener regarding the growth of OSD:

> . . . Originally conceived as a small, top-level management group to set overall policy for the Armed Forces, the Defense Department has mushroomed into a force of more than three 'divisions' of uniformed people, plus thousands of civilians . . . officer-enlisted strength of almost 12,000 . . . total number of officers and men 'borrowed' from the services by the Defense Department for various activities is *41,244*— a force two and one-half times larger than the entire Marine Corps officer strength. . . .
>
> Ten years ago, in the Defense Department hearings for fiscal 1955, DOD witnesses said there would be an 'average' of 560 military personnel assigned to OSD. . . .

Another estimate made by Representative Charles S. Gubser of California set the figure of 34,000 employees responsible to the Office of the Secretary of Defense.[2] Perhaps the disparity between these figures and those given by the *Journal of the Armed Forces* is due to the ambiguity of the terms "borrowed" and "assigned." Regardless of how the figures may be juggled by OSD, tens of thousands of military and civilian personnel now constitute the Department of Defense headquarters of the United States. Considering that the strength of OSD was less than 2,000 on June 30, 1958,[3] the growth of OSD can be likened to a runaway cancer.

JCS AUTHORITY

Walter Millis wrote that ". . . the power resides not in the uniformed officers, but in the civilian and political appointees of the Administration. . . . Before this phalanx of civilian directors, the Joint Chiefs have been immobilized. . . ."[4] He attributed much of this immobility to the inability of the Joint Chiefs to agree, but this was largely a consequence of the headless organization forced upon it. In the 1960's, when the JCS *did* agree on many significant issues the Secretary of Defense felt no restraint from overruling them. Moreover, several JCS recommendations were reversed by the Secretary of Defense not for political reasons, but for technical and "military" reasons, as was demonstrated by the TFX and the Pluto rulings when both military judgment and "cost analysis" favored the weapons which were cancelled. Rarely, however, have such rulings been revealed, the veil of policy classification and censorship hiding the marked differences between JCS and OSD. On those few occasions when the veil was lifted for a moment, the OSD public information horns were blown loudly, assuring the world that there were no real differences. The JCS, of course, has no public information outlet and is never heard from as a corporate body.

In an interview published by the *New York American* on May 9, 1965, Secretary McNamara was asked:

> Q. There have been articles taking you to task for going further than previous Secretaries and over-riding majority views of the Chiefs of Staff. Can the Secretary do that? In his recommendations to the President, can he do as he pleases?
>
> A. The fact is that I can not recall a single major decision on which I have acted contrary to the unanimous opinion of the Joint Chiefs of Staff. I can recall several instances which I have made recommendations contrary to the majority view, but none in which I have acted contrary to the unanimous view.

Eight days later, on May 17, 1965, the *Defense Management Report* carried this news item:

McNAMARA OVER-RULED FIVE UNANIMOUS DECISIONS OF JOINT CHIEFS

> Testimony to House and Senate Committees concerned with defense programs turns up the fact that Sec. of Defense Robert S. McNamara overruled the Joint Chiefs of Staff on five major programs in which they had voted unanimously in favor of— (1) procurement of 200 more Minuteman missiles (2) preproduction funds for Nike Zeus (3) procurement of two more submarines (4) proceeding with development plans and action on a new improved manned interceptor and (5) an advanced manned strategic bomber.[5]

The United States fought and won the greatest war in history without an Office of the Secretary of Defense. Coordination was largely achieved within the Joint Chiefs of Staff by professional military men. And the President himself decided the policy splits. Indeed, the necessary administrative machinery for operating our national defense already existed within the uniformed services and the *ad hoc* JCS organization which had been able to direct and win a vast two-front war. What was needed was a reorganization of *that* machinery to provide a formal system which could resolve indecision and excessive duplication. The military leaders themselves had experienced this need during the war. Instead, an entirely new and superlative civilian cap was created by the National Security Act of 1947 in the vain effort to achieve greater coordination among the professional military services.

QUESTIONS OF BASIC PHILOSOPHY

As we have seen, when unification was debated in 1946, the vision of an evil "Prussian General Staff" was conjured up by those who opposed any true kind of centralized authority. Led by the Navy, this opposition emasculated the concept of unification.[6] The end result created defense machinery which caused new military problems to emerge faster than they could be resolved. And in the name of the "civil control of the military" a premium now has been placed upon leadership of military forces by civilian amateurs. High positions in OSD are preferably filled by civilians with meager if any experience in the fields they are charged with supervising. There can be no question now of civilian control. It is absolute. The questions remaining, now that we have complete civilian control, are these: Has this organization improved our national defense? Is it truly preserving American traditions of government?

The answers must indeed be in the negative because few will deny that in our statutory efforts at unification we have gone from bad to worse and that we probably would have been far better off had the National Security Act of 1947 never been enacted at all. As for our traditions, the great powers of OSD seem to be upsetting the traditional checks and balances between the Executive and Legislative branches.

Might it not be wiser to return to our starting point and to the originally proposed centralized control of the military by the military itself with some sort of a unified general staff setup? Perhaps it is time to dust off the Collins plan and take another look at it. Reorganizing along these lines would be nothing more or less than providing the kind of control generally exercised by modern business corporations in a free society. With two levels of civilian authority, Secretary of Defense and President, above a central general staff one can hardly say that such a military office would be overly autocratic as the often heard too-much-power-for-one-man objection would imply. In fact, a more authoritative Chairman of the JCS might check a run-away Secretary of Defense. The military "board of directors," represented by the National Security Council, could always remove the president of the corporation, represented by the Chairman of the Military General Staff, as could, of course, the President or the Secretary of Defense.

SINGLE UNIFORM CONCEPT

Writing in *Newsweek*,[7] General Carl A. Spaatz, former Chief of

Staff of the Air Force, predicted that a true general staff would cause the defense dollar to go twenty-five percent farther. He pointed out that now all services, Army, Navy, and Marine Corps, have their own air forces. To achieve real unification, General Spaatz said, it would be necessary for all branches of the service to be placed under the Secretary of Defense with a Chief of Staff and a General Staff carefully selected from outstanding graduates of the National War College. General Spaatz proposed further that personnel of the General Staff should be dressed in the same uniform except for ceremonial occasions when traditional dress uniforms of the separate services might be worn. Finally, he recommended that career personnel of any service should have freedom to transfer to other services without loss of rank.

The net result in the view of this great wartime leader would be to reduce service rivalries below the danger threshold and to provide an adequate system of national defense without overtaxing the national economy.

Although General Spaatz' recommendations may sound impractical to some, as for example his preference for a common uniform, the symbolism of a common uniform could carry more significance than one might suppose. Sociologists have established that everyone gains great affection for the "in-group" of which he is a member, and each acquires a certain degree of suspicion toward the "out-group" from which he is excluded. No matter how unconscious such feelings may be, it is said to be a psychological fact that such attitudes exist.

"In-groups" identify themselves with uniforms, whether it be the charcoal grey suit of the banker, the Paris styles of the banker's wife, or the black leather jacket and boots of the motorcycle set. Distinctive dress, however casual, is adopted by each segment of society. To reduce the identifiable feature of special groups and thus the "in-group"-"out-group" friction, some institutions have resorted to the common uniform. Many schools throughout the world have long practiced the custom, as have industries, commercial enterprises, fraternal orders, and religious sects. It can be argued either way whether the uniform fosters more or less democracy, but there can be little question that, within the uniformed group itself, the uniform contributes to cooperation and social harmony.

Although not spelled out, it appears that General Spaatz would have the services run by a special corps drawn from all services, and that these be graduates of the National War College. This would indeed return the operation and administration of the military service to professional hands. Making the National War College the instrument of selection might be open to some question, however. Advanced service schools have never been used as screening instruments for subsequent assignments and to take such a step might change the whole character of the schools themselves.

It has long been felt that senior service schools should be non-competitive in order to evoke original thinking and to nurture unique ideas which might eventually provide keys to the solution of knotty national problems. Selection would require the grading and evaluating of student performance, and where grades and elimination are a feature of the education there is usually a trend toward orthodoxy and stereotyped thinking.

INTERSERVICE TRANSFER

The freedom to transfer from service to service which General Spaatz recommended could also run into snags. After all, the services have manpower tables and budgets to fit those authorized manpower spaces. When a vacancy occurs, service "A" will more likely prefer a man from its own rolls to fill the vacancy than one from service "B". A vacancy usually means an opportunity for promotion to someone and the contenders in service "A" would not look kindly toward an outsider getting the job. It is unlikely that transfers between services could ever be more than a token procedure unless the proposed general staff assumed the overall manpower and personnel authority for all armed services. Only a superior personnel authority could match the people to the spaces in all services without there being great gaps and inequities in the military units.

COMPETITION FOR THE BUDGET

Nor could one expect that a general staff would eliminate budget fights. Always, no matter what the organizational structure, there will be bureaucratic battles for the available Federal dollars. Unification, with a general staff, might not reduce interservice controversy to any appreciable extent because even here there will be sincere and serious differences among various branches or commands and these controversies, under certain circumstances, might well reach public attention. The authority of Congress to call on any citizen to testify, and the right and duty of individuals to speak the truth, should not be abridged by any legislation or Executive fiat. We should not forget the national issues brought about within the Army itself over the question of air power and the great public debates which raged for almost three decades. The campaign of Billy Mitchell is a case in point.[8] But, in the final analysis, General Spaatz' idea might provide an organizational system which would permit decision and action when such decision and action are clearly called for.

Columnist John G. Norris once pointed out [9] that each armed service has had its post-war *tour de force* with the budget makers. First the Navy brought about a congressional investigation in 1949, with complaints against Secretary of Defense Louis Johnson's decision not to build the Forrestal class carrier. As a result of this, Admiral Louis Denfield, then Chief of Naval Operations, was fired. Nevertheless after much name-calling the Navy seemed to have won its objective. At least the large carriers were eventually built.

Four years later the new Eisenhower administration began by cutting back the Air Force. General Hoyt Vandenberg, then Chief of Staff of the Air Force, dying with cancer, fought the reductions heroically but unsuccessfully before Congress. The resultant public debate however might well have had a strong influence on the restoration of the cuts the next year.

Finally, in 1954, the Army found itself the brunt of budget cuts. General Matthew B. Ridgway, Army Chief of Staff, made no public issue of this but fought bitterly "within the family." He lost, and not until he retired and wrote his most revealing book, *Soldier*[10] was the story of this in-fighting disclosed to the public.

General staff or not, there are bound to be struggles over the available dollars, and sometimes these struggles reach such proportions as to be debated in the press. This is not altogether bad. When conflicting issues are keenly and sincerely felt by professionals, it is sometimes best for the ultimate authority—the public —to study the matters in question. The American public has always been the final arbiter on any vital and contested national issue, and such ultimate public judgment has so far kept us a free and prosperous country. Should unification ever be so rigid and doctrinaire as to prevent public discussion of vital issues, it is likely that our armed forces would degenerate into ineffective orthodoxy.

SHOULD WE RETRACE OUR STEPS?

It appears that we got off on the wrong road to begin with in

1947 and the farther we go along this road of unified civilian control and coordinated military control, the further we draw away from our destination. Recognizing that something went wrong with the National Security Act, some knowledgeable observers have recommended that we retrace our steps. Henry A. Kissinger has proposed a re-merger of the Army and Air Force.[11] He suggests that "the Navy's strategic problems may remain sufficiently distinct not to require integration, and in any case resistance in the Navy to complete unification would be so bitter as to obviate its advantages."

Dr. Kissinger may be entirely correct about Navy resistance to further unification. It is now obvious that the Navy with its Eberstadt Plan put forth by the powerful Forrestal faction was successful in torpedoing the unification efforts in 1945-47. But Kissinger neglects to consider that since the days of Billy Mitchell the Air Force has struggled mightily to be freed of Army dominance, and that the Act of 1947, poor as it was, at least gave the Air Force equality with the Army and Navy. Also, that Air Force autonomy was at least one reasonable feature of the Act since by 1952 the Air Force strategic mission was recognized as paramount in terms of the budget figures then and since.

It is indeed unlikely that the Air Force would remotely entertain the notion of returning to the Army fold. Independence was a costly gain. Many fine careers were sacrificed in the long running fight for air power and autonomy. It can safely be predicted that the hard-won ultimate victory will never be docilely handed back to the Army. In fact, the resistance Kissinger estimates the Navy would raise to complete unification would certainly be no greater than the resistance the Air Force would muster against a return to the Army.

In a *Collier's* magazine article,[12] former Secretary of the Air Force, Thomas K. Finletter, offered an equally unrealistic merger between the Air Force and the Navy, although somewhat later he proposed the full treatment of a single service. About the only bilateral merger which has not been put forth seriously is one between the Army and the Navy. Accepting the bureaucratic impracticality of such a proposal, the idea has more theoretical sense than the other two schemes.

If we accept the general war/limited war dichotomy which is the current line of Army-prone thinkers such as Kissinger, Kaufman, Gavin, Ridgway, Taylor and many other writers, then the separate missions of the Army and the Navy have considerably more in common than do the separate missions of either one of those services with the Air Force. Although I do not accept the general war/limited war dichotomy, it might be interesting to pursue this hypothesis for the moment in order to demonstrate the logic which might be used for an Army-Navy marriage.

The mission of air operations, both offensive and defensive, was assigned to the Air Force by Section 208 (f) of the National Security Act of 1947 as amended.[13] This was further defined in roles and missions documents as strategic air operations, which in effect meant the delivery of nuclear weapons to an enemy heartland and defense against comparable delivery by him upon ourselves.[14] Many people conceive of the Air Force mission solely within this circumscribed strategic scope, and indeed the Act of 1947 would imply as much since supporting aviation is "otherwise assigned" to every other branch of the armed services.

So, looking at the Air Force simply as the service designed for general all-out strategic war, then the Army and Navy must be designed more for limited brush fires and tactical war and the Army-Navy merger could be logically argued on this ground. In fact, the removal of carrier aviation from strategic target systems in 1964 supports this view. Serious consideration was given at one time, for example, to the assignment of Polaris submarines to Strategic Air Command because that weapon system seemed only suitable for general nuclear war and such a mission belonged to SAC which is a "specified" Air Force command under the direction of JCS. Thus are inconsistencies born by equating a service to specific roles and missions. Suggesting mergers of services on the basis of these artificial roles and missions becomes equally futile.

Half-measures in our efforts to secure a sensible organization for national security have already been tried and found wanting. Further half-measures would only succeed in compounding an already awkward and overly-expensive system. The only real solution seems to lie in overcoming public fears of the military itself so that we may approach the issue with unbiased eyes as we would if we were to reorganize any wholly civilian institution.

ROLES AND MISSIONS CONFUSIONS

Too many have approached the issue by proposing reorganization based on a further application of the roles and missions philosophy. Kissinger proposed a revision of specific missions with his "strategic" and "tactical" alignment in the JCS. This would appeal to those who subscribe to the general-contra-limited war dichotomy now in vogue. Even some Air Force spokesmen have suggested it. Gill Robb Wilson, a former Air Force Association president, recommended a single service "with military organization based on roles and missions rather than on the color of the suit." [15]

The point to be kept in mind is that the legislation of roles and missions among the four services as recorded in the Act of 1947 and as rooted in tradition, i.e., land, sea and air missions, is as surely a part of the problem as are the colors of the uniforms associated with those missions. Once roles and missions became fixed by law, command flexibility (to adjust force compositions to suit an actual military situation or to develop new weapons to meet potentially new threats), becomes irrevocably frozen. Any adjustment to meet the changing defense situation of the dynamic world environment is fraught with exhausting legislative haggling and bureaucratic in-fighting. There is always a wild scramble for new or altered missions because these new "jobs" will determine the relative size and importance of each service. For example, the Army, Navy and Air Force each fought valiantly for control of the new ballistic missiles and the fight is even now only at a truce stage. Such nonproductive bureaucratic conflict could be largely obviated by assigning by statute just *one* role and mission to the combined services: *to provide for the defense of the United States against all foreign enemies as directed by the President.* Then a new weapon system could be constructed by a single service and assigned for operation to joint task forces as required.

One immediately asks, with a common mission for all armed services, how would weapons, supplies and responsibilities be allocated among them? Without roles-and-missions categorizations one might visualize vicious intra-service and JCS struggles at least as violent as have been experienced in the Department of Defense and in the legislative contests for budgets and responsibilities. No doubt without an appropriate decision-making authority each service would attempt to gain the wherewithal to act independently and to prepare for war without help from its sister services. Something like this existed before Pearl Harbor. Chaos could be prevented only by administrative adjudication of the differences and by decisive leadership by the JCS or a similar superior staff system.

Roles and missions, as before 1941, would cease to become a national and inter-service issue. Instead the subject would rest in its logical place, as an administrative matter for the professional leadership to decide.

In the final analysis today, even with all the efforts to abide by the prescribed roles and missions of the National Security Act and Functions Papers, the numerous kinds of military missions have inexorably become mixed up among the four services. "Strategic" warfare is now a function of Navy Polaris submarines, while the Air Force engages in small bush wars with "commando" squadrons, and the Army develops vertical take-off fighters (although the term "fighter" has not yet been used). The Marine Corps has long resisted too handicapping a definition of its roles and missions and has managed to provide a rather well-rounded and complete military force, borrowing special weapons from the Army, Navy or Air Force as needed.

MARINE CORPS OBJECTIVES

One of the telling arguments against unification has been that the Marine Corps could be administratively disbanded simply by progressively reducing its budget or its strength. Consequently Congress wrote into the Act of 1947 specific instructions that the Marine Corps "shall be so organized as to include not less than three combat divisions and three air wings" and that "except in time of war . . . the authorized strength of the Regular Marine Corps excluding retired members, is 400,000." [16] This gives the Marine Corps a unique legal status, but the elite nature of the Marines could be retained regardless of the strengthening of the JCS to provide professional management and direction of the armed services. The Marine Corps existed long before "roles and missions" became an intra-service issue and the law fixing Marine Corps strength need not be changed.

SOME SINGLE SERVICE PROS AND CONS

With our military services on a common promotion list and directed from a single military front office, military organizations could be designed and developed to meet whatever threats appeared most dangerous at any particular period. They would be, if not more perceptive, at least more flexible to the wills of the President and Congress. Both the President and Congress are now somewhat circumscribed by the roles-and-missions legislation. With a unified high command, roles and missions could be assigned by military directive to those organizations most capable of performing the tasks and the organizations would be adjusted to fit those tasks— true "task forces" would thus emerge, in fact as well as in name, composed of whatever services seemed most appropriate. Such organizations would be revised as the situation demanded without being handicapped by statutory roles and missions. For example, it might be desirable today to create a long-range missile command, utilizing whatever skilled manpower and resources are available in all the armed forces. Several years hence, a satellite command might be desirable. Later still, possibly an interplanetary command.

With a single unified service charged by law with a single mission to defend the United States, acrimonious and wasteful jurisdictional disputes would be, if not eliminated, at least reduced. Those critical disputes remaining would achieve resolution neither by statute nor by compromise, but by clear-cut military staff study and decision. Effective national military protection must be marked by unity of purpose and direction, not by indecision and argument.

A unified service, however, is anathema to both the Navy and the Marine Corps. They fear that deep-seated pride of service and hallowed tradition would go down the drain in any wholesale merger into one uniform or equivalent reorganization. Nor are these arguments without merit. It is pride of tradition that has much to do with courage and morale. We should not callously throw out such precious intangibles to achieve a new organization which may appear in one's mind to meet the principles of good management. Logical chains of command might well encompass apathetic and ineffective fighting units. Means must be found to retain the wealth of tradition and spirit we have acquired in all Services through almost two centuries of glorious and victorious military history.

QUESTIONS OF MORALE

None can gainsay, however, that General Dwight D. Eisenhower is not lacking in pride in the Army and yet he has long favored a single service. Writing in the *New York Times* [17] James Reston thus reviewed the former President's attitude toward unification:

> . . . [Eisenhower] appeared before the Senate Committee on Military Affairs on November 16, 1945, and [stated]: . . . "One of the most important and least understood factors in modern war is that it is essentially a matter of perfected teamwork. Perfected teamwork results as much from friendly association over a period of years as it does from the more obvious reasons of combined tactical training and doctrine. By unification at the top we emphasize to our soldiers,

sailors, and airmen the essential truth that each wears the uniform of the nation's fighting forces and that his natural friends and trusted associates are the others who wear that uniform, regardless of its color or design. . . . Finally, there is no such thing as a separate land, sea or air war; therefore we must now recognize this fact by establishing a single department of the armed forces to govern us all."

Reston reported further that "the President recalled this morning [16 May 1957] that he returned from World War II convinced that 'the day of the separate services was gone.' He added that he had encountered 'very fierce opposition' and that the subsequent law establishing the Defense Department did *not* meet with his desires. At that time he wanted a chief of staff for the President. He emphasized over and over again that the main thing that was needed was the power of decision to settle inevitable differences among the services."

"In war," the former President has said, "you must have decision. A bum decision is better than none. And the trouble is that when you get three [decisions] you finally get none."

Nor can anyone deny that other great military leaders who have espoused unification are lacking in pride of service or regard for tradition. Among them have been Generals Douglas MacArthur, George C. Marshall, Omar N. Bradley, J. Lawton Collins, and J. L. Devers. Certainly the many Air Force leaders such as Henry H. Arnold, Carl A. Spaatz, Nathan F. Twining, Thomas D. White, Curtis E. LeMay, Lauris Norstad, Joseph T. McNarney and George C. Kenney cannot be unaware of the need for esprit de corps in military units.

Writing on this point, Major Margaret V. Berry made a telling argument in *Air Force* magazine.[18]

Objection: that placing all military personnel in one uniform would destroy the priceless ingredient of morale and esprit de corps. This raises the question, what is the corps to which esprit attaches? All members of the United States armed forces are now, and will continue to be Americans. This is a basic loyalty, a very big corps in which the esprit is unquestionable. What lesser corps demand esprit in the national interest is a question of judgment.

Take the first example that comes to mind—the Marines. They already have land and air units. Suppose ship units were added. Would that make a difference? And if it didn't, is it likely that the only sensible solution is to put everyone in the Marines? Is a separate uniform necessary to esprit de corps? Consider the submariners—or the paratroopers, who, in the person of the present Chief of Staff of the Army and his predecessor, not to mention the present Chief of Research and Development, seem to be doing all right in the Army. Was a separate uniform necessary to give coherence to the Army Air

Corps, or the Army Air Forces in World War II? Any reader of Cecil Wooham Smith's fascinating volume *The Reason Why* will get a sense of the attachment of British regiments of the Nineteenth Century to their "regimentals," but the Tommies of the Old Contemptibles in World War I, the Desert Rats of Montgomery's Eighth Army, and the Gloucestershire Battalion in Korea suggest that regimentals were not all that important. Is it not a fact that apart from national loyalty, the esprit de corps that counts is that of the combat unit to which the soldier, sailor, or airman is attached? Arleigh Burke's DESRON 23, Curtis LeMay's Twentieth Air Force and Merrill's Marauders needed no separate uniforms.

CONCLUSIONS AND QUESTIONS

Convincing as these arguments appear, one must not overlook the fact that many loyal and able military men are devoutly determined not to lose their service identities. Moreover, as we have noted earlier those holding this view have had convincing enough arguments and sufficient political backing to get their detailed roles and missions, and even their personnel strengths written into law. Short of a national disaster this opposition to unification is not likely to dissipate through mere debate. Some means must be found of satisfying the strong drive for service identity while providing the flexibility of command necessary for optimum national security.

Reinforcing the service-identity argument is the general antimilitary bias which prefers to fracture the military establishment in order to keep it from growing "too strong" and, as this argument goes, leading the United States into a military dictatorship or at least into a "garrison State." [18] Those who hold to this school of thought should ponder the alternatives. Might we not be better off to risk trusting the military? Should we not consider military people just as prudent and sincere as we do other citizens of America? Why can't we trust the military to organize their jobs as efficiently as possible? What truth is there in the hoary fear that the American military is out to usurp civilian authority and democratic government? Must we hamstring the military with cumbersome laws and amateurish direction until we risk national defeat or blackmail by an aggressive power which seems to have no such fear of its own military profession?

CHAPTER 24

THE HYPOTHETICAL PROFESSION

If the military profession is to regain its position of respect and importance, it should establish and foster, as a first step, a military society which would have, as its major aims, professional development and progress in the military arts. Such a society should encompass all armed services, including National Guardsmen and reserves. It should also be open to civilians who devote their services to national defense. Of course, not all of the individuals in these categories could meet the prerequisites for membership set by such a society. Once established and accepted as the heart of the military profession, higher and higher entrance standards could govern professional membership.

PUBLIC EDUCATION

As a second step, and a concomitant of professionalism, military education in the public schools and colleges should be increased and become, as with the education for all other professions, a community and professional responsibility rather than a Federal program. Subsidization of military studies as with the present ROTC would decrease, and the pursuit of military knowledge in all areas would become a personal privilege of the student rather than an individual obligation. "Required" military courses would be determined by local decision and professional advice. As the prestige of the profession grew, people would voluntarily seek military knowledge rather than have it imposed upon them.

By taking these two steps, forming a comprehensive professional military society and incorporating military education into the general curricula of schools and colleges as a voluntary professional opportunity, the successful pattern of the medical profession would be emulated. Civilian degrees in military science would be offered at established levels and in many specialties. Standards of qualification for practice of the profession would gradually become a function of the society itself rather than of the national government.

The point has been made by Representative Thomas B. Curtis, a Missouri Republican, that a large portion of the training conducted in the military services is a duplication of training for civilian life and might better be conducted by public schools and colleges. Mr. Curtis noted on the floor of Congress that almost 90 percent of the military strength was assigned to noncombat jobs of one sort or another and that many of these jobs and skills were duplicated in the civilian economy.[1]

Perhaps the civilian educational system could not assume as much of the load of military training as Mr. Curtis suggests because of the many unique and highly complicated weapons and related equipment associated with arms. Much of this equipment, moreover, is classified for security purposes. But certainly a vast amount of training could be provided in the public schools along less specialized lines. I have personally devoted hundreds of hours toward training young airmen in such mundane skills as typing, engine maintenance, supply accounting, basic communications, electronics, and a host of other subjects which might far better have been taught in the public school system as Mr. Curtis recommends.

If the oft-recited purpose of public education is to prepare young people to take their places in society as productive members, this objective is not being attained with respect to the military services. Half of the male population between the ages of 18 and 26 can expect to serve in the armed forces of today. Perhaps as many as one million will make a lifetime career of military service and well over another million people will become dependent upon those careermen. What is public education doing to prepare this wide segment of our population for military life?

A professional military association, like other professional associations, could influence the establishment of appropriate courses of study in public schools, colleges, and universities. And the accreditation function could be undertaken by the professional military society as a means of assuring high quality and purposeful instruction.

The integration of military education in the public school system is anathema to most educators, many of whom feel that military training of any sort leads to, if not war, at least the creation of the "military mind." Even military history is resisted as a legitimate course of study.

In 1955 the Research Studies Institute of Air University at Maxwell Air Force Base, Alabama, conducted a survey of 815 institutions of higher education to determine how many were teaching courses in military history or policy. Only 493 replies were received and 457 of these were answered in the negative, that no such courses were being taught. The major reasons given by most of the institutions responding negatively were, first, that students were not sufficiently interested and, second, that no qualified instructors were available.[2]

The historian Theodore Ropp has indicted social scientists for their failure to give attention to the study of war in American universities. The gap in military study is wide.

> It is true of the textbooks from which the average student studies history and political science. It is true of the teachers who teach him, and it is true of the administrators who plan and finance general programs of undergraduate education. Yet few students or teachers or administrators would now deny that war has been one of the forces which has made a world of today. . . . Our generation simply cannot ignore this brand of human activity because we do not like it, or believe in it, or because it is very difficult for us to understand.[3]

No modern profession has been able to find room among the liberal arts curricula of public education until it has organized itself into a professional body and brought its needs to the attention of the public. This is true of engineering, medicine, psychology, sociology, chemistry, education and physics.[4] It is time that the military followed their examples.

In a comprehensive British study of the professions published in 1933, the army was omitted entirely "because the service which soldiers are trained to render is one which it is hoped they will never have to perform." [5] This is an all-too-typical attitude in America and one that will not likely be overcome without a professional society.

For a great country living in a dangerous world, with a stable national military establishment of 2.65 million people, an annual military budget of approximately $60 billion, and presently engaging in a limited war halfway around the world, the lack of interest expressed by public educational institutions in military education is nothing short of appalling. An active professional military society could take steps to correct this shortsightedness and apathy.

ADVANTAGES TO GOVERNMENT

The first thought that comes to mind in contemplating such a revolutionary military profession is the danger it might present to democratic government. No doubt a great professional military society, comparable to the American Medical Association, would wield considerable political influence. But need this influence be manifest outside of its own professional sphere of interest? The American Medical Association cannot be counted upon to vote as a body except on medical issues. Nor can American Bar Association ballots agree except on legal matters. Why must it be assumed, then, that the influence of a professional military association would be felt in other than professional military matters?

There have been no attempts at military *coup d'etats* in the United States since the half-hearted and abortive effort of Major John Armstrong at Newburgh in 1781. American tradition abhors the thought of government by force and violence. There have been isolated instances in America of organized groups taking over cities by force and flouting due process of law, but it hasn't taken long for public pressures to build up a reform movement and re-establish representative governments. This American tradition applies equally to all Americans, military or civilian. The fact that the military has never threatened government is rooted to this deep-seated American belief combined with a wholehearted loyalty to Constitutional processes.

There are dozens of military associations pursuing specialized purposes. To name a few, the Association of the Army, the Navy League, the Air Force Association, the American Ordnance Association, the U. S. Naval Institute, the American Military Institute, and the Air Force Historical Foundation. These associations and others each run into the tens of thousands of members. Added to these are the great veterans organizations headed by the American Legion with over one million members and followed by the substantial Veterans of Foreign Wars. Louis Smith in his renowned study, *American Democracy and Military Power*,[6] has observed that these semi-official and private associations do not represent a threat to either congressional policy or the American way of life. The influence of these associations is usually counteracted by other organizations seeking opposite goals.

But the hypothetical professional society would not be designed to influence legislation or to seek government benefits. Its goals would be to add to military knowledge and understanding, to eliminate quackery, to clarify issues and seek solutions to knotty national security problems. Its influence on government would only be incidental to the respect it would achieve as a learned profession.

One of the shining attributes of modern professional societies is the almost religious devotion to truth. This is the ethic which is essential to scientific progress and it has been adopted by all reputable professional bodies. Thus have professional associations become the conscience of the body politic, fighting bias, prejudice and phoniness at every turn in the spheres of their particular competence and interest. Professional associations are a necessary counter to all the pressure groups which play fast and loose with the facts in order to influence government to their particular selfish ends.

In order to promote progress within their profession, professional associations foster research, not infrequently even financing it, in order to broaden the horizons of their own body of knowledge. The journals of these associations report the significant research thus accomplished in order that the new knowledge may be spread and tested by the other minds and in the other laboratories of the profession. Experiments are repeated for verification and the results discussed at length in journals, bulletins, seminars and classrooms. Thus the associations become clearing houses for new knowledge, throwing out the false and the superficial, and incorporating the verifiable and proved into the living and growing body of professional knowledge. This vast professional system is truly a great national asset.

The body of knowledge gained through research and verifiable experience is next abstracted from journals and incorporated in textbooks of all descriptions. Textbooks then become the fundamental repositories of professional knowledge. And because the body of professional knowledge grows from year to year under the impetus, guidance and assistance of the many professional associations, textbooks must be constantly revised and brought up to date. Textbooks, of course, are used to train new members for the profession.

PROFIT IN RESEARCH

There are some healthy economic motivations to this whole process of professional development and search for knowledge. Research is, after all, systematic invention through multiple trial and error. Almost anything that is truly creative has a potential economic value, whether it be a new solvent for paint or an empirical formula for a rocket trajectory. But the end product of the research is not the only valuable commodity. The knowledge itself, when abstracted and incorporated into textbooks, provides monetary compensation for both author and publisher. Thus the entire cycle of professional development from the search for knowledge, to the publication of findings, to the abstraction into texts, to the teaching from the texts by professors, to the learning by students, to the practice of the profession, and finally back to the search for knowledge by practitioners and scholars—the entire cycle is boosted and accelerated at almost every step by certain monetary incentives. Without this economic attraction it is doubtful that science would bound ahead as rapidly as it has.

DRAGS ON THE MILITARY PROFESSION

Only slight economic motivation is provided for the military professional. This may seem well and good to those who continue to regard professions by the ancient criteria and feel that self-abnegation, poverty and absence of economic reward are necessary to preserve the purity of the profession. However this lack of economic motivation may likewise be a fundamental reason for its slowness to prosper as a profession. Very few students voluntarily choose the military as a life work; very few aspire to study it, write about it or teach its knowledge. Military research has only prospered when it is highly subsidized by government or when a government contract appears likely, and since few military texts are demanded by the public (or even by the profession itself), few are written and fewer published. In fact, military men are discouraged from profiting from their meager scholarly writing. The military does not present a picture of a thriving and healthy modern profession, proceeding on its own steam. Rather the military reflects a sick profession which has to be injected repeatedly with hormones and dosed with the vitamins of government funds and contracts. The profession also requires massive transfusions of new blood in the form of draftees coerced into the ranks by law.

Government cannot create or maintain a profession, any more than can government buy loyalty or pride or inspiration. A learned profession begins with the sincere dedication of its members to a search for knowledge and truth within a particular mental discipline. It prospers when those members organize into professional associations. Once organized, with each helping the other, rapid professional advance and increasingly high professional standards become possible.

In the past when civil control of the military was considerably less stultifying, the in-service military profession was able to establish, to some degree, its own standards. This professional privilege has been seriously curtailed in the modern military establishment through the multiple layers of civil control of the military. Thus the profession has lost much of its pride, dignity and self-respect. There seems no other way to regain this professional integrity than through a professional association which is neither controlled by government nor by self-interest pressure groups, but which is solely devoted to professional betterment and the quest for sound professional knowledge.

The low state to which the military profession has sunk was partially revealed to the public in 1963. The event which caused a flurry of grousing by senior military officers was of minor significance in itself. It was merely symbolic of the less obvious methods employed by the civilian leadership in OSD to thoroughly subordinate the military profession. This was the failure to appoint to a second two-year term as Chief of Naval Operations the popular Admiral George W. Anderson. Nothing required his reappointment, of course, except precedent and the fact that Admiral Anderson had performed his number one naval assignment with consummate skill, dignity and professionalism.

It was not overlooked by most observers in uniform that Admiral Anderson had not been entirely subservient to the dictates of the Secretary of Defense. Admiral Anderson had supported the joint Air Force-Navy board which four times had recommended the Boeing version of the TFX fighter aircraft over the McNamara supported General Dynamics version. The Admiral had testified for the Joint Chiefs of Staff before the Preparedness Subcommittee of the Senate along lines opposed to the views of Mr. McNamara during the nuclear test ban hearings. As one correspondent put it, ". . . Anderson wasn't reappointed simply because he wouldn't bow low enough to McNamara." [7]

It may seem fitting and proper to the casual observer for a military chief to be eased out of his post if he doesn't agree with the policies laid down by the Secretary of Defense. This kind of straight-line authority and subordination is expected within most civilian organizations and certainly within the military services themselves. But to expect such abject obedience at the expense of honest professional judgment by the top military leaders is to misread historical tradition and the laws of American civil-military relations.

In the first place, the military leader takes his supreme oath to "support and defend the Constitution of the United States against all enemies, foreign or domestic. . . ." He does not take such an oath of allegiance to the Secretary of Defense or even to the President. The officer's oath simply obliges him to ". . . faithfully discharge the duties of the office upon which [he] is about to enter," and, of course, such duties as are prescribed by his superiors. The oath leaves no doubt, however, that ultimate loyalty is pledged to the Constitution rather than any individual in the chain of command. Thus it would be improper to judge the hierarchical conduct of a military officer in his civil-military relations by the same standards one might judge the conduct, say, of an industrial manager who is expected to have no higher loyalties than to his immediate superiors.

But this is not the only area of inconsistency in the hierarchical relationship between the military men and their civilian superiors as opposed to a wholly inter-civilian relationship in an institutional environment. The Constitution does not turn over the armed forces to the Executive *en toto*. Many strings are tied to the military by Congress which, in Section 8, Article I, of the Constitution, is charged with the responsibility "to raise and support armies." Thus, by law and tradition, military leaders are required to present their honest opinions and judgments to Congressional committees when asked to testify. In the words of one correspondent writing in the *Journal of the Armed Forces,* military men are obliged to "give free, frank and full testimony based on their best professional judgment. Congress cannot properly operate unless it receives such testimony." [8]

Another cogent reason for this legal and proper independence of military chiefs in testifying before Congress is the one of internal military morale. It is axiomatic that a military commander must look after the best interests of his troops if he expects to gain their loyal obedience. Thus the thoughtful commander strives to get better living conditions, better food and more pay for his uniformed people. By and large these efforts are justified because the soldier seldom has it as good as his civilian counterpart. Be that as it may, a commander traditionally fights for the welfare of his men and they expect him to do this. Should the commander be given orders *not* to do this the morale, loyalty, and military effectiveness of his troops can confidently be expected to plummet. And it is becoming common practice for the Secretary of Defense to deter the Service Chiefs and others from testifying in support of their uniformed subordinates.

Questions of budget limitations become overriding, and of course the Secretary of Defense makes the final judgment of what the military budget should be and how it is cut up. Woe to the military man who objects to this before a Congressional committee.

In the past it has been the role of Congress to pare down the budgets proposed to it by the military departments. But since OSD has been established it has not been uncommon for Congress to vote more defense funds than were requested. The pay raise of 1965, for example, was *not* requested by OSD or the Administration. Instead, the House Armed Services Committee, chaired by Representative L. Mendel Rivers, introduced a bill which doubled the raise proposed by OSD. This was an anomalous switch. The Congress was championing the soldiers against the Secretary of Defense who testified along with most military witnesses that the nominal pay raise he proposed would be adequate. The upshot was that the Rivers Bill was passed unanimously by both committees of Congress and voted into law. It appears that Congress is more perceptive of the needs and morale of the Service than is the Secretary of Defense.

Not only does OSD's tight control of military leadership hamper the free flow of information to Congress but it discourages military professionalism. Professionalism and personal integrity are threatened when the foremost uniformed leaders are constrained to follow a party line and are smothered under a stifling civilian authority. This immoderate control does not go unnoticed in the field. Raymond Moley has written:

> What are the subordinates of these rejected chiefs to think? While an indeterminate number of officers in service are seeking another career, the discontent grows deeper. At the academies and colleges cadets and midshipmen are wondering whether it is not better to forego the long road to the top. "Why not change to MIT and then to a research corporation and at 27 find myself overruling the generals and admirals?" [9]

An ideal military profession must be able to place some constraints on political leadership, otherwise the profession is liable to degenerate into a political tool of the party in power. Brash young civilians in OSD, supremely confident of their knowledge and of their military decisions, show little respect for the generals and admirals who are gun-shy about challenging the emotional civil control premise. Service Chiefs, who, by a hollow law, are the "principal military advisors to the Secretary of Defense and the President," have their advice sought only as a "meaningless formality." [10] Their carefully studied warnings are too frequently ignored. They have nowhere to turn except to their own profession. A strong military profession would give them the needed backing to exercise their duties in accordance with Constitutional and legal principles.

PSYCHOLOGICAL COMPENSATION

A lecture to West Point cadets stands out in my memory. The period was the early thirties, marked by economic depression. Even the near-starvation level of military pay had been reduced and such governmental money-saving schemes as leave-without-pay were practiced. An officer instructor, his name long forgotten, was lecturing on the subject of military courtesy and rank. His words went something like this:

> Never fail to show respect for your military superiors. Treat them with the utmost military courtesy. Recognize and use their ranks and titles; "Sir" them and show deference to their needs and wishes. *The respect you show them is their major reward for long years of service.*
>
> They never get much pay. They work hard for an ideal, not for monetary reward, or even recognition. Life is hard for them and for their families. Few of the comforts of civilian life come to them. They are dedicated to the service of their country, and military rank is about all they have left. Don't take it away from them with bad manners.

But the close-knit isolated military profession of the thirties is no more. The modern military profession is largely integrated with the civilian society and, in effect, the rank has been taken away from the uniformed leaders. Too many civilian contemporaries look upon the military man with contempt and deny him the meager psychological income of rank and deference of former years. This leaves the serviceman shorn of any return for his years of study and labor. Is it any wonder that he adopts the policy, "If you can't lick 'em, join 'em"? Thus are yes-men born.

A true military profession would do much to restore the prestige of the serviceman, as other professions have done for their members. A military profession could defend the serviceman against unjustified attacks and harsh criticism. It would extol military virtues and give the military profession a voice that could be heard.

POLITICAL ORIENTATION OF ASSOCIATIONS

One can predict that the hypothetical military association we have been discussing would of necessity become somewhat political if for no other reason than that so many of its members would be servants of the government. One could expect that the profession would attempt to influence pay legislation or to achieve other legislation favorable to the military. Since other learned professional associations now do this, even public service professions such as education and medicine, it would be naive not to expect a revitalized military profession to act accordingly. But would not such political activity be harmful to democratic government? Would not such a society become too powerful?

There has been no tendency for other learned professions to threaten democracy or to steer the country into dangerous courses. In fact government-directed influence from learned professions has been a fundamental characteristic of democracy. They provide an expression of the will of a large body of well-informed people, and because of their professional knowledge, their moral and ethical ideals, it is usually the most healthy kind of influence upon government. It can be safely assumed that any future military association would establish and enforce high moral and ethical standards and place pressures on the government only when sincerely motivated by the most lofty principles.

CONDUCT OF THE HYPOTHETICAL ASSOCIATION

In order to visualize how this might work, let us assume that an independent professional military association has been in being since 1946. What kind of political activities might it have engaged in?

When the National Defense Act of 1947 was being considered in Congress, our postulated professional military association would likely have debated the proposal through articles in its journal, weighing the pros and cons of each proposition and providing knowledgeable, objective evaluations. This would have given the public a well-informed and balanced picture, steadying and correcting the many official positions to a reasonable course which would have been less a measure of compromise between strongly held official policies, and more designed to fulfill the national interests and improve the country's military profession. When amendments to the National Defense Act of 1947 were proposed in 1949, 1953, and 1958 the hypothetical professional military association would have analyzed this proposed legislation from a military point of view and no doubt would have noted and protested the tendency to debase the military profession by creating more, stronger, and less meaningful civilian control agencies. No doubt the association would have objected vehemently to the composition of the Hoover Commission task force in 1949, for example, because that task force which studied Defense reorganization contained no professional military members; and to the Rockefeller Committee findings in 1953 for its dearth of witnesses.[11]

Our hypothesized professional association probably would have come to the defense of the generals in Korea who, without exception, strenuously objected to the myopic political policies which dominated the conduct of that war, preventing a clear-cut military decision and dragging out the conflict to an indefinite and unsatisfactory truce, meanwhile piling up American casualties. Similarly the unsuccessful policies pursued in South Vietnam would have been debated more authoritatively. Today, civilian correspondents provide our only objective source of information.

The military association no doubt would have protested General Douglas MacArthur's summary relief. As we have seen, there is nothing illegal or unethical, as President Harry Truman implied, in a military man aspiring to the presidency of the United States. Civil control of the military was asserting itself in such a manner as to gag legitimate military comment on the conduct of the Korean war. Certainly, if the military leadership may not comment on the conduct of war, a province of its own expertise, civil control passes the point of prudence and may indeed endanger the country. MacArthur's relief was not based upon failure or refusal to obey civil direction, but rather upon his temerity to question the wisdom of his orders and to recommend other strictly military courses of action. A Gallup poll in 1951 showed that MacArthur's actions were favored by 69 percent of the people.[12] An independent military association which could not be gagged by bureaucratic edict would have debated the questioning ethic of the military code and rebutted many of the uninformed attacks on MacArthur.

One of the traditional military principles which was stigmatized and possibly destroyed by the MacArthur firing is that if an officer disagrees with his superior's orders he is duty bound to voice his disagreement to his commander. The commander then weighs the evidence presented and makes his decision. The officer finally abides by that decision, whatever it may be, and carries it out to the limit of his ability and enthusiasm. Even though the decision may run contrary to the officer's advice, the officer code compels him to carry out the decision as if it were his own.

By questioning his orders, MacArthur was simply following this very sensible code. There was never a doubt about his loyal obedience, however distasteful the civil decision. He obeyed his orders not to bomb beyond the Yalu River even at the grave risk of a catastrophic defeat for his own forces. But his unceremonious dismissal established such a precedent that the pertinent questioning code has been given a bad name. Since MacArthur's relief there have been considerably fewer disagreements with superior policies, even within the military profession itself. It has become more common practice to pay lip service to an unwelcome decision and then carry it out reluctantly. The encouragement of docile yes-men is clearly not the way to achieve a thoughtful, responsive and well-disciplined military establishment. Our hypothetical professional military society probably would have viewed the Truman-MacArthur controversy from this purely military point of view, without public or official pressure and with a minimum of passion.

Our hypothetical professional society would have attempted to resolve the inter-service jurisdictional controversies along military lines. Issues such as the B-36 controversy, the assignment of ballistic missiles to services, the responsibility for air defense, are typical. Subject to no budgetary restriction, to no pressures from civilian control, nor from business, from Congress, or local communities, the professional society would have arrived at recommendations in line with the public interests. Its recommendations would no doubt have influenced official decisions and legislation to some degree but it is hard to conceive of an association of this sort dominating government even to the extent of that, for example, of the AFL-CIO, or the American Legion, with their less objective and more political approach.

Political action is not the basic purpose of a truly professional association, although on rare occasions, such as when the American Medical Association fought socialized medicine proposals, political campaigns might be undertaken. A public issue usually receives better treatment, however, through the sober unbiased analysis of a professional society than through the heated and hastily written editorials and political speeches which too often hide the true motives. The military society envisioned would *not* be as politically oriented, as is the National Federation of Federal Employees, for example, which campaigns for its Civil Service members to fill military positions and to gain pay raises. The purpose of the military society would be to advance the art and science of the profession of arms, and incidentally to enhance the prestige of its members.

In such a diversified and specialized culture as that found in the United States, where competition for attention, interest, time and money are so characteristic of the times, few groups achieve any success unless they are organized. Wasteful labor strife progressed to useful negotiations through the organization of labor unions. Business, to hold its own against labor, likewise had to organize and consolidate its resources. And, of course, learned professions, although considerably less political, have gained prominence through the same general methods. But, paradoxically, the military, as a profession, has been highly amorphous and disorganized. Few would say that a common opinion could be gained from the military profession on any controversial subject, whether the opinion be one on strategy or the proper manner to question an order. Not only is the military split into four competing services but into variegated philosophies and doctrines of all sorts, even within those separate services. The United States would profit immensely by more unity of doctrine and purpose within its military profession as a whole, provided this were arrived at through an honest synthesis of objective thought and study. A truly professional military organization could provide such an asset.

CHAPTER 25

THE WAY AHEAD

"It is the glory of democracy," wrote Theodore R. McKeldin, former governor of Maryland, "that it has recognized ever more effectively that a man-at-arms is still a man and that the time he spends in the service of the Republic should not be an interruption, but a contribution of his development as a citizen and a member of the community, even more valuable in time of peace than he is in time of war." [1] These stirring words expressed a hope rather than a reality and the ten years since they were written have seen that hope go dimming. In every organ of its body, the military profession has been ailing and it is apt to degenerate into a mere technical vocation, if it has not done so already. As Edward L. Katzenbach put it, "The mystique—that sense of mission and that excitement of being part of a tightly knit professional body—is barely felt." [2]

SUICIDAL SOLUTIONS

Time is running out. This dangerous age may solve all of our problems with the extinction of America. In the pungent words of Julian Huxley, the "ultimate deterrent may become the ultimate detergent." But a suicidal policy, although a possible solution when disguised as something else, is unworthy of our great heritage. We did not fight our way up from the geological slime through two ice ages; stand tall to find order and beauty; create the concepts of honesty, truth, compassion and trust which have led to amicable and orderly human societies; and finally built the most fair, prosperous, and generous system of free government the world has ever known; all to throw in the towel now simply because we can't find a pat answer to the problem of nuclear war. Our paleolithic ancestors found no solution to the creeping ice but they did not lie down

341

before it. And many people feel that a policy which places principle in a secondary position to survival is tantamount to surrender at least, and suicide at most. Suicide, certainly, if at the last moment we vainly and hopelessly decide to protect our freedoms.

Far more dangerous than the chance of our accidental nuclear explosion is the social explosion which could be triggered by defense intellectuals who are tampering with our basic human values and aspirations. Perhaps they can coolly discuss the abandonment of Constitutional rights, of international police in our cities, of a world of "law" created by the votes of the Hottentots, and of uninspected disarmament. But others are deeply attached to American traditions and become emotionally upset when those traditions are threatened. World botherhood under a just world law is a beautiful ideal but it should be obvious to anyone that it is a long way off. In the meantime let us not risk the great social advances of America for a shimmering mirage. People will fight to retain their social achievements and their moral convictions. Certainly the Civil War should have convinced us that we are not immune to violent reactions when our fundamental beliefs are endangered.

NEW PURPOSE FOR CIVIL CONTROL

America was not born automatically by some sort of natural process of social gestation. America grew and developed by the blood, sweat and tears of our countless dedicated forebears. Among those who suffered most in this maturing process were members of the military. Thousands upon thousands of headstones at Arlington National Cemetery and at other graveyards throughout this land and overseas bear mute evidence of this supreme sacrifice. Now we are being told that this was all a mistake and that should we again determinedly stand up for our American principles of freedom and justice that it will lead to a nuclear holocaust, too horrible to risk for any of our noble purposes.

The military solution to self-preservation is no longer applicable, say some defense intellectuals, therefore the military profession must be denigrated, dishonored and *controlled* in order that military professionals be reduced to the status of voiceless technicians. The traditional concepts of civil control of the military come ready-made for these purposes. Alarms have rung warnings of the military-industrial complex, of the military mind, of military authoritarianism, of military narrowness and rigidity, while under the clang and confusion of these alarms the bedrock of American independence and liberty is being quietly removed.

Civil control of the military as conceived today is far different from that conceived by our Founding Fathers, or even by our fore-bears of the past century. There can be no question that America wants no military dictatorship, but this has not denied military professionals the right to aspire under due process of law to the highest office. Nor does America want military considerations always to dominate the body politic. Neither do military men desire this unbalanced military emphasis. When survival has been at stake and military power has been given its head, it has never been mis-used and the military has never failed to turn over the reins of power to civil leadership as soon as each crisis has subsided.

The harped-on fears of military domination of civil government are largely groundless simply because the military profession is the one single most dedicated American institution for the preservation of American principles.

THE SOLUTION OF WORLD GOVERNMENT

Yet it is just this dedication which hinders those who would sacrifice the United States Constitution for a chance to avoid nuclear war, who would trade the Bill of Rights for a world government which might be dominated by many countries whose people have not yet learned the basic principles of a free society.

It is not the touted "democratic processes" which assure freedom. It is the fundamental concept of trust, honesty, fair play and compassion for our fellow men. These undergird our Constitution and make it a living document. The Constitution and related laws of America would be hollow and worthless indeed unless the people wished to honor them. What kind of world government might we get should the majority of the world's citizens be composed of people whose conception of human relations in government is largely one of coercive and dictatorial rule? What kind of Praetorian Guard could we expect from an all-powerful international military system recruited world-wide? Where would be the checks and balances? These dangers frighten the American military professional even more than does nuclear war.

When will we learn that great principles are not words in a charter but deep emotional feelings? As John W. Gardner, the Secretary of Health, Education and Welfare, has written in his inspiring essay, *Self Renewal*,[3]

Young people do not assimilate the values of their group by learn-ing the words (truth, justice, etc.) and their definitions. They learn attitudes, habits and ways of judging. They learn these in intensely personal transactions with their immediate family or associates. They learn them in the routines and crises of living, but they also learn them through songs, stories, drama and games. They do not learn ethical principles; they emulate ethical (or unethical) people. They do not analyze or list the attributes they wish to develop; they iden-tify with people who seem to them to have these attributes. That is why young people need models, both in their imaginative life and in their environment, models of what man at his best can be.

Rather than risk the emotional fundamentals of our heritage by entering into pacts with those who do not share our ideals, would it not be better to impart our ideals to others so that they may share in the human advantages which come to a society which truly believes in the words on its monuments?

Do not developing countries need inspirational models just as do young people? Where are our missionaries of earlier years who passionately believed in the religious precepts they purveyed? Why should we be apologetic about a cultural heritage which has proved itself so phenomenally successful? Should we go hat in hand to the world humbly attempting to win friends by showering them with gifts and wading in the rice paddies with them? Or should we go proudly, taking a part of America with us, displaying the helping hand with a courtesy and kindliness unknown in most parts of the world?

To the military, who have established little Americas all over the globe, and who passionately believe in the great American pre-cept, there is no question raised about going native. Instead, the military attempt to bring their hosts up to higher standards of living, both spiritually and materially. For this the American sol-dier is widely admired and respected. He is a new missionary, attacked only by those who would destroy what he stands for—the preservation of a proud, strong and free America.

DEDICATION OF THE AMERICAN MILITARY PROFESSION

The American military profession rests upon the proposition that America is worth fighting and dying for. It does not debate the *degree* of fighting and dying which might be necessary to preserve America. Dying is ultimate and final. A soldier killed in a jungle war is just as dead as one killed in a holocaust. Those who preach that the degree of dying would be too much for America to endure are of little faith and courage. They have given up the struggle.

They prefer to find some sort of accommodation with the enemy through offering concessions in hopes that he will not attack. And the concessions are nothing less than those of burning our ammunition and bulldozing down our ramparts. There are bound to be other ways for human survival short of negotiating away our defenses and our birthrights.

This is not to suggest that reasonable accommodation with our rivals is not a feasible approach to world harmony. But such is the province of diplomats and statesmen, not of defense intellectuals who view diplomacy largely in terms of arms reduction. When the world's political problems are solved by the diplomats and statesmen, arms reduction will follow as a natural consequence. Arms production is the result, not the cause, of international differences.

DEDICATION OF DEFENSE INTELLECTUALS

Defense intellectuals are dedicated to the survival of humanity. They believe national survival in the traditional sense may conflict with world survival. They imperiously reserve to themselves the sole capability of understanding the solution to the nuclear war problem. And that solution, they assert, is only found through international agreement.

Defense intellectuals seeking an international solution to our nuclear dilemma should get out of the diplomats' way and get back to their laboratories where they can do the most good. Defense intellectuals who are striving mightily to control the military who stand in the way of their far-out strategies, some of which are no less than nuclear capitulation, should better devote their energies to that field in which they got their military start—weaponry. If present offensive weapons, such as thermonuclear ICBM's, threaten our extinction, then where are our *defensive* weapons? Where are the Nike Zeus and Nike "X" systems which could protect our cities? They have been "under development" for over ten years, yet not one operational antimissile is deployed. Over two billion dollars of tax money have been spent on this barren development. There is evidence that the Soviet Union has such weapons deployed, but we do not.[4]

Why don't we have these crucial defensive weapons? We don't have them because our defense intellectuals fear this will start another arms race. And what's wrong with an arms race as compared to nuclear war? A war in which we would be nakedly unprotected!

Would an arms race give too much power to an imaginary military-industrial complex? Is this why we are offered but two ultimate strategic options: holocaust or world government?

Or perhaps the defense intellectual envisions the money that might be better spent to fulfill social needs. Billions of dollars spent for ICBM's "to kill people" could feed millions of school children, for example, or could be devoted to medical research. Sir John Slessor, former Air Marshal of the Royal Air Force, responded to this argument by observing that:

> It is customary in democratic countries to deplore expenditure on armament as conflicting with the requirements of the social services. There is a tendency to forget that the most important social service that a government can do for its people is to keep them alive and free.[5]

THE BEGINNING OF A SOLUTION

No bolt from the blue will put America back on its traditional track. America has been frightened and brainwashed. America has been led to believe that nuclear extinction is bound to follow if we persist in abiding by America's principles and traditions, and that the military profession stands in the way of world peace. We can only be saved, they tell us, by laying down our arms and joining hands in one great benevolent world society. The American train is chugging off on a spur which leads to an abyss of world government, the consequences of which can be more catastrophic than Communism or nuclear war. How can we stop this headlong plunge?

The savior of our country in time of war can also be the savior in time of peace. At no risk to democratic government, the military profession can better organize itself, as have the other professions. In this way, the military profession would have an appropriate national voice and be in a position to analyze the questionable schemes and the primitive strategies now at large, leaving the country to judge. A true military profession could champion the traditional principles which have brought greatness to America and could defend its own professionals against those who would reduce them to non-citizens in order to lead America into alien paths. A true military profession could debate the scope and kind of civil control, pointing out the truth that it is not an unalloyed virtue. As with chastity, civil control can be overdone. If carried to an extreme the human race could expire.

SCHOOL OF THE WORLD

The military professional, who has served many years in foreign cultures, is not insensitive to the needs and aspirations of the less fortunate members of the human race. He has carried American ideals abroad. He has not only trained armies to defend their own countries against aggression, but he has drilled them in moral and ethical principles and in concepts of free, democratic government.

Pericles, in his oration at the funeral of the men fallen in defense of Athens, claimed that Athens was the school of Greece and praised the fallen soldiers for protecting the fountainhead of Greek culture. But the Sophists, who regarded defense as a less than primary aim of government, caused Athens to weaken and die before the troops of Macedonia. With the death of Athens, the school, all Greece succumbed, never again to rise to its ancient splendor.

America has been and can continue to be the school of mankind. It can teach the precepts of intellectual honesty, moral strength, fair play and justice, trust and compassion. Until these lessons are learned by most of mankind, a democratic world government can be no more than a wishful dream.

It will take a long time. But unless the fountainhead of America is preserved by its military profession, it will take much, much longer.

REFERENCES

CHAPTER 1

[1] J. F. C. Fuller, *Armament and History* (New York: Charles Scribner's Sons, 1945), for a perceptive account of the influence of new weapons upon civilization. Quote from Thomas Fuller (1608-1661), divine and historian, from his *Worthies of England*, p. 87.

[2] S. Paul Johnson, *Flying Squadrons* (New York: Duell, Sloan & Pearce, 1942), p. 36.

[3] *Look*, Jan. 12, 1965, p. 49.

[4] See Quincy Wright, *A Study of War* (Chicago: University of Chicago Press, 1951), Vol. 1, p. 311.

[5] See Dale O. Smith, *U.S. Military Doctrine* (New York: Duell, Sloan and Pearce, 1955), p. 18.

[6] Connor, "National Defense," *The North American Review*, Jan. 1928.

[7] Richard Stockton, VI, *Inevitable War* (New York: The Perth Co., 1932). p. 5. This monumental work, in contrast to its title, is devoted to the proposition that unpreparedness invites war. It was prophetic.

[8] *Congressional Record*, 54th Congress, First Session, April 14, 1896.

[9] I. S. Boch, a Polish economist, financier and disarmament authority, published a seven-year study. *The Future of War* (New York: Doubleday & McClure Co., 1899). See Dale O. Smith, "Background to Disarmament," *U.S. Naval Institute Proceedings*, Oct. 1956, pp. 1142-1145.

[10] New York: Doubleday Doran & Co., 1913, p. 173, in Stockton, *op. cit.*, p. 7.

[11] Brooks Emeny, "The Multi-State System," in Harold and Margaret Sprout, eds., *Foundations of National Power* (New York: D. Van Nostrand Co., Inc., 1951), p. 8.

[12] Stockton, *op. cit.*, p. 8.

[13] *Op. cit.*, p. 195.

[14] *The Impact of War* (New York: Farrar and Rinehart, Inc., 1941), p. 259.

[15] *Ibid.*, p. 259.

[16] *Crusade in Europe* (Garden City, N.Y.: Doubleday and Co., 1948), p. 456.

[17] Hans J. Morganthau, *Scientific Man vs. Power Politics* (Chicago: The University of Chicago Press, 1946), p. 119.

[18] Jordan, *op. cit.*, (and in *The Maryland Quarterly*, May 1911) was convinced that the Rothschilds ruled the "Unseen Empire" of Europe and would not permit the financial ruin of war.

[19] Eugene Burdick and Harvey Wheeler (New York: McGraw Hill Book Co., 1962).

[20] Vegetius wrote in *The Military Institutions of the Romans* (T. R. Phillips, ed., Harrisburg: The Military Services Publishing Co., 1944), p. 75, ". . . pretended conferences and deceitful appearances of truces have often been more fatal than force."

[21] W. L. Borden, *There Will Be No Time* (New York: The Macmillan Co., 1946), p. 187.

[22] *Principles of War*, tr. Hans W. Gatzke (Harrisburg: The Military Services Publishing Co., 1942), p. 25.

[23] *Surprise*, trs. Stefan T. Possony and David Vilfoy (Harrisburg: The Military Service Publishing Co., 1943).

[24] *Modern Arms and Free Men* (New York: Simon and Schuster, 1949), p. 95.

[25] New York: William Morrow and Co., 1957.

[26] *Op. cit.*, p. 263.

[27] "Winston Churchill in the House of Commons," *The Washington Post*, Jan. 16, 1951.

[28] *Ibid.*

[29] "Mencken on the Military," editorial in *The Mercury*, Sept. 1929.

[30] *Ibid.*

[31] See Harold Sprout, "Role of Military Persons and Military Ideas in American Statecraft," in Harold and Margaret Sprout, *op. cit.*, pp. 452–57.

[32] New York: The Macmillan Co., p. 4.

[33] "Leadership Training and National Security," *Army Information Digest*, Vol. 7, 1952.

[34] *Civil–Military Relations* (New York: Columbia University Press, 1954).

[35] *The Saturday Evening Post*, Oct. 31, 1953.

[36] Essay delivered to the American Association for International Conciliation, published in *McClure's Magazine*, Feb. 1910.

[37] Edward Meade Earle, ed., *Makers of Modern Strategy* (Princeton: Princeton University Press, 1948), pp. 126–127.

[38] *War As I Knew It* (Boston: Houghton–Mifflin Co., 1947), p. 335. Italics added.

CHAPTER 2

[1] Jerome G. Kerwin, ed. (Chicago: University of Chicago Press, 1948). p. 62.

[2] *Ibid.*, p. 63.

[3] With Ronald Edgerton, *War Problems in American Life* (Washington: National Council for the Social Studies, 1943), p. 43.

[4] March, 1965, p. 7.

[5] "The Garrison State," *American Journal of Sociology*, Vol. 46 No. 4 (Jan. 1941), pp. 455–68.

[6] New York: Harcourt Brace, 1949.

[7] Arthur A. Ekrich, *The Civilian and the Military* (New York: Oxford University Press, 1956).

[8] Raymond Aron, *The Century of Total War* (Garden City, N.Y.: Doubleday, 1954) p., 362.

[9] *Ibid.*, p. x.

[10] *The American Mind* (New Haven: Yale University Press, 1950), p. 431.

[11] *Soldiers and Government* (London: Eyre and Spottiswoods, 1957), p. 174.

[12] *Ibid.*, from Grant's *Memoirs*, Vol. I, p. 30.

[13] Kerwin, *op. cit.*, p. 65.

[14] *A Program for National Security*. Report of the President's Advisory Commission on Universal Military Training, Karl T. Compton, Chairman (Washington: Government Printing Office, May 29, 1947).

[15] Lewis L. Strauss, *et. al.*, *Differential Pays for the Armed Services of the United States*, Dept. of Defense (Washington: Government Printing Office, 1953).

[16] Ralph J. Cordiner, "Presentation to Armed Forces Policy Council on Professional and Technical Compensation," Dept. of Defense, mimeographed, Nov. 29, 1956. Also see "Highlights of a Modern Concept of Compensation for Personnel of the Uniformed Services," report of Defense Advisory Committee on Professional and Technical Compensation, March 1957.

[17] Kerwin, *op. cit.*, p. 71. This is delicately put by Burton M. Sapin and Richard C. Snyder as "the inappropriate application of military values, information, and interpretations at key points in the decision-making process . . ." See *The Role of the Military in American Foreign Policy* (Garden City, N.Y.: Doubleday and Co., Inc., 1954), p. 76.

[18] In 1876 Congress failed to appropriate pay for the troops. Soldiers had to borrow at usurious rates to pay their bills.

[19] Col. R. Ernest Dupuy, *History of the United States Army* (New York: Hawthorne Books, Inc., 1956), pp. 150–51.

[20] Kerwin, *op. cit.*, p. 117.

[21] *Ibid.*

[22] Capt. Robert B. Galusha, "Cambrai, Nov. 20, 1917," *Armor* Magazine, Jan.–Feb., 1965. Forty-nine tanks were first used in September 1916 and almost all conked out with mechanical trouble. Thirteen months later at Passchendale Ridge, after 3,000 guns had pumped 103,000 tons of shells in ten days on a fifteen mile front, 216 tanks were employed. They sank in a sea of mud. The British suffered 400,000 casualties.

[23] George N. Robillard, "Are We Stifling the Inventors?" *Saturday Evening Post*, June 9, 1951.

[24] H. D. Smyth, *A General Account of the Development of Methods of Using Atomic Energy for Military Purposes Under the Auspices of the United States Government* (Washington: Government Printing Office, 1945).

[25] *Ibid.*, pp. 63–78.

[26] Roger Burlingame, *General Billy Mitchell* (New York: McGraw–Hill Book Co., 1952), pp. 138, 145.

[27] Eugene M. Emme, *Hitler's Blitz Bomber* (Maxwell AFB, Ala.: Research Studies Institute, 1951).

[28] Kerwin, *op. cit.*, p. 75.

[29] Twenty-one Presidents have worn military uniforms although only five (Washington, Jackson, Taylor, Grant and Eisenhower) might be considered professionals.

[30] Walter Scott, "Personality Parade," *Parade*, Jan. 10, 1965.

[31] Anon, "Germans Still Afraid of Military Authority," *Los Angeles Times*, June 17, 1963.

[32] *Op. cit.*, p. vii.

[33] Kerwin, *op. cit.*, p. 126.

[34] *Ibid.*, p. 132.

CHAPTER 3

[1] The most comprehensive, incorporating the findings of many other studies, is Morris Janowitz' *The Professional Soldier* (The Free Press of Glencoe, Ill., 1960). One of the first valuable works of this sort was a penetrating analysis by Pendleton Herring, *The Impact of War*, *op. cit.* Louis Smith's *American Democracy and Military Powers* (The University of Chicago Press, 1951)

and Samuel P. Huntington's *The Soldier and the State* (Harvard University Press, 1957), arrived at similar conclusions, as did *Arms and Men* by Walter Mills (New York: G. B. Putnam's Sons, 1956), that the military profession is less dangerous than the stereotype suggests. The superb original research done by John W. Masland and Laurence I. Radway, *Soldiers and Scholars* (Princeton, N.J.: Princeton University Press, 1957), has been a real contribution to the literature.

[2] *Op. cit., passim.*

[3] In the Declaration of Independence he was called the "merciless Indian savage(s) whose know role of warfare is an undistinguished destruction of all ages, sexes and conditions."

[4] Janowitz, *op. cit.*, pp. 3, 4.

[5] Speech by Dr. Glenn Seaborg to the American Chemical Society, Dec. 5, 1964, in Washington, D.C. Republished in *Air Force* magazine, Feb., 1965.

[6] *New York Times*, March 21, 1965. In John A. Lang, Jr., "Public Opinion and National Security," *Air Force and Space Digest*, Sept. 1965.

[7] *Newsweek*, March 22, 1965. In *Ibid.*

[8] Harold Laswell first used the term and it struck the fancy of many others such as Samuel P. Huntington, *op. cit.*

[9] Janowitz, *op. cit.*, p. 15.

[10] Francis and Katharine Drake, "Paupers in Uniform," *Reader's Digest*, March 1965, pp. 49–53.

[11] *Op. cit.*, p. 34.

[12] *Crusade In Europe* (New York: Doubleday & Co., Inc., 1948).

[13] Supreme Headquarters Allied Forces, Europe.

[14] *Principles of Scientific Management* (New York: Harper and Bros., 1911).

[15] Janowitz, *op. cit.*, p. 45.

[16] The author participated in the NSC Planning Board debates on this question.

[17] Dave Garroway Show, 9 May 1961.

[18] Suborbital shot, May 5, 1961.

[19] 8 May 1961.

[20] Eugene M. Emme, ed., *History of Rocket Technology* (Detroit: Wayne State University Press, 1964), pp. 229n, 116.

[21] Department of Defense Release in *Newport News Times Herald*, Feb. 25, 1965.

[22] Frederick Martin Stern, *The Citizen Army* (New York: St. Martin's Press, 1957), p. 7.

[23] *Op. cit.*

[24] Stern, *op. cit.*, p. 39. It is unfortunate that Stern's own image of the military is so negative as to attribute ulterior motives even to such activities as drill and training, but the point is illustrative.

[25] Paul Leicester Ford, ed., *Jefferson's Writings* (New York, 1892, Vol. 4, p. 467) as quoted in Stern, *op. cit.*, p. 64.

[26] *Ibid.*, pp. 362-63.

[27] McCaulley, *History of England*, Vol. 3, p. 507, in Stern, *ibid.*, p. 63.

[28] Gordon A. Craig, *The Politics of the Prussian Army, 1640-1945* (Oxford, England: Oxford University Press, 1955). Also see John W. Wheeler-Bennett *The Nemesis of Power* (New York: St. Martin's Press, Inc., 1954).

[29] *Op. cit.*, p. 71.

[30] *Ibid.*, p. 80.

[31] *Loc. cit.*

[32] Pp. 3422-23, in Stern, *ibid.*, p. 119.

[33] Stern, *op. cit.*, p. 124.

[34] *Op. cit.*, p. 281.

CHAPTER 4

[1] Basil H. Liddell Hart, *Defense of the West* (New York: William Morrow & Co., 1950), for a good development of this thesis, p. 209 ff.

[2] "First Philippic."

[3] Raymond C. Senter, "The McNamara-Kennedy Doctrine," *New Republic*, Feb. 13, 1965.

[4] New York: Simon & Schuster, 1949, p. 263.

[5] Raymond Aron, *The Great Debate: Theories of Nuclear Strategy*, tr. Ernst Pawet (New York: Doubleday, 1964), describes the rebellion against military tradition.

[6] June 8, Spring Green, Wisconsin, a speech.

[7] This is the thesis advanced by Fred J. Cook, *The Warfare State* (New York: The Macmillan Co., 1962).

[8] *Op. cit.* First published in 1942.

[9] *A Social-Psychology of War* (New Haven: Yale University Press, 1943).

[10] *Ibid.*, p. 135.

[11] *Ibid.*, p. 19.

[12] Friedrich, *op. cit.*, p. 53.

[13] Dutch writer and statesman of the early 17th century whose monumental work, *De jure belli et pacis* furnished the basis for international law.

[14] Aron, *op. cit.*, p. 34.

[15] The author commanded the air division on Okinawa during this period.

[16] *Ibid.*, p. 91.

[17] *Red Alert, Dr. Strangelove, Seven Days in May, The Passion of the Hawks*, and *Fail-Safe* are a few of the titles.

[18] Editorial, *Air Force* magazine, April, 1964.

[19] " 'Strangelove'? 'Seven Days'? Not likely," *New York Times Magazine*, May 17, 1964.

[20] AFM 35-15, *Air Force Leadership* (Washington: Hq. USAF, 1948).

[21] New York: Harper and Row, 1964.

[22] *Overseas Press Bulletin*, April 25, 1964.

[23] Aron, *op. cit.*, p. 91.

[24] George A. Kelly, "The Global Civil-Military Dilema," *The Review of Politics*, University of Notre Dame, July, 1963.

[25] Pilgrims Dinner, London, Oct. 14, 1952.

CHAPTER 5

[1] "The art of war was, in fact, an integral part of Roman statecraft. . . ." F. E. Adcock, *The Roman Art of War* (Cambridge: Harvard University Press, 1940), p. 3.

[2] Jacques Pirenne, *The Tides of History*, Vol. I From the Beginning to Islam (New York: E. P. Dutton & Co., 1962), pp. 163-252.

[3] *Ibid.*, p. 320. Also see Richard A. Preston, Sydney F. Wise, and Herman O. Werner, *Men in Arms* (New York: Praeger, 1962), p. 48.

[4] Pirenne, *op. cit.*, pp. 374-380.

[5] J. F. C. Fuller, *Armament and History*, *op. cit.*, p. 45.

[6] Hadrian (117-138 A.D.) permitted veterans from the Provinces to join the Guard.

[7] It is noteworthy that Augustus reorganized the army on a completely professional basis and reduced its strength to 300,000. With this professional force he was able to keep peace in the vast Roman Empire. See Graham Webster, *The Roman Army* (Chester, England: The Grosvenor Museum, p. 29.

[8] Carlton J. H. Hayes, Marshall Whithed Baldwin, and Charles Woolsey Cole, *History of Western Civilization*, Vol. I (New York: Macmillan, 1962), p. 38.

[9] Carleton J. H. Hayes and Parker Thomas Moon, *Ancient History* (New York: The Macmillan Co., 1947), pp. 337-49.

[10] H. G. Wells, *The Outline of History*, Vol. I (Garden City, N.Y.: Garden City Books, 1956), p. 386-87.

[11] *Encyclopedia Britannica*, Vol. 19, 1956, p. 505.

[12] Lynn Montross, *War Through the Ages* (New York: Harper & Bros., 1944), p. 86.

[13] Frank Frost Abbott, *Roman Politics* (New York: Cooper Square Publishers, Inc., 1963), p. 38.

[14] Edward Gibbon, *The Decline and Fall of the Roman Empire*, Vol. I (New York: The Modern Library, n.d.), pp. 1-52.

[15] *Ibid.*, p. 98.

[16] Wells, *op. cit.*, p. 393.

[17] Paul Bernstein and Robert Green, *History of Civilization*, Vol. 1 to 1648 (Patterson, N.J.: Littlefield Adam & Co., 1961), pp. 104 ff.

[18] Wells, *op. cit.*, pp. 361-93.

[19] Hayes, Baldwin and Cole, *op. cit.*, p. 39.

[20] Gibbon, *op. cit.*, pp. 1-25. Also H.M.D. Parker, *The Roman Legions* (New York: Barnes and Noble, 1928), pp. 118-87.

CHAPTER 6

[1] Montross, *op. cit.*, pp. 287-310. Also Preston *et al, op. cit.*, pp. 111-12.

[2] For a definitive biography see John Morley, *Oliver Cromwell* (New York: The Century Co., 1901).

[3] Edward Montague, Second Earl of Manchester, "lukewarm general" of noble rank who fought for Parliament in the first years of the war and who was charged by Cromwell with losing the second battle of Newbury for "want of zeal." See Winston S. Churchill, *A History of the English Speaking Peoples*, Vol. 2 (New York: Dodd, Mead and Co., 1956), p. 255. This history provides one of the most understandable and interesting accounts of the complicated Great Rebellion.

[4] *Encyclopedia Britannica*, Vol. 6, 1956, p. 740.

[5] Churchill, *op. cit.*, p. 230. See also Will and Ariel Durant, *The Age of Reason Begins* (New York: Simon and Schuster, 1961), p. 212. Also Morley, *op. cit.*, pp. 43-58.

[6] *Ibid.*, p. 236.

[7] Maurice Ashley, *Great Britain to 1688* (Ann Arbor: The University of Michigan Press, 1961), p. 343.

[8] Robert Devereux, Third Earl of Essex, son of Queen Elizabeth's favorite.

[9] Churchill, *op. cit.*, p. 253.

[10] Morley, *op. cit.*, p. 163.

[11] *Ibid.*, p. 176.

[12] Durant, *op. cit.*, p. 215.

[13] *Ibid.*, p. 260.

[14] *Ibid.*, p. 264.

[15] Ashley, *op. cit.*, p. 351.

[16] *Ibid.*, l., p. 353.

[17] Churchill, *op. cit.*, p. 272.

[18] H. G. Wells, *The Outline of History*, Vol. II, *op. cit.*, p. 647.

[19] K. B. Smellie, *Great Britain Since 1688* (Ann Arbor: The University of Michigan Press, 1962), p. 29. Also Ashley, *op. cit.*, p. 336.

[20] Durant, *op. cit.*, p. 201.

[21] Ashley, *op. cit.*, p. 339.

[22] Morley, *op. cit.*, p. 72.

[23] Ashley, *op. cit.*, p. 352.

[24] So termed because it was that part of Parliament which was seated.

[25] Churchill, *op. cit.*, p. 277.

[26] Ashley, *op. cit.*, p. 356. Also Durant, *op. cit.*, p. 220. Edward P. Cheyney, *A Short History of England* (New York: Ginn and Co., 1960), p. 449, wrote that "Charles had never been a man on whose public faith any reliance could be placed."

[27] Ashley, *op. cit.*, p. 356.

[28] Paul Bernstein and Robert Green, *op. cit.*, p. 289.

[29] Churchill, *op. cit.*, p. 287.

[30] *Ibid.*, p. 322.

[31] George N. Clark, *The Seventeenth Century* (New York: Oxford University Press, 1961), p. 108.

[32] Churchill, *op. cit.*, p. 331.

[33] Ekrich, *op. cit.*, p. 5.

[34] Speech on Army Estimates, *Collected Works*, 1823, Vol. V, p. 16, in Howard, *op. cit.*, p. 28.

[35] *The Soldier and the State*, *op. cit.*, pp. 80 ff.

[36] Churchill, *op. cit.*, pp. 267-70.

[37] Ekrich, *op. cit.*, p. 4.

[38] Morley, *op. cit.*, p. 221.

[39] Churchill, *op. cit.*, p. 270.

[40] *Loc. cit.*

[41] *Ibid.*, p. 272.

[42] Ashley, *op. cit.*, pp. 351-57. Also Morley, *op. cit.*, p. 224.

[43] Preston, *et al.*, *op. cit.*, p. 180 for professional, nonpolitical features of NMA.

[44] Howard, *op. cit.*, p. 12.

[45] Quoted in George D. Patterson, "Should Politics be Taboo?" *U.S. Naval Institute Proceedings*, September, 1962.

[46] "War and Colleges," *Military Affairs*, Vol. IV (1940), pp. 67-75.

[47] *Loc cit.*

[48] *Loc. cit.*

CHAPTER 7

[1] Hayes, *et al.*, *op. cit.*, pp. 395-409. Also see Wells, *op. cit.*, pp. 650-652; Bernstein, *op. cit.*, pp. 336-44.

[2] Bernstein, *op. cit.*, p. 341.

[3] Wells, *op. cit.*, p. 652. Also Montross, *op. cit.*, pp. 262-292.

[4] Clark, *op. cit.*, p. 105.

[5] Theodore Ropp, *War in the Modern World* (Durham, N.C.: Duke University Press, 1959), p. 5.

[6] Charles Oman, *A History of the Art of War in the Middle Ages*, Vol. 2, 1278-1484 (New York: Burt Franklin, 1924), p. 259.

[7] *Ibid.*, p. 259.

[8] Preston, *et al.*, *op. cit.*, pp. 107-110. Also Ropp, *op. cit.*, p. 25.

[9] Clark, *op. cit.*, p. 114.

[10] Ropp, *op. cit.*, p. 29. Also see Walter L. Dorn, *Competition for Empire* (New York: Harper & Bros., 1940), pp. 81-100.

[11] Craig, *op. cit.*, p. 13.

[12] *Ibid.*, p. 22.

[13] Wells, *op. cit.*, p. 658.

[14] Alfred Vagts, *Defense and Diplomacy* (New York: King's Crown Press, 1956), p. 454.

[15] *Ibid*, p. 455.

[16] *On War* tr. O. J. Matthijs Jolles (New York: The Modern Library, 1943), p. 596.

[17] *Précis de l'art de la querre*, Vol. I, p. 395, in "Jomini" by Crane Brinton, Gordon A. Craig and Felix Gilbert, in Earle, *op. cit.*, p. 90.

[18] *Op. cit.*, p. 599.

[19] Vagts, *op. cit.*, p. 470.

[20] Ekrich, *op. cit.*, *passam*.

[21] Vagts, *op. cit.*, p. 848.

[22] *Ibid.*, p. 485.

[23] *The Nation at War* (New York: Doubleday, Doran & Co., 1932), p. 13.

[24] New Haven: Yale University Press, 1950, p. 16.

[25] New York: W. W. Norton & Co.

[26] *Op. cit.*, p. 2.

[27] *The National War College Bulletin*, 1956-57, p. 10.

[28] *History*, Vol. I (New York: Everymans, n.d.), p. 72.

[29] New York: Harper & Bros., 1959.

[30] White House Press Conference, July 29, 1965.

[31] Vagts, *Defense and Diplomacy*, *op. cit.*, p. 20.

[32] *Ibid.*

[33] *Cours de Philosophie Positive*, Vol. V, p. 44 ff. *Ibid.*, p. 53.

[34] Vagts, *Defense and Diplomacy*, *op. cit.*, p. 34.

[35] *Ibid.*

[36] *Ibid.*, p. 35.

[37] *Ibid.*, p. 36.

[38] *Ibid.*, p. 37.

[39] *Ibid.*

[40] *Ibid.*, p. 35.

[41] See General André Beaufe, "A Conception of Strategy," *Survival*, Institute of Strategic Studies, March-April 1964.

CHAPTER 8

[1] Boston: Little, Brown & Co., 1943, p. 98.

[2] *Ibid.*, pp. 98-99. Tudor historians, however, disagree with this analysis, pointing out that Spain was stronger at sea in 1600 than in 1588. See Garrett Mattingly, *The "Invincible" Armada and Elizabethan England* (Washington: The Folger Shakespeare Library, 1963, p. 25.

[3] R. Ernest Dupuy and Trevor N. Dupuy, *The Compact History of the Revolutionary War* (New York: Hawthorne Books, Inc., 1963), p. 62.

[4] *Ibid.*, p. 267.

[5] *Ibid.*, p. 264.

[6] *Ibid.*

[7] Charles A. and Mary R. Beard, *A Basic History of the United States* (New York: Doubleday, Doran & Co., 1944), p. 124.

[8] R. Ernst Dupuy, *The Compact History of the United States Army* (New York: Hawthorne Books, 1956), p. 36.

[9] *Ibid.*, p. 37.

[10] John C. Miller, *Origins of the American Revolution* (Boston: Little, Brown & Co., 1943), p. 119.

[11] Dupuy and Dupuy, *op. cit.*, p. 272.

[12] Vice Admiral T. G. W. Settle in Memorandum to Chief of Naval Personnel, May 16, 1963.

[13] Ekrich, *op. cit.*, p. 23.

[14] *Loc. cit.*

[15] *Loc. cit.*

[16] *Ibid.*, p. 194.

[17] *Ibid.*, p. 198.

[18] *Foundations of National Power, op. cit.*, p. 452.

[19] Beard, *op. cit.*, p. 126.

[20] Paragraph 1, Section 2, Article II.

[21] Paragraph 4, Section 1, Article II.

[22] Section 3, Article II.

[23] Paragraph 12, Section 8, Article II.

[24] Paragraph 2, Section 1, Article I.

[25] Thirty years of age and nine years a citizen.

[26] Howard, *Soldiers and Governments, op. cit.*, p. 14.

[57] *Op. cit.*, Preface.

[28] Louis Smith, *op. cit.*, p. 19.

[29] See Chapter 22.

[30] Huntington, *op. cit.*, p. 207.

[31] *Supra.*

[32] Huntington, *op cit.*, pp. 158-60. His narrow definition of a professional excludes Washington, Jackson and Harrison from that category. Also see Dorothy Burne Goebel and Julius Goebel, Jr., *Generals in the White House* (Garden City, N.Y.: Doubleday, 1945).

[33] This is expanded in Chapter 22.

[34] Art. XXXIX, Para. 1, Army Regulations, Dec. 31, 1836, in Huntington, *op. cit.*, p. 209.

[35] See Chapter 20.

[36] Huntington, *op. cit.*, p. 209.

[37] *Ibid.*, p. 210.

[38] *Defense and Diplomacy, op. cit.*, p. 39.

[39] *New York Times*, June 26, 1951.

[40] *Ibid.*, p. 50.

[41] *Time*, June 13, 1949. Also see Smith, *My Three Years in Moscow* (Philadelphia: Lippincott, 1950), *passim.*

[42] See *Wedemeyer Reports* (New York: Holt, 1958), for a fascinating account.

[43] This phenomenon is examined in Chapter 22, "The Military in Politics."

CHAPTER 9

[1] Walter Goerlitz, *The German General Staff* (New York: Praeger, 1953), p. v.

[2] See Vice Admiral Kurt Assmann, "Hitler and the German Officer Corps," *U.S. Naval Institute Proceedings*, tr. Capt. Roland E. Krause, May 1956.

[3] Goerlitz, *op. cit.*, p. viii. See Alvin Brown, *The Armor of Organization* (New York: Hibbert Printing Co., 1954), pp. 62-67 for a good description of the German General Staff.

[4] "Hobgoblins for the Gullible," *Air Force* Magazine, Oct., 1960.

[5] Goerlitz, *op. cit.*, p. 2.

[6] *Loc. cit.*

[7] *Ibid.*, p. 4.

[8] *Encyclopedia Britannica*, Vol. 10, 1956, pp. 256-257.

[9] Wheeler-Bennett, *op. cit.*, p. 6.

[10] Brown, *op. cit.*, p. 97.

[11] Goerlitz, *op. cit.*, p. 50.

[12] *Op. cit.*
[13] Assmann, *op. cit.*
[14] Alson J. Smith, *A View of the Spree* (New York: John Day Co., 1962), p. 175.
[15] Paul Bronsant Von Schellendorff, *The Duties of the General Staffs* (London: Harrison & Sons, 1905), *pp.* 566-567.
[16] *Ibid.*, pp. 105-118.
[17] *Op. cit.*, p. 96.
[18] Telford Taylor, *Sword and Swastika* (New York: Simon & Schuster, 1952), p. 5.
[19] A. J. Smith, *op. cit.*, p. 183.
[20] John L. Sutton, "The German General Staff in U. S. Defense Policy," *Military Affairs*, Winter, 1961.

CHAPTER 10

[1] A. J. Smith, *op. cit.*, p. 87.
[2] New York: The Macmillan Co., 1890. Second edition published in London by Constable & Co., 1913.
[3] J. M. Scammell, "Spencer Wilkinson and the Defense of Britain," *Military Affairs*, Vol. 4, 1940, pp. 129-142.
[4] *Ibid.*, p. 131.
[5] *Ibid.*, p. 130.
[6] Goerlitz, *op. cit.*, p. 100.
[7] Vegetius, *op. cit.*, p. 68.
[8] Goerlitz, pp. 102-126.
[9] *The Duties of the General Staff, op. cit.*
[10] *Op. cit.*
[11] See his preface to work by Emory Upton, *The Military Policy of the United States* (Washington: Government Printing Office, 1904). Also Scamell, *op. cit.*
[12] A. J. Smith, *op. cit.*, p. 201.
[13] Goerlitz, *op. cit.*, p. 119.
[14] *Op. cit.*
[15] See Barbara Tuchman, *The Guns of August* (New York: Macmillan, 1962), for a detailed account of this historic month.
[16] *National Security Act of 1947* (Washington: Government Printing Office, Nov. 1956), p. 7.
[17] Goerlitz, *op. cit.*, pp. 157-182.
[18] See William M. Crabbe, Jr., "Consensus Through Slogan," unpublished Ph.D. dissertation, George Washington University, June 1963.
[19] Wheeler-Bennett, *op. cit.*, pp. 14-17.
[20] Goerlitz, *op. cit.*, p. 200.

CHAPTER 11

[1] In 1788 the Comte de Mirabeau, returning to Paris after an unsuccessful mission to Berlin, coined the phrase: *"La Prusse n'est pas un pays qui a une armie, c'est une armée que a un pays."* Yet a few years later the far more militaristic state of France subdued the Prussians at Jena.
[2] J. H. Morgan's *Assize of Arms* (New York: Oxford University Press, 1946), is an analysis of the German army's activity between the two world wars. Also see Millis, *op. cit.*; and Craig, *op. cit.*
[3] *Op. cit.*
[4] Wheeler-Bennett for one.
[5] Wheeler-Bennett, *op. cit.*, p. 25.
[6] *Ibid.*, p. 67.
[7] Goerlitz, *op. cit.*, p. 215.

[8] Forty-two thousand was the strength authorized Prussia by France under the Convention of Koenigsburg.
[9] Wheeler-Bennett, *op. cit.*, p. 46.
[10] Goerlitz, *op, cit.*, p. 218.
[11] *Ibid.*, p. 223.
[12] Taylor, *op. cit.*, p. 30.
[13] *Ibid.*, pp. 40-41.

CHAPTER 12

[1] Goerlitz, *op. cit.*, pp. 234-235.
[2] *Op. cit.*, p. 36.
[3] *Ibid.*, p. 238. Also see William L. Shirer, *The Rise and Fall of the Third Reich* (Greenwich, Conn.: Fawcett Publications, 1962), p. 102.
[4] Shirer, *op. cit.*, pp. 162-3.
[5] *Ibid.*, pp. 168-9.
[6] *Ibid.*, p. 172.
[7] *Ibid.*, pp. 192-5.
[8] *Ibid.*, pp. 196-7.
[9] *Ibid.*, p. 190.
[10] *Ibid.*, p. 224.
[11] Wheeler-Bennett, *op. cit.*, p. 211.
[12] Taylor, *op. cit.*, p. 54.
[13] Shirer, *op. cit.*, p. 227.
[14] *Ibid.*, p. 244.
[15] *Ibid.*, p. 246.
[16] *Ibid.*, p. 253.
[17] *Ibid.*, p. 259.
[18] *Ibid.*, p. 262.
[19] Taylor, *op. cit.*, p. 72.
[20] Goerlitz, *op. cit.*, p. 280.
[21] *Ibid.*, p. 288.
[22] Wheeler-Bennett, *op. cit.*, p. 340.
[23] National Security Act of 1947, Nov. 1956, p. 7.
[24] *Op. cit.*, p. 299.
[25] *Ibid.*, p. 303.
[26] *Ibid.*, p. 325.
[27] Goerlitz, *op. cit.*, p. 289.
[28] *Ibid.*, p. 291.
[29] *Ibid.*, p. 294.
[30] Wheeler-Bennett, *op. cit.*, pp. 155-56.
[31] *Ibid.*, p. 355.
[32] Goerlitz, *op. cit.*, p. 298.
[33] Taylor, *op. cit.*, p. 81.
[34] Goerlitz, *op. cit.*, p. 306.
[35] *Ibid.*, p. 309.
[36] *Ibid.*, p. 311.
[37] *Ibid.*, p. 315.
[38] *Ibid.*, p. 320.
[39] *Ibid.*
[40] Wheeler-Bennett, *op. cit.*, p. 372.

CHAPTER 13

[1] Goerlitz, *op. cit.*, p. 319.
[2] *Ibid.*, p. 319.

[3] Shirer, *op. cit.*, p. 439.
[4] Wheeler-Bennett, *op. cit.*, pp. 422-423.
[5] Shirer, *op. cit.*, p. 501.
[6] Goerlitz, *op. cit.*, p. 329.
[7] *Ibid.*, pp. 515-516.
[8] *Ibid.*, p. 517.
[9] *Ibid.*, p. 518.
[10] See Emme, *Hitler's Blitz Bomber, op. cit.*, for this staff system in action. Also Richard Suchenwirth, *Historical Turning Point in the German Air Force War Effort* (Maxwell AFB, Ala.: Research Studies Institute, 1959).
[11] *Op. cit.*, p. 409.
[12] *Op. cit.*, Chapter 9.
[13] *Ibid.*

CHAPTER 14

[1] See John L. Sutton, "The German General Staff in U.S. Defense Policy," *Military Affairs*, Winter, 1961, for an expansion of this concept.
[2] *Congressional Record*, (Senate), Vol. 12, Part 10, 84th Congress, 2nd Session, July 23, 1956, pp. 13987-13992.
[3] *New York Times*, June 24, 1956.
[4] *Op. cit.*
[5] See Department of Armed Forces, *Hearing Before the Committee on Military Affairs, United States Senate*, 79th Congress, 1st Session (Washington, Government Printing Office, 1945), p. 155, for the Collins Plan. This recommended a "U.S. Chiefs of Staff" similar to the present JCS and a "Chief of Staff, Armed Forces" reporting directly to the "Secretary, Armed Forces" something like the present "Chairman, JCS" except that the "Chief of Staff, Armed Forces" would have had command over the various services as well.
[6] "A Proposal for the Next Step in Defense Reorganization," *Air University Quarterly Review*, Vol. XII, No. 2, (Summer, 1960), p. 68.
[7] *Ibid.*, p. 89.
[8] *International Security—the Military Aspect*, Special Studies, Report II of Rockefeller Brothers Fund (Garden City: Doubleday, 1958).
[9] This was an Army staff study based on a Ph.D. thesis by Maj. Lawrence J. Legere, Jr. It is one of many fine studies on the subject of unification. Legere's dissertation, "Unification of the Armed Forces," was prepared at Harvard University, 1951.
[10] Upon being designated Chief of Staff, Omar N. Bradley remarked: "I do not for a moment believe that the army is a sacred institution to be protected by the illusion that it can do no wrong. Generals are just plain people— and like anyone else they are often wrong. During the war mistakes were made—many of them. Let us remember that human nature doesn't change when you wrap it up in a uniform." Quoted from USAF Institute of Technology Information Bureau Nov. 1949, p. 31.
[11] For a fascinating picture of the Prussian General Staff in its heyday during the latter 19th Century, see Alson J. Smith, *A View of the Spree, op. cit.*
[12] *War and Peace in the Space Age* (New York: Harper & Bros., 1958), p. 263.
[13] *Loc. cit.* Also see Friedrich Ruge, "The Postwar German Navy and Its Mission," *U.S. Naval Institute Proceedings*, Vol 83, No. 10 (Oct. 1957), pp. 1035-43.
[14] *Loc. cit.*
[15] *Op. cit.*, p. 17.
[16] See Goerlitz, *op. cit.*, for Preface by Walter Millis, p. v.

[17] See the excellent study of Michael Howard, *Soldiers and Governments*, (London: Eyere and Spottiswood, 1957). Also M.R.D. Foot, *Men in Uniform* (New York: Praeger, 1961), pp. 54-58.

[18] See U.S. Commission on Organization of the Executive Branch of the Government, *Task Force Report on National Security Organization* (Washington: Govt. Printing Office, January 1949). Henceforth referred to as "Hoover Commission Report."

[19] Ferdinand Eberstadt, a New York attorney who, as a colleague of James Forrestal, was earlier instrumental in the defeat of the Collins plan.

[20] See Alvin Brown, *The Armor of Organization, op. cit.* pp. 179-180, for an interesting review of this history.

[21] U.S. Congress, Committee on Armed Services, *Hearings* on S.758, p. 113.

[22] Constitution of the United States, Section 4, Article II.

[23] James F. Byrnes, "Why We Must Give the President a Clear Road," *American*, Aug. 1945.

[24] Col. John C. Healy, "Some Reflections on the General Staff," *Air University Quarterly Review, op cit.*, p. 117.

[25] Graduation Address, Armed Forces Staff College, Norfolk, Virginia, July 2, 1952.

[26] Knight and Herzberg, *op. cit.*, p. 68.

[27] Brown, *op. cit.*, pp. 207-209.

[28] *Congressional Record*, House, July 12, 1964.

[29] Willand Edwards, "Joint Chiefs' Advice Flouted by McNamara," *Chicago Tribune*, April 27, 1965. In addition, the author served from 1961 to 1964 on the Joint Staff.

[30] *Wedemeyer Reports op. cit.*, p. 59.

[31] See Chapter 20.

[31] Appendix G of cited Hoover Commission Report included a dissenting minority on the Commission who favored a single chief of staff. Among this group were men who thoroughly understood military staff work and terminology, such as Robert P. Patterson, John J. McCloy, Chester I. Barnard, Lewis L. Strauss, and Robert E. Wood.

[32] *Op. cit.*

CHAPTER 15

[1] Frank Bowles, "The Three Great Callings," *The Editorial Record*, Journal of the American Council on Education, Washington, D.C., July 1960.

[2] R. Freeman Butts, *A Cultural History of Education* (New York: McGraw-Hill Book Co., 1947), pp. 493-97. The first state "normal" school was established at Lexington, Mass., in 1839 at the instigation of Thomas Mann.

[3] *Ibid.*, pp. 188-93.

[4] See W. S. Davis, *Life on a Medieval Barony* (New York: Harpers, 1923), *passim*.

[5] Lewis Mumford, *Techniques of Civilization* (New York: Harcourt Brace and Co., 1934), p. 81 ff.

[6] Butts, *op. cit.*, pp. 273 ff.

[7] *Ibid.*, pp. 155-57. Thomas Aquinas in his *Summa Theologia* resolved the conflict between reason and faith temporarily by placing faith on a higher unassailable plane. This was challenged by Roger Bacon in the 13th century arguing for verification by experience. The conflict is still evident in such events as the Scopes Trial of 1925.

[8] Rue Buchen and Anselm Strauss, "Professions In Process," *American Journal of Sociology*, LXVI (January, 1961), p. 326.

[9] Lloyd E. Blauche, "Patterns of Professional Education," *Higher Education*, Vol. 9, No. 1 (Sept. 1, 1952).

[10] *Encyclopedia Britannica*, 1956, Vol. 15, pp. 176-77.

[11] Henry H. Armsby, "Engineering Education in the U.S.," *Higher Education*, Vol. 9, No. 7 (Dec. 1, 1952).

[12] *Ibid.*

[13] Butts, *op. cit.*, pp. 234-47, 444-53.

[14] *Ibid.*, p. 516.

[15] *Ibid.*, pp. 636-37.

[16] Joseph A. McClain, Jr., "Legal Education in the U.S.," *Higher Education*, Vol. 9, No. 14 (March 15, 1953). Also Blauche, *op. cit.*

[17] Armsby, *op. cit.*

[18] The American Military Institute is the only one extant and its interest lies in military history rather than professionalism. A brave start was made in 1880 with the bi-service Military Service Institution of the United States but it expired in 1917.

[19] "The Challenge of Military Professionalism," *Foreign Affairs* (January, 1964).

[20] *Op. cit.*

[21] *Ibid.*, pp. 8-10.

[22] "Power, Expertise and the Military Profession," *Daedalus* (Fall, 1963).

[23] "The Military Profession Today," address to the ROTC joint commissioning ceremony at Harvard University, Cambridge, Mass., June 12, 1963.

[24] "The American Soldier," Commencement Address, June 5, 1963.

[25] Waldorf-Astoria Hotel, New York, Dec. 5, 1962.

[26] *The Soldier and the State, op. cit.*, p. 11.

[27] Originally in Sir John Winthrop Hackett, *The Profession of Arms* (London: The Times Publishing Co., 1963), p. 3.

[28] Reported in "Air Force Policy Letter," Office of the Secretary of the Air Force, Washington, D. C., Sept. 15, 1964.

[29] Huntington, *op. cit.*, p. 94.

[30] *Ibid.*, pp., 366-73.

[31] *Ibid.*, pp. 90-94.

[32] *Ibid.*, p. 84.

[33] See Samuel Edward Finer, *The Man on Horseback* (New York: Praeger, 1962), pp. 25-27.

[34] *Ibid.*

[35] Wheeler-Bennett, *op. cit.*, p. 87.

[36] Finer, *op. cit.*, p. 78.

[37] Waldemar N. Neilson, "Soldiers in Politics: A Growing Issue," *The New York Times Magazine*, October 22, 1961, p. 23.

[38] Maj. Gen. Cecil E. Combs, "On The Profession of Arms," *Air University Review*, Vol. XV, No. 4 (May-June 1964), p. 7.

[39] Finer, *op. cit.*, pp. 14-22.

[40] "The Military Rule of Obedience," *Retrospect and Prospect* (Boston: Little Brown & Co., 1901), p. 283. In Huntington, *op. cit.*, p. 73.

[41] These include the President, Vice President, persons paid by appropriations for the office of the President, heads and assistant heads of executive departments, and officers appointed by the President with the advice and consent of the Senate. See Sec. 9 of the Hatch Act (August 2, 1939, as amended; 5 U.S.C. 118 i).

[42] See Huntington, *op. cit.*, pp. 207-08 for the early attitudes toward participation of military men in politics.

[43] *Ibid.*, p. 154.

[44] Alfred Vagts, *A History of Militarism, op. cit.*, p. 15.

[45] *The Martial Spirit* (Boston: Houghton Mifflin, 1931).

[46] "The Demotion of Professionalism in War Colleges," *U.S. Naval Institute Proceedings* (March, 1965).

[47] *Op. cit.*, p. 10.
[48] *Op.,cit.*, p. 163. (Italics his.)
[49] Nov. 29, 1962.
[50] William R. Transill, *The Concept of Civil Supremacy Over the Military in the United States.* The Library of Congress Public Affairs Bulletin No. 94 (Washington: 1951), pp. 1-2.

CHAPTER 16

[1] Louis Smith, *op. cit.*, p. 3.
[2] Benjamin Jowett, tr. (New York: Modern Library, n.d.), p. 143.
[3] Speech on acceptance of Sylvanus Thayer Award, May 12, 1962. Printed in *The Airman*, Feb. 1965.
[4] Girard Lindsley McEntee, *Military History of the World War* (New York: Charles Scribner's Sons, 1937), pp. 22-24.
[5] *New York Times*, Jan. 26, 1965, p. 24.
[6] Anon., *The Armed Forces Officer* (Washington: Government Printing Office, 1950), p. 10.
[7] *The Olymthiae and Other Public Orations*, Charles Rann Kennedy, tr. (London: Henry G. Bohn, 1852), p. 60.
[8] *The Citizen Army, op. cit.*
[9] John McAuley Palmer, *Washington, Lincoln, Wilson—Three War Statesmen* (New York: Doubleday, Doran & Co., 1930), p. 375.
[10] Finer, *op. cit.*, p. 31 ff.
[11] *Armed Forces Officer, op. cit.*, p. 7.
[12] *Arms and Men, op. cit.*, p. 13.
[13] Lippman, *op. cit.*, p. 48.
[14] Upton, *op. cit.*, p. 99.
[15] *Ibid.*, p. 127.
[16] *Ibid.*, p. 246.
[17] Vagts, *Defense and Diplomacy, op. cit.*, p. 53.
[18] *Ibid.*, p. 8.
[19] *The Military Obligations of Citizenship* (Princeton: Princeton University Press, 1915), p. 5.
[20] *Ibid.*, p. 70.
[21] *Ibid.*, pp. 70-75.
[22] Speech to National Rocket Club, Washington, D. C., September 18, 1962. In *The Airpower Historian*, Vol. IX No. 4 (Oct., 1962), p. 229.
[23] *Op. cit.*
[24] *Ibid.*
[25] *Ibid.*

CHAPTER 17

[1] *Op. cit.*, p. 80.
[2] C. S. Brown, "The Social Attitude of American Generals, 1898-1940." Unpublished doctoral dissertation, University of Wisconsin, 1951.
[3] Janowitz, *op. cit.*, p. 95.
[4] *Ibid.*, p. 95.
[5] *Ibid.*, pp. 96, 103.
[6] *Ibid.*, p. 121.
[7] *Ibid.*, p. 100.
[8] *Ibid.*, p. 105.
[9] *Ibid.*, p. 106, from Masland and Radway, *Soldiers and Scholars, op. cit.*, p. 233.
[10] *Ibid.*, p. 136.

[11] *Air Force Times*, May 6, 1961, p. 29.

[12] *Ibid.*, pp. 138-39.

[13] *New York Times*, Nov. 2 and 4, 1964; *Baltimore Sun*, Nov. 2, 1964.

[14] *Op. cit.*, p. 139.

[15] *Ibid.*

[16] *Op. cit.*

[17] *New York Times*, Aug. 13, 1965.

[18] Testimony before the Rivers Committee by Ronald J. Fox, Deputy for Management Systems in the office of Assistant Secretary of the Air Force for Financial Management, and author of an in-house pay study, revealed that it would require a $374 million pay increase "to keep military pay from losing ground" and about $3 billion to return it to the same relationship it had with civilian pay in 1949. One must reflect that the 1949 relationship was far from satisfactory. See *Journal of the Armed Forces*, July 10, 1965, p. 7.

[19] General Omar Bradley, when testifying before the House Armed Services Committee in 1965 said that if a young man asked him today to recommend a service career, "I would probably change the subject." See *Journal of the Armed Forces*, July 10, 1965, p. 7.

[20] *Ibid.*, p. 181.

[21] "Adjustments to Military Pay and Allowances FY 66" (Air Force Compensation Study Group, Hqs. USAF, n.d.), p. 9.

[22] *Ibid.*, p. 24.

[23] Department of Defense figures.

[24] See Harold Lamb, *Suleiman the Magnificent* (Garden City, N.Y.: Doubleday & Co., 1951), for a vivid account of the Janissaries.

[25] Dorn, *op. cit.*, p. 100.

CHAPTER 18

[1] Ginsburg, *op. cit.*

[2] Claude Witze, "The Education of R. S. McNamara," *Air Force* Magazine (March, 1962), pp. 15-21.

[3] "The Dilemma of the Military," *Bulletin of the Atomic Scientists*, December, 1963, p. 24. This magazine has long been the principal outlet for the defense intellectuals. Raymond Senter is a pseudonym for a military analyst "who has spent more than twenty years in the aerospace field working with the military services."

[4] In Gene M. Lyons, "The Military Mind," *Bulletin of the Atomic Scientists*, November, 1963.

[5] Quote from Brig. Gen. Henry J. Reilly, "Discipline," *Liberty* Magazine, January 26, 1929.

[6] K. F. Gantz, ed., *The United States Air Force Reports on the Ballistic Missile* (New York: Doubleday, 1958), preface by General White.

[7] Princeton: Princeton University Press, 1959.

[8] Gene M. Lyons, *op. cit.*

[9] *Ibid.*

[10] U.S. Senate Committee on Armed Services, *Military Cold War Education and Speech Review Policies*, 87th Cong., 2d Sess. (Government Printing Office, 1962).

[11] *The Evening Star*, Washington, D. C., Jan. 30, 1962, and *The Washington Post*, Jan. 31, 1962.

[12] Claude Witze, "The Education of R. S. McNamara," *op. cit.*, p. 15.

[13] *Ibid.*

[14] *Ibid.*, p. 15.

[15] *Ibid.*, p. 16.
[16] "A Limit to Military Speechmaking," *Philadelphia Inquirer*, Jan. 24, 1962.
[17] *Ibid.*
[18] "On Muzzling the Military," editorial, *Saturday Evening Post*, March 24, 1962.
[19] May 16, 1964, p. 1.
[20] Author's experience.
[21] Henkin, *op. cit.*
[22] *Ibid.*, p. 7.
[23] New York: Coward McCann, Inc., 1965.
[24] *Omaha World Herald*, March 10, 1965.
[25] An example is a book by Vincent P. Rock, *A Strategy of Interdependence* (New York: Scribners, 1964), which was a version of the Phoenix Study made by IDA under government contract.
[26] New York: Harper and Brothers, 1960.
[27] Witze, *op. cit.*, p. 21.
[28] *Saturday Evening Post, op. cit.* (Italics added.)
[29] *Ibid.*
[30] "Cooperative Responsibility," editorial, *The Washington Post*, Jan. 24, 1962, p. A16. (Italics added.)
[31] "The Responsibilities of Air Power," Talk at Annual Wing Club Dinner, New York, Nov. 3, 1950.
[32] *Arms Control, Disarmament, and National Security* (New York: George Braziller, 1961).

CHAPTER 19

[1] Henry Steele Commager, *op. cit.*, p. 383.
[2] *War or Peace* (New York: The Macmillan Co., 1950), p. 186.
[3] Vagts, *Defense and Diplomacy, op. cit.*, p. 10.
[4] Sapin and Snyder, *op. cit.*, pp. 19-25.
[5] "Should We Fear the Military," *Look*, XVI, No. 6 (March 11, 1952), p. 34. In *ibid.*, p. 19.
[6] *Ibid.*
[7] " 'Military Mind' Weighed as Political Question," *The New York Times News of the Week in Review*, June 1, 1952. In *ibid.*
[8] "Generals in Politics," *The Reporter*, VI, No. 7 (April 1, 1952), pp. 33-36. In *ibid.*
[9] "Inquiry into the Military Mind," *The New York Times Magazine* (March 30, 1952), p. 53. In *ibid.*
[10] "In Defense of the Military Mind," *Harper's Magazine*, CXCIV (April 1947), pp. 341-344.
[11] Gavin, *op. cit.*, p. 76 ff.
[12] "The Dilemma of the Military," *op. cit.*
[13] Princeton: Princeton University Press, 1959.
[14] "Puzzle of the 'Military Mind'," *New York Times*, Nov. 18, 1962.
[15] *Washington Post*, Sept. 9, 1965.
[16] *New York Times, op. cit.*
[17] *Op. cit.*, pp. 15-16 and 9-10.
[18] *Op. cit.*
[19] "Power, Expertise and the Military Profession," *op. cit.*
[20] *Ibid.*
[21] July 27, 1965.
[22] *Washington Star*, July 13, 1965.
[23] George C. Wilson, "McNamara Team Extending Sphere Into Top Operating Posts," *Aviation Week*, July 19, 1965.

CHAPTER 20

[1] R. Earl McClendon, *Unification of the Armed Forces: Legislative and Administrative Developments, 1945-1949* (Maxwell Air Force Base, Alabama: Air University Documentary Research Study, 1952).

[2] The "Richardson Committee" interviewed some 800 officers from all services before the war was over soliciting views on unification. See Timothy W. Stanley, *American Defense and National Security* (Washington: Public Affairs Press, 1956), p. 72.

[3] Forrestal testimony in the Committee on Military Affairs, Senate, *Hearings on S. 84* [and] *S. 1482*, Oct. 17 to Dec. 17, 1945 (Washington: Government Printing Office, 1945), pp. 97-118. Ferdinand Eberstadt was a New York investment banker whose military experience was with the New York National Guard in the First World War, although he had served on several wartime boards as a civilian during the second conflict. His leanings can be surmised by his membership in several Navy affiliated associations such as the Navy League, the U. S. Naval Institute and the Naval Historical Foundation.

[4] Walter Millis and E. S. Duffield, eds. (New York: Viking Press, 1951).

[5] Stanley, *op. cit.*, pp. 84-85.

[6] *Ibid.*, pp. 94-95.

[7] *Armed Forces Management*, November 1959, p. 24.

[8] Sec. 202 (b), and (c) (4) NSA, 1947—10 USC 143.

[9] *Ibid.*

[10] *War or Peace, op. cit.*, p. 236.

[11] *Hearings, op. cit.*, p. 97.

[12] *Ibid.*, p. 98, Ex. 1.

[13] Sec. 101 (a), NSA 1947, *op. cit.*

[14] Italics added.

[15] *Op. cit.*

[16] Claude Witze, "Why We Need Road Signs," *Air Force*, August 1965, p. 18.

[17] Congress authorized the President to reorganize DOD and specified that the plan submitted would become law if not disapproved by Congress after a certain period. See Stanley, *op. cit.*, p. 103.

[18] U. S. President, *Message Accompanying Reorganization Plan No. 6 of 1953*, 83rd Congress, 1st Session. H.D., 136, 1953.

[19] R. Earl McClendon, *Changes in Organization for National Defense, 1949-1953* (Maxwell Air Force Base, Ala.: Documentary Research Division, Research Studies Institute, 1956), *passam.*

[20] *Soldier: The Memoirs of Matthew B. Ridgway* (New York: Harper and Brothers, 1956). Also see "Letter to the Secretary of Defense," *U. S. News and World Report*, July 29, 1956.

[21] *Op. cit.*, p. 155.

[22] *Ibid.*, p. 155.

[23] John C. Ries, *The Management of Defense* (Baltimore: The Johns Hopkins Press, 1964), p. 28.

[24] Eugene M Emme, ed., *The History of Rocket Technology* (Detroit: Wayne State University Press, 1964), p. 111.

[25] *Ibid.*, pp. 127, 137.

[26] *Ibid.*, p. 214.

[27] House Committee on Armed Services, *Hearings, 1958*, p. 6186.

[28] Ries, *op. cit.*, p. 179.

[29] "Defense Organization," *Armed Forces Management*, Nov. 1959, p. 30.

[30] *Ibid.*, p. 25.

[31] The IDA study termed "Phoenix," for example, turned up in the bookstores. See Rock, *op. cit.*

[32] *New York Times*, Sept. 5, 1963.

[33] William J. Caughlin, "Wheeler the Dealer," *Missiles and Rockets,* Sept. 13, 1965.

[34] *Washington Post,* May 15, 1965.

[35] June 11, 1962, p. 28.

CHAPTER 21

[1] *U. S. Security, Arms Control, and Disarmament* (Washington: Government Printing Office, February 1965).

[2] Donald G. Brennan, ed., *Arms Control, Disarmament, and National Security* (New York: George Braziller, 1961), p. 14.

[3] *Foreign Affairs,* April 1964.

[4] *The United States in the World Arena* (New York: Harper, 1960), p. 549.

[5] Overheard by the author.

[6] U. S. Arms Control and Disarmament Agency, *Blueprint for the Peace Race: Outline of Basic Provisions of a Treaty on General and Complete Disarmament, ACDA Publication 4* (Washington: Government Printing Office, May 1962).

[7] *Op. cit.*

[8] December 1, 1962.

[9] *The Nation's Safety and Arms Control* (New York: Viking Press, 1961).

[10] Princeton: Princeton University Press, 1962.

[11] The air-launched ballistic missile with a thousand mile range.

[12] An antiballistic missile (ABM).

[13] Orbital aircraft.

[14] This has also been termed a "finite deterrent" and a "minimum deterrent."

[15] *Foreign Affairs,* January 1965.

[16] "National Security and the Nuclear-test Ban."

[17] New York: Ace Books, 1958.

[18] Reviews by Norman Cousins, *Saturday Review,* Oct. 20, 1962.

CHAPTER 22

[1] Maj. Gen. C. V. Clifton, "Hail to the Chief," *Army,* January 1964.

[2] Sapin and Snyder, *op. cit.,* p. 53.

[3] 202 (a), NSA 1947.

[4] 203 (b), NSA 1947.

[5] Resolution of 21 October 1780, Journal of the Continental Congress, Vol. III, p. 538, from Laurence C. Moore, Laurence H. Axman and Damon M. Gunn, "Plaintiff's Response . . . in U. S. Court of Claims," *ca.* July 1965, p. 21.

[6] Louis Smith, *op. cit.,* p. 32.

[7] Act of July 15, 1870, 16 Stat. 319. This was followed by service regulations in 1876, 1896 and 1900 which further restricted political activity. The law of 1870 is sometimes pointed to as an anti-man-on-horseback measure, but the reference is questionable.

[8] Huntington, *op. cit.,* p. 246.

[9] *Ibid.,* p. 207.

[10] See Louis Smith, *op. cit.,* p. 40.

[11] William T. Sherman, *Memoirs* (Bloomington, Ind.: Indiana University Press, 1957), p. 248 ff.

[12] C. J. Bernardo and E. H. Bacon, *American Military Policy* (Harrisburg: The Military Service Publishing Co., 1955), p. 254.

[13] Finer, *op. cit.,* pp. 25-26.

[14] *New York Times,* July 26, 1951, p. 12.

[15] *Encyclopedia Britannica,* 1956, Vol. 9, p. 631.

[16] Dupuy, *History of the U. S. Army, op. cit.*, p. 159.

[17] Orvil D. Menard, "The French Army Above the State," *Military Affairs*, Winter, 1964, pp. 124-129.

[18] Dupuy, *op. cit.*, pp. 147-148.

[19] *Ibid.*, p. 146.

[20] *Ibid.*, p. 156.

[21] *Op. cit.*, p. 35.

[22] James B. Fry, "Origin and Progress of the Military Service Institution of the United States," *Journal of the Military Service Institution*, Vol. 1, 1880.

[23] Dupuy, *op. cit.*, p. 162.

[24] Huntington, *op. cit.*, p. 243.

[25] Sigmund Neuman, "Engels and Marx: Military Concept of the Social Revolutionaries," in Earle, ed., *Makers of Modern Strategy, op. cit.*, pp. 155-171.

[26] *Ibid.*, p. 155.

[27] Robert E. Beerstecher, "Revolutionary Antimilitarism in Communist Theory and Practice" (unpublished doctoral dissertation, Georgetown University, Washington, D. C., Dec. 1958), p. 527.

[28] *Ibid.*

[29] *Ibid.*, p. 528.

[30] U. S. Civil Service Commission, *Political Activity of Federal Officers and Employees* (Washington: Government Printing Office, March 1964).

[31] *Ibid.*, p. 3.

[32] Moore, Axman and Gunn, *op. cit.*, p. 21.

[33] *Ibid.*, p. 22.

[34] *Washington Post*, May 30, 1965.

CHAPTER 23

[1] Department of Defense Telephone Directory, Spring-Summer, 1965.

[2] Hanson Baldwin, "Slow-Down in the Pentagon," *op. cit.*

[3] U. S. Civil Service Commission data in *World Almanac*, 1959 (New York: New York World Telegram and the Sun), p. 76.

[4] *Arms and the State, op. cit.*, p. 401.

[5] Published by Robert C. Sellers & Associates in Washington, D. C.

[6] Ries, *op. cit.*, pp. 53-58.

[7] January 30, 1956. His remarks are applicable today.

[8] Isaac Don Levine, *Mitchell, Pioneer of Air Power* (New York: Duell, Sloan and Pearce, 1943), for an interesting account of this contest.

[9] *The Washington Post*, January 24, 1956.

[10] Harper & Brothers, New York, 1956.

[11] *Nuclear Weapons and Foreign Policy* (New York: Harper, 1957), p. 418.

[12] Should the Navy and the Air Force Merge?" May 8, 1953.

[13] Codified in section 8062 (c) of Title 10, United States Code.

[14] U. S. Air Force Bulletin No. 9, *Functions of the Armed Forces and the Joint Chiefs of Staff* (Washington: Government Printing Office, July 9, 1954). Commonly known as the Key West Agreement.

[15] "The Roles and Missions Muddle," *Air Force*, July 1956.

[16] *Op. cit.*, Sec. 206.

[17] May 16, 1957.

[18] "Unification—the Next Step," October, 1956.

[19] Quincey Wright, "The Military and Foreign Policy," in Kerwin, *op. cit.*, p. 123. "People have wanted the state's armed forces to be efficient for defense against external aggression but inefficient for domestic tyranny and have found it difficult to achieve both objectives."

CHAPTER 24

[1] *Congressional Record—House,* April 21, 1964, p. 8311.
[2] "The Teaching of Military History in Colleges and Universities of the United States," USAF Historical Studies: No. 124, p. 44.
[3] "The Teaching of Military History," *Military Affairs,* XIII (1949), pp. 14-19.
[4] A. M. Carr-Sanders and P. A. Wilson, *The Professions* (Oxford: The Clarendon Press, 1933).
[5] *Ibid.,* p. 3.
[6] *Op. cit.,* p. 242.
[7] Phil G. Goulding, *Cleveland Plain Dealer,* June 6, 1963.
[8] Louis S. Stockstill, March 27, 1965.
[9] *Newsweek,* July 1, 1963.
[10] *Ibid.*
[11] Arthur Krock, *New York Times,* May 12, 1953.
[12] Nielson, "Soldier in Politics," *op. cit.*

CHAPTER 25

[1] "Education of the Citizen Soldier," *The Educational Record,* April 1955.
[2] *Op. cit.*
[3] New York: Harper and Row, 1963.
[4] *Washington Star,* Aug. 10, 1965 quoted a story by the Soviet Military newspaper *Red Star* with photos of equipment.
[5] Quoted in John A. Lang, Jr., "Public Opinion and National Security," *op. cit.*